DESKTOP PUBLISHING
by DESIGN
VENTURA PUBLISHER® EDITION

Ronnie Shushan

Don Wright

Ricardo Birmele

PUBLISHED BY
Microsoft Press
A Division of Microsoft Corporation
One Microsoft Way
Redmond, Washington 98052-6399

Library of Congress Cataloging-in-Publication Data
Shushan, Ronnie.
    Desktop publishing by design : Ventura Publisher edition / Ronnie
  Shushan, Don Wright, Ricardo Birmele.
      p.   cm.
    ISBN 1-55615-265-5
    1. Desktop publishing. 2. Ventura publisher (Computer program)
  I. Wright, Don, date.   II. Birmele, Ricardo.   III. Title.
  Z286.D47S593   1990
  686.2'2544536--dc20   90-34885
                                                CIP

Printed and bound in the United States of America.

1 2 3 4 5 6 7 8 9   MLML   6 5 4 3 2 1

Distributed to the book trade in Canada by Macmillan of Canada,
a division of Canada Publishing Corporation.

Distributed to the book trade outside the United States
and Canada by Penguin Books Ltd.

Penguin Books Ltd., Harmondsworth, Middlesex, England
Penguin Books Australia Ltd., Ringwood, Victoria, Australia
Penguin Books N.Z. Ltd., 182–190 Wairau Road, Auckland 10, New Zealand

British Cataloging-in-Publication Data available

IBM® is a registered trademark of International Business Machines
Corporation. Microsoft® is a registered trademark of Microsoft Corporation.
Ventura Publisher® is a registered trademark of Ventura Software, Inc.

Project Editor: Jack Litewka

DESKTOP PUBLISHING
BY DESIGN

▲▲▲▲▲▲▲▲▲▲▲▲▲▲▲▲▲▲

Praise for Aldus® PageMaker® edition

▶ ▶ ▶ ▶ ▶

"Best How-To Book of 1989."— *Computer Press Association*

"A treasure trove of useful, detailed examples and tips designed to help readers create desktop-published documents that get attention. It's an enjoyable introduction to a field where taste and judgement are just as important as technical expertise; a practical, hands-on workbook with plenty of useful examples; and an excellent reference work for anyone who is designing and creating documents with PageMaker. I loved it!"— Richard Landry, Editor-in-Chief, *PC World*

"If you're still looking for an overall introductory text in desktop publishing, this may well be the best yet…. Microsoft Press simply doesn't seem to do anything but top-notch books. This is one more in a long string of high-quality texts that simply can't fail to satisfy…. A splendid book."— *Computing Now*

"The Strunk and White of desktop publishing…. A brilliantly thought-out and classically executed work…. For anyone already experimenting with desktop publishing, or contemplating doing so, it belongs in the most frequently used section of your library."
—*Woodstock Times*

"Real-life examples are liberally captioned with appropriate insights…all presented in a cogent and fluid style."—*The Page*

"An excellent resource for electronic visual communicators."
—*Step by Step Electronic Design*

To all the pioneers

scientists and artists
engineers and designers
programmers and publishers

who have shown the way

CONTENTS

Acknowledgments

No advances in technology will ever replace the information and experience shared by colleagues or the support and contribution of publishing professionals throughout the development, production, and marketing of a book such as this. Our thanks to:

All of the designers who took the time to send us their work and talk with us about both design and technological considerations.

Jack Litewka, our editor at Microsoft Press, for bird-dogging endless details with a careful eye, wisdom, and a sense of humor.

Jim Brown at Microsoft, who made it happen.

Carol Luke, who coaxed even the most ornery pages through Microsoft's L300.

Darcie Furlan, Becky Johnson, and Peggy Herman, who coordinated the production that turned electronic files, printed samples, and existing film into this book.

Russell Steele, whose production expertise and deft touch was invaluable.

Craig Bartholomew, for his initial inspiration.

William J. Teel, Jr., for his typographic and word processing skills when things got frustrating.

David Rygmyr, for his diligence and persistence in securing the required hardware.

Nancy Siadek, for her organization of the project during its initial phase.

Mary Ann Jones and Rebecca Pepper, whose editorial work on the first edition remains in many of the pages of this one.

INTRODUCTION

The computer is by all odds the most extraordinary of the technological clothing ever devised by man, since it is an extension of our central nervous system. Beside it the wheel is a mere hula-hoop.
—Marshall McLuhan

This book is about two dramatically different and wonderfully complementary tools of communication: graphic design and electronic page assembly. The first is a tradition as old as recorded history, the second a technology unimaginable to most of us even five years ago. In addition to changing the way we produce documents and publications of every kind, the combination of these tools is introducing more people than ever before to the art and technology of publishing. This volume, *Desktop Publishing by Design—Ventura Publisher Edition*, is a direct descendant of our earlier book, *Desktop Publishing by Design*, which focused on Aldus PageMaker.

Technology has always had an impact on visual communication, which is essentially what graphic design is. At every stage of the evolution of the communication arts—from prehistoric cave paintings to Gutenberg's movable type to today's computerized typesetting and imaging systems—technology has increased the potential for communication with audiences that are both broader and more specialized.

In the past, especially in the last half century or so during which graphic design as a commercial art has flourished, people entered the field through formal training in art schools and apprenticeships with experienced designers. The almost overnight proliferation of desktop-publishing technology has attracted and, through management expectations, forced many people with no training in the visual arts to take responsibility for a wide range of printed material. Increased access to publishing tools has motivated many businesses to produce in-house publications that were previously done, in whole or in part, by outside contractors. At the same time, the promise and the inevitable hype surrounding desktop publishing have raised expectations about internal and external communications of all kinds.

While expanding the number of people involved in printed communication, desktop typesetting and electronic page assembly are also dramatically changing the day-to-day operations of an increasing number of publishers, design studios, corporate art departments, and independent freelancers. Writers and editors who cannot draw a straight line find themselves assembling pages in electronic templates. Designers used to specifying type on manuscripts are setting and manipulating it themselves. Production managers used to trafficking hard copy from one department to another are wrestling with the management of electronic files. And pasteup artists with T-squares and ruling pens are, quite simply, an endangered species.

Although they approach desktop publishing from different perspectives, people within both the business community and the publishing industry share a need for two different kinds of training. This book focuses on that need. It is not a general overview of desktop publishing. It assumes that you already appreciate the potential benefits the technology offers: the ability to integrate text and graphics electronically, to see and alter on-screen what the printed page will look like, and to print that page on a variety of different printers depending upon the quality you require. The book does not try to convince you of the ways in which desktop publishing can save you time or money, enhance the creative process, or give you more control over the pages you produce. It assumes you're already convinced. Instead, it reviews the fundamental elements of graphic design for the many people without any training or experience in the visual arts who are suddenly responsible for producing—or who want to learn to produce—business publications. And it provides hands-on tutorials for using Xerox Ventura Publisher, a popular electronic page layout program for IBM-compatible computers.

There are very few rules in graphic design. A relatively subjective craft, it requires the designer to make one judgment after another based on such intangible criteria as "look" and "feel." Even if you have no inkling of the formal traditions and techniques taught in design schools, you have some personal experience with the elements designers work with—words, lines, colors, pictures.

On the other hand, there are hundreds and hundreds of rules for using Xerox Ventura Publisher. Even with its user-friendly mouse and pull-down menus, Ventura Publisher is not—for most people—a program you just jump into and start producing pages with. It requires learning which commands to use and how to respond to dialog boxes and how the same commands in different sequences produce different results.

One important quality common to designing printed pages and assembling them in Ventura Publisher is that both tasks become intuitive as you gain experience. The variety of typefaces that intimidates a novice designer, for example, becomes a rich resource once you gain a feeling for the often subtle distinctions between them. The apparent mysteries of layout grids and paragraph tags become time-saving production tools when you understand the simple principles that govern their use. Similarly, the endless rules that slow down the Ventura rookie provide control and flexibility to the experienced user.

In a sense, this book tries to simulate experience both in graphic design and in using desktop publishing tools to produce printed documents. Section 1, "The Elements of Design," is a sort of primer of visual literacy as it relates to the printed page. It provides a working vocabulary of graphic design in the context of desktop technology.

There are many techniques that can be applied in the search for visual solutions. Here are some of the most often used and easily identified:

Contrast	Harmony
Instability	Balance
Asymmetry	Symmetry
Irregularity	Regularity
Complexity	Simplicity
Fragmentation	Unity
Intricacy	Economy
Exaggeration	Understatement
Spontaneity	Predictability
Activeness	Stasis
Boldness	Subtlety
Accent	Neutrality
Transparency	Opacity
Variation	Consistency
Distortion	Accuracy
Depth	Flatness
Juxtaposition	Singularity
Randomness	Sequentiality
Sharpness	Diffusion
Episodicity	Repetition

—Donis A. Dondis,
A Primer of Visual Literacy

Think of buying a computer as like buying a car. A car just moves your body; your computer, though, is the chariot of your mind, carrying it through the whole universe. How much is your mind worth to you?
—Ted Nelson,
Computer Lib

Section 2, "A Design Portfolio," and the chapter on Creating a Grid in Section 1 show sample pages from more than a hundred documents along with notes about design elements such as grid structure, type treatment, and use of art. Although these documents can't replace personal experience, they can provide the novice designer with a sense of the many different solutions to common design problems, and they can help you develop an eye for effective combinations. All the publications were created using desktop publishing tools, although many of them incorporate traditional methods as well, such as the creation and stripping of halftones—so these samples also illustrate both simple and complex uses of the technology.

The third section, "Hands-On Projects," provides actual experience. Here you'll find seven tutorials, each with step-by-step instructions for creating a particular publication. The purpose is to help you learn and become more confident with Ventura's tools and techniques by applying them to actual documents.

This book was conceived as a resource for the Ventura user, rather than as a document to be read from start to finish. If you want to start right in working with Ventura Publisher, begin in Section 3. If you want to review publications of a particular kind, flip through Section 2. And if you want some grounding in design basics, start with Section 1. Even within each section, the chapters are organized so that you can begin at whichever point suits your needs and experience. If you stumble across an unfamiliar term, refer to the Glossary at the back of the book.

Throughout this book, we emphasize that the computer is only a tool. "Design" is not one of its default settings. Ventura Publisher can enable you to draw a straight line, but it can't tell you how heavy to make it or where to put it on the page. It allows you to place text in perfectly aligned columns, but it doesn't tell you how wide the columns should be or when to place text as one long file and when to divide it into several smaller ones. It offers hundreds of typefaces, but you must use your visual judgment to select and size the one that's right for your publication.

Visual communication of any kind, whether persuasive or informative, from billboards to birth announcements, should be seen as the embodiment of form and function: the integration of the beautiful and the useful.
—Paul Rand,
Thoughts on Design

Desktop publishing generally, and Ventura Publisher specifically, are wonderful, powerful tools, getting better—more sophisticated and easier to use—every day. These tools are only unthinking instruments of your creativity. We hope this book will help you gain some of the skill, experience, and visual discrimination needed to use them well.

THE ELEMENTS OF DESIGN

CHAPTER 1

EFFECTIVE COMMUNICATION IN AN INFORMATION ENVIRONMENT

Past	Present	Future
Data	Information	Knowledge
Control	Access	Exploration
Calculation	Presentation	Communication

—*Stuart Greene*,
Apple viewpoints

*T*he electronic age has given us an almost magical ability to store, retrieve, and analyze data. Whether you're making travel plans, checking the status of an insurance policy, or changing an assumption in a five-year plan, the computer can provide almost instantaneous answers to questions that only a decade ago might have remained unanswered for a day, a week, or even a month.

But the electronic age has not given us a paperless office. In fact, in a single year computers are said to churn out some 1200 pages of print for every man, woman, and child in the United States. Although they help us manage individual pieces of data, computers have increased our information overload.

In the midst of this overload, desktop publishing reaffirms the fundamental power of print. Print is tangible; it has a life of its own. You can read it when you want, at your own pace, and keep it for future reference. And now, with desktop publishing, the newest darling of the electronic age, you can produce more pages faster and cheaper than ever before.

But can you produce effective pages?

In the information environment, competition for the ever-shrinking attention span is fierce. We are saturated both as senders (too much to say, too little space) and as receivers (too much to read, too little time). The result is often information that is confusing, that you can't find when you need it, or that simply sits unread in a rotating stack of other communications that failed to deliver their messages. The cumulative result is an enormous amount of wasted effort. The hidden costs, whether in sales or productivity or corporate image, are difficult to calculate.

The elements that make up a successful document—careful writing, thoughtful organization, effective design—grow out of an understanding of your message, your audience, and your resources. The publication checklist below can help guide you toward that understanding. The questions it raises force you to think through a great many variables and even some unpleasant realities. Some of the answers may raise more questions. The purpose of the checklist is to help you define your communication problem so that you can use graphic design as a way of solving it. We'll briefly consider each item on the checklist after a look at a few diverse examples of effective communication.

An erroneous conception of the graphic designer's function is to imagine that in order to produce a "good layout" all he need do is make a pleasing arrangement of miscellaneous elements. What is implied is that this may be accomplished simply by pushing these elements around until something happens. At best, this procedure involves the time-consuming uncertainties of trial and error, and at worst, an indifference to plan, order, or discipline.
—Paul Rand,
Thoughts on Design

PUBLICATION CHECKLIST

- What is the purpose of your publication?

- Why is it needed?

- Who is the intended audience?

- What kind of information will your publication include?

- What kind of image do you want to project?

- Does the publication need to fit into a larger program or conform to a corporate style?

- What is the overall format?

- What kinds of art and photography—and how much— will be needed?

- What are the printing specifications?

- What will you use for camera-ready pages?

- How will the publication be reproduced?

- How will it be distributed?

- When is it needed?

- What is the budget?

The dramatically different documents reproduced on this and the following two pages illustrate the rich range of visual form that effective communication can take. Each of the four samples successfully solves a very different design problem, and their contrasting styles say a great deal about the different purpose and audience of each message.

A poster is one of the simplest and most direct forms of communication. It delivers a message that is as brief as it is bold. Although many posters rely heavily on graphics, this one is a reminder of the power of words.

The street language is well suited to the young audience; the rhythm of the words is in their own vernacular.

The typography follows the cadence of the words, so that the visual rhythm literally echoes the verbal message. Reverse type on a red background supports the jazzy rhythm and the serious message.

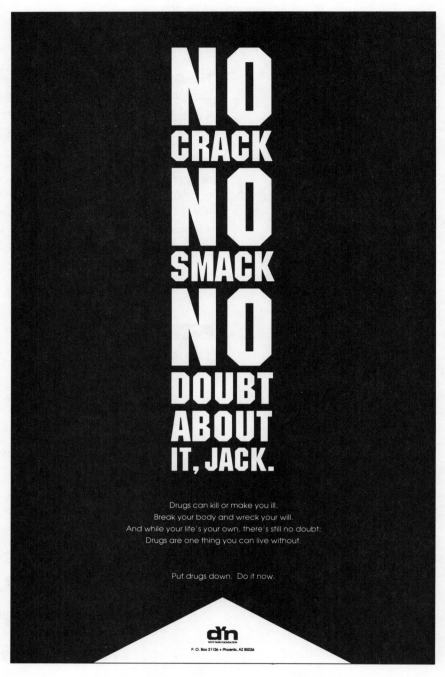

Design: Jim Parker (Phoenix, AZ)

Poster produced by the Do It Now Foundation.

Trim size: 12 by 19

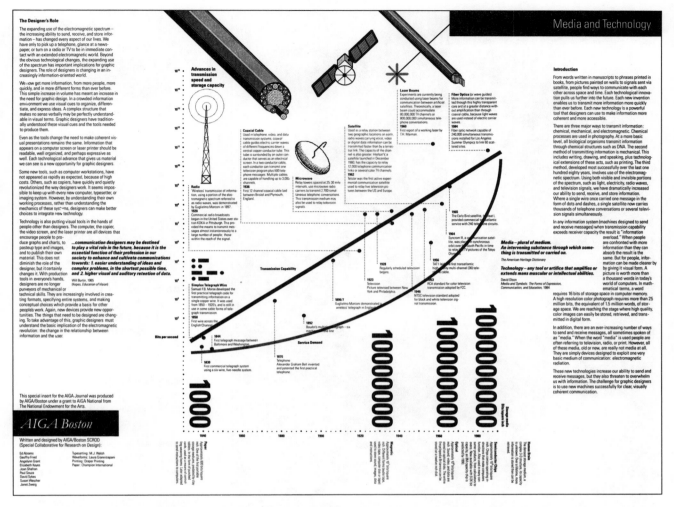

The carefully organized collection of information above is at the opposite end of the communications spectrum from the poster. The subject is media and technology; the audience is sophisticated (the document was designed as an insert for a graphic arts journal) and so is the delivery of information.

The chart encapsulates advances in transmission speed and storage capacity of media in the context of a time line. In addition to providing a great deal of information in a very small space, it cuts through the stereotypical image of charts as bland and linear.

Quotations inset between the running text and the chart provide a point of easy access in this complex page as well as another layer of historical context:

…communication designers may be destined to play a vital role in the future, because it is the essential function of their profession in our society to enhance and cultivate communications towards: 1. easier understanding of ideas and complex problems, in the shortest possible time, and 2. higher visual and auditory retention of data.
—Will Burtin, 1965

Design: Paul Souza, Ed Abrams, and Susan Wascher (Boston, MA)

Insert for the American Institute of Graphic Arts journal produced by AIGA/ Boston.

Trim size: 22 by 17

The conceptual illustration on the cover of this quarterly publication brings to bear the personal and subjective vision of the artist. It invites the reader to participate and engages the imagination.

The single-word title is very focused. It succinctly states the subject but leaves you curious as to how it will be addressed.

The overall image of the cover combines a feeling of accomplishment and success with the need for innovation and a sense of work yet to be done. Each element, as well as the whole, echoes the nature of leadership itself.

The dramatic photo composition on the cover of this PBS-series program guide has an emotional content that touches the reader in a way that straight typography cannot. The juxtaposition of a mushroom cloud against the outstretched hands of Gorbachev and Reagan evokes the terror and hope, the despair and optimism of our time. The photos also suggest the mix of historical and contemporary components in the series.

The title over the photos suggests that the series will be comprehensive. The wording is restrained and sets a tone that encourages the viewer to suspend moral judgments temporarily.

Design: Alison Kennedy (Boston, MA)

Program guide produced by WGBH and Central Independent Television.
Trim size: 8-1/2 by 11

Design: Weisz Yang Dunkelberger Inc. (Westport, CT)

Periodical published by Lefkoe & Associates, a management consulting and training organization.
Trim size: 9 by 12

What is the purpose of your publication?

Desktop publishing can be used to produce documents as diverse as calling cards and novels. This book is concerned primarily with business documents, which usually fall into several categories. Identifying the category to which your document belongs (it may be more than one) can help you develop the right approach for the purpose.

Information technology was supposed to let us taper off paper.... From 1959 to 1986 America's consumption of writing and printing paper increased from 6.83 million to 21.99 million tons, or 320 percent, while the real [GNP] rose 280 percent.

—Edward Tenner, Harvard Magazine, cited in The Computer Desk Reference & Appointment Calendar 1989

Documents that persuade
Advertisements
Invitations
Fund-raisers
Posters
Press releases
Promotional flyers
Prospectuses
Sales brochures

Documents that identify
Business cards
Certificates
Labels
Stationery

Documents that inform
Brochures
Bulletins
Curriculum listings
Fact sheets
Marketing plans
Product lists
Programs
Rate cards
Specification sheets

Periodicals that inform
Magazines
Newsletters
Newspapers
Reports

Documents that elicit response
Applications
Order forms
Surveys

Documents that provide reference
Calendars
Directories
Lists
Parts lists
Schedules
Timetables

Documents that give how-to information
Curriculum guides
Instruction manuals
Training guides

Why is your publication needed?

One of the most important questions to ask yourself is why the reader needs or wants the information in your document. If you can zero in on that need, you can use it in your headlines and art to get the reader's attention. Keeping the reader's needs in mind also helps focus your writing.

Desktop publishers get carried away with their tools. They...spend more time on the aesthetics of a document than the content of it.
—Boeing's DTP product manager, in an article in MacWEEK

In many cases the reader is at best indifferent and at worst resistant to the information you want to convey. If you acknowledge that indifference, you can try to devise some way of overcoming it. In the face of audience resistance, you might want to put extra effort and money into the cover. Or consider printing a strong opening sentence or two in large type on the cover to lure readers in. Puzzles, quizzes, and other involvement techniques can sometimes draw readers to a subject they might otherwise ignore. A headline that poses a bold question is a simpler version of this same approach and can work if your audience is likely to want to know the answer. (Readers can often be hooked by a question even if it's one they think they can answer.) Humor, where appropriate, can also cajole the audience into reading on. The technique depends on the publication, the audience, and the budget. But do try something. If you ignore audience indifference when you write and design a document, you can guarantee that it won't be read.

Who is your audience?

Unless you write like Stephen King or address a subject as important to your reader as his or her bank balance, you can't assume that your intended reader will actually read your document. You may have a target audience or even a captive audience, but you don't have a reader until you've involved that person through words or pictures or an overall impression. Identifying your audience helps you choose the techniques that engage readers. Are they colleagues? Customers? Potential investors? Clients? What style is appropriate? How much do they know about your subject? How much time are they likely to spend with your publication? What other information do they have on the subject? Is this their only source?

The business of reaching the audience is no different than before.
—Ben Bagdikian,
in a New York Times *interview about desktop publishing*

Think in terms of interaction rather than one-way communication. It doesn't hurt to think of yourself as an entertainer or a salesperson anticipating your audience's reaction. Consider readers' responses so that you can adjust your approach.

As you develop your publication, put yourself in the readers' position:

- How quickly can they pick out the highlights? Most readers scan. They want a sense of what you have to say before they make a commitment to read on. They want the highlights before the details.

- Can they find the items that are relevant to their particular concerns? Many publications have a mix of information, with different subjects, themes, or types of material. In a company newsletter, for example, one employee may be interested in educational assistance while another is concerned with after-hours security. Understanding your readers' special interests helps you organize the material.

- How quickly can they read the text? Remember the problem of information overload. Your text should be clear and lean. Less is more in print.

- Can your readers understand the information? Have you assumed knowledge they don't have?

Instruction manuals and reference books require careful organization and graphic devices that help the reader to find what he or she needs. One study of computer documentation revealed that of all the questions phoned in to the technical support staff, 80 percent were covered in the manual; the users either couldn't find the answers quickly enough or didn't understand them.

What kind of information will be included?

Different kinds of publications have different elements. A brochure for a professional conference may require a program, a workshop schedule, brief biographies of the speakers, and a map. An advertisement may consist entirely of slogans, tag lines, and little pieces of information such as prices or an address. A press release needs the name of a person to contact for more information. A technical manual needs a glossary. Review the different kinds of information—text and visual— early on so that you'll have space for all the pieces and avoid oversights.

An awareness of the elements needed in your document also affects your format and pacing. For a newsletter with several short articles and small photographs, you might choose a four-column format, whereas a newsletter with one major article and a number of short, newsy items might work best in two unequal columns. You can't possibly make an intelligent decision about format until you have a fix on the kinds of information you'll be formatting.

What kind of image do you want to project?

The layout of the circus under canvas is more like the plan of the Acropolis than anything else; it is a beautiful organic arrangement established by the boss canvas man and the lot boss.... The concept of "appropriateness," this "how-it-should-be-ness," has equal value in the circus, in the making of a work of art, and in science.
—Charles Eames

Everything about a publication, from the style of the prose to the quality of the paper it's printed on, contributes to the image it conveys about the sender. And the single most important guideline in fashioning that image is appropriateness. The elements you select and the way you assemble and reproduce them become a matter not so much of good or bad design as of design that is appropriate for your purpose and audience. Even the crammed-full, poorly printed advertisements for discount department stores cannot be dismissed as "bad" design when put to the tests of appropriate and effective communication.

If you are promoting a financial service, you want prose that is well informed and authoritative and design and printing that is prosperous without being indulgent. A company that has had a bad year, on the other hand, wants to appear careful and restrained without creating concern about quality. And you want an entrepreneurial business plan to appear energetic, bold, and thorough all at the same time.

A travel brochure for a Caribbean cruise might use color photos to suggest escape, adventure, and celebration, and an ad for a new restaurant in the theater or art district might use words and decorative motifs to project a similar experience close to home.

As you consider the elements and design of your publication, write down a list of impressions you want to make. Formal. Informal. Friendly. Playful. Elegant. Stylish. Trendy. Classic. Adventurous. Conservative. Scholarly. Provocative. Diverse. Spirited. Generous. Concerned. How do you want your audience to perceive you?

Must your publication fit into a program or conform to a corporate style?

For a new program that requires continuity—say a series of health seminars, each with a promotional mailing before the event, a seminar program distributed at the event, and a follow-up questionnaire after the event—you'll want to develop a design that establishes an identity for the series and that can be followed for each event.

The issue of corporate identity has emerged as some companies have discovered that desktop publishing encourages more creativity than their image can handle. The logo begins appearing in different sizes and positions on the page. Documents from one department have a streamlined, stylized look, whereas documents from another use Victorian clip art. The corporate response is to establish formats and design standards so that different kinds of documents—order forms, product sheets, newsletters, reports, and so on—all have a consistent look. You may feel that having to adhere to these standards puts a damper on your style, but in fact it will probably free you to concentrate on the clarity and effectiveness of the elements within the established format.

What is the overall format?

Format includes everything from the organization of material to the page size to the underlying structure, or grid, of your layout. You rarely start a publication with an idea of what the format should be; rather, the format evolves out of the material and often changes as your understanding of the publication changes.

In developing your format, consider first the common elements in the publication. How many levels of headlines will you need? How will you separate items that appear on the same page?

Readers want what is important to be clearly laid out; they will not read anything that is troublesome to read.
—Jan Tschichold,
writing in 1935, cited in
Thirty Centuries of Graphic Design

Look at the formats of other publications, keep a file of what you like, and adapt those techniques to fit your needs. Professional designers do this all the time. Don't limit your file to the kinds of publications you will produce. You may never create an accordion-fold brochure, but some aspect of the format may help you solve a problem in your own publication.

Keep in mind that readers scan printed matter, and consider techniques to facilitate this:

- A strong visual framework will separate one item from another and indicate relative importance.

- Several short stories are almost always more accessible and inviting than one long one.

- Use sidebars or boxed copy to break the text into accessible chunks.

- Every headline and caption is a hook, a potential entry point for busy readers.

- Pay attention to the pacing: Balance text with visuals, and offset "quick reads" with more demanding material.

- Use graphic devices to move the reader's eye from one place on the page to another, especially to key points or to little bits of information that you think are particularly interesting.

- Keep in mind also that many readers scan from back to front; can you get their attention in the middle of a story?

For magazines, newsletters, and other periodicals, develop your format with great care so that you can maintain a consistent style from one issue to the next. What departments and features will be included in every issue? Where will they appear?

What kinds of art or photography will be included?

You can produce professional, attractive documents without any art, but pictures unquestionably draw readers in more easily than words, and illustrations can greatly enhance your message. Art and photography can illustrate the text, provide additional information, create a mood, provoke questions in the reader's mind, and set the overall tone of a publication. Charts and graphs can squeeze a lot of facts into a small amount of space and be visually interesting at the same time. Even abstract geometric shapes can intrigue and invite and add movement to the page. Graphic devices such as borders, boxes, and tinted areas, along with icons such as arrows, bullets, and ballot boxes, all help create a strong sense of organization and move the reader from one part of the page to another. Consider these devices as ways to break up the text and make your pages more interesting, more accessible, and more informative. Keep in mind that you don't necessarily need a lot of art; often one or two strong images are more effective than half a dozen mediocre ones.

We learn language by applying words to visual experiences, and we create visual images to illustrate verbal ideas. This interaction of word and image is the background for contemporary communication.
—Allen Hurlburt,
The Design Concept

You will need to consider the amount and type of art to be used early on, because it will affect your format and will also generate loose odds and ends of text. Will you have captions? Numbers to identify figures? Sources for charts? Where will the art credits appear?

The art will affect the schedule, too. Will the printer make halftones from your black-and-white photos, or will you need to have that done? How long will it take to have color separations made? Desktop publishing is expanding into color work and scanned black-and-white photographs, but most publications created with computers still treat photos and four-color art the way they've always been treated, as a process handled by the printer.

What are the printing specifications?

Specifications—including page size, number of pages, type of binding, paper stock, quantity to be printed, and use of color, if any—are inextricably related to the overall format. Changing one often affects the other. Review your options early on with any outside vendors you plan to use (commercial printers, color separators, full-service copy centers); your specifications must be consistent with their capabilities and requirements.

If you've come to desktop publishing without any experience in working with printed materials, you'll encounter a new set of jargon as you move into printing and binding. It's just trade talk, and you'll pick it up in time. If your printer can print in four- and eight-page signatures as well as in sixteens, that might affect the number of pages you produce. If you can get a good price on an odd-size paper that works for your needs, you might want to adjust your page size. The binding you select may affect your page margins. See the Resources section in the back of this book for production guides that will help you understand the fundamentals of commercial printing.

What will you use for camera-ready pages?

For many documents, the 300-dots-per-inch output from a laser printer is sufficient for camera-ready pages. For others, you may want the higher resolution provided by an imagesetter such as the Linotronic. Again, your decision here will affect your schedule and your budget.

When you plan to use Linotronic output, be sure to run test pages of your format early on. Rules, shades, and type weight are lighter at higher resolutions, and you may want to adjust your specs when you see the early tests. You'll want to work with the service center that will provide your Linotronic output just as you do with your printer. Find out what kind of compatibility the service center requires in order to print your files—what versions of programs they use, which fonts they have, what backup you must provide, whether they use screen fonts for boldface and italic styles or require that you apply these from the Type style menu. Knowledgeable personnel at good service centers are a valuable resource and can help you troubleshoot problems early on.

How will your document be reproduced?

For any but those jobs you consider routine, talk with the printer as early in the planning as possible.... Describe your needs and ask whether your piece can be printed practically. Consider suggestions about alternate papers, design changes, and other ideas about how to save time and money.... [But] remember that they want your business. By suggesting changes which take advantage of particular presses or papers, a printer may be shaping your job to fit that shop. Keep in mind that you are getting consultation and may not be ready to write specifications.

—Mark Beach,
Getting It Printed

As is the case with many aspects of publishing, the new technology has expanded the ways in which documents are reproduced. Will you use the office photocopy machine? A full-service copy center? A quick printer with offset presses and binderies? Or a commercial printer for higher-quality reproduction? Your printing needs will be determined by the number of copies, the quality desired, and your budget.

If you will be using commercial printers on a regular basis and you are new to publishing, try to develop a working relationship with local printers and learn more about that end of the business. Printing is a fine art but an inconsistent one; even highly experienced professionals fear the nasty surprises that can happen on press. Poor communication between publisher and printer can result in poor quality. Let your printer know what you expect. If you're not satisfied with the quality, follow up after you receive printed copies to find out what the problem was. Often the printer will blame it on the paper (which is rarely as good as you'd like it to be) or on the size of the run (it is difficult to maintain certain standards in large press runs, but the printer is supposed to have quality-control mechanisms to catch problems as they come up), or on some other plausible factors. But sometimes the problem could have been avoided. Perhaps your photograph was cut off because you didn't leave enough space between your art and the trim; next time you'll know to determine the tolerance and adjust your margins accordingly. By asking, you'll let the printer know you care about quality, and you may learn something.

How will it be distributed?

Whether your document is distributed through interoffice mail, given away in stores, or sent through the mail or some other delivery service, you want the purpose to be easily discernible. What is the reader's first impression? Is a person as likely to see the back cover first as the front? If the publication is folded, will the pacing of the words and images keep the recipients moving through the folds? If a flyer is to be tacked on a bulletin board, can the headline be read from a distance?

If your document will be mailed, it must conform to postal regulations for the appropriate mailing class. This may affect the size, the way the publication is folded, the placement of the mailing label, and the amount of space for the address if the publication is a self-mailer.

An early understanding of the restrictions and requirements of your distribution method can save you time and money and can affect certain decisions about your format as well.

When is it needed?

Regardless of your experience and that of your staff, expect productivity to drop in the beginning, as everyone learns the new system.... It will probably take at least three production cycles before you can get all the kinks out.... Many organizations continue to use traditional production methods in parallel with their new desktop systems, phasing in the new methods gradually. This means you won't see your cost savings right away, but you're not putting all your eggs in one new and untested basket.
—Janet Millenson,
writing in Publish! *magazine*

Schedules are a blessing and a curse. On the one hand there is the feeling that there's not enough time to do the job the way you'd like, but on the other hand everyone knows that any project will expand to fill the time available. Scheduling is especially sensitive when you are working with new technology. Desktop publishing is supposed to shave days off of a project that would have taken a week, and weeks off of one that would have taken a month. That can happen, but not the first week you have your system. You need time to learn, time to find out what you can and can't do with your particular configuration.

Most schedules are determined backwards, starting with when you want the document in your reader's hands. You then figure in the time required for distribution, printing, and other outside services, and finally you determine not how long you *need* to create the publication, but how long you *have*.

Schedules are a reality factor. The tighter the schedule, the simpler your format should be.

What is the budget?

Money is also a reality factor. It so affects everything about a publication that it's often the first consideration. We've put it last on the checklist, not out of disregard for its importance, but out of a belief that first you should think about what you want to do, and then you should look at what you can do. It's the nature of dreams to make us reach, and even when we can't grab hold of what we want, dreams often produce good ideas that can be scaled down to fit a budget. Take your budget and your schedule seriously, but don't let them be ever-present blinders.

CHAPTER 2

THE PRINCIPLES OF TYPOGRAPHY

Typographic arrangement should achieve for the reader what voice tone conveys to the listener.
—El Lissitzky

T he ability to set type, to modify it on-screen, to compose it in pages, and then to print the result in camera-ready form is the foundation of desktop publishing. Suddenly, the fundamental building block of graphic design is in the hands of anyone with a few thousand dollars. What are we to make of this access to such a rich tradition, one developed over 500 years of practice?

The answer, of course, varies widely. Typography at its most basic is simply the selection and arrangement of typefaces, sizes, and spacing on the printed page. But faced with the raw material for a page that isn't printed, how do you style the elements so that the page is inviting and easy to read, so that the eye can distinguish the relative importance of items and pick out the ones of interest, so that the overall appearance is both varied and unified?

In addition to the utilitarian functions implied in those questions, typography also gives a page a certain personality (formal or informal, modern or classic, ornate or sturdy) and an overall feeling (dense or open, light or dramatic). How do you choose from among the many typefaces available to project the desired image and to give your publication a distinctive and recognizable personality?

As much as in any other area of graphic design, the answers come largely from experience. Some of that experience we all have as readers. A great deal more can be gained by looking carefully at how type is styled in the whole range of printed materials. And finally, the computer makes it possible to discover the nuances of type through hands-on experimentation.

Computers have given us an invaluable control over typography, but they have also made possible a counterproductive versatility. In desktop publishing we have so many typefaces available and so many special effects, we can change so readily from one size and style to another, that undisciplined typography can as easily fragment the message as help hold it together. Use the control to experiment, to find the right face and size and spacing for your purpose, but don't use the versatility to pack your pages with a half dozen or more styles that confuse more than they communicate.

The power to control typography from the desktop is all the more miraculous when you review the history of typesetting and see the

72 dots per inch (screen image)

300 dpi

1270 dpi

2540 dpi

There is a story, no doubt apocryphal, that a fifteenth-century scribe, upon examining one of Gutenberg's press sheets, exclaimed, "It's nice, but it's not calligraphy."

progression from a craftsman's handling of each individual letter to a computer operator's ability to send electrical impulses around the world. In the fifteenth century, Johann Gutenberg liberated the printed word from the painstaking craft of handscripting with what now seems the almost equally painstaking craft of individually setting each metal character. With the introduction of linotype machines in the 1880s, keyboard operators could type in the text and the machine would cast an entire line in a single slug of hot metal. Phototypesetting eliminated the actual type altogether and produced text by projecting the images of characters on light-sensitive film or paper. Today's computer-driven laser printers have turned letters into patterns of dots and computer owners and operators into typographers.

This most recent "democratization" of typography has created something of a holy war between the traditionalists and the new breed of desktop publishers. The traditionalists—designers of typefaces and graphic designers who have worked with commercial type throughout their careers—lament the distortion of letterforms in standard faces, the uneven spacing between letters and words, and the lower resolution in the type created on desktop systems. The desktop publishers see savings in time and money and, in some documents, a quality that is far superior to that of typewritten and mimeographed forms.

The real miracle, which it is the nature of holy wars to overlook, is choice. The laser printer resolution of 300 dots per inch (dpi) is perfectly adequate as well as cost effective for many newsletters, reports, bulletins, price sheets, and a great many other documents. The higher resolution of a Linotronic 100 or 300 (1270 and 2540 dots per inch, respectively) is appropriate for many brochures, books, catalogs, technical manuals, magazines, and annual reports; in these situations the desktop computer serves as the front end for commercial typesetting and still gives the user greater control and considerable savings of time and money over traditional typesetting. High-quality, commercial typesetting is still available for advertising agencies, design studios, and publishers of fine books and magazines whose products require the cleanest, sharpest, most beautifully proportioned, and costlier type. It's a matter of choosing the quality of type appropriate for your needs and budget, and then using that type as well as you possibly can.

This chapter is about the many ways of using type. The main purpose is not to put forth rules you must remember but to suggest ways of looking at type on the printed page. As Sumner Stone, the director of typography at Adobe Systems, said in a *Publish!* magazine roundtable discussion on typography, "It's like learning how to appreciate different flavors of wine." Drink up.

A VISUAL GLOSSARY OF TYPOGRAPHY

The terminology used to describe type and its appearance on the printed page is a colorful and useful jargon. As with any specialized language, it enables people to communicate unambiguously, so that the instruction "align baseline of flush right caption with bottom of art" means the same thing to everyone involved in a job. But the language of typography also describes the subtlety and diversity among letterforms. This glossary is intended to display some of that richness in the process of setting forth basic definitions.

TYPEFACE

The name of a typeface refers to an entire family of letters of a particular design. (Historically, face referred to the surface of the metal type piece that received the ink and came into contact with the printing surface.) The faces shown on this spread are resident on most Post-Script printers. Hundreds of faces are available for desktop production today; by the end of 1990, the number will be in the thousands.

Avant Garde

ABCDEFGHIJKLMNOPQRSTUVWXYZ
abcdefghijklmnopqrstuvwxyz
1234567890!$,""?
ABCDEFGHIJKLMNOPQRSTUVWXYZ
abcdefghijklmnopqrstuvwxyz
1234567890!$,""?

Bookman

ABCDEFGHIJKLMNOPQRSTUVWXYZ
abcdefghijklmnopqrstuvwxyz
1234567890!$,""?
ABCDEFGHIJKLMNOPQRSTUVWXYZ
abcdefghijklmnopqrstuvwxyz
1234567890!$,""?

Courier

ABCDEFGHIJKLMNOPQRSTUVWXYZ
abcdefghijklmnopqrstuvwxyz
1234567890!$,""?
ABCDEFGHIJKLMNOPQRSTUVWXYZ
abcdefghijklmnopqrstuvwxyz
1234567890!$,""?

Helvetica

ABCDEFGHIJKLMNOPQRSTUVWXYZ
abcdefghijklmnopqrstuvwxyz
1234567890!$,""?
ABCDEFGHIJKLMNOPQRSTUVWXYZ
abcdefghijklmnopqrstuvwxyz
1234567890!$,""?

New Century
Schoolbook

ABCDEFGHIJKLMNOPQRSTUVWXYZ
abcdefghijklmnopqrstuvwxyz
1234567890!$,""?
ABCDEFGHIJKLMNOPQRSTUVWXYZ
abcdefghijklmnopqrstuvwxyz
1234567890!$,""?

Palatino

ABCDEFGHIJKLMNOPQRSTUVWXYZ
abcdefghijklmnopqrstuvwxyz
1234567890!$,""?
ABCDEFGHIJKLMNOPQRSTUVWXYZ
abcdefghijklmnopqrstuvwxyz
1234567890!$,""?

Times Roman

ABCDEFGHIJKLMNOPQRSTUVWXYZ
abcdefghijklmnopqrstuvwxyz
1234567890!$,""?
ABCDEFGHIJKLMNOPQRSTUVWXYZ
abcdefghijklmnopqrstuvwxyz
1234567890!$,""?

Zapf Chancery

ABCDEFGHIJKLMNOPQRSTUVWXYZ
abcdefghijklmnopqrstuvwxyz
1234567890!$,""?
ABCDEFGHIJKLMNOPQRSTUVWXYZ
abcdefghijklmnopqrstuvwxyz
1234567890!$,""?

For all the variety found across thousands of typefaces, they can all be grouped into three basic styles—serif, sans serif, and script. The samples shown on these two pages suggest the variation available in each style. These samples (and the ones throughout this chapter) are PostScript fonts from Adobe Systems.

Some legibility studies have found that serif typefaces are easier to read, the theory being that the serifs help move the eye from one letter to the next without the letters blurring together. On the other hand, sans serif typefaces are generally thought to be easier to read at very large and especially at very small sizes. It's difficult to make any hard-and-fast rules because legibility is affected not only by typeface but also by size, length of line, amount of leading, amount of white space on the page, and even by the quality of the paper.

SANS SERIF

Sans serif typefaces do not have finishing strokes at the end of the letterforms. The name comes from the French *sans*, meaning "without." Sans serif faces are also referred to as Gothic.

Helvetica   Futura   Univers

Avant Garde   Franklin Gothic

Eurostile   News Gothic   Optima

SCRIPT

Script faces simulate handwriting, with one letter connected to another visually if not physically.

Freestyle Script   Zapf Chancery

SERIF

Serifs are lines or curves projecting from the end of a letterform. Typefaces with these additional strokes are called serif faces. They are also referred to as Roman faces because the serifs derived from the marks made chiseling letters into Roman monuments. (Note that when describing serif faces, the word Roman is capitalized; when describing vertical letters as distinguished from italic ones, roman is lowercase.)

Palatino   Times Roman   Garamond

New Century Schoolbook   Caslon

Bookman   Century Old Style

Goudy Old Style   Glypha

Bodoni   American Typewriter

Trump Mediæval   Galliard

Lubalin Graph   New Baskerville

SIZE

Type is measured by its vertical height, from the top of the capital letter or ascender (whichever is higher) to the bottom of the descender. That height, or size, is expressed in points. There are 12 points to a pica and approximately 6 picas to an inch.

Height Height Height Height Height Height Height **Height**

6 pt 8 pt 10 pt   12 pt   14 point 18 point   36 point   72 point

WEIGHT

Weight refers to the density of letters, to the lightness or heaviness of the strokes. It is described as a continuum: light, regular, book, demi, bold, heavy, black, extra bold. Not all typefaces are available for all weights, and the continuum varies in some faces.

HELVETICA LIGHT HELVETICA REGULAR
HELVETICA BOLD   HELVETICA BLACK

WIDTH

The horizontal measure of the letters is described as condensed, normal, or expanded. The commonly used faces—Times, Helvetica, New Century Schoolbook— are normal. Quite a few condensed faces are available in desktop publishing. And drawing programs such as Adobe Illustrator enable you to condense or expand type in any face and then import it into Ventura, a technique that is very fashionable in type design today.

CONDENSED   NORMAL   EXPANDED

SLANT

Slant is the angle of a type character, either vertical or inclined. Vertical type is called roman (in Ventura it is called Normal, and in some word-processing programs, Plain). Inclined type is called italic or oblique.

roman & *italic*

STYLE

In desktop publishing, style refers to weight, slant, and certain special effects such as outline or shadow. In a more general sense, style refers to the broad characteristics of a typeface (such as serif or sans serif) and to its distinctive personality as well (such as elegant or friendly).

STYLE   **STYLE**   *STYLE*   STYLE

STYLE   STYLE   STYLE   STYLE

FAMILY

All the variations of a single typeface—the different weights, widths, slants, and styles—constitute a type family. Some families have more styles than others, providing for considerable type contrast within a document without the need to change typefaces. In addition to the Helvetica styles shown below, the family includes Compressed, Thin, Ultra Light, and Heavy variations. Some other families with many variations are Bodoni, Futura, Univers, and Stone.

Helvetica
Helvetica Italic
Helvetica Bold
Helvetica Bold Italic
Helvetica Condensed Light
Helvetica Condensed Light Oblique
Helvetica Condensed
Helvetica Condensed Oblique
Helvetica Condensed Bold
Helvetica Condensed Bold Oblique
Helvetica Condensed Black
Helvetica Condensed Black Oblique
Helvetica Light
Helvetica Light Oblique
Helvetica Black
Helvetica Black Oblique

ANATOMY

In designing, measuring, and identifying type, a precise vocabulary is essential. Here are the basics:

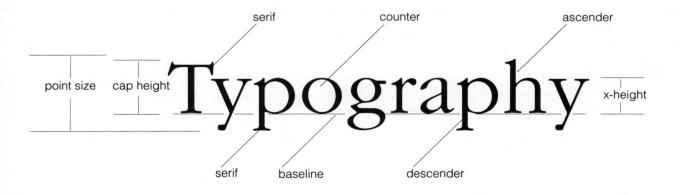

LEADING

The vertical space between lines of type is traditionally called leading (pronounced "led•ing"); in Ventura, it is called Inter-Line Spacing. It is measured in points and is expressed as the sum of the type size and the space between two lines. For example, 10-point type with 2 points between the lines is described as 10-point type on 12-point leading. It is written 10/12 and spoken "10 on 12."

Type with a generous amount of space between lines is said to have open leading; type with relatively little space between lines is said to be set tight. Type without any space between lines (such as the 10/10 and the 30/30 samples below) is said to be set solid. Leading that is less than the point size, as in the 30/26 sample, is called negative, or minus, leading; it is used primarily for large type sizes set in all caps.

10/10 Times Roman

These three type samples are all set in 10-point Times Roman. The first is set solid (10/10), the second is set tight (10/11), and the third (10/12) is set with Ventura's normal Inter-Line spacing (120% of the point size).

10/11 Times Roman

These three type samples are all set in 10-point Times Roman. The first is set solid (10/10), the second is set tight (10/11), and the third (10/12) is set with Ventura's normal Inter-Line spacing (120% of the point size).

10/12 Times Roman

These three type samples are all set in 10-point Times Roman. The first is set solid (10/10), the second is set tight (10/11), and the third (10/12) is set with Ventura's normal Inter-Line spacing (120% of the point size).

30/26 Helvetica Condensed Black

THIS DISPLAY TYPE IS SET MINUS

30/30 Helvetica Condensed Black

THIS DISPLAY TYPE IS SET SOLID

30/34 Helvetica Condensed Black

THIS DISPLAY TYPE IS SET OPEN

LINE LENGTH

The length of a line of type is called the measure and is traditionally specified in picas. Fractions of picas are expressed as points (there are 12 points to a pica), not as decimals. So a column that is 10 and one-quarter picas wide is 10 picas 3 points, specified in Ventura as 10,03.

Generally, the longer the line length, the larger the type should be.

This is set to a 12,00 measure and can be easily read with a relatively small type size. This sample is 9/11.

This is set to a 20,06 measure and needs a larger type size for ease of reading. This sample is 10/12.

This is set to a 37,10 measure and needs a larger type size to be easily read. This measure is too wide for most running text and is best used for subheads, blurbs, and other short display type. This sample is set 13/15.

ALIGNMENT

Alignment refers to the shape of the type block relative to the margins. The common settings are flush left, centered, flush right, and justified. Body text is generally set flush left or justified, but with the controls available in Ventura, flush left produces much better results.

Flush left

The lines of text are even on the left edge (flush with the left margin) and uneven, or ragged, on the right. Flush left is the recommended alignment for body text in desktop publishing. It is easy to read and allows even word spacing.

Centered

Each line is centered;
thus, both left and right margins
are ragged.
Centered text is often used
for headlines and
other display type,
as well for as formal invitations
and announcements.

Flush right

The lines of text are even on the right and uneven on the left. This alignment is sometimes used for captions, headlines, and advertising copy but is not recommended for body text. We are used to reading from left to right; if the left edge of the text is not well-defined, the eye falters, and the text is more difficult to read.

Justified

The type is flush, or even, on both the right and the left margins. Because the normal space between letters and words is altered in order to justify text, justification sometimes results in uneven spacing, with "rivers" of white space running through the type. The narrower the measure, the more uneven the spacing is likely to be, as you can see by comparing these side-by-side examples.

Justified

The type is flush, or even, on both the right and the left margins. Because the normal space between letters and words is altered in order to justify text, justification sometimes results in uneven spacing, with "rivers" of white space running through the type. The narrower the measure, the more uneven the spacing is likely to be, as you can see by comparing these side-by-side examples.

Rag left and right

A less common setting is rag left and rag right.
This is sometimes used for small amounts of display type.
It gives the page a poetic feeling without being formal.
This setting cannot be achieved automatically:
You must specify the indent for each individual line.

RULES

Rules are also typographic elements and are measured in points. With Ventura, they are most conveniently associated with particular paragraph styles. You can specify up to three rules at a time in Ventura's Ruling Line Above and Ruling Line Below dialog boxes found in the Paragraph menu. The rules can have different weights and spacing.

TYPE SPECIMEN SHEETS

Designers have traditionally relied on specimen sheets to select and specify type in their publications. "Spec" sheets, as they are known, simply display typefaces in various sizes, weights, and styles so that you can judge the appropriateness of a particular face for the publication you're about to design, as well as the readability, color, and overall look of frequently used sizes. Spec sheets are also useful when you want to identify a typeface that you see and like in another publication.

Commercial typesetters generally supply spec sheets to their customers as a sort of catalog of what is available. You can also buy books of spec sheets, and some are now available specifically for desktop publishing. (See the Resources section in the back of this book.)

Type is the first impression you have of what you're about to read. Each typeface, like a human face, has a subtle character all its own. Depending on which face you choose, the same word can have many different shades of meaning. And since you must have type in order to have words, why not make sure those words are presented in the most elegant, or the most powerful, or the softest way possible.
—Roger Black,
from an interview in Font & Function

You can also make your own spec sheets for the typefaces available on your own system or network. The little time it takes will repay you generously every time you need to design a publication. In addition to providing you with a useful resource, making spec sheets is a good way to begin learning the nuances of type.

The page at right shows one format for a spec sheet. Depending upon the kind of publication work you do, you may want to vary the components, with more or less display type, more or less running text, more or fewer small-size settings for captions, data, and so on. You may also want more variation in line length than our sample shows. Expand it to two pages, include character counts for various settings—in short, do whatever will be most useful to you. Once you have a format worked out and have set up one complete spec sheet as an electronic page, you can simply open a copy of that page for each typeface in your system, change the typeface, and then type over the identifying names for the new typeface. By using the same words and style for each sheet, you'll get a true comparison between the faces that are available to you.

In the sample, we've kerned the name of the typeface at the very top of the page, adding space between letters where needed so that none of the letters butt. You want to be able to see the shape of each letter when you use the spec sheets as an identification aid.

GARAMOND

Garamond Light
Garamond Light Italic
Garamond Bold
Garamond Bold Italic

ABCDEFGHIJKLMNOPQRSTUVWXYZ
abcdefghijklmnopqrstuvwxyz
1234567890!@#$%^&*( )+[ ] , ; " " ?

WALDEN BY HENRY DAVID THOREAU   12/14
WALDEN BY HENRY DAVID THOREAU

WALDEN BY HENRY DAVID THOREAU   caps/sm caps
WALDEN BY HENRY DAVID THOREAU

Walden by Henry David Thoreau
Walden by Henry David Thoreau

14/16

When I wrote the following pages, I lived alone, in the woods, a mile from any neighbor, in a house which I had built myself, on the shore of Walden Pond.

9/11

I lived alone, in the woods, a mile from any neighbor, in a house which I had built myself, on the shore of Walden

I lived alone, in the woods, a mile from any neighbor, in a house which I had built myself, on the shore of

11/13

When I wrote
the following pages,
or rather
the bulk of them,
I lived alone, in the woods,
a mile from any neighbor,
on the shore of Walden Pond.

36

Aa Ee Gg Tt Ww
1 2 3 4 5 6 7 8 9 $? ' '

9/11

When I wrote the following pages, or rather the bulk of them, I lived alone, in the woods, a mile from any neighbor, in a house which I had built myself, on the shore of Walden Pond, in Concord, Massachusetts, and earned my living by the labor of my hands only. I lived there two years and two months. At present I am a sojourner in civilized life again.

I should not obtrude my affairs so much on the notice of my readers if very

W 72

10/12

hen I wrote the following pages, or rather the bulk of them, I lived alone, in the woods, a mile from any neighbor, in a house which I had built myself, on the shore of Walden Pond, in Concord, Massachusetts, and earned my living by the labor of my hands only. I lived there two years and two months. At present I am a sojourner in civilized life again.

I should not obtrude my affairs so much on the notice of my readers if

11/13

When I wrote the following pages, or rather the bulk of them, I lived alone, in the woods, a mile from any neighbor, in a house which I had built myself, on the shore of Walden Pond, in Concord, Massachusetts, and earned my living by the labor of my hands only. I lived there two years and two months. At present I am a sojourner in civilized life again.

I should not obtrude my affairs so much on the notice of my

12/14

When I wrote the following pages, or rather the bulk of them, I lived alone, in the woods, a mile from any neighbor, in a house which I had built myself, on the shore of Walden Pond, in Concord, Massachusetts, and earned my living by the labor of my hands only. I lived there two years and two months. At present I am a sojourner in civilized life again.

I should not obtrude my affairs so much on the notice of

Using key letters to identify type

When using spec sheets to identify type from other publications, look for key letters that tend to be distinctive, including the T, g, and M shown here (all 60 point). Numbers and question marks are also good indicators. You quickly learn to look for the shape of the serif (straight, triangular, rounded, or square), whether the bowls of the Ps and Rs and the tails of the g's are open or closed, the contrast between thick and thin parts of the letter, and so on.

T	T	T	T	T	T
Bodoni	Bookman	Garamond	New Century Schoolbook	Palatino	Times
T	T	T	T	T	T
Avant Garde	Futura	Helvetica	News Gothic	Optima	Univers
g	g	g	g	g	g
Bodoni	Bookman	Garamond	New Century Schoolbook	Palatino	Times
g	g	g	g	g	g
Avant Garde	Futura	Helvetica	News Gothic	Optima	Univers
M	M	M	M	M	M
Bodoni	Bookman	Garamond	New Century Schoolbook	Palatino	Times
M	M	M	M	M	M
Avant Garde	Futura	Helvetica	News Gothic	Optima	Univers

The color of type

The addition of a second color (or several colors) can enhance the typographic design of a publication in many ways. But even when printed in black and white, type has a color on the printed page. Color in this sense means the overall tone, or texture, of the type; the lightness or darkness, which varies from one typeface and style to another; and also the eveness of the type as determined by the spacing. Spec sheets provide valuable guides to the color of different typefaces, which, as you can see in the samples below, varies considerably.

A large rose-tree stood near the entrance of the garden: the roses growing on it were white, but there were three gardeners at it, busily painting them red. Alice thought this a very curious thing, and she went nearer to watch....
—Futura Light

A large rose-tree stood near the entrance of the garden: the roses growing on it were white, but there were three gardeners at it, busily painting them red. Alice thought this a very curious thing, and she went nearer to...
—Goudy Old Style

A large rose-tree stood near the entrance of the garden: the roses growing on it were white, but there were three gardeners at it, busily painting them red. Alice thought this a very curious thing, and she went nearer to...
—Optima

A large rose-tree stood near the entrance of the garden: the roses growing on it were white, but there were three gardeners at it, busily painting them red. Alice thought this a very curious thing, and she went nearer...
—Palatino

A large rose-tree stood near the entrance of the garden: the roses growing on it were white, but there were three gardeners at it, busily painting them red. Alice thought this a very curious thing, and she went nearer to...
—Garamond

A large rose-tree stood near the entrance of the garden: the roses growing on it were white, but there were three gardeners at it, busily painting them red. Alice thought this a very curious thing...
—Avant Garde

A large rose-tree stood near the entrance of the garden: the roses growing on it were white, but there were three gardeners at it, busily painting them red. Alice thought this a very curious thing...
—Univers

A large rose-tree stood near the entrance of the garden: the roses growing on it were white, but there were three gardeners at it, busily painting them red. Alice thought this a very curious thing, and she went nearer...
—Franklin Gothic Demi

A large rose-tree stood near the entrance of the garden: the roses growing on it were white, but there were three gardeners at it, busily painting them red. Alice thought this a very curious thing, and she went nearer...
—Helvetica

A large rose-tree stood near the entrance of the garden: the roses growing on it were white, but there were three gardeners at it, busily painting them red. Alice thought this a very curious thing, and she went nearer to watch....
—New Baskerville Bold

A large rose-tree stood near the entrance of the garden: the roses growing on it were white, but there were three gardeners at it, busily painting them red. Alice thought this a very curious thing...
—Souvenir Demi

A large rose-tree stood near the entrance of the garden: the roses growing on it were white, but there were three gardeners at it, busily painting them red. Alice thought this a very curious thing...
—Bookman Demi

A large rose-tree stood near the entrance of the garden: the roses growing on it were white, but there were three gardeners at it, busily painting them red. Alice thought this a very curious thing, and she went nearer to watch....
—Glypha

A large rose-tree stood near the entrance of the garden: the roses growing on it were white, but there were three gardeners at it, busily painting them red. Alice thought this a very curious thing, and she went nearer to watch....
—Century Old Style Bold

A large rose-tree stood near the entrance of the garden: the roses growing on it were white, but there were three gardeners at it, busily painting them red. Alice thought this a very curious thing and she went ...
—Am. Typewriter Bold

A large rose-tree stood near the entrance of the garden: the roses growing on it were white, but there were three gardeners at it, busily painting them red. Alice thought this a very curious...
—Futura Extra Bold

The many personalities of type

Typefaces clothe words. And words clothe ideas and information…. Typefaces can do for words, and through words for ideas and information, what clothes can do for people. It isn't just the hat or tie or suit or dress you wear. It's the way you put it on…and its appropriateness to you and to the occasion that make the difference. And so it is with type. A type library is a kind of wardrobe with garments for many occasions. You use your judgment and taste to choose and combine them to best dress your words and ideas.
　　　　　—U&lc, June 1980, cited in an Adobe poster

Every typeface has its own personality, a look that makes it more or less suited for a particular type of publication. Confident, elegant, casual, bold, novel, romantic, friendly, stylish, nostaligic, classic, delicate, modern, crisp…the possibilities are endless. You have only to know the feeling you want, select an appropriate face, and then test it for legibility and effectiveness within your overall design.

The faces shown on these pages merely suggest the range available to today's desktop publisher. Having to choose from the many faces available can be intimidating to new designers. Begin by using a few faces and learning them well: how to achieve contrast through different styles and spacing within those families, which letter pairs require kerning, which counters fill in at small sizes, and so on.

Take note of typefaces you like in other publications and identify them using a type book. Then gradually add new faces to your system, learning their unique subtleties as you did the few faces that you started with. As one designer cautioned in the same *Publish!* round-table on typography quoted earlier in this chapter, "There are only two kinds of typefaces: those you know how to use and those you don't."

GEOMETRY AND PRECISION
WHEN YOU WANT THE CUTTING EDGE

USE AVANT GARDE. IT'S MODERN WITHOUT BEING FORMAL AND GIVES A PAGE A VERY CRISP LOOK. IT SETS BEST IN ALL CAPS AND BENEFITS FROM KERNING SO THAT THE LETTERS SNUGGLE UP TIGHT AGAINST ONE ANOTHER.

A REPORT THAT SUGGESTS
The Writer Has Big Shoulders

would work well in Bookman. It's a sturdy, highly legible typeface, used in many newspapers and often described as a workhorse because it's so versatile. In both its light and bold faces, it has relatively little contrast between the thick and thin strokes.

WHEN YOU WANT TO KNOW THE SCORE

MACHINE IS THERE TO DELIVER IT IN A VERY BOLD WAY. IT IS A FACE WITH NO CURVES, ONLY ANGLES, AND IT SETS VERY CONDENSED. IT SHOULD BE USED FOR SHORT DISPLAY COPY ONLY AND NO SMALLER THAN 18 POINT (WHICH IS WHY THIS 9-POINT DESCRIPTION IS SET IN HELVETICA LIGHT RATHER THAN IN MACHINE). FOR BEST VISUAL RESULTS, MACHINE SHOULD BE KERNED. IN THE SAMPLE ABOVE, WE'VE KERNED TO TIGHTEN UP BOTH THE LETTER AND THE WORD SPACE.

This message demands your immediate attention...

and so it is set in American Typewriter, which has the immediacy of a standard typewriter face but is more sophisticated. Type sets more economically, with more words per line, in this face than in true typewriter faces such as Courier.

If the plan is to
GET ON THE FAST TRACK

try Lubalin Graph Demi. It's actually a serif version of Avant Garde with a square, Egyptian-style serif that is both modern and utilitarian. (Both Lubalin Graph Demi and Avant Garde were created by renowned designer Herb Lubalin.)

LIGHT AS THE ESSENCE OF SUNSHINE
AND BOLD AS A MOONLESS NIGHT

is the broad personality of Futura. It's a classic typeface: Born of the machine age in the twenties, it continues to be a designer favorite. Its versatility ranges from advertising to editorial, from fashion to technology. It comes in a wide selection of weights and widths. An all-time favorite combination is Futura Light and Extra Bold, shown above. This text is Futura Light Condensed.

If the need is to be
DRAMATIC AND SOPHISTICATED
AT THE SAME TIME

then look no further than the Bodoni family. It is very urban, with a touch of the theatrical. This is especially true with Bodoni Poster, used above. This text is in Bodoni Bold.

THE ANNUAL MESSAGE FROM
THE EXECUTIVE OFFICES

might well be set in Garamond. It's an extremely graceful, refined, and legible face that suggests the confidence that comes from success. The italic face is highly legible (many italic faces are not), as you can see from these few lines set in Garamond Light Italic.

The efficiency of type

The number of characters per line varies from one typeface to another, even when the same size type is specified. A typeface that has a relatively high character count per line is said to set efficiently (or tightly or economically), and is likely to look smaller than a less efficient typeface set in the same size.

Traditional type charts (and some books on typography) provide tables for determining the character count of each typeface in various sizes and line lengths. These may not translate with 100 percent accuracy to your desktop system because there are subtle differences in the same typeface from one manufacturer to another. Still, they can be helpful for determining the relative efficiency of different faces, as well as the approximate character count for your type specifications.

The words in these twelve blocks of text are exactly the same, and each text block is set 10/12. But the length varies from 10 to 15 lines because some typefaces set more economically than others, with more characters per line. Note also that the type in the shortest text block does not look the smallest. A condensed typeface with a large x-height sets tighter than a noncondensed face but still looks larger.
—Times Roman

The words in these twelve blocks of text are exactly the same, and each text block is set 10/12. But the length varies from 10 to 15 lines because some typefaces set more economically than others, with more characters per line. Note also that the type in the shortest text block does not look the smallest. A condensed typeface with a large x-height sets tighter than a noncondensed face but still looks larger.
—Garamond

The words in these twelve blocks of text are exactly the same, and each text block is set 10/12. But the length varies from 10 to 15 lines because some typefaces set more economically than others, with more characters per line. Note also that the type in the shortest text block does not look the smallest. A condensed typeface with a large x-height sets tighter than a noncondensed face but still looks larger.
—New Baskerville

The words in these twelve blocks of text are exactly the same, and each text block is set 10/12. But the length varies from 10 to 15 lines because some typefaces set more economically than others, with more characters per line. Note also that the type in the shortest text block does not look the smallest. A condensed typeface with a large x-height sets tighter than a noncondensed face but still looks larger.
—Helvetica Condensed Light

The words in these twelve blocks of text are exactly the same, and each text block is set 10/12. But the length varies from 10 to 15 lines because some typefaces set more economically than others, with more characters per line. Note also that the type in the shortest text block does not look the smallest. A condensed typeface with a large x-height sets tighter than a noncondensed face but still looks larger.
—Futura

The words in these twelve blocks of text are exactly the same, and each text block is set 10/12. But the length varies from 10 to 15 lines because some typefaces set more economically than others, with more characters per line. Note also that the type in the shortest text block does not look the smallest. A condensed typeface with a large x-height sets tighter than a noncondensed face but still looks larger.
—News Gothic

The samples on these two pages show the relative efficiency of a number of popular faces, with the serif faces across the top and the sans serif faces across the bottom. (All are from Adobe Systems.) Note that the more efficient faces have a smaller x-height; in addition to getting more characters per line, these faces require less leading because there is more built-in white space between the lines.

When efficiency is extremely important, consider using a condensed face with a large x-height. Note that the Helvetica Condensed Light sample looks larger than some of the others even though it sets the most economically.

The words in these twelve blocks of text are exactly the same, and each text block is set 10/12. But the length varies from 10 to 15 lines because some typefaces set more economically than others, with more characters per line. Note also that the type in the shortest text block does not look the smallest. A condensed typeface with a large x-height sets tighter than a noncondensed face but still looks larger.

—Palatino

The words in these twelve blocks of text are exactly the same, and each text block is set 10/12. But the length varies from 10 to 15 lines because some typefaces set more economically than others, with more characters per line. Note also that the type in the shortest text block does not look the smallest. A condensed typeface with a large x-height sets tighter than a noncondensed face but still looks larger.

—New Century Schoolbook

The words in these twelve blocks of text are exactly the same, and each text block is set 10/12. But the length varies from 10 to 15 lines because some typefaces set more economically than others, with more characters per line. Note also that the type in the shortest text block does not look the smallest. A condensed typeface with a large x-height sets tighter than a noncondensed face but still looks larger.

– Bookman

The words in these twelve blocks of text are exactly the same, and each text block is set 10/12. But the length varies from 10 to 15 lines because some typefaces set more economically than others, with more characters per line. Note also that the type in the shortest text block does not look the smallest. A condensed typeface with a large x-height sets tighter than a noncondensed face but still looks larger.

—Helvetica

The words in these twelve blocks of text are exactly the same, and each text block is set 10/12. But the length varies from 10 to 15 lines because some typefaces set more economically than others, with more characters per line. Note also that the type in the shortest text block does not look the smallest. A condensed typeface with a large x-height sets tighter than a noncondensed face but still looks larger.

—Univers

The words in these twelve blocks of text are exactly the same, and each text block is set 10/12. But the length varies from 10 to 15 lines because some typefaces set more economically than others, with more characters per line. Note also that the type in the shortest text block does not look the smallest. A condensed typeface with a large x-height sets tighter than a noncondensed face but still looks larger.

—Avant Garde

STYLING TYPE IN VENTURA

It is very difficult to give general rules for specifying type. The variables are so numerous—the kind of publication, the nature of the audience, the size of the page, the type of reading material, the relationship of text to white space, how the text is broken up, the resolution of the output, the quality of the printing, and on and on and on.

Outside of design school, there are two basic ways to learn about styling type. The first is to examine printed material and note what, to your eye, does and doesn't work. Does the type get your attention? Is it easy to read? Does it help move your eye from one part of the page to another and clarify the relationship between different items? Do special typographic effects further the communication or are they gratuitous? You'll find comments about how type is used in many of the samples reproduced in the next several chapters of this book (and also in some of the books listed in the Resources section). This kind of commentary seems more useful to us than general rules.

The second way to learn about type is to experiment. Desktop publishing facilitates experimentation to an unprecedented degree, which alone is likely to speed the learning curve of anyone coming into the field of graphic design today. Even a seasoned designer may need several settings before getting just the right relationship of display to body text, the desired contrast between captions or sidebars and the main story, and the balance of size, leading, and column width for the amount of text on a page. With commercial typesetting, both the cost and the turnaround time severely limit the ability to test different possibilities; when you work on the desktop, the time is your own (which, to be sure, can be a mixed blessing), and the cost of laser printouts is a few cents each.

You should take advantage of this ability to experiment once you are comfortable with the mechanics of changing and controlling type in Ventura. (See the Projects section for hands-on practice with the mechanics.) In fact, "playing" with type styles is a good way to learn both the mechanics of the program and the nuances of type. In addition to creating spec sheets as described earlier in this chapter, experimenting with different type settings in the early stages of any particular project is likely to be a good investment of time. Use text in whatever stage it exists, or use a file of dummy type.

A file of dummy type can consist of *lorem ipsum* text such as you'll see in many of the samples documents we created for this book. Some designers actually prefer using *lorem ipsum* to real text in the early stages because it encourages people to focus on the format and design, rather than on reading the copy.

When you begin to develop the format for a project, try two or three different typefaces with several settings. If you know you need a

---

TIP

Keyboard shortcuts to access Ventura's modes can save you time when you are testing different specifications. Use the following shortcuts to move from mode to mode.

Frame Setting	Ctrl-U
Paragraph Tagging	Ctrl-I
Text Editing	Ctrl-O
Graphic Drawing	Ctrl-P

relatively small text size, try 9/10, 9/11, 10/11, 10/12. In Ventura you can specify both type and leading in point and fractional point increments; an extra half point may be just what you need to achieve the proper balance.

You will often find it useful to experiment with the spatial relationships of your format's design elements. For instance, vary the margins and the space between columns. Try different headline treatments in relation to the body text—different sizes and styles, with different amounts of space between the headline and the text. The size of the headline should be proportional to the column width, the body text size, and the length and importance of the story.

Once you have a text block or a number of different text elements formatted, you can copy them, paste them on another page, and change the type specs for comparison. No lesson in any book will teach you as much as the comparisons you make of these printouts.

Learn early on to use the Paragraph menu's Spacing dialog box to specify paragraph indents and space between paragraphs or between different text elements, such as headlines and body text. For many new users, the familiar typewriter functions of the space bar and the carriage

MEASURING TYPE

As mentioned previously, type is measured vertically, in points, and line lengths are measured in picas. Of course you can measure lines and page elements other than type in inches as well, but because type size and line length are so interrelated, it is useful to become comfortable with picas and to be able to visualize in that system of measure. If you have not worked with points and picas before, you will soon appreciate the small unit of measure this system provides:

12 points = 1 pica

6 picas = 1 inch

To measure type in printed samples, you will need a type gauge, a special ruler with several slots running for most of its length and various sizes (usually ranging from 5 or 6 to 15 points) marked along the sides of different slots. You can buy a type gauge in any art supply store; they're very inexpensive. (The most common one is called a Haberule.) When using a type gauge, keep in mind that the conversion from picas to inches is slightly different from that on the computer: 6 picas (72 points) is 0.996 inches on a traditional type ruler; the conversion has been rounded off in most desktop publishing systems, where the 72 dots-per-inch resolution of many monitors converts so easily to 72 points to the inch.

return seem easier, but it is virtually impossible to maintain consistency using them, or to remember, when you compare different samples, how much space you inserted. (When several people work on the same job, space bar and carriage return spacing can really wreak havoc.) You'll be amazed at how quickly you can specify indents and spacing. (See Project 4 and Project 5 for practice with paragraph typography.)

A HANDFUL OF TYPOGRAPHIC CONVENTIONS

If you're a writer or editor used to working on a typewriter or word processor or a designer used to sending manuscripts out to someone else to typeset or new to publishing altogether, you should remember these typographic conventions:

• **Space between sentences** One space after a period at the end of a sentence is sufficient. It's difficult to get used to this if you've spent years pressing a typewriter space bar twice between sentences, but typesetting requires only one space after periods, question marks, exclamation points, and colons.

• **Dash** Type Ctrl-] to get a long dash—also called an em dash—rather than typing two hyphens as you do on a typewriter. For an en dash, used to indicate continuing or inclusive numbers such as 1988–1991, type Ctrl-[.

• **Quotation Marks and Apostrophes** Type Ctrl-Shift-[to open a quotation and Ctrl-Shift-] to close a quotation. This will give you true "typeset" quotation marks designed for the font you are using instead of straight, "typewriter-style" marks. When you place text in Ventura from a word-processing program, you can get typeset-style quotation marks automatically by selecting the Auto-Adjustments option to Both in the Options dialog box, but you will need to use the keyboard sequence for quotation marks that you type in Ventura.

For single quotation marks, the keyboard sequence is Alt-Shift-096 to open the quote and Alt-Shift-039 to close the quote. (The numbers must be typed using the numeric keypad.)

For an apostrophe, use the close single-quote sequence: Alt-Shift-039.

• **Common typographical symbols** There are several symbol characters you will find handy. Type Ctrl-Shift-C to insert a copyright symbol (©), Ctrl-Shift-2 to insert a trademark symbol (™), or Ctrl-Shift-R to insert a registered symbol (®) into your text.

TIP

Do not press the space bar numerous times to indent paragraphs, align text or numbers in columns, or create hanging indents. What appears aligned onscreen may not be aligned on the printed page. In addition to the options available through the Paragraph menu Tab Settings dialog box, use the following typographic spaces as needed:

Space	Keystoke combination
em	Ctrl-Shift-M
en	Ctrl-Shift-N
figure	Ctrl-Shift-F
thin	Ctrl-Shift-T

For most people, setting tabs properly is more difficult than specifying indents and line spacing, but if you need tabs, you won't get them right until you learn to use the Tab Settings dialog box, accessed from the Paragraph menu on the main screen. Don't even be tempted to use the space bar to set tabs; it simply won't work reliably with proportionally spaced text. (See Projects 3 and 5 for hands-on practice with tabs.)

For complex documents, use the dialog box options found in the Paragraph menu to specify various type elements. You can open a test chapter, change whatever style specifications you want for your next sample, and those styles will automatically be changed throughout the chapter. (See Projects 4 and 5 for working with style sheets.)

And, as we will say many times throughout this book, get ideas from other publications. If you see headlines or body text that has the feeling you want, use a type book to identify the typeface, measure the size and leading with a type gauge, run out a sample on your computer, and begin building your type design from that base.

TYPOGRAPHIC REFINEMENTS

Part of what distinguishes well-executed typography is the fine-tuning of details that we generally take for granted, such as hyphenation and the space between letters and words. This section will briefly address some of those details.

Hyphenation

You can turn hyphenation on and off through Ventura's Paragraph menu Alignment dialog box. If you have Ventura Professional Extensions and expanded (LIM) memory, you will be able to use the included Edco hyphenation directory. This directory is a list of 130,000 English words; it allows you direct control over where in a word hyphenation occurs and the minimum length a word has to be for Ventura to hyphenate it.

Soft rag	Hard rag
The first type sample has a soft rag, with relatively little difference between the short and long lines; hyphenation is used to make every line as long as possible without forcing the text to be justified on the right margin. The second sample has a hard rag, with some of the lines much shorter than others, because hyphenation is not allowed.	The first type sample has a soft rag, with relatively little difference between the short and long lines; hyphenation is used to make every line as long as possible without forcing the text to be justified on the right margin. The second sample has a hard rag, with some of the lines much shorter than others, because hyphenation is not allowed.

TIP

To add a discretionary hyphen, which Ventura will insert only if a line break occurs at that point, set an insertion point and then type Ctrl-Hyphen. To delete an undesirable hyphen (such as one that occurs in an already hyphenated word), insert a discretionary hyphen immediately preceding the word to force the word to the next line (or edit the text to pull up all of the word to the line on which it begins).

With a very hard rag, you may sometimes want to fill a hole at the end of a short line for a more even appearance, and you can do this by adding a discretionary hyphen. It's called discretionary because Ventura inserts it only if the word breaks at that point; if later editing causes the word to fall anywhere other than the end of the line, Ventura won't insert the hyphen. See the marginal tip for how to insert a discretionary hyphen.

A few caveats for end-of-line hyphenation:

- Don't hyphenate words in headlines and other display text.
- Don't hyphenate captions set to a very short measure.
- Don't hyphenate more than two consecutive lines.
- Do observe the proper conventions for word division. Use an unabridged dictionary and a good style manual. (See the Resources section at the end of this book.)

Pay attention to headlines

Because they are set large, headlines often require some typographic refinement. It's not simply that their size and styling make them such a dominant element on the page but also that larger-size type in general requires special attention.

Editorially, the purpose of a headline is to attract the reader's attention, to make the subject immediately apparent, and to indicate the relative importance of items. Visually, headlines add variety to page design and in the absence of art may be the primary graphic device a designer has to work with in setting a tone and style.

TIP

When you experiment with headline sizes in Ventura, remember to keep the leading proportional to the larger sizes. You may want to set the headline's Inter-Line Spacing (from the Paragraph menu's Spacing dialog box) to the same size as the headline itself. At the same time, make sure that the Above and Below spacings are set to 00,00 picas.

There are many ways to achieve visual emphasis with headlines: type size, typeface, line length, surrounding white space, and use of rules and banners are a few. You will see these and many other techniques in the samples reproduced later in this book. Whichever approach you select, your headlines will almost surely require attention to the spacing between letters, words, and lines. As much as any other aspect of typography, spacing in display type distinguishes amateurs from professionals.

In general, large type sizes require proportionately less leading than body text. Ventura's automatic leading of 120%, which works very well for 10- or 11-point reading text, would result in more than 7 points of lead in a 36-point headline. Especially when headlines are set in all caps, they usually look better set solid or with minus leading so that the lines hold together as a unit.

Large type sizes also generally require kerning, the process of adjusting the space between individual letters for better overall balance. The shape of some letter pairs, such as Wo, Ya, and Tu, makes the space between the letters seem too big. The shape of other letters, such as Mi and Il, makes the letters seem too close together. Mechanically, it is very easy to adjust the space in Ventura (see the tip on the next page), but how much to add or delete is a subjective visual judgment.

TIP

To add or delete space between letter pairs in Ventura, first select a range of letters and then press and hold a Shift key while you type a right or a left arrow key. Pressing the right arrow key moves the letters in the selected range farther apart; pressing the left arrow does the converse.

When you kern, the goal is to achieve an overall balance of spacing across the entire headline. One approach is to imagine pouring sand between the letters and then to add or delete space so that there would be a nearly equal volume of sand between each pair. Another approach is to visually isolate three letters to see if the space on both sides of the center one is equal; you can quickly "scan" an entire headline this way.

In the samples below, the top two are set 30/30, the bottom two 20/20. The samples with the tighter leading hold together much better as a unit and are easier to read.

The top two samples have not been kerned. The unkerned Times Roman setting (top left) is better balanced than the unkerned Helvetica Condensed setting to its right; in general, serif typefaces are more forgiving of spacing imbalances because the serifs form a visual connection between the letters. Compare the kerned and unkerned samples in each typeface to see where we've added and removed space. In the Helvetica version of the word DETAIL, for example, we've closed up the ET and the TA and opened up the IL so the word doesn's seem to have a "hole" in it.

HEADLINES WITH ATTENTION TO DETAIL

Spacing is too open

Good spacing

HEADLINES WITH ATTENTION TO DETAIL

HEADLINES WITH ATTENTION TO DETAIL

Spacing is too open

Good spacing

HEADLINES WITH ATTENTION TO DETAIL

Understanding leading

In the early days of typesetting, "leading" described the thin strips of lead inserted between lines of hot metal type. In commercial typesetting, leading is measured from baseline to baseline as the total of the type size plus the space between lines.

Ventura's leading (called Inter-Line Spacing) is also measured from the baseline of one line to the baseline of the line below it. The default leading is 120% of the specified font size (in the example below, the 20-point type has default leading of 24 points); but you can specify any value you want for the leading.

24 points lead ——— This type has default 120% Inter-Line spacing

24 points lead ———

Ventura ensures consistent line spacing when there is more than one size type in a given line through an option called Grow Inter-Line To Fit, found in the Paragraph Typography dialog box. In such a line, inter-line space is based on the largest type size in the line.

In the sample below left with 10/11 body text and a 48-point inital cap, Grow Inter-Line To Fit is off. It is on in the sample below right (with a 14-point word inserted for emphasis in 10-point running text), and Ventura has set the entire text block with 16 points of Inter-Line Spacing to accommodate the larger word.

W hen you have an initial cap, whether it is raised above the text or dropped in it, specify the same leading for the cap as for the body text.

If you insert a larger size text style for emphasis in a text block, turn on Grow Inter-Line to Fit to accommodate the larger size.

A few words about emphasis

When used for emphasis, boldface, italic, underline, and all caps can sometimes have the reverse effect of what is intended.

Boldface is generally the most effective way to make type stand out. Its usefulness in **headlines** needs little comment. It can also be used to emphasize **keys words, names, or events in running text,** either as a leadin or interspersed throughout the text as it is in this paragraph. (Note, however, that some typefaces, such as the Palatino used here, do not have much contrast between the bold and regular face.) Like anything else, too much can undermine the intended effect; too much boldface also makes the page look uneven and dark. In addition, when used in small sizes, boldface type can fill in the open space in letters such as o, e, and b; this is of particular concern when using a 300 dots-per-inch printer for final output, when using paper that absorbs a lot of ink (such as newsprint), and in poorer-quality printing in general.

Italic type may be the most misused of all forms of emphasis because it is actually softer, not bolder, than roman text. The calligraphic nature of italic text also makes it relatively difficult to read. Used for captions, quotes, display type, marginalia, leadins, and other short items, *italic type can provide a subtle contrast to the main text, but it does not provide emphasis.* As is the case with boldface, some typefaces have more contrast than others between their italic and roman styles; the Palatino used here is one of them.

ALL CAPS works well in headlines but should be avoided for sustained reading. Words set in upper and lower case have distinctive and recognizable shapes. WORDS SET IN ALL CAPS LOOK LIKE RECTANGLES OF DIFFERENT LENGTHS AND ARE MORE DIFFICULT TO READ, ESPECIALLY IN RUNNING TEXT, WHERE THERE ISN'T MUCH WHITE SPACE. It's fine to use all caps sparingly to get attention or emphasize a headline. But don't overdo it.

<u>Underlining</u> is a holdover from typewriters, where it is one of the few means of emphasis available. Even with the many other typographic techniques in electronic publishing, underlining can be useful when there are many different elements, as in the Garamond spec sheet earlier in this chapter, and in the presentation of data and other complex information. The underline style in Ventura, however, can be heavy and be set too close to the body text in many typefaces. If it appears this way to you, a different way to use underlining is to draw a hairline (.25 point) rule with the Graphic mode line tool. Remember, though, that if you edit the text, you'll have to move the underline manually.

> In this type sample, we used <u>Underline</u> from within Ventura's Text mode.
>
> In this type sample, we used a hairline-weight rule to <u>underline these words</u>.

Widows and orphans

Widows and orphans are colloquialisms for words or sentences that are visually isolated. The two terms are defined a little differently in different sources. We define a widow as a short line at the end of a paragraph, or the last line of a paragraph when it is isolated at the top of a column or page. Widows have traditionally been considered bad form because they make the type appear uneven on the page and in some situations interrupt the reader's eye movement. Widows are less of a problem in ragged right text than in justified text, especially when there is space between paragraphs. The widow in this paragraph, for example, is acceptable to us; if it were the last or the first line in a column, we would have eliminated it by cutting or adding to the text. In advertising and display typography, widows should always be eliminated.

We define an orphan as the opening line of a paragraph isolated at the bottom of a column or page. Orphans can interrupt the reader's eye movement at the beginning of a new thought and they should be eliminated by editing the text, either to force the orphan to the next column or to pull up additional lines of the paragraph.

SPECIAL CHARACTERS & SYMBOLS

Ventura Publisher gives you access to extended character sets that enable you to incorporate special symbols—registered trademarks, British pound and Japanese yen signs, accents used in foreign languages, and so on—in your documents.

Here is a list of characters commonly available. It gives the equivalent character among text, Zapf Dingbats, and Symbol fonts, alongside the ASCII number associated with each character. For more information about how to use these characters in your work, see Project 3 in Section 3 of this book.

Normal	ASCII	Symbol	Dingbat	Normal	ASCII	Symbol	Dingbat	Normal	ASCII	Symbol	Dingbat
	<32>	(Space)	(Space)	<	<60>	<	♣	X	<88>	Ξ	✳
!	<33>	!	✂	=	<61>	=	†	Y	<89>	Ψ	✳
"	<34>	⊇	⑩	>	<62>	>	✝	Z	<90>	Z	✳
#	<35>	#	✄	?	<63>	?	†	[	<91>	[	✳
$	<36>	∃	✂	@	<64>	≅	⊞	\	<92>	∴	✳
%	<37>	%	☎	A	<65>	A	✡	]	<93>	]	✳
&	<38>	&	✆	B	<66>	B	✢	^	<94>	⊥	✳
'	<39>	∋	✍	C	<67>	X	✣	_	<95>	‾	✿
(	<40>	(	✈	D	<68>	Δ	✤	'	<96>	‾	✾
)	<41>	)	✉	E	<69>	E	✥	a	<97>	α	❀
*	<42>	∗	☞	F	<70>	Φ	◆	b	<98>	β	❂
+	<43>	+	☞	G	<71>	Γ	◇	c	<99>	χ	✳
,	<44>	,	✌	H	<72>	H	★	d	<100>	δ	✳
-	<45>	−	✍	I	<73>	I	☆	e	<101>	ε	✳
.	<46>	.	✎	J	<74>	ϑ	✪	f	<102>	φ	✳
/	<47>	/	✏	K	<75>	K	☆	g	<103>	γ	✳
0	<48>	0	✐	L	<76>	Λ	✦	h	<104>	η	✳
1	<49>	1	☜	M	<77>	M	★	i	<105>	ι	✳
2	<50>	2	➔	N	<78>	N	✧	j	<106>	φ	✳
3	<51>	3	✓	O	<79>	O	✫	k	<107>	κ	✳
4	<52>	4	✔	P	<80>	Π	☆	l	<108>	λ	●
5	<53>	5	✗	Q	<81>	Θ	✳	m	<109>	μ	○
6	<54>	6	✘	R	<82>	P	✺	n	<110>	ν	■
7	<55>	7	✗	S	<83>	Σ	✳	o	<111>	o	❑
8	<56>	8	✘	T	<84>	T	✴	p	<112>	π	❐
9	<57>	9	✚	U	<85>	Υ	✶	q	<113>	θ	❑
:	<58>	:	✛	V	<86>	ς	✵	r	<114>	ρ	❏
;	<59>	;	✜	W	<87>	Ω	✸	s	<115>	σ	▲

Normal	ASCII	Symbol	Dingbat
t	<116>	τ	▼
u	<117>	υ	◆
v	<118>	ϖ	❖
w	<119>	ω	◗
x	<120>	ξ	❘
y	<121>	ψ	❙
z	<122>	ζ	❚
{	<123>	{	❛
|	<124>	|	❜
}	<125>	}	❝
~	<126>	~	❞
Ç	<128>	*(blank)*	*(blank)*
ü	<129>	ϒ	❡
é	<130>	′	❢
â	<131>	≤	❣
ä	<132>	⁄	❤
à	<133>	∞	❥
å	<134>	ƒ	❦
ç	<135>	♣	❧
ê	<136>	♦	♣
ë	<137>	♥	♦
è	<138>	♠	♥
ï	<139>	↔	♠
î	<140>	←	①
ì	<141>	↑	②
Ä	<142>	→	③
Å	<143>	↓	④
É	<144>	°	⑤
æ	<145>	±	⑥
Æ	<146>	″	⑦
ô	<147>	≥	⑧
ö	<148>	×	⑨
ò	<149>	∝	⑩
û	<150>	∂	❶
ù	<151>	•	❷
ÿ	<152>	÷	❸
Ö	<153>	≠	❹
Ü	<154>	≡	❺
¢	<155>	≈	❻
£	<156>	…	❼
¥	<157>	⏐	❽
¤	<158>	⎯	❾
ƒ	<159>	↵	❿
á	<160>	ℵ	➀
í	<161>	ℑ	➁
ó	<162>	ℜ	➂
ú	<163>	℘	➃
ñ	<164>	⊗	➄
Ñ	<165>	⊕	➅
ª	<166>	∅	➆
º	<167>	∩	➇
¿	<168>	∪	➈
“	<169>	⊃	➉
”	<170>	⊇	➊
‹	<171>	⊄	➋
›	<172>	⊂	➌
¡	<173>	⊆	➍
«	<174>	∈	➎
»	<175>	∉	➏
ã	<176>	∠	➐
õ	<177>	∇	➑
Ø	<178>	®	➒
ø	<179>	©	➓
œ	<180>	™	➔
Œ	<181>	∏	→
À	<182>	√	↔
Ã	<183>	⋅	↕
Õ	<184>	¬	➘
§	<185>	∧	➙
‡	<186>	∨	➚
†	<187>	⇔	➛
¶	<188>	⇐	➜
©	<189>	⇑	➝
®	<190>	⇒	➞
™	<191>	⇓	➟
„	<192>	◊	➠
…	<193>	〈	➡
‰	<194>	®	➢
•	<195>	©	➣
–	<196>	™	➤
—	<197>	∑	➥
°	<198>	⎛	➦
Á	<199>	⎜	➧
Â	<200>	⎝	➨
È	<201>	⎡	➩
Ê	<202>	⎢	➪
Ë	<203>	⎣	➫
Ì	<204>	⎧	➬
Í	<205>	⎨	➭
Î	<206>	⎩	➮
Ï	<207>	⎪	➯
Ò	<208>	*(blank)*	*(blank)*
Ó	<209>	〉	➱
Ô	<210>	∫	➲
Š	<211>	⌠	➳
š	<212>	⎮	➴
Ù	<213>	⌡	➵
Ú	<214>	⎞	➶
Û	<215>	⎟	➷
Ÿ	<216>	⎠	➸
ß	<217>	⎤	➹
Ž	<218>	⎥	➺
ž	<219>	⎦	➻
/	<220>	⎫	➼
(blank)	<221>	⎬	➽
(blank)	<222>	⎭	➾

CHAPTER 3

CREATING A GRID: THE UNDERLYING STRUCTURE OF PAGE COMPOSITION

A major virtue of the grid system is the discipline it imposes on the untrained designer. As a teacher of publication design, I have found that it is only when the student divides and analyzes the space he is working with that he is able to achieve a cohesive design solution.
—Allen Hurlburt,
The Grid

There is nothing mysterious about a grid. It is simply an underlying structure that defines where to put things on the page. A letter typed on an old manual typewriter uses a grid; so does a handwritten list on a sheet of paper in which you note the names of items on the left and the costs on the right. Although grids used in publication design can be considerably more complex than that, they can also be that simple.

The grid itself is a series of nonprinting vertical and horizontal lines that divide the page. This technique has been the dominant approach to publication design for at least twenty years, primarily because it provides such an effective way of organizing the page and speeds up layout time considerably. A well-constructed grid can make a lot of decisions for you—where to place the headlines, text, and art and how to handle the many details that inevitably turn up. A grid gives a publication a planned, cohesive look and helps ensure consistency from one page to the next. It also sets visual ground rules that everyone involved in a publication can follow.

The grid system is perfectly matched to designing on computers, where the basic unit is a square pixel. It works on the same principle as modular furniture, storage units, and old-fashioned wooden building blocks. In fact, constructing and using a grid has the same tactile tidiness and infinite variety as playing with blocks.

Of course, not all graphic designers use the grid system in their work. Some use other formal techniques, such as perspective, and some use a more intuitive, more purely aesthetic approach to page design. In general, however, designers find it far easier to introduce diversity and visual interest to a formal grid than to impose order and balance on a free-form approach.

This chapter looks at the grids found in a wide variety of publications, some of them real, some of them hypothetical documents created for this book. (The real publications carry a credit identifying the designer and the purpose of the document; the hypothetical publications, which generally use a Latin *lorem ipsum* file for running text, do not carry that credit.) The chapter begins with simple one-column grids and proceeds to increasingly complex formats. By following the progression from simple to complex, you should get a good feel for how grids work and how to use them in your publications.

Because grids provide the underlying structure of the page, we've used them as a sort of lens for looking at the other elements of page composition—typography and art. Type size and leading are inextricably related to column width, as are the size and position of graphic elements. So although the organizing principle of this chapter is grids, you will also find information about styling type and working with art. Terms that may be unfamiliar to some readers, whether having to do with graphic design or electronic page assembly, are defined in the glossary.

Throughout the chapter there are blueprints for grids that you can adapt for your own needs. Each blueprint is based on one of the hypothetical documents; your own documents may have different elements. If you use a different typeface, it might look better a little smaller or a little larger than the one in the document on which the blueprint was based. If your headline is longer than the one in the sample, you might need to adjust the space between the head and the text. The blueprints are only guidelines; as you change one element, be sure to reevaluate the others to see if additional changes are needed.

Before moving on to the structure of the page, we'll look at the shape of the page and the elements that are often found on it.

THE ANATOMY OF A PAGE

Designing and assembling pages, whether by hand or on a computer, is more than a mechanical or electronic task. It's a way of looking at a page as having a certain size, shape, and proportion.

Look through the printed material around you and you'll see that most of the pages are 8.5 by 11 inches, the same size as the letters we read and the memos we send. It's the most efficient cut of paper, it stacks up in newsstand racks with other printed material, and it fits nicely in files. But it's the vertical, or portrait shape—more than the size—that feels so familiar.

Although the page itself is usually vertical, in multipage documents the reader sees two facing pages as a horizontal unit with the slight interruption of the gutter down the center. Take advantage of this wider, more expansive unit as you organize your material and design the actual pages. And think of consecutive pages as part of a three-dimensional whole that exists in time as the reader turns the pages.

In addition to its shape, the printed page has a vocabulary that enables editors, designers, layout artists, and printers to communicate unambiguously about a job. Turn the page for a visual glossary of terms you're likely to encounter in this book and elsewhere.

THE ANATOMY OF A PRINTED PAGE

Byline The author's name, which may appear after the headline or at the end of an article.

Overline (also called a kicker or eyebrow) A brief tag over the headline that categorizes the story.

Headline The title of an article.

Deck (also called a tag line) A line that gives more information about the story.

Stick-up cap An enlarged initial letter extending above the body text.

Bleed art A photo, drawing, or tint that runs off the edge of the page.

Picture window A rectangle that indicates the position and size of art to be stripped into the page.

Caption The text describing a photograph or illustration.

Body text The main text, also called running text.

Folio The page number.

Running foot A line across the bottom of the page that helps orient the reader within a document. Here it contains the folio and date.

Verso Left-hand page (literally, the reverse, with the right-hand page considered the front).

Alley The space between columns.

Wraparound text Copy that wraps around a graphic.

Subhead A phrase that identifies a subtopic.

Inside margin The space between the binding edge of the page and the text.

THE COMPANY BULLETIN

Cover story

The Headline Goes Here

Optional secondary lines follow the headline to guide the reader into the story.

by John Hamilton

Lorem ipsum dolor sit amet, consectetuer adipiscing elit, sed diam nonummy nibh euismod tincidunt ut laoreet dolore magna aliquam erat volutpat. Ut wisi enim ad minim veniam, quis nostrud exerci tation ullamcorper suscipit lobortis nisl ut aliquip ex ea commodo consequat.

Duis autem vel eum iriure dolor in hendrerit in vulputate velit esse molestie consequat, vel illum dolore eu feugiat nulla facilisis at vero eros et accumsan et iusto odio dignissim qui blandit praesent luptatum zzril delenit augue duis dolore te feugait nulla facilisi. Lorem ipsum dolor sit amet, consectetuer adipiscing elit, sed diam nonummy nibh euismod tincidunt ut laoreet dolore magna aliquam erat volutpat.

Ut wisi enim ad minim veniam, quis nostrud exerci tation ullamcorper suscipit nisl ut aliquip ex ea commodo consequat. Duis autem vel eum iriure dolor in hendrerit in vulputate velit esse molestie consequat, vel illum dolore eu feugiat nulla facilisis at vero eros et accumsan et iusto odio dignissim qui blandit praesent luptatum zzril delenit augue duis dolore te feugait nulla facilisi.

Nam liber tempor cum soluta nobis eleifend option congue nihil imperdiet doming id quod mazim placerat facer possim assum. Lorem ipsum dolor sit amet, consectetuer adipiscing elit, sed diam nonummy nibh euismod tincidunt ut laoreet dolore magna aliquam erat volutpat. Ut wisi enim ad minim veniam, quis nostrud exerci tation ullamcorper suscipit lobortis nisl ut aliquip ex ea commodo consequat. Duis autem vel eum iriure dolor in hendrerit in vulputate velit esse molestie conse-

quat, vel illum dolore eu feugiat nulla facilisis at vero eros et accumsan et iusto odio dignissim qui blandit praesent luptatum zzril delenit augue duis dolore te feugait nulla facilisi. Lorem ipsum dolor sit amet, consectetuer adipiscing elit, sed diam nonummy nibh euismod

Duis autem vel eum iriure

Ttincidunt ut laoreet dolore magna aliquam erat volutpat.Ut wisi enim ad minim veniam, quis nostrud exerci tation ullamcorper suscipit lobortis nisl ut aliquip ex ea commodo consequat. Duis autem vel eum iriure dolor in hendrerit in vulputate velit esse molestie consequat, vel illum dolore eu feugiat nulla facilisis at.

Vero eros et accumsan et iusto odio dignissim qui blandit praesent luptatum zzril delenit augue duis dolore te feugait nulla facilisi. Lorem ipsum dolor sit amet, consectetuer adipiscing elit, sed diam nonummy nibh euismod tincidunt ut laoreet dolore magna aliquam erat volutpat. Ut wisi enim ad minim veniam, quis nostrud exerci tation ullamcorper suscipit lobortis nisl ut aliquip ex ea commodo consequat. Duis autem vel eum iriure dolor in hendrerit in vulputate velit esse molestie consequat, vel illum dolore eu feugiat nulla facilisis at vero eros et accumsan et iusto odio dignissim qui blandit prae-

The caption helps entice the reader into the text of your story and also provides information about the art and photography.

8 JANUARY 1989

Sidebar A smaller story inside a larger one, boxed with its own headline to set it apart from the main text. (It can be positioned anywhere on the page.)

Breakout (also called a pull quote, blurb, or callout) A sentence or passage excerpted from the body copy and set in large type.

Top margin The distance from the top trim to the top of the text area. Running heads and feet and folios are often positioned in the top or bottom margin.

THE COMPANY BULLETIN

Running head A line of text across the top of the page that helps orient the reader within a document. It might include the document's title, author, chapter, subject of current page, or page number.

This display type is another technique to grab the reader's attention and pull him or her into the article.

Sidebar heading is centered over the text in the sidebar

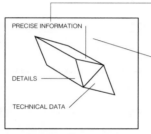

PRECISE INFORMATION

DETAILS

TECHNICAL DATA

Callout A label that identifies part of an illustration.

Leader A rule that moves the eye from a callout to the part of the illustration it describes.

Sequat, vel illum dolore eu feugiat nulla facilisis at vero eros et accumsan et iusto odio dignissim qui blandit praesent luptatum zzril delenit augue duis dolore te feugait nulla facilisi.

Lorem ipsum dolor sit amet, consectetuer adipiscing elit, sed diam nonummy nibh euismod tincidunt ut laoreet dolore magna aliquam erat volutpat. Ut wisi enim ad minim veniam, quis nostrud exerci tation ullamcorper suscipit lobortis nisl ut aliquip ex ea commodo consequat.

Duis autem vel eum iriure dolor in hendrerit in vulputate velit esse molestie consequat, vel illum dolore eu feugiat nulla facilisis at vero eros et accumsan et iusto odio dignissim qui blandit praesent luptatum zzril delenit augue duis dolore te feugait nulla facilisi. Lorem ipsum dolor sit amet, consectetuer adipiscing elit, sed diam.

Nonummy nibh euismod tincidunt ut laoreet dolore magna aliquam erat volutpat. Ut wisi enim ad minim veniam, quis nostrud exerci tation ullamcorper suscipit lobortis nisl ut aliquip ex ea commodo consequat.

The caption helps entice the reader into the text of your story and provides additional information about the art and photography.

❖ ❖ ❖

sent luptatum zzril delenit augue duis dolore te feugait nul ummy nibh euismod tincidunt ut laoreet dol magna aliquam erat volutpat.

Ut wisi enim ad minim veniam, quis nostrud exerci tation ullamcorper suscipit lobortis nisl ut aliquip ex ea commodo consequat. Duis autem vel eum iriure dolor in hendrerit in vulputate velit esse molestie consequat, vel illum dolore eu feugiat nulla facilisis at vero eros et accumsan et iusto odio dignissim qui blandit praesent luptatum zzril delenit augue duis dolore te feugait nulla facilisi. Lorem ipsum dolor sit amet, consectetuer adipiscing elit, sed diam nonummy nibh euismod tincidunt ut laoreet dolore magna aliquam erat volutpat. Ut wisi enim ad minim veniam, quis nostrud exerci tation ullamcorper suscipit lobortis nisl ut aliquip ex ea

Continued on page 11

JANUARY 1989 9

Dingbat A decorative or symbolic device used to separate items on the page or denote items in a list.

Outside margin The space between the outside trim and the text.

Continued line (also called jumpline) A line of text indicating the page on which an article continues. Its counterpart on the continuation page is a carryover line identifying the story that is being continued.

Bottom margin The space between the bottom trim and the baseline of the last line of text.

Drop cap An enlarged initial letter that drops below the first line of body text.

Screen (also called tone) A tint, either a percentage of black or a second color, behind text or art.

Printing rule A rule that traps a screen or surrounds a text block or a piece of art.

Page trim The edge of the page. In commercial printing, the size of the page after it is cut during the binding process.

Gutter The space between two facing pages.

Recto Right-hand page.

ONE-COLUMN GRIDS

The fewer the columns, the easier a grid is to work with. A simple one-column format requires relatively little planning and allows you to place text quickly. When done well, this format has an unstudied, straightforward look in which the hand of the designer is relatively invisible. That lack of "fuss" suggests a serious purpose that is appropriate for business plans, reports, proposals, press releases, announcements, simple manuals, and various forms of internal communications. Even when you use a two-column grid for these types of documents, consider a one-column format for the opening page to create the feeling of a foreword. When you mix grids in this way, be sure to maintain consistent margins throughout.

The generous margins and leading and the frequent subheads make this page very open for a one-column format. The text is 10/16 Helvetica with an 8-pica left margin and a 7-pica right margin.

The sans serif Helvetica face used here has a straightforward look that is well suited to factual or practical information. By comparsion, the serif type in the sample on the facing page suggests a narrative, essay-like writing style.

The 6-point rules at the top and bottom give the page structure. Note that with an anchor such as this you can vary the depth of the text from one page to the next and still maintain continuity of page format.

The justified text balances the overall openness, creating a strong right margin that completes the definition of the image area. The page would not hold together nearly as well with ragged right text.

Charts and diagrams (not shown) run as half or full pages centered left to right.

Design: Wadlin & Erber (New Paltz, NY)

Page from a manual that addresses the subject of radon occurrence in homes for an audience of building inspectors, architects, and contractors.
Trim size: 8-1/2 by 11

REDUCING INDOOR RADON

UNIT I

RADON OCCURRENCE AND HEALTH EFFECTS

Introduction

Radon is a colorless, odorless, and tasteless gas produced by the normal decay of uranium and radium. It is a naturally occuring radioactive gas produced in most soil or rock which surrounds houses. As a result, all houses will have some radon. It is an inert gas, which means it tends to be chemically inactive. Since radon is not chemically bound or attached to other materials, it can move easily through all gas permeable materials.

Radioactive Decay

Radioactive decay is the disintegration of the nucleus of atoms in a radioactive element by spontaneous emission of charged particles, often accompanied by photon (gamma) emission. As these charged particles are released, new elements are formed. The radioactive decay chain for radon begins with **uranium** producing **radium**, which in turn produces **radon**. Each of these elements has a different "half-life" (the time required for half of the atoms of a radioactive element to decay). The "half-life" is important because its length determines the time available for decay products to be dispersed into the environment.

Types of Radiation

The three types of radiation are gamma, beta, and alpha.

Gamma radiation is photon "parcels of energy" which operate at much higher energy levels than visible light. These rays are relatively high in penetrating power. They can travel much more deeply into objects than alpha or beta particles, and can pass through the body.

Beta radiation involves an energized particle emitted from the nucleus of a radioactive atom. It has a negative charge, and has a mass equal to one electron. Beta particles have medium penetrating power, and can penetrate up to about 0.5 centimeter of surface tissue, or about a millimeter of lead.

1

The simpler grids are generally "quiet." They don't allow for as much variety in art and headline treatment as the multicolumn formats, but with the typefaces, rules, and other simple graphic devices available in desktop publishing these pages can be effective and smart-looking.

Keep in mind that longer lines are more difficult to read than shorter ones because the eye has to travel farther from the end of one line to the beginning of the next. One-column pages risk becoming dense, dull, and uninviting. To compensate for this, use generous margins and space between lines and a relatively large typeface (10 to 13 points). Space between paragraphs also helps keep the page open.

The Past, Present and Future of Lotteries
People prefer to play on-line games

Three quarters of all lottery revenues in North America now come from on-line games.

1981
1983
1985
1987

Lottery sales are booming. In North America, the combined annual revenues from state-run lotteries have risen from approximately $3 billion in 1980 to over $15.7 billion in 1987.

Approximately 75 percent of the total revenues generated by North American lotteries is now derived from on-line games. The attraction of the on-line games lies in the daily drawing of the Numbers game and the frequent, multimillion-dollar jackpots of the Lotto games. These huge and enticing Lotto jackpots are the result of the top-prize pot "rolling over." The pot rolls over when all the numbers drawn were not picked by any player, and the unclaimed money rolls back into the pot for the next drawing. Rollovers cause wagering on the game to soar which, in turn, pushes the jackpot even higher until, finally, one or more lucky players win by matching the numbers drawn and the prize money is paid.

Outside of North America, those lottery jurisdictions that have added on-line technology to their operations have experienced great increases in revenues. For example, GTECH provided the first lottery-specific on-line system in Asia for Singapore Pools, Singapore's government-owned lottery company. The accompanying chart demonstrates the impact in sales gained by Singapore Pools after the GTECH network began operation.

In May 1986, Singapore Pools added on-line games. By the end of the year its sales had climbed 1600%, to average $8 million Singapore per week.

$8 million

on-line operations begin

months

5

The continuous running text in this sample requires a different treatment than the broken blocks of copy on the facing page. The inset art shortens the line length and makes the page more readable than it would be if the text were solid.

The margins are 6 picas top and bottom and 7 picas left and right.

The text is 12/16 Times Roman with a ragged right margin.

The headline treatment borrows editorial and typographic techniques used in magazines, with the contrasting style and size unified by the flush right alignment. The relationship of the two sizes is very nice here: The headline is 24-point Times Roman, and the tag line is 18-point Times Roman italic.

The chart, graph, and angled type were created in Adobe Illustrator. The ability to create dramatic, three-dimensional art for charts and graphs without having to be a technical illustrator is a great asset of desktop technology.

Design: Tom Ahern (Providence, RI)

Page from a capabilities brochure for GTECH, which provides on-line games for lottery networks.
Trim size: 8-1/2 by 11

Wide-margin one-column

A one-column grid with a wide margin is perhaps the most useful of all the designs in this book for internal reports, press releases, proposals, prospectuses, and other documents that have unadorned running text and need to be read fast. You may be tempted, with desktop publishing, to take something you used to distribute as a typewritten page and turn it into a multicolumn format, simply because you can. The danger is that you'll devote time to layout that would be better spent on content. As the hypothetical documents on the next three pages show, this simple one-column format can be smart, authoritative, and well planned. And though the line length is long, the white space provided by the wide margin gives the eye room to rest and makes the copy more inviting to read.

This format is especially well suited for single-sided documents that are either stapled or intended for three-ring binders. Use the left side of the page for the wide margin so that the space will look planned. (If you use the right side, it may look as though you ran out of copy and couldn't fill the page.) Although none are shown in these pages, headlines and subheads could extend into the margin for visual interest. So could short quotes, diagrams, and even small photos. When you want to make extensive use of the margin in this way, consider the "one + one-column" format discussed later in this section.

Extremely open leading facilitates quick scanning of a press release (on facing page), which usually commands less than a minute of the reader's time. The body text here is 11/20 Times Roman. With this much leading you probably would not want space between paragraphs; so you need an indent that is markedly wider than the space between lines. The indent in the sample shown is 3 picas for all paragraphs except the first.

The first paragraph is not indented. With flush left text, you rarely need to indent the opening paragraph or any paragraph that immediately follows a headline or a subhead. An indent would create an unnecessary visual gap at a place where the start of a new paragraph is obvious to the reader. To achieve this in running text where your paragraph indent is specified, for example, as 1 pica, you will need to select the opening paragraph and change its first line indent to 0.

The logo treatment can vary. The symbol could be flush with the left edge of the 6-point rule; a company name or logo could run across the top of the page, replacing the symbol and release line shown. (See the following page for an example.)

The headline should be short and straightforward. This is not the place to be clever.

The names of contacts for more information are positioned on a grid of two equal columns within the single-column format. The type is 9/12 Helvetica for contrast with the body text. If there is only one contact to list, position it in the right column of the two-column grid and move the "for immediate release" line to the left column.

The blueprint for this page appears on the following spread.

XYZ Corporation Announces New Plant Opening

For more information contact:

High Profile Publicity
Ann Millard
5432 Schoolhouse Road
Santa Monica, CA 92131
213-555-4664

XYZ Corporation
Marilyn Ferguson
1104 Beltway Drive
Los Angeles, CA 92111
213-555-3030

SANTA MONICA, CA. OCTOBER 10, 1990—Lorem ipsum dolor sit amet, consectetuer adipiscing elit, sed diam   nonummy nibh euismod tincidunt ut laoreet dolore magna aliquam erat volutpat. Ut wisi enim ad minim veniam, quis nostrud exerci tation ullamcorper suscipit lobortis nisl ut aliquip ex ea commodo consequat. Duis autem vel eum iriure dolor in hendrerit in vulputate velit esse molestie consequat, vel illum dolore eu feugiat nulla facilisis at vero eros et accumsan et iusto odio dignissim qui blandit praesent luptatum zzril delenit augue duis dolore te feugait nulla facilisi. Lorem ipsum dolor sit amet, consectetuer adipiscing elit, sed diam nonummy nibh euismod tincidunt ut laoreet dolore magna aliquam erat volutpat. Ut wisi enim ad minim veniam, quis nostrud exerci tation ullamcorper suscipit lobortis nisl ut aliquip ex ea commodo consequat.

Duis autem vel eum iriure dolor in hendrerit in vulputate velit esse molestie consequat, vel illum dolore eu feugiat nulla facilisis at vero eros et accumsan et iusto odio dignissim qui blandit praesent luptatum zzril delenit augue duis dolore te feugait nulla facilisi. Nam liber tempor cum soluta nobis eleifend option congue nihil imperdiet doming id quod mazim placerat facer possim assum. Lorem ipsum dolor sit amet, consectetuer adipiscing elit, sed diam nonummy nibh euismod tincidunt ut laoreet dolore magna aliquam erat volutpat. Ut wisi enim ad minim veniam, quis nostrud exerci tation ullamcorper suscipit lobortis nisl ut aliquip ex ea commodo consequat. Duis autem vel eum iriure dolor in hendrerit in vulputate velit esse molestie consequat, vel illum

The basic grid for the documents on this page is the same as the one used for the press release. Tighter leading here (11/15 Times Roman) is balanced with a full line space (15 points) between paragraphs.

The business plan above has 6 picas between the left trim and the rule. The text block is 12 picas from the top trim.

Boldface subheads are the same size as the body text. Omitting paragraph space after the subheads visually connects each subhead to its respective text block.

The company name is 14-point Times Roman bold italic.

The caption is inset in the box around the art (a style commonly found in reports and business plans) and set in 10/12 Times Roman italic.

In the proposal at right, the art is the full column width with the caption (10/13 Times Roman italic) in the margin. Note the alignment of the date, folio, rules at the top and bottom of the page, and left margin of the caption. This alignment is important: It creates an implied border that gives structure to the page.

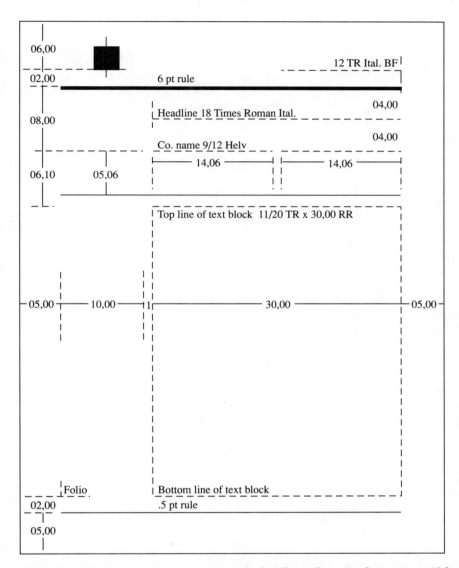

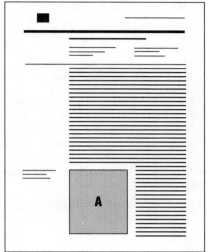

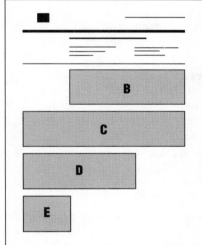

This blueprint shows the grid and type specifications for the press release on the preceding spread. The documents on the facing page use the same grid (except as noted in the annotations) but, for the most part, different type sizes.

A mixed grid structure is useful even in this simple format. Divide the text column into two equal units with a 1-pica space between. This creates two additional grid lines for placing small text and sizing art.

Blueprint measurements throughout the book are given in picas unless otherwise noted. The notation "x 30,00" describes the measure, or length, of a text line. "RR" denotes a ragged right margin.

Guidelines for placing art on this grid

- Size all art to one of the following widths:
  A: 14,06 (Ventura notation for 14 picas 6 points)—half the width of the text column with 1 pica between the art and the wraparound text
  B: 30,00—the full width of the text column
  C: 41,00—from the left edge of the 6-point rule to the right margin
  D: 25,00—from the left edge of the 6-point rule to a point 1 pica short of the midpoint of the text column
  E: 10,00—in the wide margin (if you have small mug shots)

- Avoid placing half-column art in the text column. Small charts and illustrations should be boxed with a 0.5- or 1-point rule to the sizes suggested.

- Placement is best at the bottom of the page, as shown in the examples at left. The top of the page is acceptable; the middle is not.

- For art that extends the full width of the column, the space between the text and the art should be equal to or greater than the leading.

- Place captions in the margin or inset them in a box around the art, as shown. Captions generally should be set one size smaller than the body text with tighter leading. Italic or a contrasting typeface is often used.

Attention to graphic detail makes the designer's hand more apparent in these documents than in the ones on the preceding pages. Both use a strong organization identity for external communication.

The large vertical headline fills the wide margin and establishes a distinctive style for a series of information sheets. Vertical type should always read upward unless the words themselves suggest downward motion.

The underlined headlines and bullets (which are gray) add variety to the simple page design.

Bulleted paragraphs with hanging indents are very effective when a message can be broken down into small chunks of information. The text immediately following the bullet should align exactly with subsequent lines.

The typeface is Palatino throughout.

IMAGESET :
First in Digital Graphic Design and Desktop Publishing

GRAPHIC DESIGN SERVICES

■ ImageSet provides professional graphic design services for creating state-of-the-art computer graphics and page layouts for a variety of businesses, firms, and publications.

■ Brochures, newsletters, magazine covers, advertisements, menus, logos, annual reports, and corporate identity programs can be designed from start to finish by our graphic design department. If there is a special design problem, ImageSet will find a solution.

■ ImageSet offers electronic design templates that can be purchased and modified for a client's use. Design templates are preformatted designs that can be quickly adapted to just about any publication task (newsletters, flyers, price lists, etc.).

■ ImageSet offers graphic design consultation for companies and individuals using desktop publishing technology. ImageSet can provide graphic design consultancy to assist the client in designing templates for newsletters, brochures, logos, or even help develop a coherent corporate identity program which can be utilized for all the client's desktop publishing applications.

■ Should the need arise, ImageSet offers individual and group instruction on computer graphics and page layout programs.

DESKTOP PUBLISHING SERVICES

■ ImageSet offers an output service of high resolution print for individuals and organizations whose publishing tasks demand higher quality typeset than laser printer (300 dpi) resolution. To implement this service, ImageSet utilizes a Mergenthaler Linotype L100 commercial laser phototypesetting device.

*Design:
Mark Beale,
ImageSet Design
(Portland, OR)*

*One of a series of information sheets in the promotional literature for ImageSet Associates.
Size: 8-1/2 by 11*

A distinctive logo gives this simple page a unique personality. The descriptive line explains the otherwise cryptic name.

The black and gray border echoes the logo style and gives structure to what would otherwise have been an overly loose composition. Borders provide a very simple and effective way to add graphic interest and importance to a page. To create a gray border in Ventura, such as the one used here, create a Ruling Box Around the frame, giving it a Pattern of 1. The technique is similar to that used for the coupon in Project 5 later in this book.

Initial caps add variety to the text and help draw the reader into the page. Like the bullets in the sample above, the initial caps facilitate the "quick scan" nature of information presented in short paragraphs.

The typeface, Galliard throughout, has a calligraphic feeling that is more friendly than formal.

Thanks for re-enlisting in the Giraffe Campaign

To show you how much we appreciate that, we've enclosed our official H.W.C.S.F.F.* telling the world that your membership in the Giraffe Project is in good standing and that you're entitled to all the rights and privileges thereof.

You'll also find an updated membership card, an *Instant Giraffe Citation* and a new campaign button — we're assuming that you, like so many other members, have been hit up for your old button by a friend or one of your kids.

People's faces do light up when they see Giraffe stuff — instead of letting them take yours, you can use the enclosed order form to get them their own buttons, mugs, shirts — and memberships. And don't forget to order more *Instant Giraffe Citations* yourself. Members who are using these report maximum satisfaction in being able to cite a Giraffe on-the-spot for meritorious action.

There will be exciting New Ideas and new "giraffenalia" in your upcoming year's worth of *Giraffe Gazettes*. We think you'll be surprised and delighted.

Keep scouting for new Giraffes and reporting your sightings to Giraffe Headquarters. We couldn't do the job without you.

And thanks again for your renewed vote of confidence in Giraffeness.

* *Handsome Wall Certificate Suitable For Framing*

*Design:
Scot Louis Gaznier
(Langley, WA)*

*Page acknowledging membership in the Giraffe Project, an organization that encourages people to "stick their neck out for the common good."
Size: 8-1/2 by 11*

Centering text inside a border creates a more formal image. The style of the border subtly changes the look of a page; experiment with the borders in Ventura and clip art files to find a style appropriate for your needs.

The justified text and centered headline add to the formality. Positioning the border slightly off center keeps the design from being quite so rigid.

On subsequent pages the border would be repeated and the position of the first line of text would remain constant, leaving the space occupied by the headline open.

The 33-pica line length is the widest of the one-column formats shown in this section. The density of the running text (11/15 New Century Schoolbook) is maximum for a readable page, and you should avoid paragraphs longer than the last one shown here (11 lines).

The inset text helps relieve the density of the long text lines. Use this device on as many pages as possible in a document with this wide a column.

This blueprint defines the guidelines for the proposal above.

Charts, graphs, financials, and other art should be centered horizontally within the text block, inset at least 2 picas from the left and right margins. Graphics of various sizes can be accommodated, as shown in the schematics at far right. If you have data or art on several consecutive pages, placing them in the same vertical position on the page suggests care and planning. (It also takes a little more time.)

Southside Coolant Incorporated

A Proposal for Temperature Control in the Mesa School District

Lorem ipsum dolor sit amet, consectetuer adipiscing elit, sed diam nonummy nibh euismod tincidunt ut laoreet dolore magna aliquam erat volutpat. Ut wisi enim ad minim veniam, quis nostrud exerci tation ullamcorper suscipit lobortis nisl ut aliquip ex ea commodo consequat. Duis autem vel eum iriure dolor in hendrerit in vulputate velit esse molestie consequat, vel illum dolore eu feugiat nulla facilisis at vero eros et accumsan et iusto odio dignissim qui blandit

Praesent luptatum zzril delenit augue duis dolore te feugait nulla facilisi. Lorem ipsum dolor sit amet, consectetuer adipiscing elit, Sed diam nonummy nibh euismod tincidunt ut laoreet dolore magna aliquam erat volutpat. Ut wisi enim ad minim veniam, quis nostrud exerci tation ullamcorper suscipit lobortis nisl ut aliquip ex ea commodo consequat. Duis autem vel eum iriure dolor in hendrerit in vulputate velit esse molestie consequat, vel illum dolore eu feugiat nulla facilisis at vero eros et accumsan et iusto odio dignissim qui blandit praesent luptatum zzril delenit augue duis dolore te feugait

Nulla facilisi. Nam liber tempor cum soluta nobis eleifend option congue nihil imperdiet doming id quod mazim placerat facer possim assum. Lorem ipsum dolor sit amet, consectetuer adipiscing elit, sed diam nonummy nibh euismod tincidunt ut laoreet dolore magnaAliquam erat volutpat. Ut wisi enim ad minim veniam, quis nostrud exerci tation ullamcorper suscipit lobortis nisl ut aliquip ex ea commodo consequat. Duis autem vel eum iriure dolor in hendrerit in vulputate velit esse molestie

Consequat, vel illum dolore eu feugiat nulla facilisis at vero eros et accumsan et iusto odio dignissim qui blandit praesent luptatum zzril delenit augue duis dolore te feugait . Lorem ipsum dolor sit amet, consectetuer adipiscing elit, sed diam nonummy nibh euismod tincidunt ut laoreet dolore magna aliquam erat volutpat. Ut wisi enim ad minim veniam, quis nostrud exerci tation ullamcorper suscipit lobortis nisl ut aliquip ex ea Commodo consequat. Duis autem vel eum iriure Dolor in hendrerit in vulputate velit esse molestie consequat, vel illum dolore eu feugiat nulla facilisis at vero eros et accumsan et iusto odio dignissim qui blandit praesent luptatum zzril delenit augue duis dolore te feugait nulla facilisi. Lorem ipsum dolor sit amet, consectetuer adipiscing elit, sed diam nonummy nibh euismod tincidunt ut laoreet dolore magna aliquam erat

3

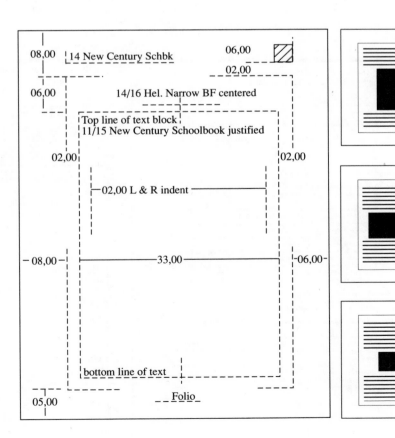

One-column grid with display heads

Many complex reports and proposals contain straight running text separated by subheads that recur throughout the document. The wide, one-column measure is ideal for the running text, and when the subheads are set fairly large and given plenty of white space and structural rules, the effect is well organized and easy to scan.

The highly structured report shown below contains a single topic on each page, with two recurring subheads placed in the same position on every page. You can adapt this format for a less structured document, placing the topic headline anywhere on the page with running text continuing from one page to the next as needed.

Bulleted text is used here to summarize the contents of each page. This technique works particularly well in long documents: The reader can make a horizontal pass through the pages for the highlights and then drop vertically into the running text for details. The ballot boxes are 11-point Zapf Dingbats.

The rules and generous white space (3 to 4 picas above each 0.5-point rule) provide a strong horizontal grid that facilitates scanning.

Art can be centered in the text column or inset on one side with the text wrapped around it, as shown in the schematics below.

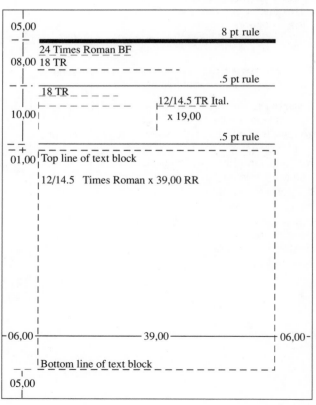

One + one-column grid

The combination of one narrow and one wide column might be considered either a one- or a two-column grid. The narrow column isn't a true text column, but it is wide enough to use for different kinds of text, graphics, and display type without crowding.

Whether you set up this format as one or two columns on the screen may well depend on the length of the document. In a long document with a great deal of running text, it may be more expedient to have Ventura flow the majority of your text in a single column, leaving you to place smaller paragraphs as they are required. In a short document, it may be just as easy to let Ventura place the text in both columns, leaving you to make only slight spacing adjustments.

Whatever you call it and however you set it up, keep this format in mind. It's extremely useful for a wide variety of reports, newsletters, bulletins, and data sheets.

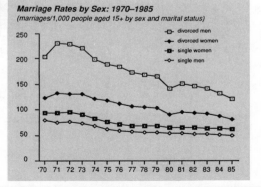

THE NUMBERS NEWS
6

A Publication of American Demographics
Martha Farnsworth Riche, Editor   Diane Crispell, Associate Editor

June 1988   Volume 8 Number

Will fewer couples tie the knot this June?

inside:

■ *How are population projections tracking?* (page 6)

■ *Regions shift in per capita income (page 2)*

■ *Women's labor force patterns approach men's (page 3)*

Divorced people are still more likely to marry than single people, but the gap is narrowing

Businesses that depend on married couples for a market need some hard rethinking: **the marriage rate continues to decline, the number of unmarried couples continues to increase, and divorced people are waiting longer to remarry.**

Final marriage statistics for 1985, produced by the National Center for Health Statistics, all point downward. Barbara Foley Wilson, who wrote the report ("Advance Report of Final Marriage Statistics, 1985"), said it was depressing to write: **Marriages dropped substantially in every region, almost every month, in most states, and for every marital status group.** To put these figures in context, remember that preliminary figures for 1986 and 1987 show the drop in the marriage rate continuing (*Numbers News*, Vol. 8, No. 5).

About two-thirds of the newly married were marrying for the first time; most of the rest had been divorced. However, as the chart shows, marriage rates are far higher for divorced persons: divorced men have higher marriage rates than divorced women, and single women have higher marriage rates than single men. **Marriage rates have declined for all these groups since the early 1970s, falling by about one-third for single people to nearly one-half for divorced men.**

Most people are now aware that young people are waiting longer to marry: the mean age at first marriage was 24.0 for women in 1985 and

Marriage Rates by Sex: 1970–1985
(marriages/1,000 people aged 15+ by sex and marital status)

- □ divorced men
- ◆ divorced women
- ■ single women
- ◇ single men

The Numbers News (ISSN 0732-1597) is published monthly. Copyright 1988 by American Demographics, Inc. All rights reserved. Reproduction without permission is prohibited. Subscription rate: $149 per year first class, subscribers outside the U.S., Canada and Mexico add $20. For subscription information or change of address contact American Demographics P.O. Box 68, Ithaca, NY 14851. Telephone (607) 273-6343. Editor/Publisher: Martha Farnsworth Riche, Research Editor: Thomas Exter, Associate Editor: Diane Crispell, Conference Editor: Ellen Marsh, Research Assistant: Janet McClafferty, Production Manager: Stephane Major, Marketing Director: Camilla Walter.

This newsletter uses the narrow column on the cover for headlines, contents listings, and story highlights. On inside pages the use is even more versatile, accommodating charts, graphs, news items, product notes, and conference listings.

The narrow column is 11,06, the wide column is 29 picas, and the space in between is 1 pica. The inside margins are 4,06, wide enough to accommodate the holes for a three-ring binder.

The tinted boxes run the full column measure without rules. Once you adopt this style, you should maintain it throughout. Text inside the boxes is indented 1 pica at both the left and right margins.

The logo uses the currently popular technique of enlarging the initial caps in an all cap name. Here the caps drop below the other letters, and tie in with the large issue number, a good device for quick reference and continuity.

The 2-point rules at the bottom of the page enclose publishing and masthead information. This type can be as small as 5 or 6 points.

Design: Carol Terrizzi (Ithaca, NY)

The Numbers News *is published monthly by American Demographics.*
Trim size: 8-1/2 by 11

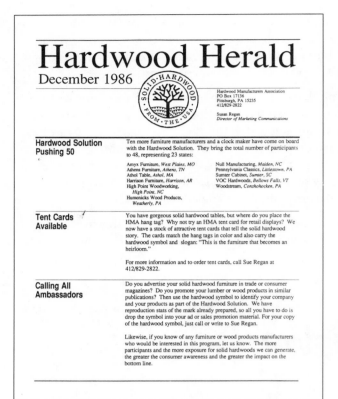

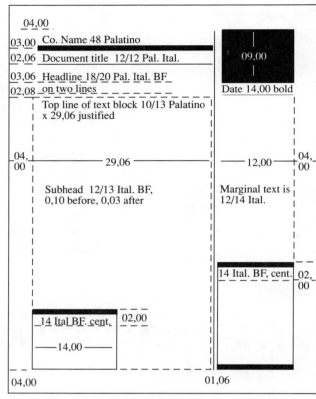

A deep space at the top of the page for the company identification, a narrow column for headlines and overhanging rules, and a wide column for information add up to a very simple, very effective use of desktop publishing.

The text column is divided into two equal columns for listings. The address above the text area follows this grid line.

The main headline and running text are Times Roman; the marginal heads are Helvetica Narrow.

The text column is 29 picas. The outside margins are 3 picas, and the top and bottom margins are 4 picas.

Design: Agnew Moyer Smith (Pittsburgh, PA)

The Hardwood Herald is published by the Hardwood Manufacturer's Association. Trim size: 8-1/2 by 11

This blueprint matches the monthly report on the facing page. You can adapt the grid for either of the other publications shown in this section by reversing the narrow and wide columns and adjusting the margins.

The text is Palatino throughout.

The bold rules are 4 point, the lighter ones are 0.5 point.

The sales highlights box in the lower left has a 1-pica standoff for the text wraparound. The type in the sample is 12/14, with 1,03 left and right indents. The tab is set at 7 picas.

The type in the contents box is 10/11.5 italic with 1,03 left and right indents, a leadered tab at 9 picas, and 6 points after each listing.

The screens in both of the boxes are 10% (a frame background pattern of 1).

You can use four art sizes, as shown above. Another approach is to hang the art from a horizon line, as in the second schematic.

Instructions for producing a newsletter or report using a one + one-column format can be found in Project 3 later in the book.

University Press

The Monthly Report on Sales, Promotion, and Product Development

March 1990

Political History and Economics Titles Continue to Boost Overseas Sales

Lorem ipsum dolor sit amet, consectetuer adipiscing elit, sed diam nonummy nibh euismod tincidunt ut laoreet dolore magna aliquam erat volutpat. Ut wisi enim ad minim veniam, quis nostrud exerci tation ullamcorper suscipit lobortis nisl ut aliquip ex ea commodo consequat. Duis autem vel eum iriure dolor in hendrerit in vulputate velit esse molestie consequat, vel illum dolore eu feugiat nulla facilisis at vero eros et accumsan et iusto odio dignissim qui blandit.

Praesent luptatum zzril delenit augue duis dolore te feugait nulla facilisi. Lorem ipsum dolor sit amet, consectetuer adipiscing elit, sed diam nonummy nibh euismod tincidunt ut laoreet dolore magna aliquam erat volutpat. Ut wisi enim ad minim veniam, quis nostrud exerci tation ullamcorper suscipit lobortis nisl ut aliquip ex ea commodo consequat.

Duis autem vel eum iriure dolor in hendrerit in vulputate velit esse molestie consequat, vel illum dolore eu feugiat nulla facilisis at vero eros et accumsan et iusto odio dignissim qui blandit praesent luptatum zzril delenit augue duis dolore te feugait nulla facilisi. Nam liber tempor cum soluta nobis eleifend option congue nihil imperdiet doming id quod mazim placerat facer possim assum. Lorem ipsum dolor sit amet, consectetuer adipiscing elit, sed diam nonummy nibh euismod tincidunt ut laoreet dolore magna aliquam erat volutpat.

London office to open this summer

Ut wisi enim ad minim veniam, quis nostrud exerci tation ullamcorper suscipit lobortis nisl ut aliquip ex ea commodo consequat. Duis autem vel eum iriure dolor in hendrerit in vulputate velit esse molestie consequat, vel illum dolore eu feugiat nulla facilisis at vero eros et accumsan et iusto odio dignissim qui blandit praesent luptatum zzril delenit augue duis dolore te feugait nulla facilisi. Lorem ipsum dolor sit amet, consectetuer adipiscing elit, sed diam nonummy nibh euismod tincidunt ut laoreet dolore magna aliquam erat volutpat.

Ut wisi enim ad minim veniam, quis nostrud exerci tation ullamcorper suscipit lobortis nisl ut aliquip ex ea commodo consequat. Duis autem vel eum iriure dolor in hendrerit in vulputate velit esse molestie consequat, vel illum dolore eu feugiat nulla facilisis at vero eros et accumsan et iusto odio dignissim qui blandit praesent luptatum zzril delenit augue duis dolore te feugait nulla facilisi. Lorem ipsum dolor sit amet, consectetuer adipiscing elit, sed diam nonummy nibh euismod tincidunt ut laoreet dolore magna aliquam erat volutpat. Ut wisi enim ad minim veniam, quis nostrud exerci tation ullamcorper suscipit lobortis nisl ut aliquip ex ea commodo consequat.

Duis autem vel eum iriure dolor in hendrerit in vulputate velit esse molestieerat volutpat. Ut wisi enim ad minim consequat, vel illum dolore eu feugiat nulla facilisis at vero eros etis ac.

University Press authors Jonathan Pritchard and Michelle Colibier are honored by the United States Library of Congress; see page 6.

Overseas Sales

FY 85	16,365
FY 86	25,347
FY 87	36,897
FY 88	47,356
FY 89	59,000

TWO-COLUMN GRIDS

Two-column grids have a more designed and polished look than the one-column formats, yet they don't require a great deal of planning and can be assembled fairly quickly in Ventura. They're useful for a wide variety of publications, including newsletters, brochures, annual reports, bulletins, menus, fact sheets, and catalog listings. When done well, they can range from honest simplicity to punchy straightforwardness. When done poorly, they can be boring or heavy-handed.

With two equal columns, the line length in an 8.5- by 11-inch page is usually between 16 and 21 picas, depending on the margins and the space between the columns. The type can drop down to 10/12 and still be quite readable. These factors make this format very economical in that you can fit quite a lot of text on a page. The greatest danger of the

Each editorial topic is contained on a single page, giving this brief annual report a simple, consistent, accessible style. The text does not have to fill out to the bottom margin. When your message can be broken down into one and two page units, this is a very effective format that is quite simple to produce.

The narrow margins (3 picas on the outside and bottom, 5 picas on the inside) work here because of the undersized page, the simple design, the open leading, and the white space at the top of the page. You wouldn't want margins any narrower than this, and without the compensating factors just mentioned wider margins would be essential.

The inset photos with wraparound text keep the running text from being too symmetrical. The depth of the photos varies according to the picture and the amount of text on the page. Photos can also run the full column width or extend halfway into the second column.

The body text is 10/14 Times Roman with 36-point initial caps. The headlines are 22 point.

PATIENT SERVICES

A kidney patient faces hardships that most healthy people never encounter. The Kidney Foundation of Maryland attempts to help these patients by providing an extensive array of patient programs and services.

The second annual Kids Having Fun Camp for pediatric renal patients was held during the weekend of August 23 at the pastoral YMCA Camp Letts in Edgewater, Maryland. This year's camp attracted 13 young renal patients from a three-state area. Smiles were abundant as the youngsters enjoyed a care-free weekend away from the all-too-familiar medical environment. Exciting activities such as horseback riding and boating, as well as the more traditional sports of tennis, softball and volleyball, thrilled the campers and volunteers alike. The camp also provided a respite from the constant demands imposed by kidney disease on the patients' parents.

December is an unlikely time to have a picnic. The Kidney Foundation, however, chose to beat summer's heat and hold a " Picnic in December" for its annual patient party for the second consecutive year. The University of Maryland Medical School Teaching Facility was the site for the party attended by special guests Mr. and Mrs. Santa, who presented gifts donated by Santa Claus Anonymous, to over 40 children. Volunteers from Maryland Casualty Company portrayed the visitors from the North Pole, as well as a snowman and other storybook characters. The Boys Latin Magicians' Guild provided entertainment that delighted the entire audience.

The Patient Emergency Assistance Program provided one-time grants to kidney patients in need of financial help. Patients were awarded nearly $2,000 in emergency grants.

The Medication Discount Program allowed dialysis, transplant, and chronic kidney disease patients to purchase medication at the lowest possible cost. Patients were registered for the program by their physicians. Under this program, all prescription drugs related to the patient's kidney condition can be purchased at wholesale price through the Kidney Foundation, which pays the pharmacist's fees and handling costs.

Transplant and dialysis patients also received free medical identification jewelry. This jewelry alerts medical personnel to the patient's kidney condition and is especially valuable in emergency situations.

Young kidney patients from Maryland and Washington, D.C. had an opportunity to show off their creativity in the Foundation's "Gift of Life" poster contest, held on November 15 at the Top of the World Trade Center in Baltimore. The youngsters' artwork was displayed and judged by such celebrities as Ken Matz of WMAR-TV and Bob MacAvan of the Baltimore Blast.

Eight-year-old Mario Velez, of Baltimore, won third prize in his category and was awarded a trip for his entire family to the Six Flags Power Plant in Baltimore. First prize winners in each category advanced to the National "Gift of Life" poster contest in Washington, D.C.

PUBLIC EDUCATION

K idney disease is an intricate and complex subject. One of the Kidney Foundation's primary responsibilities is to educate the public about kidney disease and the benefits of organ donation.

Over 78,000 Americans die each year of kidney disease. Many of these patients die because a suitable organ donor cannot be found. As a result, the Kidney Foundation has expanded its efforts to promote voluntary organ donation through its "Give the Gift of Life" campaign.

In December and January the Maryland affiliate participated in a nationwide campaign based on the theme, "Sign an organ donor card....It's one New Year's resolution that's easy to keep." The Foundation distributed public service announcements to the major Baltimore TV stations and to radio stations across the state. Public service ads and fact sheets were also provided to area newspapers.

Public information efforts were intensified during Organ Donation Awareness Week in April. NKF-Maryland held an organ donor sign-in at Johns Hopkins Hospital, and area radio stations gave frequent air play to public service announcements about organ donation. Although April marked the height of the organ donor campaign, "Gift of Life" materials were used extensively by the media throughout the year.

Health fairs provided an excellent opportunity for Foundation representatives to personally

speak with the public about kidney disease and organ donation. During the year Kidney Foundation staff and volunteers were on hand at many health fairs throughout the area. The KF newsletter, refreshed with a new format, continued to inform thousands of readers with interesting information about kidney disease issues and the many activities of the Foundation. Educational brochures, on topics ranging from "Transplantation" to "Nutritional Considerations for the Patient on Dialysis," were available to the public free of charge.

The KF Membership Drive held in the spring featured an effective plea for funds by WMAR-TV anchorman Ken Matz and infant kidney patient Jason Ogle. The drive culminated in May, with a three-night phone-a-thon from the offices of the Baltimore Gas and Electric Company. Friends of the Foundation generously responded to the drive, contributing a total of nearly $10,000 to the fight against kidney disease.

Since organ donation is a key step in solving the problem of kidney disease, the Foundation strongly supported the efforts of Delegate Paula Hollinger to pass a state law regarding the "routine inquiry" issue. The law now states that parents of a deceased minor must be approached by a hospital medical staff member concerning post-mortem organ donation.

Design: Carl A. Schuetz, Foxglove Communications (Baltimore, MD)

Pages from the annual report of the National Kidney Foundation of Maryland. Trim size: 7-1/2 by 10

two-column grid, however, is that you will try to fit in too much text and create pages that are dense and difficult to read. When in doubt, add an extra pica to the margins rather than to the text block.

With two columns you have more options in both the size and placement of headlines. You need to be careful, however, of the position of the heads—they shouldn't be too close to the top or the bottom of a column. (The very top of a column is, of course, okay.) Also, take care that headlines in adjoining columns do not align with one another.

The off-center page created by a wide outer margin adds variety and sophistication to a two-column grid. This format is especially well suited to house organs.

A tight grid structure and well-defined image area is established by the extension of visual elements into the side and top margins and by the strong graphic treatment of the folios at the bottom of the page.

The graphic style of the breakout, folios, and logo and the contemporary headline treatment with bracket-style rules give the format a personal signature, as well as a consistency of visual style from one page to the next. The overall feeling is restrained without being bland.

Photos can be sized as shown here; mug shots can be half-column width with wraparound text filling out

the other half column. The rules around the photos crisp up the otherwise soft edges.

The text is Palatino throughout.

Design: Michael Waitsman,
Synthesis Concepts (Chicago, IL)

The Wildman Herald *is the national newsletter of Wildman, Harrold, Allen & Dixon, a law firm.*
Trim size: 8-1/2 by 11

THE
WILDMAN
HERALD

March 1988

Judge Turner and his wife Kay (right) enjoy themselves at the Federal Bar Association reception following the swearing-in ceremony.

In 1967 Turner hired on with the firm of Canada, Russell & Turner (Memphis predecessor of Wildman, Harrold), where his father Cooper Turner had helped establish a thriving practice. He became a partner in 1974, the year of his father's death.

In 20 years of private practice with the firm, Turner earned a reputation as one of the Mid South area's top civil litigators. Working in state and federal courts throughout the region, he ran the gamut — commercial and corporate cases, products liability, banking, insurance defense, you name it. His most recent success was the recovery of a summary judgment in favor of Richards Medical Company, requiring that

The ABA declared him "well qualified," a rating not often given, and the nomination sailed through the Judiciary Committee and the full Senate.

Richards' parent company turn over $13 million in pension plan assets to Richards. (The parent has appealed.)

Over the years Turner has also found time for various civic endeavors. He worked in the successful campaigns of Rep. Don Sundquist, a Memphis-area congressman, and he has filled numerous offices and

committee positions with the local bar, which he now serves as president.

With this kind of background, Turner was as ready as one can be for the intricate and sometimes intrusive process of becoming a federal judge. "There was a form for Department of Justice, a form for the FBI, a form for the ABA, a form for the Federal Bar Association..." the nominee recounted with a weary sigh. Scores of friends and family members were interviewed by men in dark suits. Detailed financial disclosure forms had to be completed.

After being put through the washer and dryer, though, he emerged clean — and more. The ABA declared him "well qualified," a rating not often given, and once the Senate finally got past the logjam over the Battle of Bork, the Turner nomination sailed through the Judiciary Committee and the full Senate.

A few days before his swearing in, Turner, along with another large gathering of the legal profession, attended the funeral of Judge Marion Boyd. The father of Memphis partner Boots Boyd, Judge Boyd was the first man to occupy the seat which Judge Turner now occupies. He was known for his honesty, fairness, timeliness, and strictness in sentencing. As the eulogist reviewed Judge Boyd's long career of public service, Turner felt a special kinship with his early predecessor. "I would like to be seen after a number of years as being completely honest, with a good temperament, polite and courteous, as one who knows his law and does his work and comes up with fair results. If I can do all of that I will be a great judge."

Because of his caseload, with 370 civil cases and an unknown number of criminal cases awaiting him when he first arrived, it is difficult to see how Judge Turner will find time for his hobbies, which include tennis, bird hunting, and gardening. But he vows to make time for his family, who have been his biggest boosters throughout the long nominating process: wife Kay Farese Turner, herself a practicing attorney, and five children, Park (18), Alexandra (14), Oliver (13), Christian (12), and Whitney (9).

Looking back on his private practice, Turner noted that leaving the firm was not easy. "I have practiced law with most of the lawyers here longer than I have been with anyone else in my life, and I've liked it. I've liked the firm, and I respect the integrity of the lawyers here. I hope I'll be lucky enough to enjoy my job as judge as much as I have enjoyed practicing law."

Janet Wilson has something special to remember, too. "Can you believe it?" she marvelled. "I put the President on hold!"

Firm Promotes Valuable European Contacts
by Robert Keel

In November, 1987, Tom Smith of the New York office and Bob Keel of the Toronto office visited Rome and London. The visit to Rome was arranged by Keel to introduce Smith to clients of the Toronto office. Moreover, Keel Cottrelle maintains an office in Rome in association with Avvocato Francesco Ruggieri and Avvocato Giovanni Iasilli. The trip therefore, presented an opportunity to introduce this affiliated office to a member of the national management committee. Indeed, Bob and Tom were delighted to discover that there are now two affiliated offices in Italy because Avv. Ruggieri now maintains an office in Milan. Avv. Ruggieri made it clear that both the Rome and Milan offices are available to anyone in the firm, either for business or merely to drop in to get acquainted. The Rome office is in the center of the city at 95 Via Barberini, which is just around the corner from the American Embassy.

While they were in Italy, Keel and Smith devoted a considerable amount of time to client business. Among other things, Bob introduced Tom to a number of multi-national corporate clients. As you might expect, the trip was not all work. The hospitality extended to them by clients and by Avv. Ruggieri and Avv. Iasilli was delightful and occupied a considerable amount of otherwise billable hours. Moreover, Tom's wife Terry, who also made the trip, convinced Tom to take a side trip to Venice.

After Rome, Tom, Terry and Bob flew on to London. This time, it was Smith's turn to show Keel around. Tom visited his business acquaintances at Shell International. Bob and Tom also visited an acquaintance at Hambros Bank. They spent some time with representatives of Network Security Management Limited, which is based in London. Keel managed to squeeze in visits with a number of business acquaintances who are now doing business in London.

With our expanding practice and our shrinking world, our European contacts will assume increasing importance. We should all be aware of the global networks that are in place.

Left to right:
Bob Keel,
Giovanni Iasilli,
Tom Smith, and
Francesco Ruggieri.

Four wide-margin, two-column designs

Wide margins are the foundation for an open, two-column format that is very appealing and highly readable. All four documents in this section were designed using the grid in the blueprint on the following spread, but the kind of information, the intended audience, and the style of the publications differ considerably.

The most varied and dynamic of the four designs (facing page) divides the vertical grid into horizontal story areas. This modular format requires more time and planning to execute than the others; you may have to adjust the depth of the text blocks several times to balance all the elements on the page.

The overall busyness of the design elements is appropriate here because it evokes the adventure of travel. You can create a more conservative look with this horizontal format by using a simpler nameplate and more uniform art styles. The format works for all-text documents, too, though to very different effect.

The nameplate at the top of the page uses the multiple headline style commonly found in magazines, including a list of the contents and the "Summer Specials" stamp, which is similar to the diagonal banner on many magazine covers. Deft handling of typography is critical in composing so many elements with varying emphasis into a unified, readable whole.

The pictures use the grid effectively precisely because they break out of it. The mountains seem more expansive because they exceed the margins; the balloon seems to float off the page. The range of art styles, from realistic to schematic, adds to the feeling of adventure that a travel bulletin wants to project.

The type used throughout is Futura. Alternating Light, Extra Bold, and Oblique in the headlines creates a colorful contrast without introducing another typeface. The unity of a single type family balances the complex nameplate treatment and the different styles of art.

Type specifications
Nameplate overline: 16-point Futura Light
Going: 96-point Light
Places: 36-point Futura Extra Bold Oblique
Contents: 14/14 Extra Bold
Lead story headline: 28/29 Light
Second story head: 18/18 Extra Bold
Body text: 10/12.5 Light

Instructions for producing a newsletter that uses a wide-margin, two-column format can be found in Project 4.

GOING PLACES

RIVERBOAT RACES

GRAND TETONS

GREAT BARRIER REEF

AROUND THE WORLD IN SO MANY WAYS

Lorem ipsum dolor sit amet, consectetuer adipiscing elit, sed diam nonummy nibh euismod tincidunt ut laoreet dolore magna aliquam erat volutpat. Ut wisi enim ad minim veniam, quis nostrud exerci tation ullamcorper suscipit lobortis nisl ut aliquip ex ea commodo Consequat. Duis

PLUS THE MANY ADVENTURES THAT AWAIT YOU CLOSE TO HOME

Autem vel velit esse molestie Consequat, vel illum dolore eu feugiat nulla facilisis at vero eros et accumsan et iusto odio dignissim qui blandit praesent luptatum zzril delenit augue duis dolore te feugait nulla facilisi. Lorem ipsum dolor sit amet, consectetuer adipiscing elit, sed diam nonummy nibh euismod tincidunt ut laoreet dolore magna aliquam erat volutpat. Ut wisi enim ad minim veniam, quis nostrud exerci tation ullamcorper suscipit lobortis nisl ut aliquip ex ea commodo consequat.

Duis autem vel eum iriure dolor in hendrerit in vulputate velit esse molestie consequat, vel illum dolore eu feugiat nulla facilisis at vero eros et accumsan et iusto odio dignissim qui blandit

praesent luptatum zzril delenit augue duis dolore te feugait nulla facilisi. Nam liber tempor cum soluta nobis eleifend option congue nihil imperdiet doming id quod mazim placerat facer pos assum.

Lorem ipsum dolor sit amet, consectetuer adipiscing elsed diam nonummy nibh euismod tincidunt ut laoreet magna aliquam erat volutpat. Ut wisi enim ad minveniam, quis nostrud exerci tation ullamcorper suscipit lobortis nisl ut aliquip ex ea commodo

What We've Accomplished

Lorem ipsum dolor sit amet, consectetuer adipiscing elit, sed diam nonummy nibh euismod tincidunt ut laoreet dolore magna aliquam erat volutpat. Ut wisi enim ad minim veniam, quis nostrud exerci tation ullamcorper suscipit lobortis nisl ut aliquip ex ea commodo consequa te feugait nulla facilisi.t.

The Centerville Nursing Home

Duis autem vel eum iriure dolor in hendrerit in vulputate velit esse molestie consequat, vel illum dolore eu feugiat nulla facilisis at vero eros et accumsan et iusto odio dignissim qui blandit praesent luptatum zzril delenit augue duis dolore te feugait nulla facilisi. Lorem ipsum dolor sit amet, consectetuer adipiscing elit, sed diam nonummy nibh euismod tin-

cidunt ut laoreet dolore magna aliquam erat volutpat. Ut wisi enim ad minim veniam, quis nostrud exerci tation ullamcorper suscipit lobortis nisl ut aliquip ex ea commodo consequat te feugait nulla.

Duis autem vel eum iriure dolor in hendrerit in vulputate velit esse molestie consequat, vel illum dolore eu feugiat nulla facilisis at vero eros et accumsan et iusto odio dignissim qui blandit praesent luptatum zzril delenit augue duis dolore te feugait nulla facilisi. Nam liber tempor cum soluta nobis eleifend option congue nihil imperdiet doming id quod mazim placerat facer possim assum.

Job Training Program for Disadvantaged Youth

Lorem ipsum dolor sit amet, consectetuer adipiscing elit, sed diam nonummy nibh euismod tincidunt ut laoreet dolore magna aliquam erat volutpat. Ut wisi enim ad minim veniam, quis nostrud exerci tation ullamcorper suscipit lobortis nisl ut aliquip ex ea commodo consequat. Duis autem vel eum iriure dolor in hendrerit in vulputate velit esse molestie consequat, vel illum dolore eu feugiat nulla facilisis at vero eros et accumsan et iusto odio dignissim qui blandit praesent luptatum zzril delenit augue duis dolore te feugait nulla facilisi. Lorem ipsum dolor sit amet, consectetuer adipiscing elit, sed diam nonummy nibh euismod tincidunt ut laoreealiquam erat volut

What We Need to Do

Ut wisi enim ad minim veniam, quis nostrud exerci tation ullamcorper suscipit lobortis nisl ut aliquip ex ea commodo consequat. Duis autem vel eum iriure dolor in hendrerit in vulputate velit esse molestie consequat, vel illum dolore eu feugiat nulla facilisis at vero eros et accumsan et iusto odio dignissim qui blandit praesent luptatum zzril delenit augue duis dolore te feugait nulla facilisi.

Capital Fund

Lorem ipsum dolor sit amet, consectetuer adipiscing elit, sed diam nonummy nibh euismod tincidunt ut laoreet dolore magna aliquam erat volutpat. Ut wisi enim ad minim veniam, quis nostrud exerci tation ullamcorper suscipit lobortis nisl ut aliquip ex ea commodo consequat. Duis autem vel eum iriure dolor in hendrerit in vulputate velit esse molestie consequat, vel illum dolore eu feugiat nulla facilisis at vero eros et accumsan et iusto odio dignissim qui blandit praesent luptatum zzril delenit augue duis dolore te feugait nulla facilisi.

Lorem ipsum dolor sit amet, consectetuer adipiscing elit, sed diam nonummy nibh euismod tincidunt ut laoraliquam eratorem Lorem ipsum dolor sit amet, consectetuer adipiscing elit, sed diam nonummy nibh euismod tincidunt ut laoreet dolore magna..

ipsum dolor sit amet, consectetuer adipiscing elit, sed diam nonummy nibh euismod tincidunt ut laoreet dolore magna aliquam erat volutpat. Ut wisi enim ad minim veniam, quis nostrud exerci tation ullamcorper suscipit lobortis nisl ut aliquip ex ea commodo consequat. Duis autem vel eum iriure dolor in hendrerit in vulputate velit esse molestie consequat, vel illum dolore eu feugiat nulla volutpat.orem ipsum dolor sit amet, consectetuer adipiscing elit, sed diam nonummy nibh euismod tincidunt ut laoreet dolore magna aliquam erat volutpat. Ut wisi enim ad minim veniam, quis nostrud exerci tation ullamcorper suscipit lobortis nisl ut aliquip ex ea commodo consequat. Duis autem vel eum iriure dolor in hendrerit in vulputate velit esse molestie consequat, vel illum dolore eu feugiat

Staff Expansion

Ut wisi enim ad minim veniam, quis nostrud exerci tation ullamcorper suscipit lobortis nisl ut aliquip ex ea commodo consequat. Duis autem vel eum iriure dolor in hendrerit in vulputate velit esse molestie consequat, vel illum dolore eu feugiat nulla facilisis at vero eros et accumsan et iusto odio dignissim qui blandit praesent luptatum zzril delenit augue duis dolore te feugait nulla facilisi. Lorem ipsum dolor sit amet, consectetuer adipiscing elit, sed diam nonummy nibh euismod tin

duis dolore te feugait nulla facilisi. Nam liber tempor cum soluta nobis eleifend option congue nihil imperdiet doming id quod mazim placerat facer possim assum. Lorem ipsum dolor sit amet, consectetuer adipiscing elit, sed diam nonummy nibh euismod tincidunt ut laoreet dolore magna aliquam erat volutpatillum .

This document shares the dignified simplicity found in the annual report reproduced at the beginning of the two-column grid section. It is designed to accommodate a subject head over a 0.5-point rule at the top of each page. If you omit that head, leave the rule in place.

The text seems to hang from the rule under the main headline. This strong structure provides consistency from page to page regardless of the column depth. The variable column depth gives you flexibility and speed when you assemble the pages on screen.

The banner, the main headline, and the rule below that headline extend 3 picas past the left text margin shown in the blueprint on the facing page. The banner is 2 picas deep with 14-point Garamond Bold type.

The main headlines are 30-point Bodoni Bold.

The body text is 10/13 Helvetica Light. The subheads are 10/12 Helvetica Black under 0.5-point rules.

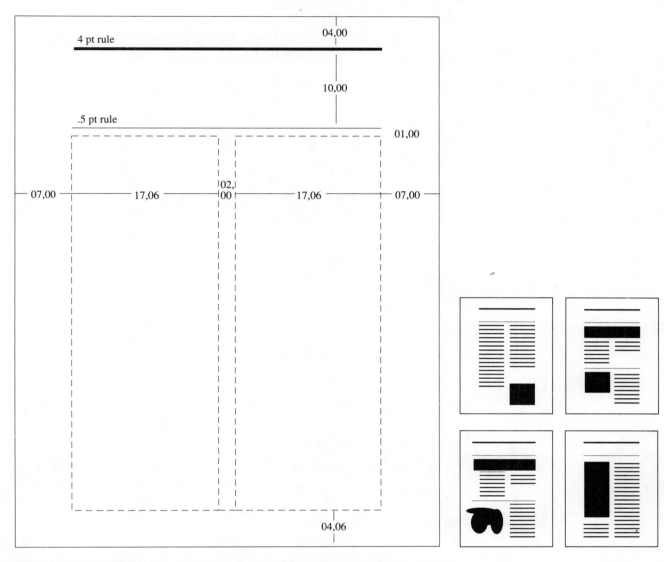

The blueprint above shows the basic grid for the four documents on the previous three and following two pages.

The column width (17,06) is excellent for easy reading.

The generous margins require a generous space between the columns.

The grid is centered on the page. If you shift the grid to one side for an off-center page, the wider margin can be used for annotations, notes, small pieces of art, and other marginalia.

A variation with a more structured nameplate and headline treatment is shown on the next spread.

Art can be placed on the grid as shown in the schematics or as shown in the sample pages.

1989 PROGRAM OF EVENTS

SCHOOL OF PHYSICAL SCIENCES

SOUTHEAST STATE UNIVERSITY
70TH SCIENTIFIC FORUM

MONDAY, MAY 8, 1989   FULTON AUDITORIUM

MORNING PROGRAM

7:45 Registration
Hendrerit in vulputate velit esse molestie consequat, vel illum dolore eu feugiat.

7:45 Continental Breakfast
Nonummy nibh euismod tincidunt ut laoreet dolore magna aliquam erat volutpat. Ut wisi enim ad minim.

9:00 Introduction
Veniam, quis nostrud exerci tation ullamcorper suscipit lobortis nisl ut aliquip ex ea commodo consequat. Duis autem vel eum iriure dolor in.

10:00 Break
Hendrerit in vulputate velit esse molestie consequat, vel illum dolore eu feugiat nulla facilisis at vero eros et accumsan et iusto odio dignissim qui.

10:30 Opening Address
Blandit praesent luptatum zzril delenit augue duis dolore te feugait nulla facilisi. Lorem ipsum dolor sit amet, consectetuer adipiscing elit, sed diam.

12:00 Open House and Lunch
Nonummy nibh euismod tincidunt ut laoreet dolore magna aliquam erat volutpat. Ut wisi enim ad minim.

AFTERNOON PROGRAM

2:00 Overview of Seminars
Veniam, quis nostrud exerci tation ullamcorper suscipit lobortis nisl ut aliquip ex ea commodo consequat.

3:00 Faculty Roundtable
Duis autem vel eum iriure dolor in hendrerit in vulputate velit esse molestie consequat, vel illum dolore eu feugiat nulla facilisis at vero eros et accumsan et iusto odio dignissim qui blandit praesent luptatum zzril delenit augue duis dolore te feugait nulla facilisi. Nam liber tempor cum soluta.

4:00 The Year in Review
Option congue nihil imperdiet doming id quod mazim placerat facer possim assum. Lorem ipsum dolor sit amet.,

4:30 Agenda for the Nineties
Consectetuer adipiscing elit, sed diam nonummy nibh euismod tincidunt ut laoreet dolore magna aliquam erat volutpat. Ut wisi enim ad minim veniam, quis nostrud exerci tation.

5:00 Discussion Period
Ullamcorper suscipit lobortis nisl ut aliquip ex ea commodo consequat. Duis autem vel eum iriure dolor in hendrerit in vulputate velit esse.

EVENING PROGRAM

6:30 School of Chemistry Buffet
Consequat, vel illum dolore eu feugiat nulla facilisis at vero eros et.

8:00 Class Reunion
Et iusto odio dignissim qui blandit praesent luptatum zzril delenit augue duis dolore te feugait nulla facilisi. Lorem ipsum dolor sit amet, con.

Programs with many items briefly described, like the one shown here, work very well in this two-column format. The column measure is wide enough to contain the agenda listings on single lines, but short enough so that the indented descriptions run over, creating visual separation between the headings.

A classic, traditional feeling appropriate for an academic program is created by the centered text in the open space at the top of the page and by the use of Garamond, a very refined and graceful typeface.

Nameplate type
1989 Program: 18-point Garamond
Top rule: 4.00 fractional points
School of...: 12 points
Southeast State...: 18/21
Date and place: 10 points
Bottom rule: 0.50 fractional points

The three subheads (Morning Program, etc.) are 10-point Garamond small caps. The double rules below them are 0.50 fractional points, to match the weight of the double rules. You should maintain consistency in line weight throughout a page. The typeface underscore would be too heavy here.

The boldface time for each part of the program adds a different color to the type, which keeps the page from being too monotonous.

The program listings are 10/12 Garamond. The event after the time is tabbed to 3 picas from the left margin; the descriptive copy is set with a 3-pica left indent so that it is flush with the tabbed text.

The space between listings in the sample is specified as 1 pica paragraph space before each event heading and 4 points after it.

A newsletter style is adapted here for a sales department's monthly bulletin. The rules, bold heads with tag lines, and initial caps dress up and give a newsy image to what could be a pedestrian report.

The highly structured nameplate shows another way of using the open space at the top of the grid. (See the blueprint detail below right for specifications.)

The strong headline treatment requires white space around the various elements and makes separation of headlines in adjoining columns essential.

The initial caps are 60-point Helvetica Condensed Black. Often found in the editorial pages of magazines to highlight points of entry on a page, initial caps are generally underused in business publications. They are especially effective in complex pages such as this sample.

The wide, 3-pica paragraph indent is proportional to the initial cap. Be aware that very narrow letters (such as I) and very wide letters (M and W) will not conform to this proportion. The price of a truly professional document is editing to avoid these letters. Really.

The body text is 10/12 Bookman.

The box around the illustration uses a 2-point rule and a frame background pattern of 1. The headline is 10-point Helvetica Black Oblique, and the descriptive lines are 9/9 Helvetica Light with Helvetica Black numbers. The caption is 10/12 Bookman italic, centered.

The centered folio (10-point Helvetica Light) and the flush right continued line (9-point Helvetica Light Oblique) are aligned at their baselines 2 picas below the bottom margin.

THE GREAT OUTDOORS STORE

Month in Review

July 1989

BRISK START FOR CAMPING AND BACKPACKING EQUIPMENT

Fewer travelers abroad spurs sales in do it yourself activities.

Lorem ipsum dolor sit amet, consectetuer adipiscing elit, sed diam nonummy nibh euismod tincidunt ut laoreet dolore magna aliquam erat volutpat. Ut wisi enim ad minim veniam, quis nostrud exerci tation ullamcorper suscipit lobortis nisl ut aliquip ex ea commodo consequat. Duis autem vel eum iriure dolor in hendrerit in vulputate velit esse molestie consequat, vel illum dolore eu feugiat nulla facilisis at vero eros et accumsan et iusto odio dignissim qui blandit praesent luptatum zzril delenit augue duis dolore te feugait nulla facilisi.

Lorem ipsum dolor sit amet, consectetuer adipiscing elit, sed diam nonummy nibh euismod tincidunt ut laoreet dolore magna aliquam erat volutpat. Ut wisi enim ad minim veniam, quis nostrud exerci tation ullamcorper suscipit lobortis nisl ut aliquip ex ea commodo consequat. Duis autem vel eum iriure dolor in hendrerit in vulputate velit esse molestie consequat, vel illum dolore eu feugiat nulla facilisis at vero eros et accumsan et iusto odio dignissim qui blandit praesent luptatum zzril delenit augue duis dolore te feugait nulla facilisi. Nam liber tempor cum soluta nobis eleifend option congue nihil imperdiet doming id quod mazim placerat facer possim assum.

Lorem ipsum dolor sit amet, consectetuer adipiscing elit, sed diam nonummy nibh euismod tincidunt ut laoreet dolore magna aliquam erat volutpat. Utwisi enim ad minim veniam, quis nostrud wisi enim ad minim veniam, quis nostrud exerci tation ex ea commodo

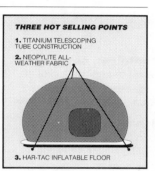

THREE HOT SELLING POINTS

1. TITANIUM TELESCOPING TUBE CONSTRUCTION

2. NEOPYLITE ALL-WEATHER FABRIC

3. HAR-TAC INFLATABLE FLOOR

The newly introduced two-person model X-2000-2 tent

WEATHERMAN PREDICTS ANOTHER HOT SUMMER. EXPECT BOOST IN WATER SPORTS GEAR

Jump in on the action in the new colorful inflatable water toys.

Nonsequat. Duis autem vel eum iriure dolor in hendrerit in vulputate velit esse molestie consequat, vel illum dolore eu feugiat nulla facilisis at vero eros et accumsan et iusto odio dignissim qui blandit praesent luptatum zzril delenit augue duis dolore te feugait nulla facilisi.

Lorem ipsum dolor sit amet, consectetuer adipiscing elit, sed diam nonummy nibh euismod tincidunt ut laoreet dolore magna aliquam erat volut. Lorem ipsum dolor sit amet, consectetuer adipiscing elit, sed diam nonummy nibh euismod tincidunt ut laoreet dolore magna

1   Continued on page 3

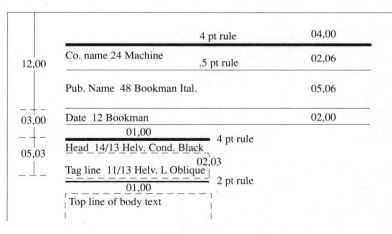

Wide-measure two-column grids

When you need to put a lot of running text or data on a page but still want a fairly simple format, consider a two-column grid with narrow margins and wide columns. You can see from the documents in this section—a newsletter, a catalog, an instruction sheet, and a journal—how adaptable this grid is to many different kinds of publications. Each of the examples uses this format in a completely different way and creates a very different image through typography and art.

A self-contained cover story emphasizes the importance of the topic, in this case a substantial contribution to a small boarding school.

The sidebar inset in the two-column grid is used here to quote the donor. The box is 14 picas wide with a 12,06 column measure. The use of a second color, blue, for the italic type draws the reader's attention to this statement.

Blue is also used in the banner, with reverse type, and for the display text.

The typeface on the cover is Galliard throughout.

A bolder, busier style for an inside story is created by the large headline, the recurrent subheads, and the bold rule around the photo. The banner, headline, and subheads print in blue.

The column width—22 picas—is the absolute maximum for running text on an 8.5- by 11-inch page. With a rule down the center of the page, you don't have to align the text in adjoining columns.

Other pages of the newsletter use a three-column grid, maintaining the banner, page frame, and rules between columns for continuity.

Mixing grids within a publication in this way accommodates a mix of short and long stories and different-size pictures and gives the publication a varied texture.

The body text is Galliard. The headlines are Helvetica Black Oblique.

Design: Scot Louis Gaznier (Langley, WA)

Pages from The Solebury School newsletter. Trim size: 8-1/2 by 11

The Newsletter

EDITOR: *Daniel Lusk* • ASSOCIATE EDITOR: *Jean Shaw Gaznier '53* • DESIGN: *Scot Louis Gaznier*

SPRING 1988

Pledge to Build New Dorm Spurs Board to Consider Long-Range Capital Campaign

A RECENT PLEDGE of $250,000 for capital construction by Carol Chianese VanDuyne '52 has provided the impetus for the trustees of Solebury School to look into the feasibility of launching a full-scale campaign.

A feasibility study to explore options and create plans for faculty and student housing is going forward at this time, according to Bruce Bergquist, HEAD OF SCHOOL.

The study, authorized by the BOARD OF TRUSTEES at its January meeting, will consider three options with respect to improvement of present boys' living quarters: to renovate the existing facility, to rebuild the present dormitory, or to construct a new building in a different location on campus.

Bruce said that the Planning Committee has met frequently since the Board meeting, has selected an architect to act as consultant for the study, and is currently exploring options for location of a new building. It also is reviewing the feasibility of a new wing for the current dorm, which he said seems at this point a less likely option for providing the housing needed to meet both immediate and long-range goals for the school.

The Board also authorized preparation of a more formal long-range plan by administration and Board leadership. A written document is being created to clarify and project long-range goals for future development of the school — in essence to update and focus a long-range plan completed in 1985 by an ad hoc committee of students, faculty, administration and Board members.

When completed, the current study will provide schematics of a proposed new building, lay out a timetable for construction, and project costs.

Bruce anticipates completion of the study by April 15, in time for the Board to decide in May which of the options under consideration to include in a case statement

"I have made this decision because I believe in Solebury's future, and I feel fortunate and proud to be able to help the school reach its goals in such a substantial way. I also want this pledge to be used as an incentive for others to reach as deeply as they can into their own pockets and help. My two years at Solebury gave me more of a total education than any schools before or after that time. I want to make certain that students just like me continue to be able to have the Solebury experience. I am just as certain that all of you reading this have much to thank Solebury for. It helped us create our future as adults, and now it is time for us to repay that debt and help Solebury's future."*

being prepared by Bruce and BOARD CHAIRMAN Bill Berkeley. The latter statement will present the case for a capital campaign for the school.

Balanced Budget

While the tenor of the Board's open session in January was cautious, dominated by realistic assessment and close examination, there was an obvious undercurrent of excitement. For the first time in a decade a Board faced the prospect of a balanced budget — a budget that not only projected realistic income figures and expenditures that do not exceed income; it also projected nominal salary increases and substantial reduction of indebtedness.

Members acknowledged a need to improve on the current rate of annual giving, citing a general caution on the part of donors that reflects current economic trends in the country. The Board targeted annual giving donations in the $5,000 – $10,000 range as critical to the continuing, improved health of the school.

Given a balanced budget for the coming fiscal year, and given long-range goals, the Board is considering major steps involving possible construction of new facilities in order to accomodate the proposed growth of the student body.

With Carol VanDuyne's pledge of $250,000 already a beginning for a capital campaign, the question now before the Board is whether the time is right for proceeding with a major fund drive that will accomodate the growth of the student body, enhance the quality of life for faculty, and in the process affect the growth of curriculum and programs and focus more clearly the character of the school.

The present challenge, said Bruce, "is to clarify our priorities and to act on them. In looking a long way, and we know what we want. Now we have some even harder decisions to make."

CLEVE: SOMETHING EXTRA

CLEVE IS ONE of those talented part-time people there have been so many of in our little history. We tend to take them, once they are here, for granted. And, when they are specialists like Cleve Christie, we may not even know their names, much less meet them.

Cleve is easy to talk about because the numbers we can use are beautiful: 18 and 2, 22 and 1. Those are the season records, wins and losses of his Solebury boys varsity basketball team for the past two seasons.

Yet, while those are pretty numbers, they are far from being the whole story of Cleve's impact on his players or even on our school; they aren't even the interesting part.

Coaching our team is only one of the things Cleve does, and one might hurry to say that, while it may appear to be the shiny part, it is not a separate thing from the other parts of his life.

ROMEO AND JULIET'S

Dignified, tough, and generally soft-spoken, Cleve works for the Trenton Housing Authority and manages a number of public housing projects. That's a very important part of his life. He has always made things happen.

He grew up in Trenton in a neighborhood that used to be known as *Dogpatch*. He lived with his grandmother on Southard Street, not far from where he took me for lunch — a cafe called Romeo and Juliet's. Cleve says the place wz. smaller when he was a kid and used to shovel snow for the people who owned it.

He recalls that he and his friends had one of the first basketball courts in the area. When a couple of houses were moved out of the neighborhood, they asked the township for some dirt to cover the bricks and refuse that were left behind. The Ewing Township trucks brought dirt and dumped it in huge piles and went away. Cleve says he organized the kids, got the lemonade, and together they spread out that dirt to make a court.

"When the township people saw our initiative," he recalls, "they came and put up baskets. Putting in time on the court kept me out of trouble."

LOFTY GOALS

Like many young kids, his idols were the basketball super stars of the day – Elgin Baylor, Jerry West, Bob Koosy — immortals of the game. "You set lofty goals, and if you

get halfway there, you're a lot farther than you might have been."

In high school, Cleve "lettered" in basketball and soccer, and continued to play basketball during the 4 $^1/_2$ years he was in the Air Force, stationed in Istanbul, Turkey. Twice he made the service all-star team. He returned then to Trenton, married, but left again to go back to school. He attended High Point College and graduated from Ashmore Business College in Thomasville, North Carolina.

Coaching grew quite naturally, he says, out of playing (he still plays in a couple of 30-and-older type leagues, "to get rid of hostilities," and to be with friends) and out of concern for kids.

Since 1970 he has coached in the Unlimited League, a part of the Trenton summer basketball program. His Merryman team has won the championship three times.

Besides coaching from 1984–1986 in the Pro-Am League in Camden — a development league for young professionals sponsored by the National Basketball Association (NBA) — Cleve coached for five years (1981–1986) in the Police Athletic League (PAL) for girls 12 years and under.

Cleve now directs the Summer Program. He says it "helps a lot of guys to get into college." NBA fans will recognize the names of John Battle of the Atlanta Hawks and Roy Hinson of the Philadelphia 76ers, both of whom are graduates of his summer program.

ROLE MODELS

Cleve is very conscious that he is a role model for kids and young people. "In the inner city, the only role models are the guys dealing drugs with their pockets bulging with money. I know it was tough when I came up — but not tough compared to now. I stay involved and give them some time; I have their ear.

For a time he was the director of an after-school pro-

The two-column grid is used in this book catalog to create an extremely open, well-organized, easily referenced format.

The long line length (maximum measure is 20,06) minimizes runover lines, so it's easy to pick out the title, author, and other details in each listing.

The small type size (8/11 Friz Quadrata) helps contain the lines, but the leading and white space are designed so that readability isn't compromised. This typeface has a good contrast of boldface to light-face that makes the book titles stand out. The use of boldface, roman, italics, and all caps is handled care-fully to delineate clearly what could have been a hodgepodge of details.

The hard left edge created by the type and the hairline rules contrasts with the openness of the very uneven right margin. Open at the top and the bottom, the page has a strong sense of verticality, which is emphasized by the weight of the category heads.

The headline type is Aachen Bold. The weight of the headlines is emphasized by the bold rules below. Note that in a two-line head the length of the bold rule is determined by the short second line; the hairline rule above the bold rule extends to the maximum measure.

The faceted sphere, with its mathematical precision and crystalline structure, is appropriate for the scientific line of books being sold. The art was created using graphic design software and imported as a PICT file. Because PICT-file tones print differently on LaserWriters and Linotronics (the final output was from an L300), the Pro3D art was kept a little lighter and lower in contrast on-screen than was desired in the printed piece.

Design: John Odam (San Diego, CA)
Catalog from Academic Press, Harcourt Brace Jovanovich, Publishers.
Trim size: 24-3/4 by 11 inches, folded twice

PHYSICAL SCIENCES

THE REWIRING OF AMERICA
The Fiber Optics Revolution
C. David Chaffee
Atlantic Information Services, Inc., Washington, D.C.
1987, 256 pages, **$17.47** ($24.95)
ISBN: 0-12-166360-4

THE FOUNDATIONS OF MAGNETIC RECORDING
John C. Mallinson
Center for Magnetic Recording Research, University of California, San Diego
1987, 175 pages, **$20.97** ($29.95)
ISBN: 0-12-466625-6

ELECTRONS IN SOLIDS
An Introductory Survey
Second Edition
Richard H. Bube
Stanford University, California
1988, 328 pages, **$27.65** ($39.50)
ISBN: 0-12-138552-3

ENCYCLOPEDIA OF PHYSICAL SCIENCE AND TECHNOLOGY
edited by
Robert A. Meyers
TRW Electronics and Defense Sector, Redondo Beach, California
1987, 15-volume set, **$1750.00** ($2500.00)

HANDBOOK OF DIGITAL SIGNAL PROCESSING
ENGINEERING APPLICATIONS
edited by
Douglas F. Elliott
Rockwell International Corporation, Anaheim, California
1987, 999 pages, **$94.50** ($135.00)
ISBN: 0-12-237075-9

ISOTOPE CHRONOSTRATIGRAPHY
Theory and Methods
Douglas F. Williams and Ian Lerche
University of South Carolina, Columbia
W.E. Full
Wichita State University, Kansas
May 1988, 333 pages, **$34.97** ($49.95, tentative)
ISBN: 0-12-754560-3

HISTORICAL SEISMOGRAMS AND EARTHQUAKES OF THE WORLD
edited by
W.H.K. Lee
U.S. Geological Survey, Menlo Park, California
H. Meyers
National Oceanic and Atmospheric Administration Boulder, Colorado
K. Shimazaki
University of Tokyo, Japan
1988, 528 pages, **$31.50** ($45.00)
ISBN: 0-12-440870-2

COMPUTER SCIENCE

PROLOG FOR PROGRAMMERS
Feliks Kluźniak and Stanisław Szpakowicz
Warsaw University, Poland
With a contribution by Janusz S. Bien
Paperback Reprint: $17.47 ($24.95)/ISBN: 0-12-416521-4
1987, 320 pages
Casebound: **$47.25** ($67.50)/ISBN: 0-12-416520-6
1985, 400 pages

INTRODUCTION TO COMMON LISP
Taiichi Yuasa and Masami Hagiya
Kyoto University, Japan
translated by
Richard Weyhrauch and Yasuko Kitajima
1987, 293 pages, **$20.97** ($29.95)
ISBN: 0-12-774860-1

U.S. and Canadian Customers
CALL TOLL FREE
1-800-321-5068
During normal working hours, weekdays only.
In Missouri, Alaska, or Hawaii
call 1-314-528-8110.
*For detailed sales and discount information
call our National Sales Desk
at 1-619-699-6345*

THE WRITER'S GUIDE TO DESKTOP PUBLISHING
Kathy Lang
Mayflower Computing Consultants, Looe, Cornwall, England
In Paperback: $13.97 ($19.95)/ISBN: 0-12-436275-3
1987, 184 pages

COLOR AND THE COMPUTER
edited by
H. John Durrett
Interactive Systems Laboratories, San Marcos, Texas
1987, 299 pages, **$41.30** ($59.00)
ISBN: 0-12-225210-1

PARALLEL COMPUTER VISION
edited by
Leonard Uhr
University of Wisconsin-Madison
1987, 320 pages, **$20.97** ($29.95)
ISBN: 0-12-706958-5

MATHEMATICS AND ECONOMICS

MATHEMATICS FOR DYNAMIC MODELING
Edward Beltrami
State University of New York at Stony Brook
1987, 277 pages, **$19.25** ($27.50)
ISBN: 0-12-085555-0

RANDOM SIGNAL ANALYSIS IN ENGINEERING SYSTEMS
John J. Komo
Clemson University, South Carolina
1987, 302 pages, **$27.97** ($39.95)
ISBN: 0-12-418660-2

ALGEBRAIC D-MODULES
A. Borel et al.
Princeton University, New Jersey
Volume 2 in the PERSPECTIVES IN MATHEMATICS Series
1987, 355 pages, **$23.10** ($33.00)
ISBN: 0-12-117740-8

THE BOOK OF SQUARES
Leonardo Pisano
(Fibonacci)
An annotated translation into Modern English by
L.E. Sigler
Bucknell University, Lewisburg, Pennsylvania
1987, 124 pages, **$13.97** ($19.95)
ISBN: 0-12-643130-2

INDUSTRIAL POLICY OF JAPAN
edited by
Ryutaro Komiya and Masahiro Okuno
University of Tokyo, Bunkyo-ku, Japan
Kotaro Suzumura
Hitotsubashi University, Kunitachi, Tokyo, Japan
Kazuo Sato
Rutgers University, Newark, New Jersey
March 1988, 590 pages, **$34.97** ($49.95, tentative)
ISBN: 0-12-418650-5

MACROECONOMIC THEORY
Second Edition
Thomas J. Sargent
University of Minnesota and Federal Reserve Bank, Minneapolis and Hoover Institution Stanford University, California
1987, 528 pages, **$31.15** ($44.50)
ISBN: 0-12-619751-2

AN INTRODUCTORY THEORY OF SECURITY MARKETS
J.D. Duffie
Stanford University, California
April 1988, 350 pages, **$27.65** ($39.50, tentative)
ISBN: 0-12-223345-X

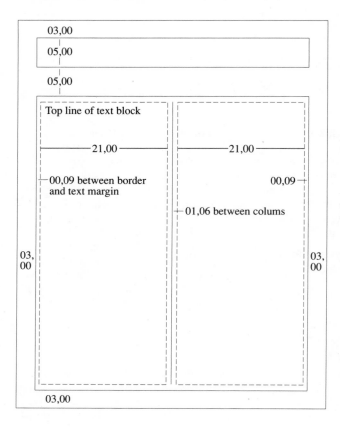

This blueprint was used for both documents on these two pages.

Equal margins on all four sides work best in this format. If you vary from that, do it decisively, as in a deep top margin, rather than subtly.

The depth of the panel at the top of the page and the space between the panel and the text block can vary depending on the elements to be included.

Art is best sized to the width of a single column. Small diagrams can be accommodated as shown in the instruction sheet at right. Art can also be inset in the text, like the quote in the page below.

The illustrations in the instruction sheet were scanned with a Datacopy 730 and then inserted separately. Using a scanner in this way provides an opportunity to test sizes in the layout and to eliminate elements of the art that are unnecessary. The printer strips in the halftones to match the size and position in the layout.

Type specs for instruction sheet
Company name: 18-point Bookman with 20-point caps
Headline: 16/15 Helvetica Black
Subheads: 12-point Helvetica Black
Text: 10/10 Helvetica Light with 6 points between paragraphs, Helvetica Black numbers, and a 1,04 hanging indent
Numbers in diagrams: 18-point Helvetica Black

The journal page at left is obviously designed for an audience predisposed to sustained reading.

The white box for the inset quote is the same width as the text columns. The 12-point rule anchors the quote so that it doesn't float in empty space. The type is 16/18 Helvetica Condensed Bold, centered, and contrasts with the classic feeling of the rest of the page.

The running text is Palatino. The initial cap is 96-point Zapf Chancery followed by a 5,06 pica indent.

 The Journal of Contemporary Mythology

Winter 1990

In Search Of The Modern Myth

By Raymond Chavoustier

> We have not even to risk
> the adventure alone,
> for the heroes of all time have
> gone before us.
> The labyrinth is thoroughly
> known. We have only to follow
> the thread
> of the hero path,
> ... and where we had thought
> to be alone,
> we will be with all the world.
> —Joseph Campbell

23

AUTOMATIC ICE MAKER INSTALLATION KIT
FOR TWO-DOOR SIDE-BY-SIDE REFRIGERATOR

IMPORTANT

The refrigerator must be level to ensure proper operation of the ice maker. See your owner's manual.

TOOLS YOU WILL NEED

Phillips head screwdriver
Drill with 1/4" bit
Adjustable open-end wrench
Needlenose pliers

PARTS LIST

1. Harness and fill-tube grommet.

2. Water supply unit with hose nut, rubber washer, water valve, and compression nuts.

3. Rectangular clip (4) for end assembly unit and split grommet (2).

4. Screws and nuts (See screw identification chart on page 3).

5. Fill spout.

6. Plastic fill tube for ice maker harness.

STEPS IN THIS PROCEDURE

Ut wisi enim ad minim veniam, quis nostrud exerci tation ullamcorper suscipit lobortis nisl ut aliquip ex ea commodo consequat. Duis autem vel eum iriure dolor in hendrerit in vulputate velit esse molestie consequat, vel illum dolore eu feugiat nulla facilisis

1. At vero eros et accumsan et iusto odio dignissim qui blandit praesent luptatum zzril delenit augue duis dolore te feugait

2. Nulla facilisihendrerit in vulputate velit esse molestie . Lorem ipsum dolor sit amet, consectetuer adipiscing elit, sed diam nonummy nibh euismod tincidunt ut laoreet dolore magna aliquam erat volutpat.

3. Ut wisi enim ad minim veniam, quis nostrud exerci tation ullamcorper suscipit lobortis nisl ut aliquip ex ea commodo consequat.

4. Duis autem vel eum iriure dolor in hendrerit in vulputate velit esse molestie consequat, vel illum dolore eu feugiat nulla facilisis at vero eros et accumsan et iusto odio dignissim qui blandit praesent luptatum zzril delenit augue

5. Duis dolore te feugait nulla facilisi.Lorem ipsum dolor sit amet, consectetuer adipiscing elit, sed diam nonummy nibh euismod tincidunt ut laoreet dolore magna

1

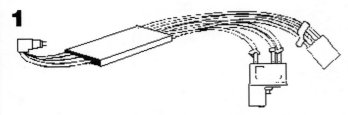

Ut wisi enim ad minim veniam, quis exerci tation

2

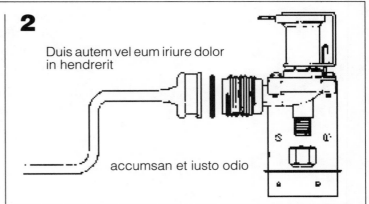

Duis autem vel eum iriure dolor in hendrerit

accumsan et iusto odio

3

Ut wisi enim ad minim veniam, quis exerci tation

4

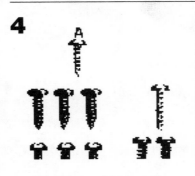

accumsan et iusto odio

5

Duis autem vel eum iriure dolor in hendrerit

6

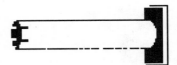

Nulla facilisihendrerit in vulpu

THREE-COLUMN GRIDS

The three-column grid is the most common format in publishing, widely used in magazines, newspapers, newsletters, catalogs, and annual reports. It is popular because it is so flexible, allowing you to place headlines, art, boxed copy, and other elements across any one, two, or even all three columns. This enables you to break the material into small chunks or modules, using various graphic devices to indicate the relative importance of items and relationships between them.

In the short line length, usually 12 to 14 picas, type sets efficiently in relatively small sizes (9- or 10-point type is frequently used for running

This informal, three-column format shows the value of simplicity. With the controls available in desktop publishing, these pages are probably easier to produce than a single-column typewritten document. A stapled, four-page statement of purpose, this was created when the organization first converted to desktop publishing. Three years later, they print the same information in an 11-by-17, three-color folder with computer-drawn art .

The horizontal rules provide a consistent structure that is balanced by open, ragged right type. The two-column heads, the angled, bit-mapped initial caps, and the playful art keep the three-column grid from feeling rigid and also suggest the personality of a foundation trying to reach young people.

The headline type is Bookman (with open spacing in the foundation's name). The running text is Avant Garde, a sans serif face with a large x-height. When generously leaded, as it is here, it is distinctive and iniviting.

Lists of names work very well in the three-column format.

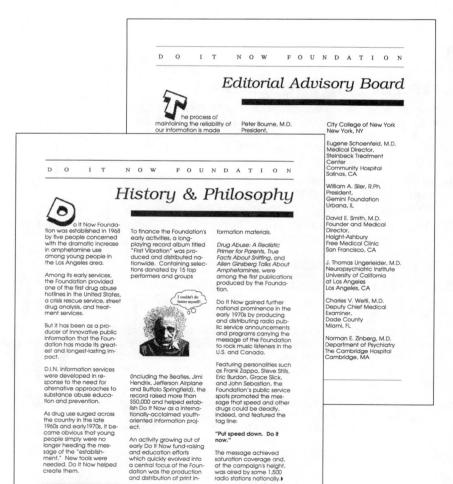

Design: Jim Parker (Phoenix, AZ)

Pages from a statement of purpose by the Do It Now Foundation.
Trim size: 8-1/2 by 11

text) that is still easy for readers to scan. The three-column grid also accommodates small pictures and large ones equally well, so that a really terrific photo can be given adequate space while a not-very-good mug shot can be kept appropriately sized to the width of a single column. This range enables you to use contrast in sizing art as a design element.

So why doesn't everyone use a three-column grid? One of the disadvantages of the format is that so many people do, and it can be difficult to devise a style that distinguishes your publication from all the others.

Page frames and column rules create a classic, three-column newsletter format. A second color, used for banners, breakouts, art, and sidebar tints, adds to the appeal.

Note the many devices used to vary the page composition: inset art, two-column tables and breakouts, sidebars that run the full page width in a two-column format rather than a three-column one. Note

also how the horizontal rules turn into the page on one or both sides of the center column; often, the facing page runs the horizontal rule across all three columns for contrast.

The shatter outline of the art (below left) contrasts sharply with the page structure. In general, irregularly shaped art helps keep a tight grid from being too rigid.

The reverse type in the banners is Avant Garde with open letter spacing, which greatly improves the legibility of reverse type. The breakout is Avant Garde italic, the headlines are Helvetica, and the running text is Times Roman.

Design: Jim Parker (Phoenix, AZ)

Pages from Newservice, *published by the Do It Now Foundation. Trim size: 8-1/2 by 11*

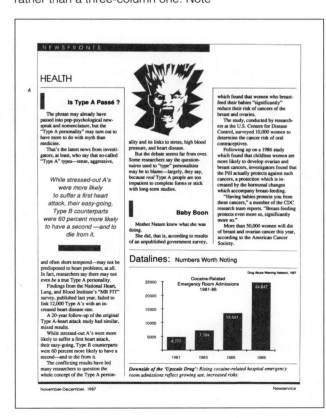

Modular verticals

The easiest way to lay out a three-column page is to run the text continuously in vertical columns. And one of the easiest ways to keep those verticals from being dull is through the use of tones. Whether shades of gray or a second color, tones can be used to separate, isolate, emphasize, or unify. Three different treatments are shown on these two pages.

The tones used in headline banners both unify and separate different elements on the page. The headline banners in this newsletter are 8-point rules (which print 60% black) on top of 20% black boxes, which vary in depth according the length of the headline. The two-line heads are centered in 3,09-deep boxes, the one-line heads in 3,00-deep boxes. You can leave a master banner for each headline size on the pasteboard of your document, and then make copies of them as needed.

The caption also prints in a 20% box. A three-line caption fits in the same 3,09 box as a two-line head.

Nashville, the type used for the publication name, is from Compu-graphic. When Nashville is set tightly, its slab-serif style works well, and the word "NewsBeat" has been kerned to bring out that characteristic. The date, set in 9-point Futura, is set with 200% letter space for additional contrast with the type above.

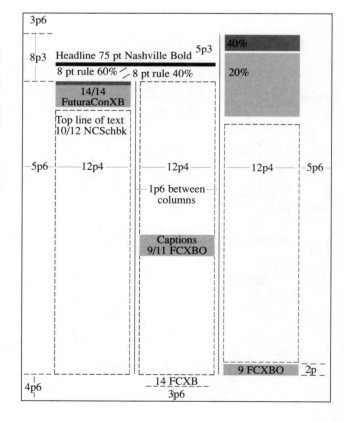

Art, headlines, and color tints are placed loosely in the grid to create a collage-like feeling in the first sample. The effect is casual and gives an inviting sense of the unexpected, which is relatively rare in three-column newsletters.

Color is a strong element in this design. The tone unifying the two related stories under a single headline is orange; it drops out to create a white border around the photos, which print over a blue tint. The two-column headline, initial caps, 8-point rules, and exclamation point also print in orange. The logo prints orange and blue.

The distinctive logo collages small sans serif type, boxed and angled, over the larger Roman-style title. An effective way to integrate the company and newsletter names, this device is relatively easy to execute if you have a good eye for proportioning type.

The Times Roman running text is set in relatively narrow columns surrounded by generous white space. For contrast, the display type is set in a bold Helvetica.

In the bottom sample, the tone is used behind secondary material—the issue highlights on the cover and sidebars on inside pages—rather than behind features.

The structured rules, justified text, and even column bottoms represent a completely different approach to page design than the previous sample. Each sets a style appropriate for its audience.

Design (top): Tom Ahern (Providence, RI)

Dateline *is published quarterly by GTECH Lottery.*
Size: 8-1/2 by 11

Design (bottom): Kimberly Mancebo, Robert Bryant Associates (Campbell, CA)

TeleVisual Market Strategies *is published by Telecommunications Productivity Center.*
Size: 8-1/2 by 11

Introducing the horizontal

A true grid has a precise horizontal structure that is generally determined by the type specifications of the dominant text face, so that a given number of lines will fit in each grid unit. The construction of the grid must also take into account the space between grid units. For example, if your type is 10/12, each grid unit and the space beween two units will be in multiples of 12 points, or 1 pica. If your type is 11/13, then the grid units will be in multiples of 13 points, obviously a less convenient measurement to work with.

If you want to study an expertly used horizontal grid, see the Pitney Bowes publication toward the beginning of the Brochure section in Chapter 5.

Visual elements are sized to fit different combinations of these units, allowing for varied sizes and shapes which, because of their relationship to the underlying structure, are in proportion to one another and to the page as a whole. In some ways, the truly modular grid simplifies layout more than the mostly vertical structures apparent in many of the samples reproduced in this book. But an orthodox grid is also more difficult to construct. If you find the mathematically determined horizontal structure confusing or inhibiting, then adopt a more informal approach to placing the elements vertically on the page. If, on the other hand, you are drawn to the possibilities inherent in the technique introduced on these and the following two pages, you'll find a number of useful books listed in the resource section.

The sample on the facing page is built on an 18-unit grid, with 3 vertical divisions and 6 horizontal ones. This schematic shows the placement of the sample's visual elements on the grid. You can see how the structure facilitates decision making by suggesting both size and placement; note also how the design overrides the grid when needed. Turn the page for additional diagrams, grid specifications, and another, very different design based on the same grid.

Type Specifications

Overline: 10/12 Avant Garde reverse, centered, with
   Tracking: Looser by 2.0 EMS
Publication name: 48-point Avant Garde, with Tracking:
   Tighter by 0.2 EMS
Story heads: 24/24 Bodoni Bold Italic
Body text: 10/12 Bodoni
Captions: 11/12 Bodoni Bold Italic

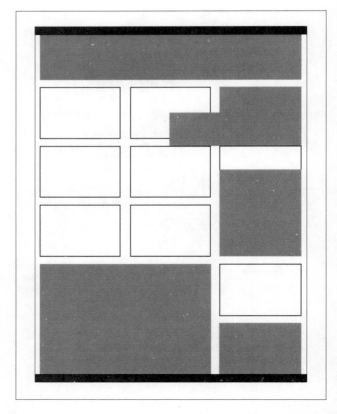

Triangle Hotel Trumpet

EAT, DRINK AND BE MERRY

Lorem ipsum dolor sit amet, consectetuer adipiscing elit, sed diam nonummy nibh euismod tincidunt ut laoreet dolore magna aliquam erat volutpat. Ut wisi enim ad minim veniam, quis nostrud exerci tation ullamcorper suscipit lobortis nisl ut aliquip ex ea commodo consequat.

Duis autem vel eum iriure dolor in hendrerit in vulputate velit esse molestie consequat, vel illum dolore eu feugiat nulla facilisis at vero eros et accumsan et iusto odio dignissim qui blandit praesent luptatum zzril delenit augue duis dolore te feugait nulla facilisi. Lorem ipsum dolor sit amet, consectetuer adipiscing elit, sed diam nonummy nibh euismod tincidunt ut laoreet dolore magna aliquam erat volutpat. Ut wisi enim ad minim veniam, quis nostrud exerci tation ullamcorper suscipit lobortis nisl ut aliquip ex ea commodo consequat.

Duis autem vel eum iriure dolor in hendrerit in vulputate velit esse molestie consequat, vel illum dolore eu feugiat nulla facil at vero eros et

accumsan et iusto etei odio dignissim qui blandit praesent luptatum zzril delenit augue duis dolore te. feugait nulla facilisi. Nam liber tempor

Sunday Jazz Brunch

FROM BIG BAND TO ROCK 'N ROLL

Duis autem vel eum iriure dolor in hendrerit in vulputate velit esse molestie consequat, vel illum dolore eu feugiat nulla facilisis at vero eros et accumsan et iusto odio dignissim qui blandit praesent luptatum zzril delenit augue duis dolore te feugait nulla facilisi.

Lorem ipsum dolor sit amet, consectetuer adipiscing elit, sed diam nonummy nibh euismod tincidunt ut laoreet dolore magna aliquam erat volutpat. Ut wisi enim ad minim veniam, quis nostrud exerci tation

ullamcorper suscipit lobortis nisl ut aliquip ex ea commodo consequat. Duis autem vel eum iriure dolor in hendrerit in vulputate velit esse

All-Night Buffet

molestie consequat. Lorem ipsum dolor sit amet, consectetuer adipiscing elit, sed diam nonummy nibh euismod tincidunt ut

Baoreet dolore magna aliquam erat volutpat. Ut wisi enim ad minim laoreet dolore magna aliquam erat veniam, quis nostrud eu feugiat nulla facilisis at vero eros et accumsan et

New Year's Gala in the Ballroom

Morning-After Room Service

This is a good place for the placement of a pull quote from the text

Lorem ipsum dolor sit amet, consectetuer adipiscing elit, sed diam nonummy nibh euismod tincidunt ut laoreet dolore magna aliquam erat volutpat. Ut wisi enim ad minim veniam, quis nostrud exerci tation ullamcorper suscipit lobortis nisl ut aliquip ex ea commodo consequat. Duis autem vel eum iriure dolor in hendrerit in vulputate velit esse molestie consequat, vel illum dolore eu feugiat nulla facilisis at vero eros et accumsan et iusto odio dignissim qui blandit praesent luptatum zzril delenit augue duis dolore te feugait nulla facilisi. Lorem ipsum dolor sit amet, consectetuer adipiscing elit,

in hendrerit in vulputate velit esse molestie consequat, vel illum dolore eu feugiat nulla facilisis at vero eros et accumsan et iusto odio dignissim qui blandit praesent luptatum zzril delenit augue duis dolore te feugait nulla facilisi. Nam liber tempor cum soluta nobis eleifend option

nostrud exerci tation ullamcorper suscipit lobortis nisl ut aliquip ex ea commodo consequat. Duis autem vel eum iriure dolor in hendrerit in vulputate velit esse molestie consequat, vel illum dolore eu feugiat nulla facilisis at vero eros et accumsan et iusto odio dignissim qui blandit prae

nostrud exerci tation ullamcorper suscipit lobortis nisl ut aliquip ex ea commodo consequat. Duis autem vel eum iriure dolor in hendrerit in vulputate velit esse molestie consequat, vel illum dolore eu

sed diam nonummy nibh euismod tincidunt ut laoreet dolore magna aliquam erat volutpat. Ut wisi enim ad minim veniam, quis nostrud exerci tation ullamcorper suscipit lobortis nisl ut aliquip ex ea commodo consequat. Duis autem vel eum iriure dolor

congue nihil imperdiet doming id quod mazim placerat facer possim assum. Lorem ipsum dolor sit amet, consectetuer adipiscing elit, sed diam nonummy nibh euismod tincidunt ut laoreet dolore magna aliquam erat volutpat. Ut wisi enim ad minim veniam, quis

sent luptatum zzril delenit augue duis dolore te feugait nulla facilisi. Lorem ipsum dolor sit amet, consectetuer adipiscing elit, sed diam nonummy nibh euismod tincidunt ut laoreet dolore magna aliquam erat volutpat. Ut wisi enim ad minim veniam,

1   2   3

4

Page composition within an 18-unit grid such as the one discussed on these four pages can vary considerably. The page at left and schematic 1, above, show picture placement in which the horizontal and vertical structures are balanced. The second schematic shows a strong horizontal arrangement; the third, a strong vertical. In the fourth, one column is used only for headlines, captions, and small photos, creating still another look.

Research Paper

Lorem ipsum dolor sit amet, consectetuer adipiscing elit, sed diam nonummy nibh euismod tincidunt ut laoreet dolore magna aliquam erat volutpat. Ut wisi enim ad minim veniam, quis nostrud exerci tation ullamcorper suscipit lobortis nisl ut aliquip ex ea commodo consequat.
   Duis autem vel eum iriure dolor in hendrerit in vulputate velit esse molestie consequat, vel illum dolore eu feugiat nulla facilisis at vero eros et accumsan et iusto odio dignissim qui blandit praesent luptatum zzril delenit augue duis dolore te feugait nulla facilisi.
   Lorem ipsum dolor sit amet, consectetuer adipiscing elit, sed diam nonummy nibh euismod tincidunt ut laoreet dolore magna aliquam erat volutpat. Ut wisi enim ad minim veniam, quis nostrud exerci tation ullamcorper suscipit lobortis nisl ut aliquip ex ea commodo consequat.
   Duis autem vel eum iriure dolor in hendrerit in vulputate velit esse molestie consequat, vel illum dolore eu feugiat nulla facilisis at vero eros et accumsan et iusto odio dignissim qui blandit praesent luptatum zzril delenit augue duis dolore te feugait nulla facilisi. Nam liber tempor cum soluta nobis eleifend option congue nihil imperdiet doming id quod mazim placerat facer possim assum.
   Lorem ipsum dolor sit amet, consectetuer adipiscing elit, sed diam nonummy nibh euismod tincidunt ut laoreet dolore magna ut laoreet dolore magna aliquam erat ea commodo consequat.
   Duis autem vel eum iriure dsent luptatum zzril delenit augue duis dolore te feugait nulla

TEST RESULTS	Grp A	Grp B	Control
Uptatum zzril delenit augue	1,745	1,398	1,598
Dolore eu feugiat nulla	4,978	2,467	1,028
Tincidunt ut ladolore wisi enim	3,684	1,746	5,896
Tin vulputate velit esse	2,678	3,986	1,038
Dignissim qui blandit praesent	3,794	1,840	2,096
Uptatum zzril delenit augue	1,493	2,047	3,208
Dolore eu feugiat nulla	2,067	2,067	3,906
Total	17,376	13,982	20,387

NARRATIVE

Amet consectetuer adipiscing elit, suscipit lobortis nisl ut aliquip ex commodo consequat. Duis autem vel eum iriure dolor in hendrerit in vulputate velit esse molestie consequat, vel illum dolore eu feugiat nulla facilisis at Vero eros et

sectetuer adipiscing elit, sed diam nonummy nibh euismod tincidunt ut lcommodo consequat. Duis autem aoreet dolore magna aliquam erat volutpat. Ut wisi enim ad minim

continued on following page

FURTHER RESEARCH

Accumsan et iusto odio dignissim qui blandit praesent luptatum zzril delenit augue duis dolore te feugait nulla facilisi.
Lorem ipsum dolor sit amet, consectetuer adipiscing elit, sed

CONCLUSIONS

Diam nonummy nibh euismod tincidunt ut laoreet dolore magna aliquam erat volutpat. Ut wisi enim ad minim veniam, quis nostrud exerci tation ullamcorper suscipit lobortis nisl ut aliquip ex ea commodo consequat. Duis facilisi.

Lorem ipsum dolor sit amet, tincidunt ut laoreet dolore magna aliquam erat volutpat. Ut wisi enim ad minim veniam,

The sample at left uses the grid on the facing page to create horizontal divisions for text blocks. A text block can run any number of grid units, and need not fill the entire unit. But regardless of the depth of the text, rules separating text blocks are placed at the midpoint of the space between two grid units.

The banner runs from the top margin to the midpoint of the space between the first two horizontal grid units. A hairline horizontal rule is placed midway between the last grid unit and the bottom margin.

The headline is 60-point American Typewriter, reversed out of the 60% black banner.

The body text is 10/12 New Century Schoolbook.

Subheads are 12-point Helvetica Black, aligned at top with the top of a grid unit. The running text in these text blocks is 10/12 Helvetica Light. The text in the table is 10/24, creating a full line space between each item so that this text aligns with running text in the adjacent column.

Grid units and type size are designed in relation to one another. The first detail here shows how 10/12 text fits in the grid units used in the samples on these two pages. For the sake of comparison, the second detail shows 10/14 text in the same 10/12 grid; you can see that with the increased leading, the grid no longer works. Both details are shown full size.

With Line Snap on, all frames that you place on the page will align with the page's Body Text Inter-Line spacing.

Lorem ipsum dolor sit amet, consectetuer adipiscing elit, sed diam nonummy nibh euismod tincidunt ut laoreet dolore magna aliquam erat volutpat. Ut wisi enim ad minim veniam, quis nostrud exerci tation ullamcorper suscipit lobortis nisl ut aliquip ex ea commodo consequat.

Duis autem vel eum iriure dolor in hendrerit in vulputate velit esse molestie consequat, vel illum dolore eu feugiat nulla facilisis at vero eros et accumsan et iusto odio dignissim qui blandit praesent luptatum zzril delenit augue duis dolore te feugait nulla facilisi. Lorem ipsum dolor sit amet, consectetuer adipiscing elit, sed diam nonummy nibh euismod tincidunt ut duis laoreet dolore magna

1

Lorem ipsum dolor sit amet, consectetuer adipiscing elit, sed diam nonummy nibh euismod tincidunt ut laoreet dolore magna aliquam erat volutpat. Ut wisi enim ad minim veniam, quis nostrud exerci tation ullamcorper suscipit lobortis nisl ut aliquip ex ea commodo consequat.

Duis autem vel eum iriure dolor in hendrerit in vulputate velit esse molestie consequat, vel illum dolore eu feugiat nulla facilisis at vero eros et accumsan et iusto odio dignissim qui blandit praesent luptatum zzril delenit augue duis dolore te feugait nulla facilisi. Lorem ipsum dolor sit

2

This grid was used for the samples in this section. Although all the units are of equal size, elements placed on the grid need not be. The grid is constructed as follows:

Margins: 3 picas top and bottom, 4 picas side

Columns: three, 1,06 space between

Horizontal grid units: 8,09 deep beginning at top margin, 1 pica between units

Hairline vertical rules from top to bottom margin: 1 pica outside left and right margins and, where appropriate, between columns

Horizontal rules (Triangle Hotel sample on preceding spread): 1,03 deep; top rule flush with top grid unit; bottom rule just below last grid unit.

Note that the grid is slightly asymmetrical along the vertical axis. In the Triangle Hotel sample on the preceding spread, the 1,03-deep horizontal rule fills the space between the bottom grid unit and the bottom margin. In the Research Paper at left, a hairline rule visually fills the space at the bottom of the page. If you were to use this grid without horizontal rules to balance the space, you would probably want to shift the entire grid down 9 points to center it on the page.

A mixed grid

Varying the column width within a single page has many uses. It accommodates different kinds of material, allows for a varied page design, and can inspire you to organize the components of your document in a way that strengthens the intrinsic relationships and forms contrasts among them. In the sample shown below, the mixed grid is both functional and dramatic.

Sidebar vignettes set to a 13-pica measure are inset in a single wide column that provides the background narrative in this annual report. The sidebars, which run throughout the report, are human-interest stories. On other pages not shown, some sidebars are styled as two single columns that face each other across the gutter, others as two singles in the outer columns of facing pages.

The two different settings are unified by a single typeface (Goudy Old Style), generously leaded, yet they are styled for considerable contrast: The larger, roman type in the wide measure is justified and prints in warm brown; the smaller, italic type is ragged right and prints in black. The italic caption at the bottom of the page is set to the wide measure and prints in brown.

Design: Tom Lewis (San Diego, CA)
Page from the Medic Alert Annual Report.
Trim size: 8-1/2 by 11

Design (facing page): Edward Hughes, Edward Hughes Design (Evanston, IL)
Pages from the Roosevelt University Annual Report.
Trim Size: 8-1/4 by 11-5/8

R E P O R T   T O   T H E   R E A D E R

"My membership is like insurance coverage - the very best protection, and for a reasonable cost. I'm sure all the members feel as I do - grateful there is an organization called Medic Alert."

That's how one member described the secure feeling enjoyed by the more than 2.6 million people worldwide who wear the Medic Alert emblem. For 32 years, Medic Alert has warned health professionals about patients' special medical conditions, saving thousands of lives and sparing needless suffering. "As an EMT," another member wrote, "I know how much Medic Alert helps emergency personnel. If people would only realize how important it is for us to know their medical problems in an emergency maybe more would wear Medic Alert emblems."

In recent years, Medic Alert's emergency medical identification system has substantially improved operations management and product and service quality. The Foundation's quest for excellence is ongoing.

MEDIC ALERT'S NEW SERVICES This year, Medic Alert launched plans to diversify into services that capitalize on the Foundation's ability to manage an accurate, confidential medical data base. In August, in 1987, Medic Alert began

MEDIC ALERT PROTECTS TRANSPLANT RECIPIENT

Eleven years ago, a New Zealand school girl named Ann Crawford became ill with the flu. Unlike many flu victims for whom the malady is a fleeting annoyance, Ann suffered permanent lung damage. She fell prey to a series of infections that strained her breathing and weakened her heart.

In the years that followed, Ann endured a revolving door of hospital treatments. Her doctors experimented with megadose drug therapies to clear her frequent infections, but her lungs continued to worsen. Eight years

after her bout with the flu, Ann's health had become so fragile that few expected her to survive the winter.

Only 19, Ann was not ready to give up. She had read up on the latest advances in thoracic surgery and transplant technology. She wondered, " Why not start all over again with a new heart and lungs?"

Ann's enthusiasm sparked support from the Lions Club in her area, which agreed to help finance the cost of her surgery. She traveled to the United Kingdom for the operation, and returned home with a new heart and lungs. Shortly after, she penned Pumps & Bellows, a detailed account of her illness and transplant operation.

This brave young woman from New Zealand, is breathing easier these days. But she will always require anti-rejection drugs to ensure that her body will not declare war on her new organs. In a medical emergency, responders need to know instantly of her transplant operation and drug regimen to administer proper treatment.

That is why Ann, like many others around the world, wears a Medic Alert emblem. After years of hospital stays and bed rest, the young New Zealander takes every precaution to protect her most treasured gift, a second chance at life.

From Evangeline: Thanks to Medic Alert my husband is alive today. He was in a very bad car accident. The paramedics saw his Medic Alert necklace and found his wallet card. His seat belt and his Medic Alert tag saved his life.

Asymmetrical three-column

Generally, asymmetrical three-column grids have two wide columns and one narrow one. This produces a slightly more interesting and an inherently more variable look than three equal columns, especially when you consider the possibilities that derive from combining two columns, whether two equal columns or one wide and one narrow.

The underlying structure is two 11-pica columns and one 18-pica column. When the wide column is combined with the inside narrow column, the resulting 31-pica measure provides additional flexibility in page composition.

The depth of the photographs remains constant from page to page, although the depth of the captions varies. Good photographs, well-printed, result in the rich blacks and grays evident here.

The captions are styled as display type, reversed out against the gray background.

The uneven bottoms of the three columns helps balance the tight structure created by the strong horizontal line across the top of the page, the strong left edge of the type columns (which is emphasized by the elongated page), and the tabbed folios that bleed off the bottom of the page.

Note that single-digit numbers are indented so that all numbers align right. This typographic refinement is all the more needed here with the hanging indent.

As precise as this format is, the pages are relatively easy to assemble. Having two standardized picture sizes minimizes art decisions, and the uneven bottoms speed up page assembly.

The slightly elongated page, elegant gray paper, and high-quality printing create an image that is both distinctive and consequential. Fine printing on excellent paper stock is essential to provide an even gray background throughout and to hold the crisp detail on the small, reverse-type numbers seen here and in reverse hairline rules used on tables (not shown).

Director **Geraldine Piorkowski** (left) and Associate Director **Rod Esbrook** (right) of Counseling & Testing and Career Planning & Placement Director **Arthur Eckberg** (center) will administer a three-year "Career Analysis & Placement Project" funded by the Irvin Stern Foundation.

Roosevelt University student **Kendy Kloepfer** met some of the requirements for a major in theatre by taking classes at the Lou Conte Dance Studio, home of the Hubbard Street Dance Company. Cooperative agreements with local institutions enable University students to earn degree credits while learning from experts unique to Chicago.

Two narrow outer columns and a wide center column create a somewhat specialized three-column grid. The layout implies that the center item is the most important one. In the pages shown here, the outer columns are used to present contrasting viewpoints on the same subject, an editorial approach that works particularly well in this format. The outer columns could also be used for quotes and other marginalia, for resources related to the main story, brief listings, short profiles or news items, and so on.

The justified text in these pages adds to the formality of the subject matter and to the point-counterpoint approach of the editorial.

The blueprint gives dimensions and type specs for the nameplate on the cover. On subsequent pages, as in the one shown below left, the top of the text block is 9 picas from the top trim, so that would be the dimension to use for the top margin on the page setup.

The Bodoni and Bookman headlines were condensed on the horizontal axis and then placed. The document title was cropped to clip off the bottom of the letters, which makes the type look like it is emerging from behind the rule.

The Avant Garde ID lines on the cover and inside page were set with open letter and word spacing so that the "Educational Advancement" line filled the three-column measure.

The depth of the framed illustrations on both pages is a guideline only. The placement of visuals in the center column is best at the bottom of the page, although the top is also acceptable.

Space between art, captions, rules, and adjacent body text is often a difficult detail in page assembly unless you are working on a very precise grid. The closer any two elements are to each other, the more related they will seem to the reader. In these samples, the caption is closer to the picture frame below it than to the rule above, and the rule is closer to the caption than to the preceding text.

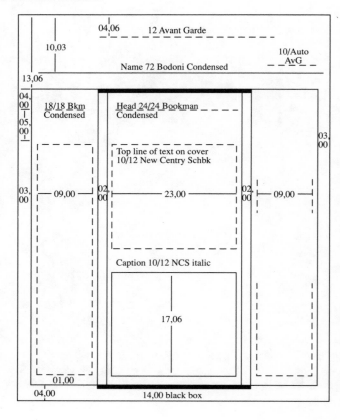

ASSOCIATION

BULLETIN

TEACHERS
ADMINISTRATORS
COUNSELORS

PARENTS
SOCIAL WORKERS
PSYCHOLOGISTS

EDUCATIONAL ADVANCEMENT IN AMERICA

A Case for Gradual Growth in Our Schools

Feugait nulla facilisi. Nam liber tempor cum soluta nobis eleifend option congue nihil imperdiet doming id

quod mazim placerat facer possim assum. Lorem ipsum dolor sit amet, consectetuer adipiscing elit, sed

Diam nonummy nibh euismod tincidunt ut laoreet dolore magna aliquam erat volutpatUt wisi enim ad minim veniam, quis nostrud exerci tation ullamcorper suscipit lobortis nisl ut aliquip ex ea commodo conse

A Primer for School Administrators in the Nineties

Torem ipsum dolor sit amet, consectetuer adipiscing elit, sed diam nonummy nibh euismod tincidunt ut laoreet dolore magna aliquam erat volutpat. Ut wisi enim ad minim veniam, quis nostrud exerci tation ullamcorper suscipit lobortis nisl ut aliquip ex ea commodo consequat.

Duis autem vel eum iriure dolor in hendrerit in vulputate velit esse molestie consequat, vel illum dolore eu feugiat nulla facilisis at vero eros et accumsan et iusto odio dignissim qui blandit praesent luptatum zzril delenit augue duis dolore te feugait nulla facilisi. Lorem ipsum dolor sit amet, consectetuer adipiscing elit, sed diam nonummy nibh euismod tincidunt ut laoreet dolore magna aliquam erat volutpat. Ut wisi enim ad minim veniam, quis nostrud exerci tation ullamcorper suscipit lobortis nisl ut aliquip ex ea commodo consequat.

Duis autem vel eum iriure dolor in hendrerit in vulputate velit esse molestie consequat, vel illum dolore eu feugiat nulla facilisis at vero eros et accumsan et iusto odio dignissim qui blandit praesent luptatum zzril delenit augue duis dolore te

Aliquip ex ea commodo consequat. Duis autem vel eum iriure dolor in hendrerit in vulputate velit esse mo

The Wisdom of Revolutionary Change in Education

Autem vel eum iriure dolor in hendrerit in vulputate velit esse molestie consequat, Vel illum dolore eu feugiat nulla facilisis at vero eros et accumsan et iusto odio dignissim qui blandit praesent luptatum zzril delenit augue duis dolore te feugait nulla facilisi.

Lorem ipsum dolor sit amet, consectetuer adipiscing elit, sed diam nonummy nibh euismod tincidunt ut laoreet dolore magna aliquam erat volutpat.

Narrow outer columns in a three-column grid are useful for publications as diverse as catalogs and technical journals.

In text-heavy publications, such as the one shown below, the narrow outer column can provide much-needed white space when reserved for art, captions, breakouts, and marginalia.

When you wrap ragged right text around a rectangular graphic, you get a much neater appearance if the graphic juts into the flush left margin.

The body text in the sample is 10/12 Galliard. The display type is Futura Condensed Extra Bold, set in 30-, 14-, and 10-point sizes. The captions are 10/12 Futura Heavy.

A classic catalog format on the facing page uses rules, art, white space, and the edge of text blocks to frame pictures. The art and text requirements dictate the size, the only restraints being the vertical rules (and even those can be violated effectively).

The blueprint shows measurements for the sample below. To set up the format, specify 4 pica side margins, and 3 columns with 1,06 space between; then override the default column widths with the measurements given in the blueprint.

The grid for the catalog on the facing page is similar, but the left edge of the text is flush with the column rules, which drop out behind the text. This maintains the structure of the rules while providing maximum measure for copy. To construct this grid, position the vertical rules, including those in the page frames, at these intervals: 3,00; 17,00; 17,00; 11,00; 3,00.

The type reinforces the impression of variety, with six different faces used. From top to bottom, they are Futura Condensed, Aachen Bold, Avant Garde, Palatino Italic, Franklin Gothic Heavy, and American Typewriter.

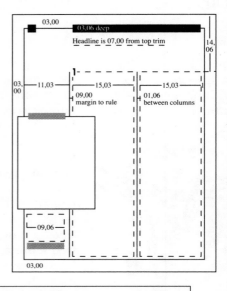

03,00
03,06 deep
Headline is 07,00 from top trim
14,06
03,00 — 11,03 — 15,03 — 15,03
09,00 margin to rule
01,06 between columns
09,06
03,00

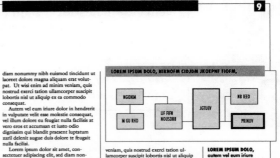

8   CD ROM TECHNOLOGY REPORT

AUDIO DELIVERY SYSTEMS FOR THE 1990S

Tem ipsum dolor sit amet, consectetuer adipiscing elit, sed diam nonummy nibh euismod tincidunt ut laoreet dolore magna aliquam erat volutpat. Ut wisi enim ad minim veniam, quis nostrud exerci tation ullamcorper suscipit lobortis nisl ut aliquip ex ea commodo consequat. Duis autem vel eum iriure dolor in hendrerit in vulputate velit esse molestie consequat, vel illum dolore eu feugiat nulla facilisis at vero eros et accumsan et iusto odio dignissim qui blandit praesent luptatum zzril delenit augue duis dolore te feugait nulla facilisi. Lorem ipsum dolor sit amet, consectetuer adipiscing elit, sed diam nonummy nibh euismod tincidunt ut laoreet dolore magna aliquam erat volutpat.

Duis autem vel eum iriure dolor in hendrerit in vulputate velit esse molestie consequat, vel illum dolore eu feugiat nulla facilisis at vero

LOREM IPSUM DOLO

UT WISI ENIM AD
veniam, quis nostrud exerci tation ullamcorper suscipit lobortis nisl ut aliquip ex ea commodo consequat. Duis autem

eros et accumsan et iusto odio dignissim qui blandit praesent luptatum zzril delenit augue duis dolore te feugait nulla facilisi. Nam liber tempor cum soluta nobis eleifend option congue nihil imperdiet doming id quod mazim placerat facer possim assum. Lorem ipsum dolor sit amet, consectetuer adipiscing elit, sed diam nonummy nibh euismod tincidunt ut laoreet dolore magna aliquam erat volutpat. Ut wisi enim ad minim veniam, quis

nostrud exerci tation ullamcorper suscipit lobortis nisl ut aliquip ex ea commodo consequat. Duis autem vel eum veniam, quis nostrud exerci tation ullamcorper suscipit feugiat nulla facilisis at vero eros et blandit praesent luptatum zzril delenit augue duis dolore te feugait nulla facilisi.

Ut wisi enim ad minim veniam, quis nostrud exerci tation ullamcorper suscipit lobortis nisl ut aliquip ex ea commodo consequat.

FIDELITY V STORAGE
Amet, consectetuer adipiscing elit, sed diam nonummy nibh euismod tincidunt ut laoreet dolore magna aliquam erat volutpat. Ut wisi enim ad minim veniam, quis nostrud exerci tation ullamcorper suscipit lobortis nisl ut aliquip ex ea commodo consequat. Duis autem vel eum iriure dolor in hendrerit in vulputate velit esse molestie consequat, vel illum dolore eu feugiat nulla facilisis at vero eros et accumsan et iusto odio dignissim qui blandit praesent luptatum zzril delenit augue duis dolore te feugait nulla facilisi. Lorem ipsum dolor sit amet, consectetuer adipiscing elit, sed diam nonummy nibh euismod tincidunt ut laoreet dolore magna aliquam erat volutpat. Ut wisi enim ad minim veniam, quis nostrud exerci tation ullamcorper suscipit lobortis nisl ut aliquip ex ea commodo consequat. Duis autem vel eum iriure dolor in hendrerit in vulputate velit esse molestie consequat, vel illum dolore eu feugiat nulla facilisis at vero eros et accumsan et iusto odio dignissim qui blandit praesent luptatum zzril delenit augue duis dolore te feugait nulla facilisi. Lorem ipsum dolor sit amet, consectetuer adipiscing elit, sed

diam nonummy nibh euismod tincidunt ut laoreet dolore magna aliquam erat volutpat. Ut wisi enim ad minim veniam, quis nostrud exerci tation ullamcorper suscipit lobortis nisl ut aliquip ex ea commodo consequat.

Autem vel eum iriure dolor in hendrerit in vulputate velit esse molestie consequat, vel illum dolore eu feugiat nulla facilisis at vero eros et accumsan et iusto odio dignissim qui blandit praesent luptatum zzril delenit augue duis dolore te feugait nulla facilisi. Lorem ipsum dolor sit amet, consectetuer adipiscing elit, sed diam nonummy nibh euismod tincidunt ut laoreet dolore magna aliquam erat volutpat. Ut wisi enim ad minim veniam, quis nostrud exerci tation ullamcorper suscipit lobortis nisl ut aliquip ex ea commodo consequat.

Duis autem vel eum iriure dolor in hendrerit in vulputate velit esse molestie consequat, vel illum dolore eu feugiat nulla facilisis at vero eros et accumsan et iusto odio dignissim qui blandit praesent luptatum zzril delenit augue duis dolore te feugait nulla facilisi. Lorem ipsum dolor sit amet, consectetuer adipiscing elit, sed diam nonummy nibh euismod tincidunt ut laoreet dolore magna aliquam erat volutpat. Ut wisi enim ad minim

LOREM IPSUM DOLO, NIRNOFM CIDJDM JKOEPNF FIOFM,

NGIDKM   NB IEEO
UF FIFN NOUSDBI   JGTUEV
M GU KHD   PRINUV

veniam, quis nostrud exerci tation ullamcorper suscipit lobortis nisl ut aliquip ex ea commodo consequat. Duis autem vel eum iriure dolor in hendrerit in vulputate velit esse molestie consequat, vel illum dolore eu feugiat nulla facilisis at vero eros et accumsan et iusto odio dignissim qui blandit praesent luptatum zzril delenit augue duis dolore te feugait nulla facilisi. Lorem ipsum dolor sit amet, consectetuer adipiscing elit, sed diam nonummy nibh euismod tincidunt ut laoreet dolore magna aliquam erat volutpat dolore te feugait nulla facilisi.

PLAYBACK ENVIRONMENT
Ut wisi enim ad minim veniam, quis nostrud exerci tation ullamcorper suscipit lobortis nisl ut aliquip ex ea commodo consequat. Duis autem vel eum iriure dolor in hendrerit in vulputate velit esse molestie consequat, vel illum dolore eu feugiat nulla facilisis at vero eros et accumsan et iusto odio dignissim qui blandit praesent luptatum zzril delenit augue duis dolore te feugait nulla facilisi. Lorem ipsum dolor sit amet, consectetuer adipiscing elit, sed diam nonummy nibh euismod tincidunt ut laoreet dolore magna aliquam erat volutpat. Ut wisi enim ad minim veniam, quis nostrud exerci tation ullamcorper suscipit lobortis nisl ut aliquip ex ea commodo consequat. Duis autem vel eum iriure dolor in hendrerit in vulputate velit esse molestie consequat, vel

LOREM IPSUM DOLO,
autem vel eum iriure dolor in hendrerit in vulputate velit esse molestie consequat, vel illum consectetuer adipiscing elit, sed diam nonummy nibh euismod tincidunt ut laoreet dolore

9

The Most Realistic Stuffed Animals You Ever Saw

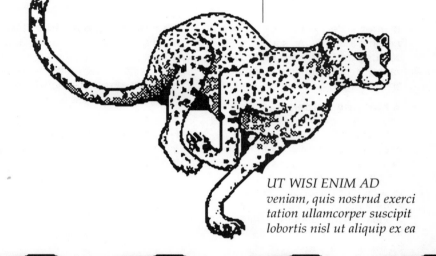

UT WISI ENIM AD veniam, quis nostrud exerci tation ullamcorper suscipit lobortis nisl ut aliquip ex ea

LOREM IPSUM DOLOR SIT AMET, sectetuer adipiscing elit, sed diam nonummy nibh euismod tincidunt ut laoreet dolore magna aliquam erat volutpat. Ut wisi enim ad minim veniam, quis nostrud exerci tation ullamcorper suscipit lobortis nisl ut aliquip ex ea commodo consequat. Duis autem vel eum iriure dolor in hendrerit in vulputate velit esse molestie consequat, vel illum dolore eu feugiat nulla facilisis at vero eros et accumsan et iusto odio dignissim qui blandit praesent luptatum zzril delenit augue duis dolore te feugait nulla facilisi. Lorem ipsum dolor sit amet, consectetuer adipiscing elit, sed diam nonummy nibh euismod tincidunt ut laoreet dolore magna aliquam erat

UT WISI ENIM AD veniam, quis nostrud exerci tation ullamcorper suscipit

LOREM IPSUM DOLO, autem vel eum iriure dolor in hendrerit in vulputate velit esse molestie consequat, vel illum consectetuer adipiscing elit, sed diam

FOUR-COLUMN GRIDS

Four-column grids are even more versatile than three-column formats. They provide an opportunity for varied page design within the same publication and for dramatic contrast among visual elements of different sizes. These grids are used frequently in magazines, newspapers,

Boxed sidebars work extremely well in a four-column setting, and can be sized with considerable variety depending on the number and depth of the columns used.

A half-page sidebar is printed against a gray tone, with two narrow columns at the bottom combined to accommodate tables. Note that the box extends beyond the page frame, a technique you see frequently in graphic design today. Here those extra 9 points make it possible for the text set in the four-column format to run at the same 9-pica measure as the unboxed text. (Usually you lose a few points to the box.)

The "At a Glance" headline is used repeatedly over charts and graphs, which, with their captions, are self-contained items. A three-column treatment is shown, although other sizes are used as well.

The Times Roman running text is set 8/10 ragged right. Text this small really requires the narrow 9-pica column measure. Tables, captions, and headlines are set in a sans serif face for contrast.

Repeating headlines are inset between gray rules, with shorter rules on each end providing a spot of red that livens up the mostly text pages. The second color is repeated in charts and rules under initial caps.

Display type at the top of News Briefs pages, like the one shown below right, are tickertape-style previews of the stories on that page.

Design: Kimberly Mancebo, Robert Bryant Associates (Campbell, CA)

Pages from TeleVisual Market Strategies, *published ten times per year by Telecommunications Productivity Center. Trim size: 8-1/2 by 11*

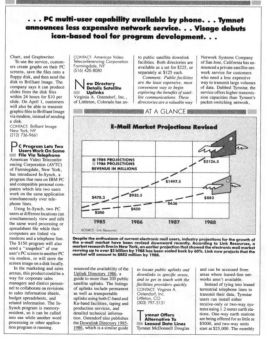

and newsletters. They are also well-suited to reference material, directories, price sheets, and other documents that require collecting many small items on a page.

But four-column grids are also more demanding to work with and require more decisions throughout the design and production process. Inherent in their flexibility, also, is the need for balance, proportion, and a deft handling of detail.

Narrow columns also require special care with typography. The type size should be relatively small, to be in proportion to the column width, and so the face must be chosen for ease of readability. With relatively few words in a line, you need to watch for excessive hyphenation. Generally, you should avoid more than two hyphens in a row. Also, a narrow column accentuates the uneven spacing inherent in justified text, so choose that style with caution.

The ease of combining running text set to a two- and a four-column measure is a definite advantage of the four-column grid. As in the previous sample, serif and sans serif faces are used for contrast.

The bold 2-point rules and unusual folio and publication identification in the upper right corner add to the distinctive and contemporary look of the page.

The graphic combines bit-mapped, graduated-tone, and geometric art.

Design: John Odam (San Diego, CA)

Page from Verbum, *published quarterly.*

Trim size: 8-1/2 by 11

try, are losing a battle to stay alive against foreign clothing manufacturers. "Since 1980, 3,000 apparel/textile companies have closed their doors and 350,000 jobs have been lost. Of the $170 billion trade deficit, $20 billion is in the apparel industry.... In 1974, 80% of the shoes sold in this country were made in this country. Now more than 80% of the shoes are imports and footwear manufacturing in this country is practically dead." VanFossen was vice president of Corporate Information Services at Wolverine Worldwide, makers of Hush Puppies shoes, when he analyzed the company's declining competitiveness in marketplace would only be turned around with a fully automated factory. The design of the footwear in 3-D appeared to be the answer. "If I could design a shoe in 3-D, then I would have the data I needed to drive an automated factory," he concluded. "Everything you needed to know about price of material, what you had to do with it, how you had to stitch it together — I'd have all this information. That was what I was after."

In 1983 VanFossen started Computer Design Inc. in Grand Rapids, MI which was partially financed at that time by Wolverine. CDI installed their first system about five years ago at H.H. Cutler Co. of Grand Rapids, a childrens' wear company. Since then they have installed more than 50 systems in the U.S. and Europe. The CDI system is IBM PC-based, and the software starts at about $25,000. The designer can visualizes garment in 3-D on the screen and the program will automatically create 2-D flat pattern pieces. According to Jerry Johnson, vice president of Marketing at CDI, "On our CAD systems today designers can design fabrics, then wrap those fabrics onto a model to actually see how it would look. Change colors and try it again in minutes, not hours or days as it now takes to re-paint or recolor fabric designs. Change necklines, sleeves, add pockets, take pockets away...all of these functions can be performed on our computer. These functions can greatly reduce product development time."

INTUITION AND INFORMATION IN FASHION DESIGN

Jackie Shapiro became one of the first fashion designers in the United States to explore the application of the computer with fashion design when she picked up her first Macintosh in 1984. She first used the computer to help develop her own line called "GARB", or Global Apparel Resource Bank, and even then she claimed that the computer was a vital part of her design process. "GARB has taken available technology and applied it...for designing clothing. To experiment and explore an infinite number of design solutions. To visualize...garments before making them. To coordinate one silhouette with another. To create, store and retrieve frequently used images: bodies, basics, prints, parts, stuff (garment treatments). To scale for measurements for pattern specification detail. To design labels, logos, illustrate...and to write this."

But using a computer alone does not make one a great de-

13

VERBUM 2.2

CUSTOMERS LIKE TO DESIGN IT THEMSELVES

One Southern California store blends fashion design with a novel marketing approach. The store's name is Softwear Swimwear and they sell custom swimsuits "designed" on a computer.

Liz Norling and Gary Leeds opened a swimwear boutique which featured an unusual gimmick of allowing customers create their own sportswear. "Not necessarily a gimmick but a new twist." Liz corrected me. "In order to succeed in this day and age in retail, one needs a unique idea." The customer's image in a swimsuit would be scanned into a color computer program, and the customer could then select from 300 fabric patterns which can be projected on the scanned image of the sportswear on the computer monitor. That way the customer would know exactly what the swimsuit would look like before it's made.

Fashion trends change quickly, and this is one way for

the customer to keep up with the fashion...or start his or her own trend.

"There are problems created by using the computer," acknowledged Norling. "We are working on a solution to the two dimensional look of the person on the screen. There is also a problem of confusing the customer with so many possibilities of color and fabric that it's hard for them to make a decision on which suit they

want. We also tend to get into trouble by taking colors from the screen...and then finding out that we do not have the color in stock."

The customer can see three suits on the screen at one time to compare and evaluate which one looks best. The customer's image can also be saved in the computer and pulled up at a later time for design another suit. "This is a good feature" Norling says, "as the store's sales volume can be larger. If they like all three swimsuits they may buy all three! Overall, I think the addition of the computer system to our retail store is a great one as many customers are highly excited about designing their own clothing."

The flexible size of art in a four-column grid is used to good advantage in this signage manual, where similarities and contrasts in visual details are the heart of the message. In the pages shown, note the possibilities for grouping photos as well as the variety of sizes.

Strong perspective lines in many of the photos lead your eye back into the distance. This depth illusion separates the photographs from the surface of the page. The severity of the grid structure, with the bolder-than-usual column rules, in turn enhances the perception of depth in the photos.

The vertical rules also delineate sections, as seen in the top page.

The text is Times Roman throughout, with italic captions set on a narrower measure with open leading for contrast to the running text. The white space makes it possible to run headlines the same size as body text so that they do not compete with typographic elements in the art.

*Design:
Denise Saulnier,
Communication
Design Group
Limited
(Halifax, Nova
Scotia)*

Pages from A Guide to Better Signs *published by the City of Halifax.
Size: 8-1/2 by 11*

Neon Signs

Fabrics

A fluorescent powder added to the glass tubing will produce yellow, green, rose and gold light. Very deep rich colours are produced by using coloured glass tubing to add to the colour of the gas.

When neon is used as a window sign, the glass tubing is attached to a sheet of clear acrylic which is suspended from the top of the window and is connected to the transformer by thin wires. Some sign makers prefer to enclose the entire neon sign in a clear acrylic box.

Certain gases (neon, argon, krypton, helium and xenon) contained in a glass vacuum tube will produce a coloured glow when an electrical current is passed through them. In the fabrication process, the glass tubing is heated and can be bent to virtually any shape. The air is removed from the tube and the gas inserted. A transformer is attached, which controls the transmission of electric current to the tube. Paint is used to cover areas of glass tubing which need to remain dark. Various gases produce different colours: neon is red-orange; argon is violet; argon and mercury together are blue; helium is gold; xenon is pale blue; krypton and argon together are purple.

Painted/printed: Fabrics such as cotton canvas, flag nylon, acrylic fabric and vinyl-coated polyester in a variety of colours can have lettering painted or silkscreen printed on and can then be sewn into flags, banners and awnings. Awnings are stretched across frames made of construction steel fixed to the building wall. Awnings can be manufactured to fit the building on which they will be installed and can be made in a wide variety of shapes.

Illuminated awnings use translucent vinyl-coated polyester to transmit light from shielded fluorescent or incandescent lights installed inside the awning. New finishes, materials and technologies have made this one of the most versatile

39

Chapter 6
Lighting techniques

Planning for the illumination of signs is an integral part of the sign design process. Signs, when well lit, can add liveliness to our streets. They create a mood of festivity, drama, excitement and warmth while contributing to the profile of our commercial districts at night.

The row of frosted glass globes lining the front of this restaurant provides general lighting for customers and passers-by, while lighting the building's signs at the same time.

One technique of sign illumination is to light the entire building front on which the sign is installed. In some cases there will be enough ambient light spilled on the building from adjacent light sources to allow the sign to be read. (Street number signs can often be read because they are lit by street lights or lights over doorways.)

Decorative lamps can be installed on the exterior of buildings where they will create an atmosphere of warmth or excitement, highlight the architectural details of the building front, as well as lighting both the building's signs and the sidewalk area. Low wattage incandescent bulbs installed in rows or groups are another technique of providing general lighting for buildings and signs which were traditionally used on theatre marquees.

When lighting only the sign itself, spotlights are an efficient solution. Strong focus lights are used to illuminate the sign face from above, the sides or below. Care should be taken in placing spotlights in order to avoid reflection on the sign face. The spotlights should be shielded from the eyes of the viewers. Electrical cables attached to the spotlights should be hidden from sight, incorporated in the sign

support and fed into the building at a location as close to the sign as possible. Advance planning can usually ensure that there won't be any unsightly electrical cables draping from the sign to the building or running along the building front.

Interior lit signs with opaque backgrounds and illuminated letters are a refined alternative to the typical electric back lit sign.

Metal faced channel letters with built in light sources mounted away from the walls, create a rather soft halo of light with the letters in silhouette.

Exposed neon lights can be formed to virtually any shape, and require very little maintenance.

Above: Shielded spots light the fascia sign but protect the viewer from any glare.

Right: A projecting sign and a fascia sign are lit by a set of four spots. The electrical cable is fed along the sign support and then directly into the wall.

Above: Channel letters containing neon tubing make an effective sign for both day and night.

The need to accommodate different kinds of editorial material often suggests the use of a four-column grid. The pages shown demonstrate the ease of combining two- and four-column settings.

The contents pages use the narrow measure for the short program descriptions on the left-hand page, and the wider measure for a tidy listing of the publication contents on the right. Contrasting column widths provide an immediate visual clue to the reader that these are different kinds of material. Art is sized to both column widths for variety and visual contrast, and the silhouetted dancing figures break the grid and float above it.

Note the implied horizon line that runs across all four pages, 11 picas from the top trim.

The short listings in the Program Highlights work especially well in narrow columns. The boldface dates are Helvetica Black, the listings are Garamond with boldface heads. Garamond is used for the contents page and running text in feature stories as well.

The music headline is Futura Condensed Extra Bold; the Program headline on the facing page is Futura Bold. Display typefaces with a variety of styles enable you to create subtle contrasts within the same type family.

Optical character recognition software (OCR) is a key component in the production cycle. The designer uses a DEST scanner to capture text from typewritten copy that is provided by the client. They

experience only about a 3 percent error, which the designer attributes to their using clean, double-spaced copy typed in a big, round face (they use Pica) and output on an impact printer. (With smaller faces and dot matrix output, the counters of letters tend to fill in, resulting in error rates as high as 20 percent.) The text is checked for spelling and typesetting conventions (single space after periods, and so on) in Microsoft Word before it is inserted onto the magazine layout.

Design: Tom Suzuki (Falls Church, VA)

Pages from Worldnet *magazine, published bimonthly by the United States Information Agency.*
Trim size: 8-1/4 by 10-3/4

PROGRAM HIGHLIGHTS

Monday, August 1

CinemAttractions
Hosts Steve March and Pat Kelley preview the hottest scenes from American theaters

Tuesday, August 9

National Gallery of Art
David Smith, one of the most prolific American sculptors of this century, was a pioneer of free-standing, open metal forms. His life is explored

ed the massive, movable forms he called "mobiles," created his last great sculpture for the East Building of the National Gallery. The program traces the evolution of this signature work.   11.30 GMT

Wednesday, August 17

Jazz at the Smithsonian

Thursday, August 25

Wild America
Every summer when Pacific salmon make their massive spawning run, up to a hundred brown bears—the largest carnivores in North America—line up along the McNeil River in Alaska to feast on the fish.   11.00 GMT

MUSIC MUSIC MUSIC

The Forum Presents Fridays, Hour

Sing along with Coolidge, Judy Collins Flack and more. Forum Presents and exciting show top entertainment ing the old favor new hits sung by the stars who the music fame Filmed in p each Forum f one entertain an interrupt of song: sw such as "Kill and "Send it gospel hymn "Amazing G in the Servic and sagas City of Ne "American Each brings ba all from t house—

WORLDNET

VOLUME II, ISSUE 5   AUGUST/SEPTEMBER 1988

CONGRESS: WE, THE PEOPLE
Meet the men and women, senators and congressional representatives elected by their fellow citizens to serve in Congress, the legislative branch of the United States government.

ADAM SMITH'S MONEY WORLD
Adam Smith, that is to say, George J. W. Goodman, knows his business—which is wisely and wittily explaining the ins and outs of high finance. Goodman's credo is: "Economics is boring; money is fascinating."

JAZZ AT THE SMITHSONIAN
The golden age of jazz, the improvisational music rooted in blues, band music and ragtime, is recreated in special concerts by talented performers such as Art Farmer, Red Norvo, Mel Lewis and Alberta Hunter.

GEORGE MICHAEL'S SPORTS MACHINE
George goes out to the ball games—the opening of the 1988 football season and baseball's championship World Series. George also gets the inside scoop on every fall sport.

Alexander Calder's "Mobile" (detail on front cover) is the focal point of The National Gallery of Art East's atrium.

CONTENTS

The cover and an inside flap show the contrasting but unified look in a folder that uses the four-column grid to combine two- and four-column settings.

The GTE logo on the cover is aligned left with the type. The underlying grid will almost always suggest an appropriate placement for loose items on the page.

The large, Palatino italic type on the cover shows off the calligraphic nature of this typeface.

The text in the narrow columns hugs the column rules, creating a very crisp left edge that emphasizes the verticality of the page. The loose ragged right margin makes the left edge seem stronger still in comparison.

The horizontal lines running through the map contrast with the strong verticality of the text above. Note the implied vertical edge of the map, aligned left with the second column of text. The map and rules print gray on the inside flap, with different colored dots denoting the locations listed. The cover map, surrounded by graduated tones of color that suggest the dimensionality of the earth, prints as green lines against white, with the background rules in gray.

Design: Weisz Yang Dunkelberger Inc. (Westport, CT)

Pages from The World of GTE, Year-End Highlights.
Trim size: 11 by 33-3/4, double gatefold

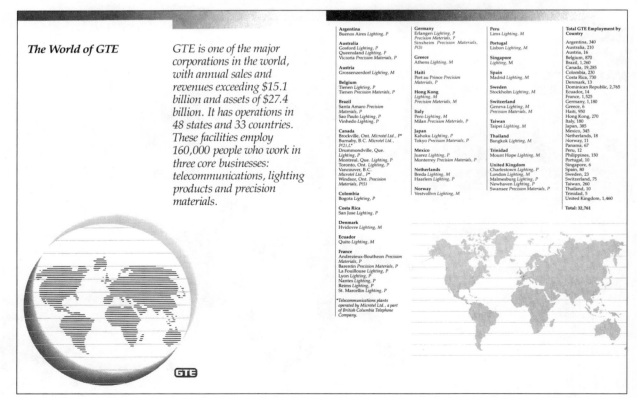

The World of GTE

GTE is one of the major corporations in the world, with annual sales and revenues exceeding $15.1 billion and assets of $27.4 billion. It has operations in 48 states and 33 countries. These facilities employ 160,000 people who work in three core businesses: telecommunications, lighting products and precision materials.

Argentina
Buenos Aires *Lighting*, P
Precision Materials, P

Australia
Gosford *Lighting*, P
Queensland *Lighting*, P
Victoria *Precision Materials*, P

Austria
Grossenzerdorf *Lighting*, M

Belgium
Tienen *Lighting*, P
Tienen *Precision Materials*, P

Brazil
Santa Amaro *Precision Materials*, P
Sao Paulo *Lighting*, P
Vinhedo *Lighting*, P

Canada
Brockville, Ont. *Microtel Ltd.*, P*
Burnaby, B.C. *Microtel Ltd.*, P(2),L*
Drummondville, Que.
Lighting, P
Montreal, Que. *Lighting*, P
Toronto, Ont. *Lighting*, P
Vancouver, B.C.
Microtel Ltd., P*
Windsor, Ont. *Precision Materials*, P(5)

Colombia
Bogota *Lighting*, P

Costa Rica
San Jose *Lighting*, P

Denmark
Hvidovre *Lighting*, M

Ecuador
Quito *Lighting*, M

France
Andrezieux-Boutheon *Precision Materials*, P
Barentin *Precision Materials*, P
La Fouillouse *Lighting*, P
Lyon *Lighting*, P
Nantes *Lighting*, P
Reims *Lighting*, P
St. Marcellin *Lighting*, P

Telecommunications plants operated by Microtel Ltd., a part of British Columbia Telephone Company.

Germany
Erlangen *Lighting*, P
Sinsheim *Precision Materials*, P(3)

Greece
Athens *Lighting*, M

Haiti
Port au Prince *Precision Materials*, P

Hong Kong
Lighting, M
Precision Materials, M

Italy
Pero *Lighting*, M
Milan *Precision Materials*, P

Japan
Kahoku *Lighting*, M
Tokyo *Precision Materials*, P

Mexico
Juarez *Lighting*, P
Monterrey *Precision Materials*, P

Netherlands
Breda *Lighting*, M
Haarlem *Lighting*, P

Norway
Vestvollvn *Lighting*, M

Peru
Lima *Lighting*, M

Portugal
Lisbon *Lighting*, M

Singapore
Lighting, M

Spain
Madrid *Lighting*, M

Sweden
Stockholm *Lighting*, M

Switzerland
Geneva *Lighting*, M
Precision Materials, M

Taiwan
Taipei *Lighting*, M

Thailand
Bangkok *Lighting*, M

Trinidad
Mount Hope *Lighting*, M

United Kingdom
Charlestown *Lighting*, P
London *Lighting*, M
Malmesburg *Lighting*, P
Newhaven *Lighting*, P
Swansee *Precision Materials*, P

Total GTE Employment by Country

Argentina, 340
Australia, 210
Austria, 16
Belgium, 870
Brazil, 1,260
Canada, 19,285
Colombia, 230
Costa Rica, 730
Denmark, 13
Dominican Republic, 2,765
Ecuador, 14
France, 1,525
Germany, 1,180
Greece, 6
Haiti, 950
Hong Kong, 270
Italy, 180
Japan, 385
Mexico, 345
Netherlands, 18
Norway, 11
Panama, 67
Peru, 12
Philippines, 150
Portugal, 10
Singapore, 6
Spain, 80
Sweden, 23
Switzerland, 75
Taiwan, 260
Thailand, 10
Trinidad, 5
United Kingdom, 1,460

Total: 32,761

One narrow + three wide columns for oversize pages

In a tabloid publication, the four-column grid provides a relatively wide measure for reading text, especially when one column is narrow as in the page shown here.

The body text is 10/13 New Baskerville, a graceful face with a light weight. It makes this oversize, mostly text page inviting and easy to read. The generous use of boldface in the running text emphasizes the "people" focus of the publication and facilitates scanning.

The display type is Helvetica Condensed Black.

The rules for the page frame and columns are a little bolder than is usually found, and the inside rules for the narrow columns run all the way to the page frame. The rigidity of that structure is balanced by white space and appropriately sized type. Note also how the initial caps interrupt the column rule.

The distinctive large folio reverses out of a box, which prints in a second color used also for the page frames, the initial caps in the headlines, and the ballot boxes signalling the end of each piece.

The bold, silhouette-style illustration, used throughout the publication, helps small images hold up on the oversize pages.

Design: Kate Dore, Dore Davis Design (Sacramento, CA)

Page from Communique, *published by Sacramento Association of Business Communicators.*
Trim size: 11 by 17

2

IABC Board

President
Robert L. Deen
Deen & Black
444-8014

First Vice President
Tracy Thompson
Carlson Associates
973-0600

Vice President/Programs
Tamra Weber
Deen & Black
444-8014

Vice President/ Professional Development
Mary Closson
The Packard Group
484-8709

Vice President/ Membership
Terri Lowe
Crocker Art Museum
449-8709

Vice President/ Communications
Pat Macht
AmeriGas/Cal Gas
686-3553

Vice President/ Academic Affairs
Jeff Aran
Sacramento Board of Realtors
922-7711

Treasurer
Diana Russell
Pacific Legal Foundation
444-0154

SYNERGY Chair
Della Gilleran
Della Gilleran Design
446-4616

Past President
Betsy Stone
Sutter Health
927-5211

Staff Secretary
Barbara Davis
Creative Consulting
424-8400

Delegates At Large:
Cindy Simonsen
Hanson Simonsen
451-2270

Rick Cabral
Connolly Development, Inc.
454-1416

Colleen Sotomura
The Sierra Foundation
635-4755

Newsletter Editors
Marisa Alcalay
Mercy San Juan Hospital
537-5245
Mary C. Towne
California Veterinary Medical Association
344-4985

Newsletter Design & Layout
Kate Dore
Dore Davis Design
920-3448

IABC *Communiqué*
January/February 1988

About Sacramento Communicators

Jolaine Collins, past president of the IABC Denver chapter and a recent addition to IABC Sacramento, will represent District 6 on the IABC Professionalism Committee. **Jan Emerson** has moved from Foundation Health Plan to a new position with the publications department at Sutter Health. **Dan Brown,** Group Director of Public Affairs for Aerojet General, will be the 1988 President of the new Sacramento chapter of the Public Relations Society of America.

IABC 1988 president **Robert Deen** and **Christi Black** have formed the partnership of Deen & Black, Communications and Public Affairs. Christi is the former executive director of the American River Parkway Foundation. They will be joined by IABC member **Tamra Weber,** former Communications Director for United Way, who will be an associate, and **Colleen Jang,** a recent CSU Chico communication graduate and member of the student IABC chapter. The new firm is located in an office building at 2212 K Street recently pur-

chased by fellow IABC member **Della Gilleran** (who will chair SYNERGY in 1988).

Terri Lowe of the Crocker Art Museum is interested in volunteers to assist with Crocker's 1988 Bike-a-Thon fundraiser, scheduled for June. **Robert Deen** will chair the overall event, with IABC'ers **Jolaine Collins** and **Janice White.** Terri's number is 449-8709.

Stacey Eachus, former IABC Sacramento member who went to San Diego in June for a position with the National Cash Register Company, has returned to Sacramento in a public relations position with the California Association of Health Facilities.

The **CSU Chico student chapter** has expressed an interest in repeating the successful exchange program in which students were matched for a day with IABC Sacramento members

to observe a typical work day.

The Sacramento Communications Council has been restructured as a quarterly meeting of the presidents of the dozen professional communications organizations involved, and will be chaired by the IABC president.

The **IABC's annual international conference** will finally be closer to home in 1988 — Anaheim. It should be an interesting one as the proposed IABC/PRSA merger comes to a head.

Mark your calendars now for upcoming **IABC Sacramento luncheons,** held the first Thursday of each month: Feb. 4, March 3, April 7, and May 5. ■

(Have something to contribute? Send information to Communicator Column, c/o editor, IABC Sacramento, P.O. Box 160481, Sacramento, Ca. 95816.)

Chapter Business

Meet the 1988 IABC Board of Directors

The IABC Sacramento Board of Directors serves on a calendar year basis. Being involved is an important part of the IABC experience, and members are encouraged to contact board members to find out more about the areas of activity outlined below.

Immediate Past President Betsy C. Stone will represent IABC Sacramento at the District level, and as circumstances dictate will speak for the chapter on the proposed IABC/PRSA merger. She is also responsible for organizing the District 6 conference for 1990 which Sacramento will host. **Robert L. Deen, the chapter president** is responsible for group's overall direction and functioning.

1st Vice President Tracy Thompson oversees administrative matters and special projects at the president's direction.

Treasurer Diana Russell is responsible for the chapter's finances, including coordinating with the SYNERGY management team.

Vice President, Communications, Pat Macht is responsible for the chapter newsletter, all media relations (meeting notices, awards, etc.), and for any and all activities which relate to the chapter's image and visibility.

Vice President, Membership, Terri Lowe, directs membership recruiting

efforts, including correspondence, planning, renewal program, roster, and special efforts as required.

Vice President, Programs, Tamra Weber, surveys the membership for their interests and selects luncheon speakers accordingly, coordinates arrangements, and ensures that monthly meeting notices go out in a timely manner.

Vice President, Academic Affairs, Jeff Aran serves as a liaison to local universities and coordinates with the IABC student chapter at CSU Chico.

Vice President, Professional Development, Mary Closson, develops seminars and programs to enhance members' professional skills and abilities, and conducts the annual membership survey.

Della Gilleran, 1988 SYNERGY Chair, is responsible for the overall direction and management of SYNERGY, Sacramento's coalition-based special event for the communications profession.

Delegates at Large: Rick Cabral, Cindy Simonsen, and Colleen Sotomura serve as at-large members of the board and take responsibility for special assignments as needed.

The board is responsible for the functioning and direction of the Chapter. Members are encouraged to discuss concerns or make suggestions to any board member at any time. ■

Plan On Being Active in 1988

The best way to meet new people, learn new skills and become a part of new groups is through active volunteerism.

Working together on projects gives you a chance to get to know people and for them to get to know you and your skills, capabilities and interests.

IABC/Sacramento encourages members to be involved in both IABC activities and general community activities. Consider your options:

The IABC chapter conducts ongoing efforts such as the scholarship and communications (including the newsletter). The board members responsible for these areas are listed in each issue of the newsletter, with their phone number, and all are interested in hearing from those who want to help.

Community involvement — IABC/Sacramento encourages members to accept leadership positions in community organizations such as United Way, KVIE, March of Dimes, etc. These members deserve and need the support of fellow chapter communicators and the chapter is often approached directly by organizations in need of volunteers.

To help you get involved, the chapter needs to know about your interest. Contact the appropriate board member directly, or let Chapter President Robert Deen know.

Make being an active volunteer part of your plan for self improvement in 1988! ■

Using the center columns

In this four-column grid, photos are enlarged to a two-column measure. The text in the narrow outer columns frames the pictures, and the generous white space provides an opportunity to dramatize the shape of the photos against the structure of the page.

The digitized photos, which are reproduced from a laser printout, need a layout in which the overall composition has more impact than the individual parts. Sizes and placements were chosen for dramatic contrast, with a passive close-up against an active middle shot on the cover and a dancing full-figure long shot against a close-up on the inside page.

The logotype gives the name FLASH a strong identity and emphasizes the action and boldness implied by in the name. The typeface, Bodoni Poster, doesn't come with a true italic, so FLASH was typed in Adobe Illustrator and shifted on a horizontal axis with the shear tool to create an oblique. The word was given a white fill with no stroke and placed over the black panel to create the reverse type. Note that the serifs of the F and the H bleed off the left and right edges of the banner, which themselves have been stretched beyond the text margins.

Futura, used in the story headline and names of the models, is forever stylish. It has graced the cover of virtually every fashion magazine at one time or another. Placing the type on a 15-degree angle creates an additional dimension, a layer that seems to float above the rectilinear grid of the logo, text columns, rules, and photos. Keeping all the names and the headline on the same angle creates organized spontaneity rather than random movement.

MAY/JUNE 1988

MANNER continued from page 1

we can send them right away to clients here that are willing to use brand new people. That starts the ball rolling, and if things start to click right away, they stay in New York. If things don't happen immediately, we ask them to go to Europe and develop a strong book, learn how to really model, and then come back to New York. We deal with several agencies in Milan, Paris and Germany and we try to send models to the appropriate agency. Each individual model is different of course, and how much time each one would stay in Europe varies. It can take a couple of months or even a couple of years to get started. The truth of the matter is, if you are a real good model, you don't need a strong book, you need to have a look that works in New York. If you are a brand new model, and you have that look, you can start to work immediately. We are very lucky to have models like that.

If any men are interested in being with our agency

BILLY HAIRE

FLASH

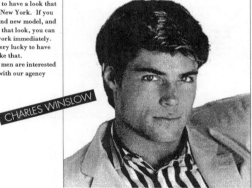

CHARLES WINSLOW

they should send a couple a pictures in the mail. Don't spend alot of money on pictures - snapshots will do - put your stats on the back, and send them in. You'll get an answer quickly, usually within a week after we receive them. We answer all mail that we get, but a warning, more than 99% of the people who send in pictures receive a "no."

If you are interested in modeling in New York, you should just take a deep breath, swallow, and come. You can go on and on wonder and worry, but if you want to model you should come here and see everybody and find out what your chances are. But don't kid yourself. If the answer is "no" the answer is "no". Don't get the attitude of "Well, I'll show them!" The business is much too rough for that kind of attitude. Chances are you won't show them, they'll show you.

MANNER is located at
874 Broadway
New York, NY 10003
(212) 475-5001

9

Bodoni, used for the running text, is hard to beat for typographic elegance. Its alternating thicks and thins give this newsletter a distinctive look—fashionable but not trendy. The type just feels like Fred Astaire dancing. Bodoni needs open leading (10/13 was used) to take advantage of its tall ascenders and descenders without sacrificing legibility.

The logo treatment is adapted as a visual "prop" throughout the publication. On the page above, for example, it becomes a stage on which one of the models dances. The stylized lightening bolt from the logo provides an additional motif that can be used decoratively.

The photographs were scanned and then retouched in a photo-retouching program. In the Charles Winslow photo, for example, the background was removed to create a silhouette, and the neck area was lightened. Billy Haire's feet were given some tone (they were white in the original).

The blueprint on the next page provides the basic grid structure for this and the following design, which conveys a very different image than the one shown here. For type specs for this design, refer to the commentary on these two pages, rather than the ones in the blueprint. Note also that the cover banner here has been stretched 2 picas beyond the side margins defined in the blueprint.

Design: Don Wright (Woodstock, NY)

Pages from Flash, *a bimonthly newsletter for models published by Nautilus Books, designed as a "Page Makeover" for* Publish! *magazine.*
Trim size: 8-1/2 by 11

The business report at right and on the facing page uses the same four-column grid as the fashion newsletter on the previous spread but to very different effect.

The report title in the nameplate is spaced to fill the banner. In Ventura, you can insert a thin space (which varies from one font to another) by pressing Ctrl-Shift-T. In the sample, we inserted five spaces.

On page 2, the banner is 2,06 deep, with the same fonts and letterspacing as the nameplate type but dropped down to 14 point. The top of the text block is 5 picas from the top of the banner.

The charts and graphs were created with 10-point Futura Light type.

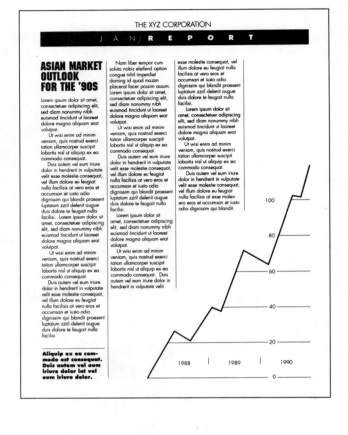

The blueprint shows the details for the sample on the facing page. The same column structure is used for the newsletter on the preceding page.

The basic column width is 10,03. In addition to combining the center columns for art as shown on these samples, you could combine any two or three columns for variable art sizes and self-contained sidebar material.

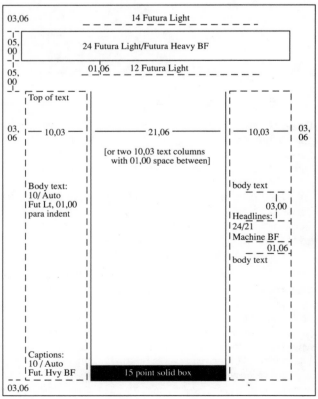

PRODUCTION LANDMARK FOR THE XYZ MACHINE: 100,000 UNITS

Lorem ipsum dolor sit amet, consectetuer adipiscing elit, sed diam nonummy nibh euismod tincidunt ut laoreet dolore magna aliquam erat volutpat. Ut wisi enim ad minim veniam, quis nostrud exerci tation ullamcorper suscipit lobortis nisl ut aliquip ex ea commodo consequat.

Duis autem vel eum iriure dolor in hendrerit in vulputate velit esse molestie consequat, vel illum dolore eu feugiat nulla facilisis at vero eros et accumsan et iusto odio dignissim qui blandit praesent luptatum zzril delenit augue duis dolore te feugait nulla facilisi.

Lorem ipsum dolor sit amet, consectetuer adipiscing elit, sed diam nonummy nibh euismod tincidunt ut laoreet dolore magna aliquam erat volutpat. Ut wisi enim ad minim veniam, quis nostrud exerci tation ullamcorper suscipit lobortis nisl ut aliquip ex ea commodo consequat. Duis autem vel eum iriure dolor in hendrerit in vulputate velit esse molestie consequat, vel illum dolore eu feugiat

Aliquip ex ea comi-modo es consequat. Duis vel ex eat com modovel eumet.

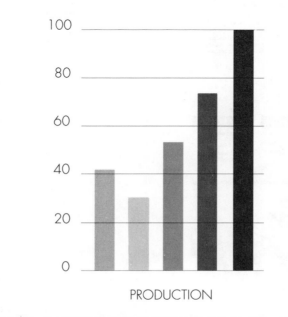

PRODUCTION

Aliquip ex ea commodo est consequat. Duis autem vel eum iriure dolor int vel eum iriure dolor.

nulla facilisis at vero eros et accumsan et iusto odio dignissim qui blandit praesent luptatum zzril delenit augue duis dolore te feugait nulla facilisi. Nam liber tempor cum soluta nobis eleifend option congue nihil imperdiet doming id quod mazim placerat facer possim assum.

DO YOU KNOW YOUR CUSTOMER?

Lorem ipsum dolor sit amet. Consectetuer adipiscing elitt. Sed diam nonummy nibh euismod tincidunt ut laoreet dolore magna aliquam erat volutpat. Ut wisi enim ad minim veniam, quis nostrud exerci tation ullamcorper suscipit lobortis nisl ut aliquip ex ea commodo consequat. Duis autem vel eum iriure dolor in hendrerit in

Vulputate velit esse molestie consequat, vel illum dolore eu feugiat nulla facilisis at vero eros et accumsan et iusto odio dignissim qui blandit praesent luptatum zzril delenit augue duis dolore te feugait nulla facilisi. Lorem ipsum dolor sit amet, consectetuer adipiscing elit, sed diam nonummy nibh euismod suscipit lobortis nisltincidunt ut laoreet dolore magna aliquam erat volutpat.

Within the four-column format you can balance strong vertical and horizontal material, as in the sample on the facing page. The image area for visuals in the first three horizontal units is almost square (9 by 9,03), a nice proportion in this grid, although other sizes are possible.

The layout in the Safety Tips page could be used as an expanded contents page, with the cover story in the text column and four different stories, briefly described with art from each, in the outer two columns. When using this technique, which is very effective, the cover art can be repeated inside or can be a detail from a piece of art that runs with the story.

The word "Safety" is 18-point Bookman Italic. In order to inset it in the T of "Tips," we created a T with an elongated bar across the top by drawing a black box over the top of an I. In doing this, we encountered WYSIWYG problems: the manually created T aligned with the I on-screen but not in the printed page. We went through several trial-and-error adjustments before an incorrect on-screen image produced a correct printed page.

Events listings are well suited to the narrow measure, as shown in the sample flyer below left. And short introductory copy is still quite readable in one wide column.

The clip art was altered to allow for text in the upper right corner of the image area by our merely erasing that part of the image.

The column specifications for the listings use the same measurements as the four-column format in the blueprint. The headline and listing specifications are shown in the details below.

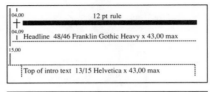

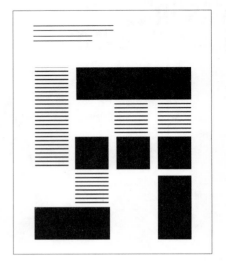

The blueprint specifications are for the Safety Tips sample. You can divide the space in other ways to balance the vertical and horizontal divisions; the schematic below shows another possible arrangement. Don't forget white space as an element in the grid.

Public Hearings on Zoning and Land Use

The Green County Planning Commission will hold a series of public hearings on coordinating zoning ordinances and land use throughout the county. Green County is the first in New England to address these issues from a county-wide perspective and with a view toward the needs and future of the entire region. The public is encouraged to attend and to comment at the hearings. Written testimony can be brought to the hearings or sent to the commission's offices at the address listed below. The agenda will include:

- Natural resources in an age of changing supply and demand.
- The requirements of site review in the 1990's and beyond.
- Parks, recreation, and wilderness areas: new definitions for the future.
- Incentives for low-income housing.

Monday	Tuesday	Wednesday	Thursday
June 13	**June 14**	**June 15**	**June 16**
Madison	**Cooperstown**	**North River**	**Winchester**
7:00 - 9:00 PM	6:30 - 8:30 PM	7:00 - 9:00 PM	7:00 - 9:00 PM
Town Hall	Community Center	George Washington	Town Hall
245 Main Street	186 River Road	High Auditorium	45 Church Street
		Broadview and Elm	

GREEN COUNTY PLANNING BOARD
23 Center Street
Madison, New Hampshire
25876
307/466-8798

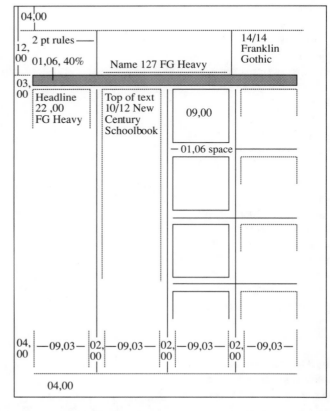

Summer 1989

Safety **TIPS**

from
Timberline
Power & Light
Co.

Tools and Hazards of the Trade

Lsectetuer sed adipiscing elite in sed utm diam nonummy nibh euismod tincidunt ut laoreet dolore magna aliquam erat volutpat. Ut wisi enim ad minim veniam, quis nostrud exerci tation dolor in ullamcorper suscipit lobortis nisl ut aliquip ex ea commodo feugiat consequat. Duis autem vel eum iriure dolor in hendrerit in vulputate velit esse molestie vero consequat, vel illum dolore eu feugiat nulla facilisis at vero eros et accumsan et iusto odio dignissim qui blandit.

Praesent luptatum zzril delenit augue duis dolore te feugait nulla facilisi. Lorem ipsum dolor sit amet,et zzril delenit consectetuer adipiscing elit, urt sed diam nonummy nibh euismod tincidunt ut laoreet dolore magna aliquam erat volutpat.

Ut wisi enim ad minim veniam, quis nostrud exerci tation ad minim ullamcorper suscipit lobortis nisl ut aliquip ex ea facilisi. Lorem ipsum commodo Duis autem vel eum iriure dolor iscingin hendrerit in vulputate velit esse molestie consequat, vel illum dolore eu feugiat nulla facilisis at vero eros et

Consequat duis aute vel eum iriure dolor in hendrerit in vulputate velit esse

Molestie consequal illum dolore eu feugiat nulla facilisis at vero eros et accumsan et iusto odio dignissim qui blandit praesent

Tatum zzril delenit augue duis dolore te feugait nulla facilisi. Nam liber tempor cum

Lorem ipsum dolor sit amet, consectetuer adipiscing elit, sed diam nonummy nibh euismod tincidunt ut laoreet dolore magna aliquam erat volutpat.

Ut wisi enim ad minim veniam, quis nostrud exerci tation ullamcorper suscipit

MIXED GRIDS

Grids with multiple and variable column widths can handle the widest range of elements, partly because the columns combine to produce so many different page arrangements. These grids allow for several different widths of text, which in turn allow for more contrast in type sizes and faces to distinguish components from one another. And of course the possibilities for picture placement are even more varied in size and scale than those of the text.

This type of grid is particularly useful in publications such as catalogs, which have many different kinds of elements that need to be distinguished from one another. The format also encourages browsing, with numerous headlines and art providing multiple entry points for busy readers.

Constructing this sort of grid requries a careful analysis of the material to determine the format. And executing the design requires a good eye for balance. This is "breaking the rules" territory and can backfire if you don't know what you're doing.

This five-column grid accommodates newsletter-style essays alongside catalog listings, with short quotes and 19th-century engravings adding verbal and visual personality to the pages. The result is lively, inviting, and well-organized.

The variable column width is the key to the diverse page composition. From rule to rule, the narrow outer columns are 7 picas, the wider inner columns are 10,06. With 6-point margins between the text and rules, this creates four different measures for use in this publication:

- 6,00 (a single narrow column used for quotes)
- 9,06 (a single wider column used for product listings and for the continuation of essays from a previous page)
- 20,00 (two wide columns used for essays and product listings)
- 16,06 (one narrow and one wide column, used for listings).

In fact, additional combinations are available by combining three wide columns, one narrow and three wide, and, of course, all five columns.

Note the contrast in typeface among the different kinds of text. The essays are Palatino for both body text and headlines (which print blue), with Bodoni initial caps (also blue). The product listings are various weights of Futura.

The engravings are traditional clip art, photostatted and pasted onto camera-ready pages. Matching 19-century thematic art with contemporary subject matter provides a subtle visual humor, reinforced by placement which invariably breaks the grid.

The short quotes in the narrow columns include humor, anonymous aphorisms, and testimonials from satisfied customers.

Design: Barbara Lee,
Folio Consulting (Englewood, NJ)
Pages from the SuperLearning Newsletter/Catalog.
Trim size: 8-1/2 by 11

Self-Hypnosis

Self-hypnosis can be the royal road to self-mastery. A good man to learn with is Lee Pulos, Ph.D., professor, psychologist, past president of the Canadian Society of Clinical Hypnosis.

Learn the classical approach on Side A. Then on Side B, experience Pulos' original double induction – two voices weaving in and out, in counterpoint, to help you understand the power of indirect suggestion.

Creative Thinking & Problem Solving
Get your creative juices flowing with hypnotic imagery, suggestion, dream programming. Create solutions instead of problems.
TAPE 401 $12.95

☛ Sports Excellence
Weekend sport or competitive athlete – you can sharpen performance with the same training Pulos used to coach Team Canada.
TAPE 403 $12.95

Recover Quickly and Stay Well
Accelerate your body's natural healing processes. How to team up with your subconscious to maintain and improve all-round health.
TAPE 404 $12.95

Sleep & Dream Enhancement
Insomnia? Sink into a whole new level of deep, comfortable sleep. Enjoy more pleasant, positive dreams. You owe it to yourself to try this drugless way to good quality sleep.
TAPE 405 $12.95

Subtle Seducer, Procrastination
Banish the wiles of procrastination. Instead of kicking yourself, get a kick out of accomplishment. Don't procrastinate! Order this one today!
TAPE 406 $12.95

Self-Talk

Positive self-talk is a secret that life's winners have always known.
What you say to yourself and what you believe is what you achieve.

Let Dr. Pulos turn your self talk into a powerful, positive route to achievement. Affirmations are in a 3D Holosonic surround of Superlearning-type music. SideA: guided relaxation with active participation. Side B: positive self-talk statements you can listen to anywhere.

☛ Improving Self-Esteem and Self-Image
Strengthen self-esteem, build a good self image to help you succeed in any endeavor and enjoy life to the fullest.
TAPE 413 $12.95

Successful Selling
Learn how to meet challenges head on with a positive attitude, prepare yourself fully for each situation and make it easy for people to say YES! The positive Self-Talk in this program is the secret shared by those at the top in sales.
TAPE 411 $12.95

Creative Thinking
Tap into the unused 90% of your creative brain power. Positive self-talk can open your mind to a wealth of new ideas.
TAPE 412 $12.95

"The Pulos system has been invaluable, to myself and to many of our key employees."
Peter H. Thomas, Chairman Century 21 Real Estate

Superlearning 450 7th Ave. New York, NY 10123 212 279-8450 9

The Book that Started It All!

Music & the Art of Learning
Dissolve learning blocks and relax into the optimal state for learning (side A).

The Famous Superlearning music – music to learn faster by – music to reduce stress – beautiful music performed by world class orchestras (side B).
TAPE 101 $13.95

The Beat of Memory
How to put any material you want to learn into the rhythmic Superlearning format. A short demo of Continental menu terms so you know exactly how a lesson should sound (side A). Better than a metronome, this timer tape with four second clicks helps you pace material correctly (side B).
TAPE 102 $13.95

Superlearning
A do-it-yourself book that reads like an adventure story. Reveals the secrets of fast, stress-free learning and ultra performance. More than 800,000 copies sold.

"Superlearning…Super reading" — Gannett

"Highly readable" — Psychology Today

Hardcover 100 $14.95

The All-Music Tape
Find out how good it feels to start tapping unused capabilities with Superlearning music. Heighten learning, relaxation, visualization. Get in an ideal state for mental training for sports and creative performance.
TAPE 103 $13.95

Very Special Limited Offer…
Help someone else get started!
Buy any two of the Basic Superlearning Tapes – 101, 102, 103 – and we'll send you the hardcover Superlearning Book free!
A $43.00 value for only $27.95

"Even if you're on the right track, you'll get run over if you just sit there."
Will Rogers

ORDER FORM

All NY state residents must pay sales tax

Shipping/ Handling:
First item: $2.00
$.75 per item thereafter
$10.00 maximum

Quantity	Item No.	Price	Total

Subtotal	
Discount (if applicable)	
NY Sales Tax	
Shipping/Handling	
Total	

Payment must be made in US Dollars (either U.S. money orders or checks in U.S. funds payable through a U.S. bank). Canadian money orders or checks accepted in equivalent U.S. funds. Sorry – no billing or COD.

Save! On orders of $50 or more, deduct 10%
On orders of $75 or more, deduct 15%
(not including shipping & handling)

Charge Orders – Call (212) 279-8450

Charge card: ____American Express ____Visa ____Mastercard

Valid from: ________ to ________

Signature: ____________________

Card Number: [ ][ ][ ][ ][ ][ ][ ][ ][ ][ ][ ][ ][ ][ ][ ]

Phone: ____________ Date: ____________

Name: ____________________

Address: ____________________
(please print)

City: ____________ State: ____________

Zip: ____________

Code — ABCDE

Superlearning 450 7th Ave. New York, NY 10123 212 279-8450 11

Magic (cont. from p. 2)

will and the imagination are in conflict, the imagination always wins. The task of the will, it seems, is to make a conscious decision. Then, the task of the imagination is to gather all one's forces, conscious and subconscious, physical, emotional, and mental, to bring that goal into reality.

Today, people are proving Coue's law for themselves. They are beginning to know that the pictures we hold inside ourselves, the scenarios we imagine, have a potent influence not just on the functioning of our minds and bodies, but also on the style and nature of our life experience. Imagination is funny, and we bet you'll hear much more about it in the coming decade. We've only begun to understand imagination. But it does appear that almost anyone can learn to use imagination and bring his life closer to the heart's desire. ✻

Super Relief the Natural Way

Head hurt? Let chiropractors Catherine Sweet and Lisa Pete help you keep a clear head. Find out what kind of headache you suffer from. Discover how various body systems are involved. Learn how you can help yourself with nutrition, herbs, reflex points, acupressure, and other easy-to-practice techniques. What to do when you feel pain coming on. How to ease a full blown headache. Best of all, how to prevent many headaches. Includes reflex point chart.
TAPE 740 $11.95

How to Sharpen Imaginary Senses

"Whatever you do, don't think about a pink elephant!"

Right away, many of us would have trouble keeping visions of pink pachyderms from prancing into mind. That's a reverse way to prove to people that they can visualize. Another, sometimes used by imagery expert Vera Fryling, M.D., is to exclaim, "Oh, someone just threw purple paint on your car!"

As more and more people use imagery rehearsal to improve performance in everything from learning and business to intimate relationships, some are feeling left out because they "can't visualize" or "can't hear a sound in my head." There are remedies.

To begin with, good imagery rehearsal involves all five senses. To improve your imaginative capacity, consider which is your dominant sense. Is your main connection to the world visual? Or audio? Or kinesthetic, through the sense of touch?

When conjuring imaginary experiences, rely first on your dominant sense, just as you do in the outside world. Then start to add the others. If you have difficulty bringing in a sense,try practicing it with the crossover method. If you're an audio type, imagine talking with someone close to you. Listen awhile, then without straining, try to let the image that goes with the voice rise in your mind. Or imagine hearing your special song. Then let the scene that made it special come to you.

If you're the kinesthetic type, imagine running your hands up and down the sides of an oak tree, feeling the rough bark. Then let the image grow between your hands. Or try it with a long, thin icicle sliding between your fingers. Or a heavy ball in one hand.

If you're a visual type, reverse the above exercises. Or conjure any of the myriad things in the world, then add sound, touch – and smell and taste too.

You do have movies in your mind, some experts assert, even if you don't think so. It's just that your images are so fleeting that you're not aware of them. "Such people are turning images into words," says imagery therapist Sally Edwards. The mind labels so quickly that the image goes unperceived. Edwards suggests taking a few minutes a day to practice turning off verbal noise. Just look around, don't name or label. Just see objects, lines, colors, movements.

Learning to sharpen all five of your senses will add power to your imaginary rehearsal. A little practice can also enrich your experience of the outside world. ✻

6 Superlearning 450 7th Ave. New York, NY 10123 212 279-8450

New Musical Memory Booster
(cont. from p. 4)

received books in French and is featured in such magazines as "Paris Match." He's travelled through Europe, South and North America and the East seeking out new ideas, new techniques. But he's best known for bringing Sophrology into sports, an area where success – or failure, is dramatic and very visible.

Years before mental training was fashionable, Abrezol started coaching tennis players and skiers with Sophrology. Word of some remarkable achievements got around the peaks and valleys of Abrezol's tight-knit land. He was asked to coach four members of the Swiss Olympic team, not a powerhouse at the time. At the 1968 Winter Olympics at Grenoble, three of the four won medals. The sensible Swiss stuck with Sophrology and in the 1972 Sapporo Olympics, three more medals were won.

Abrezol, a mountain climber and swimmer himself, went on from there, coaching professionals and amateurs of every stripe: golfers, skeet shooters, boxers, stunt fliers, canoeists, cyclists. As for the Olympics, by 1987, his trainees had garnered 114 medals.

Still active in mental coaching, still training other medical people, still fulfilling his role as a healer to his patients, Abrezol seems to be increasingly interested in seeking out ways to bring forth the "possible human" now, the human that could be, if we started using not the 90%, but – Abrezol insists – the 99% of our capacity that lies waiting within us.

For more data:

The International Sophrology Institute
381 Park Avenue South
New York, NY 10016
718-849-9335 ✻

Better Than Twenty Winks

What's better than twenty winks? A six-second way to relax called the Quieting Reflex (QR) by its creator, Dr. Charles Stroebel, a Connecticut psychiatrist. QR is simple, deceptively so, says Stroebel who maintains it can take six months' practice before you get it down perfectly and experience the full health benefits. The benefits seem more than worth the minimum effort. Reversing the body's stress reactions as you go through the day can alleviate or ward off many common complaints – hypertension, back trouble, ulcers, migraines and tension headaches. Stroebel himself devised QR almost as a last resort to conquer his excruciating chronic headaches. Stress, of course, is a factor in many, maybe most, physical problems. Beyond that, when you're not uptight, you can perform better during the day – and enjoy the evening. Thanks to QR, Stroebel says he's "involved in lots of things that normally would have pushed me to the exhaustion point."

The six steps of QR:

1. Become aware that you are tense.
2. Say to yourself, "Alert mind, calm body."
3. Sparkle and smile inwardly to relax your face.
4. Relax your jaws and inhale, imagining the air coming up through the soles of your feet, to the count of three.
5. Imagine the air coming up your legs into your belly and stomach.
6. Exhale, letting jaws, tongue, shoulders go limp, feeling heaviness leave the body.

For more information see:

QR: The Quieting Reflex — G.P. Putnam's Sons. ✻

Super Sports

Tennis Flow by Dyveke Spino
Increase enjoyment and performance with mental training. Play centered, stress-free tennis. Imagery rehearsal to enhance concentration and improve your stroke. Part of Spino's top-rated tennis course.
TAPE 321 $12.95

Creative Running by Dyveke Spino
Pointers for stress-free running. Exercises to increase energy and avoid injury. Visualization to attune yourself to motion. For all who like to move in the outdoors.
TAPE 322 $12.95

Creative Running II by Dyveke Spino
"If you're a jogger, you will love it. Imagery experiences for transcending pain and awakening the heroic. I listen at home and afterwards go out and run as smoothly as a deer for as long as I want."
– Gene Bruce. East/West Journal.
TAPE 323 $12.95

Superlearning 450 7th Ave. New York, NY 10123 212 279-8450 7

A collage-style approach

Within the basic three-column structure, this format allows the designer to nestle variable-width text blocks around art as needed. The large page size makes it possible to present several items on a single page, which reinforces the thematic organization of material and encourages browsing as well.

For this particular publication, the format solves the problem of placing a great many loose elements on the page—each of the items on the page shown includes the publishing information, the book cover, a brief one-paragraph review, text and art excerpted from the book being reviewed, and captions. The collage-style approach is a visual signature of the magazine from which this book spins off.

The underlying structure for this collage-style page is three 17-pica columns.

A pragmatic use of rules and boxes helps organize the disparate elements and separate one item from another. Boxes and silhouettes that overhang the rules create a dimensionality that lightens up the densely packed pages.

Design decisions are required for almost every text block in a grid used with this much flexibility. While most grids dictate the placement of elements on the page, this grid provides but a subtle understructure for the multitude of elements.

The type is from the Helvetica family, an ideal choice for its efficient word count and its legibility in small sizes as well as for the variety afforded within a single type family. The introduction of a second typeface to such a complex page could easily create chaos.

Design: Kathleen O'Neill

Pages from Signal, *a book created by Whole Earth Review.*
Trim size: 10-1/2 by 12-1/8

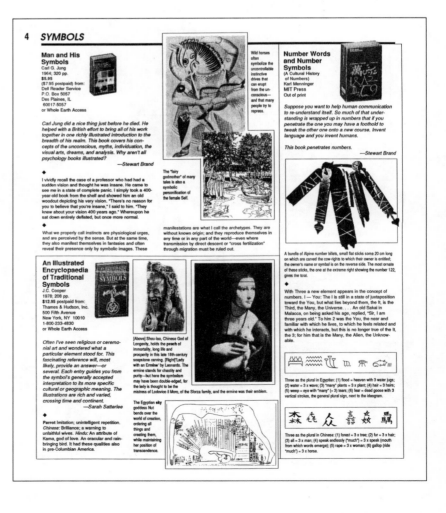

Playing with frames

This three + two-column format plays with rules to create frames within frames. The underlying grid is very symmetrical and modular, but the elements break through it and out of it in many different and sometimes subtly humorous ways. The resulting playfulness is especially useful in balancing the medical, scientific, and fundamentally difficult subject of aging.

Three 10-pica columns are used for the short items that make up this news section of a monthly magazine. Items whose headlines run across two or three columns take on more importance than those with single-column heads. The column width of the "featured" stories varies: two or three 10-pica columns, one 20-pica column, and two 14,06 columns are all used.

The narrow outer margins (4 picas from rule to rule) are used exclusively for captions. Brevity is essential in lines that rarely contain more than a single word.

The overall effect, which is very open and accessible, is achieved by sacrificing a considerable amount of text space. A distinct advantage of the format, not seen in the pages reproduced here, is that it creates a strong contrast when editorial and advertising pages face each other on the same spread.

Art almost invariably breaks out of the grid, creating a variety of depth illusions. Type, too, can appear to move through a three-dimensional page: The clipped-off bottoms of the "Anti-Aging" headline (left) make the type appear to be moving down through the box.

The body text is Helvetica with Futura headlines.

The paper is a heavy, noncoated, gray stock, which adds considerable bulk to a 36-page magazine. Blue and burgundy, used for banners, headlines, and tones behind the featured items, add color and reinforce the modular structure. Another similarly formatted section in the magazine uses green and purple.

Design: Regina Marsh (New York, NY)

Pages from Longevity, *published monthly by Omni International. Trim size: 8-1/4 by 10-3/4*

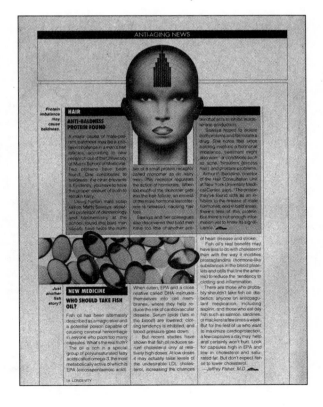

Variable column width

When you have variable-length components and want to contain each one within a single column, you can let the length of each item dictate the column width. Putting together such a page is a little like doing a jigsaw puzzle. This layout would be exceedingly expensive and time-consuming using traditional typesetting and pasteup. But the ability to vary text and frame elements in Ventura gives you extraordinary on-screen control over the width and depth of each column. You assemble this kind of page from left to right, and then make adjustments as needed.

The key to balancing all the elements on the page is to establish some horizontal constants in either text placement or illustration depth. In addition to unifying the page, these horizontal guidelines will help keep you from getting lost in a sea of choices.

A horizontal grid is used to balance the elements in variable-width columns on the the two pages shown here. The headings for all items sit on a baseline 4,06 from the top of the page. The first line of body text sits on one of three baselines, all measured from the top trim: 11,00; 27,06; or 39,00.

The margins are 3 picas for the sides and bottom and 4 picas for the top.

The text is 10/12.5 with headlines in Helvetica Condensed Black and body text in Helvetica Condensed. Condensed sans serif faces are a good choice for short copy in narrow columns.

The Allsport title was set in Helvetica Condensed Black in Freehand, further condensed, rotated, and then placed in the document.

The rules are 1 point—heavier than usually found—in order to give more structure to the page.

ALLSPORT

Lorem ipsum dolor sit amet, consectetuer adipiscing elit, sed diam nonummy nibh euismod tincidunt ut laoreet dolore magna aliquam erat volutpat. Ut wisi enim ad minim veniam, quis nostrud exerci tation ullamcorper suscipit lobortis nisl ut aliquip ex ea commodo consequat.

Duis autem vel eum

Duis autem vel eum iriure dolor in esse hendrerit in vulputate velit esse molestie consequat, vel illum dolore eu feugiat nulla facilisis at vero eros et accumsan et iusto odio dignissim qui blandit praesent luptatum zzril delenit augue duis dolore te feugait nulla facilisi.

Lorem ipsum dolor sit amet, consectetuer adipiscing elit, sed diam nonummy nibh euismod tincidunt ut laoreet dolore magna aliquam erat volutpat. Ut wisi enim ad minim veniam, quis nostrud exerci tation ullamcorper suscipit lobortis nisl ut aliquip ex ea commodo consequat.

Duis autem vel eum iriure dolor in hendrerit in vulputate velit esse molestie consequat, vel illum dolore eu feugiat nulla facilisis at vero eros et accumsan et iusto odio dignissim qui blandit praesent luptatum zzril delenit augue duis dolore te feugait nulla facilisi. Nam liber tempor cum soluta nobis eleifend option congue nihil imperdiet doming id quod mazim placerat facer possim assum. Lorem ipsum dolor sit amet, consectetuer adipiscing elit, sed diam nonummy nibh euismod tincidunt ut laoreet dolore magna

Lorem ipsum

Aliquam erat esse volutpat. Ut wisi enim ad minim veniam, quis nostrud exerci tation ullamcorper suscipit lobortis nisl ut aliquip ex ea commodo consequat.

Duis autem vel eum iriure dolor in hendrerit in vulputate velit esse molestie consequat, vel illum dolore eu feugiat nulla facilisis at vero eros et accumsan et iusto odio dignissim qui

Duis autem vel eum iriure dolor in hendrerit in vulputate velit esse molestie lorem ipsum

Blandit praesent luptatum zzril delenit augue duis dolore te feugait nulla facilisi. Lorem ipsum dolor sit amet, consectetuer adipiscing elit, sed diam nonummy nibh euismod tincidunt ut laoreet dolore magna Lorem ipsum dolor sit amet, consectetuer adipiscing elit, sed diam nonummy nibh euismod tincidunt ut laoreet dolore magna aliquam erat

volutpat. Ut wisi enim ad minim veniam, quis nostrud exerci tation ullamcorper suscipit lobortis nisl ut aliquip ex ea commodo consequat.

Duis autem vel eum iriure dolor in hendrerit in vulputate velit esse molestie consequat, vel illum dolore eu feugiat nulla facilisis at vero eros et accumsan et iusto odio dignissim qui blandit praesent luptatum zzril delenit augue duis dolore te feugait nulla facilisi. Lorem ipsum dolor sit amet, con-

Ut wisi enim ades min ut wisi enim ad min

Sectetuer adipiscing elit, sed diam nonummy nibh euismod tincidunt ut laoreet dolore magna aliquam erat volutpat.

Ut wisi enim ad minim veniam, quis nostrud exerci tation ullamcorper suscipit lobortis nisl ut aliquip ex ea commodo consequat. Duis autem vel eum iriure dolor in hendrerit in.

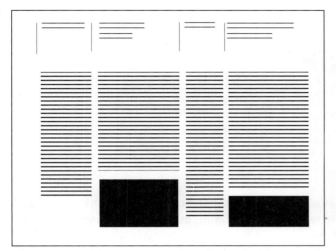

In the schematics above, the approach is to establish a horizon line for the headlines and for body text and then to hang copy from those lines in variable column widths. Art is sized to match the text width in each column, with variable heights but with a common baseline and a fixed amount of space between the bottom of the text and the top of the art.

The left-most schematic shows the same approach in a vertically oriented page. Another approach is to have even bottoms and ragged tops, with art and headlines providing another horizontal constant at the top of the page.

Duis au

liriure dolor in hendrerit in vulput

Autem vel eum iriure dolor in hendrerit in vulputate velit esse molestie consequat, vel illum dolore eu feugiat nulla facilisis at vero eros et accumsan et

quis nostrud exerci tation ullamcorper suscipit lobortis nisl ut aliquip ex ea c minUt wisi enim

Diam nonummy nibh euismod tincidunt ut laoreet dolore magna. Lorem ipsum dolor sit amet, consectetuer adipiscing elit, sed diam nonummy nibh euismod tincidunt ut laoreet dolore magna aliquam erat volutpat. Ut wisi enim ad minim veniam, quis nostrud exerci tation ullamcorper suscipit lobortis nisl ut aliquip ex ea commodo consequat.

Duis autem vel eum iriure dolor in hendrerit in vulputate velit esse molestie consequat, vel illum dolore eu feugiat nulla facilisis at vero eros et accumsan et iusto odio dignissim qui blandit praesent luptatum zzril delenit augue duis dolore te feugait nulla facilisi.

Lorem ipsum dolor sit amet, consectetuer adipiscing elit, sed diam nonummy nibh euismod tincidunt ut laoreet dolore magna aliquam erat volutpat. Ut wisi enim ad minim veniam, quis nostrud exerci tation ullamcorper suscipit lobortis nisl ut aliquip ex ea commodo consequat.Duis autem vel eum iriure dolor in hendrerit in vulputate velit esse molestie consequat, vel illum dolore eu

Feuga

Feugiat nulla facilisis at vero eros et accumsan et iusto odio dignissim qui blandit praesent.

Lorem ipsum dolor sit amet

luptatum zzril delenit augue duis dolore te feugait nulla facilisi. Nam liber tempor cum soluta nobis eleifend option congue nihil imperdiet doming id quod mazim placerat facer possim assum. Lorem ipsum dolor sit amet, consectetuer adipiscing elit, sed diam nonummy nibh euismod tincidunt ut laoreet dolore magna aliquam erat volutpat.

Ut wisi enim ad minim veniam, quis nostrud exerci tation ullamcorper suscipit lobortis nisl ut aliquip ex ea commodo consequat. Duis autem vel eum iriure dolor in hendrerit in vulputate velit esse molestie consequat, vel illum dolore eu feugiat nulla facilisis at vero eros et accumsan et iusto odio dignissim qui blandit praesent luptatum zzril delenit augue duis dolore te esse.

Vulputate velit esse molestie consequat, vel illum dolore eu feugiat nulla facilisis at vero eros et accumsan et iusto odio dignissim qui blandit praesent luptatum zzril delenit augue duis dolore te feugait nulla facilisi. Nam liber tempor cum soluta nobis eleifend option congue nihil imperdiet doming id quod mazim placerat facer possim assum.

Lorem ipsum dolor sit amet, consectetuer adipiscing elit, sed diam nonummy nibh euismod tincidunt ut laoreet dolore magna aliquam erat volutpat. Ut wisi enim ad minim veniam, quis nostrud exerci tation ullamcorper suscipit lobortis nisl ut aliquip ex ea commodo consequat. Duis

iusto odio dignissim qui blandit praesent luptatum zzril delenit augue duis dolore te feugait nulla facilisi. Lorem ipsu dolor sit amet con- secteadipis- cing elit, se.

CHAPTER 4

THE CIRCULAR NATURE OF PLANNING AND DOING

In describing electronic page composition, many books and manuals depict a neatly linear process of creating master pages, placing edited text and finished graphics, making a few refinements, and then printing out final pages to send off to the printer. The demonstrations of page layout programs are even more misleading. Innocent spectators stand wide-eyed, mouths agape as a demonstrator pours text into pages that seem to compose themselves as if by magic. Everything falls into place without a loose end in sight. How could anyone resist a tool that makes page layout so utterly simple, so fantastically tidy?

The reality of producing almost any publication is considerably different. Rather than being linear, the process is a circular one involving trial and error as well as numerous revisions to make all the elements work together. This case history should give you a better picture of that reality. It shows, for example, that some of the most important design work goes on before you put pencil to paper or turn on the computer and involves simply thinking through the problem of how to get your audience's attention. It looks at the overlapping steps of developing the concept, planning the design, testing the plan with text and graphics in various stages of development, refining the design, altering the text and graphics to fit the refined plan, and then making whatever changes are necessary—in the individual elements as well as the design itself— as all the pieces come together in final form.

Solving a design problem is much like running a maze. The designer selects a line to follow only to learn that the constraints he encounters send him back to probe another direction until he finds a clear path to the solution.

—Allen Hurlburt

The final version of the brochure described in this chapter may look as effortless as the slickest computer-show demonstration, but there was nothing linear about the process of creating it. Unlike a jigsaw puzzle, in which a single fixed piece completes the task, this publication evolved into its final form, and almost everything about it changed at least a little along the way.

The process described in this case history is quite specific to the particular publication. At each stage, our approach grew out of the unique problems and goals of the project and the division of duties among the different people involved. Every project and every team will use a process that is different, sometimes a little different and sometimes dramatically different. The goal of this chapter is simply to reveal the circular and overlapping nature of the two main facets of the work— planning and doing.

Background: the need, the purpose, and the concept

The New York City Charter Revision Commission was created to study and propose revisions to the city charter. The commission knew that most New Yorkers had never heard of the charter and were not likely to be informed about the proposals that would be on a voter referendum. The purpose of the publication was to increase voter awareness about how the charter affected city government and why it was being changed. Recognizing audience apathy was the first step toward finding an appropriate way to deliver the message.

We were hired as the editorial and design team because of our background in working with interactive techniques—puzzles, games, quizzes, and so on. These activities provide an effective if somewhat subversive way to engage people in a subject they might otherwise not be inclined to read about. Each activity tends to have a different "look," and so in addition to breaking up the text, the activities also vary the texture from one page to the next.

PROJECT AT A GLANCE: THE VOTER'S GUIDEBOOK

Description	An educational brochure produced for The New York City Charter Revision Commission.
Purpose	To increase voter awareness of changes in the city charter that were to be voted on in the coming election.
Specifications	8-1/2 by 11, 16 pages, 2-color, newsprint, suitable for self-mailing. Initial print run: 200,000.
Audience	Citizens in all five boroughs.
Distribution	Bulk distribution through citizen groups, unions, schools, libraries, and civic organizations. "Copies on request" promoted through city payroll, phone bill stuffers, and public service announcements.
Design Objectives	To involve people in a generally tedious subject.
Devices to Achieve Goal	• Puzzles and games as both editorial and design elements. • A modular editorial format to create many entry points for readers. • A strong, tight format to unify disparate elements. • Bold headlines and borders. • A photo of a landmark and a unique headline style to highlight each borough, with a map motif to unify all five of them.
Typeface	Body text: Times Roman. We chose this face because it is serious, sets tightly, and reproduces well in a wide range of situations, making it a safe choice for inexpensive newsprint.
	Headlines: New Century Schoolbook, condensed in Adobe Illustrator. We chose condensed type because some headlines were fairly long, and we didn't want to sacrifice point size for line length.

Presentation sketch: a miniature booklet

The commission gave us a 3500-word essay on city government and the process of charter revision and a list of concepts and facts that the activities should explain. Every activity had to satisfy two criteria: It had to be fun to do, and it had to deliver information about the charter.

In designing the pages, our first step was to divide the single, continuous narrative into short, self-contained stories. Very few people read a brochure (or any publication other than a book) from cover to cover. Each story is a potential entry point, each headline an opportunity to hook the audience.

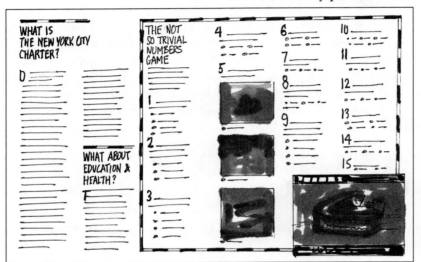

We wanted each spread to carry a small chunk of the text and a related activity. Establishing a relationship between the text and its accompanying activity wasn't always possible, but it was useful to start with that as the organizing principle. Creating a dozen individual stories from the single long one required only a little rewriting because the text had clear and natural divisions. This is not always the case.

Doing early sketches by hand helps you to focus on the big picture, rather than on the mathematical details required in setting up an electronic page.

Although the publication was to be 8-1/2 by 11 inches, we did the presentation sketch at one-fourth that size, with each two-page spread on half of an 8-1/2- by 11-inch page. And we did it by hand rather than on the computer. Computer layouts are unforgiving of imprecision and have a way of looking more cast in stone than is the case at an early stage. Working by hand sometimes helps you to focus on the big picture rather than on the details of spacing and alignment that the computer encourages you to attend to. And working small, when you're working by hand, is simply faster and emphasizes the preliminary nature of the presentation. (Interestingly, people also seem to get a kick out of the tiny pages.)

The pencil sketch (actually, it was done with colored markers) showed the position of each story and activity. It showed the bold borders and the strong headlines surrounded by generous white space as well as the use of red as a second color. Writing and positioning the real headlines at this early stage contributed to everyone's feeling that the concept and design worked. The individual pieces were right, and the pacing was right. Although no real text or art was in place, everyone got a sense of what the publication would look and feel like to the reader. Some stories and placements changed along the way, but this early sketch reflected the tone and structure of the final publication.

A few holes were left in the sketch for activity concepts that hadn't been developed. This was, thankfully, a client with a minimalist attitude toward meetings, and we'd scheduled a brainstorming session immediately following the presentation to fill in those holes.

The manuscript for the original essay had not been created in a word processor, so we keyboarded the text at this stage. We did the first edit in Microsoft Word and printed out galleys with the text in 13-1/2-pica columns for the commission to review along with the sketch.

ANOTHER APPROACH

In the early stages of a project, you'll often want to explore more than one concept. For *The Voter's Guidebook*, we briefly entertained the idea of creating a takeoff on the *New York Post*. Given the number of New Yorkers who follow the infamous Post-style headlines, such a blatant simulation of it, while not a true parody, was sure to get attention.

Several considerations quickly ruled out the idea. The most important was that the design concept would have dictated the contents, rather than the other way around. Much of the information the Charter Revision Commission wanted to convey didn't lend itself to tabloid-style headlines. This meant that we would have had to delete material we wanted to include, write headlines that were inappropriate, or include some headlines that didn't follow through on the concept.

A takeoff on the New York Post *was briefly considered as an alternative approach.*

The *Post* takeoff would also have required writing new copy to carry out the concept and using more photos than the budget allowed. There simply wasn't time or money to execute it.

Further, no one was truly comfortable with the idea. It seemed a little brazen and somehow inappropriate for a city commission to model itself, however tongue in cheek, on a daily tabloid.

We anticipated these problems when we sketched out the idea. But when you edit yourself too much in the early stages of a project, you sacrifice both good ideas and *esprit de corps*. Part of the design process requires striking a balance between anticipating what your client (or boss or editor or communications director) wants and taking some risks. A good working relationship has a free flow of ideas that inspires everyone involved. Daring visuals and bold concepts loosen people up and are catalysts for problem solving. The *New York Post* concept, although discarded, got the project off to a creative, upbeat start. That feeling carried over to the puzzle brainstorming session that followed the design presentation and was largely maintained throughout the project.

The first dummy: copy fitting

After the galleys and presentation sketch were approved, we put each individual essay and activity in its own word-processor file. In a modular publication in which every item is self-contained rather than continuous from one page to the next, fitting the copy into the allotted spaces usually requires cutting or adding text. If the stories had been threaded together in a single document, changes to the line count in one story would have rippled through subsequent stories, requiring much moving back and forth among pages to retrieve errant lines (and risking the kinds of errors that computers should minimize).

While we were still working out some of the design elements, we did a rough electronic dummy to facilitate the copy fitting. It's generally recommended that copy fitting be done in the word-processing program, and when extensive editing is required, we agree. But one of the great advantages of electronic layout is seeing the copy in place. When you cut copy and see the lines on the pasteboard flow up neatly to fill the column, you know that the copy fits and you get a nice feeling of completeness. If the editing and design functions in your office are clearly separated, however, you may not have this choice.

The first electronic dummy substituted temporary rules and headline type for the real ones that were to be created in Illustrator. By this time, we had dropped some art shown on the presentation sketch for these pages.

At this point, the master pages had three 13-1/2-pica columns (which later changed to 13 picas to allow for more white space). The text for each story was in place, but other details had to be simulated. The map rules above the headlines and in the box borders hadn't been worked out, so we used a bold dashed line to simulate them. The New Century Schoolbook headlines, which were to be created in Adobe Illustrator, had not yet been completed, so we used Helvetica instead.

Simulating the unresolved design elements at this point gave us—and the client—a chance to read the copy in the context of the layout and to evaluate the layout with the copy in place.

The presentation dummy: refining the design

The brochure had been conceived as 24 pages, including a pull-out poster in the center. When the poster idea proved unworkable, we were left with 20 pages. Because publications are generally printed in signatures of 8 or 16 pages, printing 200,000 twenty-page brochures would have wasted an unconscionable amount of paper. After exploring the possibility of expanding or shrinking the brochure, everyone agreed that less was more (this is almost always the case in publication work, as it is in other endeavors), and we dropped down to 16 pages.

Changing the page count midway through a project inevitably solves some problems and creates others. Here, in a nutshell, were the effects that the reduced page count had on *The Voter's Guidebook*:

- We eliminated the weaker activities and were left with the really good, solid, fun stuff.

- We had to juggle the position of some essays and activities. Several crossover spreads had art or stories on facing pages that could not be broken up. When you eliminate one page before a spread that has to stay together, you have to find some other page to fill in. In the course of this juggling, we had to put one puzzle with a lot of specific details about the charter earlier in the brochure than we would have liked, but all decisions have their trade-offs.

- Copy that had been edited to fit in the 24-page dummy had to be edited again to fit the new page count. This kind of reworking is part of the process of publication design, and desktop publishing makes it infinitely easier and cheaper to accomplish than the traditional method, where every change requires that you send out for new type and mechanically paste up the new version.

At this stage, we created the map rules that were to frame the various components. Once we saw them in place, however, we felt they were too bold a device to use throughout, and we decided to substitute a simple double-rule border for the games. The double rule echoed the map rules but was subtler, and so kept the pages from looking too heavy and busy. The two types of borders were exactly the same depth so that they aligned horizontally across the page.

The headline type and initial caps—condensed New Century Schoolbook—were placed as Encapsulated PostScript files. (Each headline and each initial cap was a separate file.) These were to be in red, the second color. Again, we felt that having red headlines and initial caps for every item would be too busy, so the games had black headlines and no initial caps.

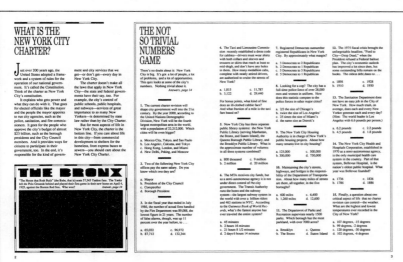

Final page proofs used black boxes to indicate the position of photos that would be stripped in by the printer. The position of the Bronx sidebar changed from the original sketch to the final. And, as a result of deadline pressures, the decorative numbers in the quiz were replaced by rules, which were easier to create.

As a result of these changes, the contrast in rules and color for the two types of material—running text and activities—provided a visual organizing cue for the reader.

Some of the games and puzzles had not yet been completed, so for the presentation dummy we filled in these holes with a pencil sketch of each activity and the working introductory copy.

The final pages

Desktop publishing enabled us to show the commission more complete proofs for approval earlier in the cycle than would have been possible using traditional typesetting and pasteup methods. This paid off handsomely by minimizing corrections at the final stage. Still, changes were requested, and although they were relatively easy to make on-screen, printing pages was extremely slow. (At the time we were working with a relatively slow LaserWriter Plus printer.) Up against the deadline, we printed type patches and pasted in small corrections by hand rather than waiting for a graphics-intensive page to print. (The headlines, initial caps, and borders imported were all electronically-generated graphics; the photographs, however, were stripped in by the printer.)

A strong center axis on the cover makes the offset compass rose, with the commission's logo inside, more prominent. The map and compass rose were created and placed electronically. The logo was pasted in by hand.

Starting text on the cover, as on the page shown below left, can be an effective way to get the reader's interest. The text must be very strong for this technique to work and must be carefully designed for visual effect.

The back cover is designed as a self-mailer and uses the most universally popular of all puzzles to draw the reader in. When solved, the crossword reveals a message in the shaded squares that reads: "Vote on charter change in 88." Someone who solves the puzzle but never opens the brochure will still get the most important message of the guidebook.

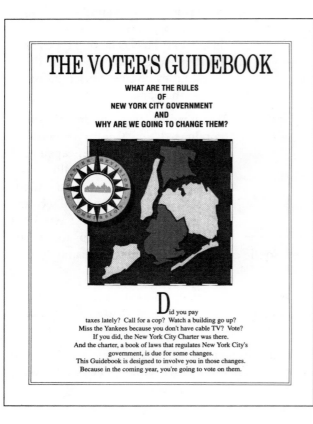

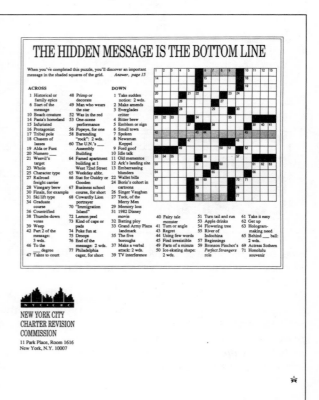

The printed pages for the spread shown throughout this chapter in various stages of its evolution: A trivia quiz reminds readers of the sheer size of city government by supplying such facts as the number of false alarms answered by the fire department and the amount of trash generated, on average, by each citizen every day.

The headlines and initial caps are 36-point New Century School-book, created and condensed to 60% on the horizontal axis in Adobe Illustrator. The heads and caps for primary text print in red to help unify the short essays that run throughout the 16 pages. The activity headlines print in black.

The position of the opening line of text for the essays remains constant throughout the booklet.

The map rules over the essays and around the borough boxes were created in Illustrator from a double hairline rule with black rectangles dropped in. Alignment is critical.

Boxes around the activities use hairline rules. Note that the map rules and the open rules of the boxes align exactly.

Rules crossing the gutter between two pages required manual pasteup for alignment.

The running text for the essays is 11/13 Times Roman set in 13-pica columns. Because they have a map rule above but not around them, these text blocks have a more open look than the activities, which are enclosed in boxes. Eleven-point type was difficult to read on-screen but worked much better in the overall design than 10- or 12-point type.

The text for activities is 10/12 Times Roman. The column width is a half-pica shorter than the width used for the essay text, and the space between columns is also a half-pica shorter, to compensate for the space occupied by the rules around the activity.

Decorative rules, which print in red, separate numbered text blocks in the quiz. For these dividers we copied the rectangle used in the map rule and pasted it repetitively in the quiz.

Borough headlines were created individually in Illustrator to give each borough a different personality. Press type can also be used to create this effect.

WHAT IS THE NEW YORK CITY CHARTER?

J ust over 200 years ago, the United States adopted a framework and a system of rules for the operation of our national government. It's called the Constitution. Think of the charter as New York City's constitution.

It explains who gets power and what they can do with it. That goes for elected officials like the mayor and the people the mayor appoints to run city agencies, such as the police, sanitation, and fire commissioners. It goes for the people who approve the city's budget of almost $23 billion, such as the borough presidents and the City Council members. And it provides ways for citizens to participate in their government, too. In the end, it's responsible for the kind of govern-

ment and city services that we get—or don't get—every day in New York City.

The charter doesn't make all the laws that apply in New York City—the state and federal governments have their say, too. For example, the city's control of public schools, public hospitals, and subways—services of great importance to so many New Yorkers—is determined by state law rather than by the City Charter.

But for most aspects of life in New York City, the charter is the bottom line. If you care about life in this city—from commercial development to shelters for the homeless, from express buses to sewers—you should care about the New York City Charter.

THE BRONX

"The House that Ruth Built" (the Babe, that is) seats 57,545 Yankee fans. The Yanks left the Polo Grounds behind and played their first game in their new home on April 4, 1923, against the Boston Red Sox. Who won? *Answer, page 14*

THE NOT SO TRIVIAL NUMBERS GAME

There's no doubt about it: New York City is big. It's got a lot of people, a lot of problems, and a lot of opportunities. This quiz looks at some of the city's numbers. Nothing trivial about it.
Answers, page 14

1. The current charter revision will shape city government well into the 21st century. By the year 2000, according to the United Nations Demographic Division, New York will be the fourth largest metropolitan area in the world, with a population of 22,212,000. Which cities will be even bigger?

a. Mexico City, Tokyo, and Sao Paulo
b. Los Angeles, Calcutta, and Tokyo
c. Hong Kong, London, and Miami
d. New Delhi, Peking, and Moscow

2. Two of the following New York City offices pay the same salary. Do you know which two they are?

a. Mayor
b. President of the City Council
c. Comptroller
d. Borough President

3. In the fiscal year that ended in July 1986, the number of actual fires handled by the Fire Department was 89,088, the lowest figure in 21 years. The number of false alarms, though, was up 11 percent over the year before, to . . .

a. 65,022   c. 96,972
b. 87,712   d. 132,344

4. The Taxi and Limousine Commission recently established a dress code for cabbies—drivers must wear shirts with both collars and sleeves and trousers or skirts that reach at least to mid-thigh, with no holes in them. How many medallion cabs, complete with neatly attired drivers, are authorized to cruise the streets of New York?

a. 1,815   c. 11,787
b. 5,122   d. 29,440

For bonus points, what kind of fine does an ill-clothed cabbie face? And what fraction of a mile is the taxi fare based on?

a. 2/3 the size of Chicago's
b. twice the size of Los Angeles'
c. 25 times the size of Miami's
d. the same size as Detroit's

5. New York City has three separate public library systems: the New York Public Library (serving Manhattan, the Bronx, and Staten Island), the Queens Borough Public Library, and the Brooklyn Public Library. What is the approximate number of volumes in all three systems combined?

a. 800 thousand   c. 9 million
b. 2 million   d. 20 million

6. The MTA receives city funds, but as a semi-autonomous agency it is not under direct control of the city government. The Transit Authority runs the buses and the subway system—the largest subway system in the world with over a billion riders and 463 stations in NYC. According to the *Guinness Book of World Records*, what's the fastest anyone has ever traveled the entire system?

a. 45 minutes
b. 2 hours 16 minutes
c. 21 hours 8 1/2 minutes
d. 2 days 6 hours 14 minutes

7. Registered Democrats outnumber registered Republicans in New York City. By approximately what margin?

a. 3 Democrats to 2 Republicans
b. 2 Democrats to 1 Republican
c. 5 Democrats to 3 Republicans
d. 5 Democrats to 1 Republican

8. Looking for a cop? The city has a full-time police force of over 28,000 men and women in uniform. How does this statistic compare to the police forces in other major cities?

a. 2/3 the size of Chicago's
b. twice the size of Los Angeles'
c. 25 times the size of Miami's
d. the same size as Detroit's

9. The New York City Housing Authority is in charge of New York's public housing projects. About how many tenants live in city housing?

a. 125,000   c. 500,000
b. 300,000   d. 750,000

10. Maintaining the city's streets, highways, and bridges is the responsibility of the Department of Transportation. About how many miles of streets are there, all together, in the five boroughs?

a. 600 miles   c. 6,400
b. 1,260 miles   d. 12,600

11. The Department of Parks and Recreation supervises nearly 1500 parks. Which borough has the most parkland, with over 7000 acres?

a. Brooklyn   c. Queens
b. The Bronx   d. Staten Island

12. The 1975 fiscal crisis brought the unforgettable headline, "Ford to City—Drop Dead," when the President refused a Federal bailout plan. The city's economic outlook has improved a lot since then, but some outstanding bills remain on the books. The oldest debt dates to . . .

a. 1898   c. 1928
b. 1910   d. 1950

13. The Sanitation Department does not have an easy job in the City of New York. How much trash does, on average, each and every New Yorker generate each and every day? (Hint: The world leader is Los Angeles with 6.6 pounds per person.)

a. 6.2 pounds   c. 2.2 pounds
b. 4.5 pounds   d. 1.8 pounds

14. The New York City Health and Hospitals Corporation, established in 1970 as a semi-autonomous agency, is the only municipal health care system in the country. Part of that system, Bellevue Hospital, is the nation's oldest public hospital. What year was Bellevue founded?

a. 1736   c. 1836
b. 1786   d. 1886

15. Finally, a question about one critical aspect of life that no charter revision can control—the weather. What are the highest and lowest temperatures ever recorded in the City of New York?

a. 107 degrees, -15 degrees
b. 99 degrees, -2 degrees
c. 120 degrees, -30 degrees
d. 102 degrees, -6 degrees

2

3

A DESIGN PORTFOLIO

SECTION 2

INTRODUCTION TO THE PORTFOLIO

You will find in this portfolio a broad selection of publications, from businesses both large and small, with designs that range from simple to complex. The samples were chosen with an eye to variety—different types of messages from many kinds of businesses including those concerned with health, education, manufacturing, sales, service, entertainment, politics, fashion, real estate, law, and art. Some were designed by freelance designers, others by corporate art departments, and still others by top design studios. The level of graphic sophistication varies considerably. A modest layout is often presented side by side with an ambitious one because each represents an appropriate solution to a specific communication need.

Some of the publications were created using Ventura Publisher, some were created using other page layout software, some were created using a mix of traditional and electronic methods. It can't be said often enough that the technology is only a tool—a remarkable tool to be sure, but still only a tool. And the focus of this portfolio is not so much how the pages were created, but the choices that the designers made along the way.

Before turning to those specifics, it is worth looking behind the documents to the stories of how some organizations and individuals have integrated desktop publishing into their work. Geiger International, for example, is a furniture design firm in Atlanta. In 1985 they were planning a major revision of their product guide and price list. Previously, price lists had been typeset outside and laboriously pasted up by the two-person art and design department. Without really knowing anything about desktop publishing (they hadn't even heard the term), they did know that if they could do the price lists themselves, in-house, they'd have a database that could be updated as needed. Manfred Petri, their new vice president of design, had seen the LaserWriter at an office equipment show in Germany, and he was convinced that it really could produce what was called "near typeset quality." Pamela Bryant, an executive assistant in sales, was recruited to translate Petri's paper-and-pencil guidelines into electronic form. She had no graphic design experience and no computer experience beyond word processing. What she

If we are to communicate quickly and clearly (as we must, if we are to retain our audience), then we must accept the fact that WHAT we say is integral with HOW we say it. Visual form and verbal content are inseparable.... Graphic design is not something added to make the pages look lively. It is not an end in itself. It is the means to an end—that of clear, vivid, stirring communication of editorial content.

—Jan White,
Designing for Magazines

Three people [should] be trained to educate and support the others in a work group: a computer-oriented person (to handle hardware and software problems); a designer or graphic artist (to support others in the use of templates and style sheets, among other tools); and a production person (to help manage the document flow). That way, the computer wizard learns about publishing, the publishing people learn about computers, and the rest of the staff has more than one person to go to in times of need.
—Barbara Hawkins, quoted in Publish! *magazine*

did have was an interest in learning what this new technology could do. The typesetting for the price list redesign would have been $30,000, so the savings on type alone more than covered the purchase of what became their first desktop publishing system. There are still two people in the design department (Bryant being one of them)—doing more publication work than they'd previously done plus many thousands of dollars worth of typesetting. (A page from a current Geiger price guide is on the opening spread of Chapter 7.)

The brief history of desktop publishing is full of such stories—not only of cost savings but also of shifting careers such as Pam Bryant's. Beverly Kay Rubman had been a secretary for organizations as diverse as the FBI and MTV when she and her husband Ken, an ad salesman, started a business in 1986 with an IBM XT, a Hewlett-Packard LaserJet, Word Perfect, and Ventura Publisher. Within four years they'd grown from doing word processing at a per-page rate to a full-service graphic design, typesetting, and computer-training operation with eight computers. Although Beverly Rubman has no formal training in graphic design, a good eye has enabled her to take advantage of the quick learning curve that desktop publishing can afford novice designers. (Samples of her work appear in the Folders section in Chapter 5 and the Financials section in Chapter 7.)

Depending on your point of view, it is either easier or more difficult to move into desktop publishing today than it was in 1985 or 86. Easier because the tools are more advanced, and there's plenty of evidence that in trained hands those tools can produce high-quality work. But the choices are more various—and hence more complex—and the expectations are so much higher.

Even so, organizations with a definable need and a sensible approach to phasing in the technology tend to realize the benefits they had anticipated. Kathy Tomyris, of the Mill Valley, California gardening emporium Smith & Hawken, writes of 50 percent savings in signage costs and of the ease of producing a wide variety of product information sheets consistent with the high standards of the store's merchandise and the smart image of their mail-order catalog. (The catalog is still produced using traditional typesetting; samples of their product information sheets are in Chapter 7.) Ann Wassmann Gross, a graphic designer at The Art Institute of Chicago, notes that they began using desktop production for gallery labels alone, and within two years were producing half of the museum's printed materials in-house, using an outside typesetter's Linotronic 300 for final pages. (A folder and a brochure from the Art Institute are in Chapter 5.)

Jim Parker, the executive director of the Do It Now Foundation in Phoenix, believes desktop publishing literally saved his organization. A not-for-profit educational publisher of materials on drug and alcohol abuse, Do It Now supports its operations from publication sales. In 1984, dwindling resources and soaring costs forced the foundation to lay off the last of its staff artists and layout people, leaving a skeletal staff of four. Then came desktop publishing. Not only did Do It Now survive, it survived to see increased publication sales, numerous design awards, and the building of a new national headquarters. "If I sound proud," Parker reflects, "I guess I am. I'm also grateful that I got the opportunity to develop my publication ideas myself, without the need for costly intermediaries. If I sound like a devotee, I guess I'm that, too. You'd probably sound just the same if you'd come as close as I did to presiding over the demise of a valuable organization because of a lack of cost-effective tools to develop, design, and keep current a publication roster of some 120 titles."

Freelance designers and small design studios with a wide variety of clients have a somewhat different experience with desktop publishing than organizations using it for their own publishing and communications needs. One issue for many designers is whether or not they want to become typesetters and, to the degree that they do, how to bill that service back to the client. It's not so much a question of quality anymore but of efficiency.

While many companies use already-in-place IBM-compatibles for desktop publishing, professional designers have gravitated more toward the Macintosh environment, both for its ease of use and for its early lead in graphic programs. So there simply aren't as many professional designers working in Ventura as in Quark Express or PageMaker. But those designers who have chosen Ventura heartily endorse its speed and power. Donna Kelly, of Zetatype in San Francisco, abandoned PC PageMaker for Ventura's facility preparing and revising text files, its sophisticated style tags, and its superior typographic controls. (Kelly's work appears in Chapters 5 and 6.) Carol Finkelstein, who also has a small desktop publishing business in San Francisco, found that working in Ventura gave her an edge in a community where many potential clients had Ventura and most professional designers didn't. (You'll find two of Finkelstein's pieces in Chapter 5.)

Michael Sullivan, on the other hand, moves back and forth between PCs and Macs in his Cambridge, Massachusetts, design studio. Sullivan finds the conventional wisdom—that you do short pieces on the Mac in PageMaker and long ones on a PC in Ventura—oversimplified. He finds Ventura much faster for producing short pieces with a lot of tabs and rules. And he may design the format for a long document in PageMaker and then execute it in Ventura. When he's not sure what the design will be and wants to develop it on the computer, he uses PageMaker—whereas both the strength, and the difficulty, of Ventura is that it requires you to figure out how you can get the computer, rather than the computer operator, to lay the piece out. Ventura also provides an efficient platform for the technical documents his studio designs. Sullivan will work out several approaches from text and graphic files supplied by the client, and then after the client approves one design, Sullivan creates the style sheets in Ventura. The client then implements the design, with art direction from Sullivan's studio as needed. With this kind of relationship, designers get paid to design and the client saves money by doing

This technology is a force that is going to move everybody up to where we will begin to expect and receive a higher level of sophistication in all areas of our printed communication.

*—Roger Black,
from an interview in* Font & Function

There is…an instant…when an idea comes alive! If you freeze it…too soon, it's still unformed and incomplete. Premature. But if you play around too much, you'll wind up with something over-worked…. You lose touch with the vitality of the original impulse, or cover it up so that no one else but you sees it. You have to catch the moment on the wing, so to speak.

—Michael Green,
Zen & the Art of Macintosh

the labor-intensive production in-house. (You'll find samples of Sullivan's work in all three Portfolio chapters.)

Many large corporations have graphic departments that work with other corporate divisions in much the way that Michael Sullivan works with his clients. At Shearson Lehman Hutton, the Graphic and Print Communications group designs documents for "clients" throughout the corporation. In the case of repetitive documents where the client will do the ongoing production, the design prototype is accompanied by a customized information packet. The packet is a desktop novice's dream: a style sheet on disk, an electronic template into which new text can be flowed, a printout of a sample document annotated with tag names, a printout of a word-processor file with tags prior to the text, and a list of tags with a definition of each one. (Two of Shearson's newsletters appear in Chapter 6.)

Many of the contributors to this section acknowledge with good humor their role as pioneers in exploiting the tools of electronic publishing, puzzling through traditional editorial and design considerations one minute and technological challenges the next. Those challenges aren't limited to exploring the cutting edge of technology. They include coping with bugs and getting the most of equipment that perhaps isn't state of the art. Frank Kendig, a writer and editor with many years of experience in magazine publishing, tells of using a non-PostScript printer to proof pages that would ultimately be printed on a high-resolution PostScript imagesetter. What made it not only possible but also relatively efficient was his understanding of the nuances of font technology and of the depth of Ventura's stylesheets. (Pages from that publication, *Science Digest*, appear in the Magazine section of Chapter 6, along with more examples of Kendig's technological resourcefulness.)

In the time that we've been collecting the portfolio samples, the quality of desktop-published pages has improved dramatically. That's partly a function of the technology, partly a result of the increasing experience of users, and partly a result of the attraction of more and more professional designers to electronic tools. It's important, however, not to pass over a simple and modest approach if it is appropriate to your needs and especially if it matches the level of your skill, either as a designer or as a technological pioneer. It's far better to produce a well-executed modest design than to make a mess of a more ambitious one.

In the following pages, the commentary accompanying the sample documents focuses primarily on design elements—grid structure, type styling, and so on. But you'll also find notes on various software programs and production methods used in some of the publications as well as notes about color, paper stock, and other production values not readily apparent. Each sample is reproduced as large as possible while still allowing room for annotations about the work. Inevitably, both impact and detail are lost in reduction. Of course, color is lost as well. Your imagination is the bridge that will translate the reproductions and notes into solutions for your own publishing needs.

CHAPTER 5

PROMOTIONS: FLYERS, POSTERS, FOLDERS, AND BROCHURES

Promotional literature is the most image-conscious of all publications. Here, more than anywhere else, the medium really is the message. That doesn't mean that the words don't count, but it does mean that the art, the graphic design, the texture of the paper, the color of the ink, and the overall production values make a first impression that it's difficult for the text to overcome if that impression is off the mark.

Of course, the image and production values that are appropriate vary tremendously. At one end of the spectrum, the category includes simple flyers that grass-roots organizations and small businesses leave under car windshield wipers; at the other end are slick four-color brochures distributed by large corporations to prospective clients. Both extremes, and everything in between, share the need to consider carefully the image they want to convey in order to produce the desired effect.

Promotional literature also presents a conceptual challenge that is rarely found in other kinds of business publications. If you can discover some unique perspective on your event, service, or product, you can turn that into an original and effective promotional idea. This is where catchy slogans, visual metaphors, and all the other tricks of Madison Avenue are used to good advantage. To be sure, if you're promoting a financial service or a funeral home, the style will be decidedly different than for a local eatery or theater group. But regardless of how frivolous or somber the concern, a fresh perspective on it will gain attention and set it apart from the competition.

FLYERS & POSTERS

You can look at flyers as modest posters, and posters as flyers on a grand scale. Though their budgets may differ dramatically, flyers and posters share the challenges inherent in any single-page promotion. To be effective, they have to deliver the strong graphic impression of a well-designed cover and the clear, concise information of a data sheet. Without the graphic appeal, the promotion will get lost amid all the other messages competing for the prospect's time and money; without the clear information, the flyer or poster becomes a piece of art, interesting to look at, perhaps, but probably not very effective.

Flyers and posters in this section

- *California Association of Midwives*—a photographic mandala for a fashion show fund-raiser
- *Student Recital*—the easy appeal of borders
- *VideoFashion Monthly*—using company stationery for a monthly flyer
- *WGBH Brown Bag Lunches*—a simple format that works
- *DesignSystems corporate résumé*—the flexibility of a good table-making system
- *AIGA poster*—the drama of life-size bit-mapped art
- *WPFW poster*—using type design for a jazzy 10th anniversary promotion

For hands-on instructions for creating a flyer with a coupon, see Project 5 in Section 3.

A scanned photo, copied and manipulated to create a mandala-like image, is a dynamic graphic technique for flyers and posters that is relatively easy to create. The digitized image was rotated and flopped in a paint program to create four versions oriented in different directions. Each version was saved as a separate file and imported into the electronic layout, where they were then composed into a single image.

The four corners created by the negative space of the art inside the 8-point-rule box provide an effective way to organize the type. The vertical rules add additional structure that keeps the type from floating in space.

The type and art print black against a shocking pink background, enhancing the playful feeling that sets the tone for the fashion show benefit.

The typeface is Garamond with a Futura Extra Bold headline.

Design: John Odam (San Diego, CA)

Flyer for a benefit auction for the California Association of Midwives. Trim size: 8-1/2 by 11

CALIFORNIA ASSOCIATION OF MIDWIVES

BENEFIT FASHION SHOW AUCTION

FASHIONS BY MANAGOS
Designer Christine Anderson-Nieto will be present

Music by Melissa Morgan

SATURDAY MAY 2ND, 1987 3PM AT TALBOT'S RESTAURANT 530 NORTH HIGHWAY 101, LEUCADIA
TICKETS $8. PER PERSON

Proceeds to benefit California Association of Midwives public outreach. For more information call Paula Tipton-Healy 944-3987 Carol Schrammel 264-2464

Name

Address

Phone

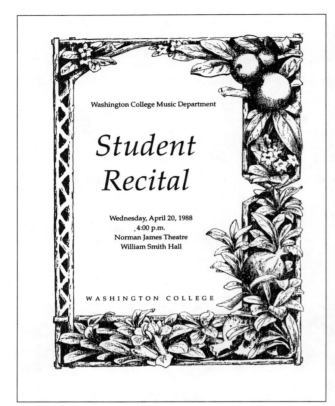

Borders from electronic or traditional clip art provide a quick, easy, and effective way to dress up a simple message. The one here is from *Victorian Pictorial Borders*, a book of public domain art published by Dover Press. The designer simply photocopied the art to the desired size, ran out type on a laser printer, pasted the two together on an 8.5- by 11-inch page, and photocopied the result.

The large Palatino headline is easy to read. It combines modern and classical elegance in a style that works well with the floral border and is appropriate for the event.

When considering borders from the ever-expanding clip art universe, keep in mind that you can use and modify segments of them to bracket and separate text.

A photostat of the company stationery provides the logo at the top of the page, the address line at the bottom, and space in between for a simply formatted information sheet (above right). The type, composed in Ventura, and a black-and-white glossy photo are pasted onto the stat. That finished page is photocopied on colored paper to produce an inexpensive mailer and package stuffer for a monthly video magazine.

The type combines two standard faces: Times Roman (also known as Dutch on some printers) for the title and volume number and Helvetica (also known as Swiss) for the rest of the text.

The main frame is the 8.5- by 11-inch page. The text to the right of the photo is in a separate frame. The paragraph tags remain the same every month; only the tab settings for the designers' names have to be created for each new flyer.

Design (above left): Diane Landskroener (Chestertown, MD)

Flyer for a recital at Washington College. Trim size: 8-1/2 by 11

Design (above right): Michael Adelberg, Videofashion Monthly (New York, NY)

Flyer for video magazine. Trim size: 8-1/2 by 11

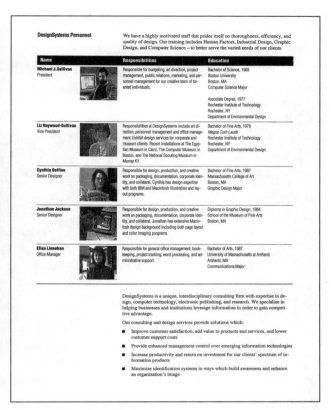

This simple format (above left), printed on brown kraft paper, announces events in a series of "brown bag lunch" lectures and demonstrations. The format establishes a strong identity for the series and is easy to execute for each event.

The shadowed box is a very simple attention-getting graphic. It is left in place on the template for the flyer so that only the type needs to be added for each new event.

The information above and below the boxed copy identifies the series and sponsor and is also a standing item in the template. It prints in red, so it looks stamped on.

The type is all from the Helvetica family.

A one-page corporate résumé for a design studio (above right) is as carefully organized as the technical manuals the firm designs. In fact, the résumé was produced by adapting a table-making system created for one of their client's manuals.

The basic page design divides the margin-to-margin widths into six equal columns, each with a 6,06-pica text area and a 0,06-pica column margin. Columns can be combined to allow for tables ranging from one to six column units. In the résumé, the Responsibilities and Education columns are each two units wide; the introductory and summary copy at the top and bottom are each four units wide.

A mnemonic naming system used for tags defines columns by their start and end positions. For example, @COL3-4 indicates a column beginning in unit 3 and ending in unit 4 (in the résumé, the Responsibilities column). The type specs for most tags are identical, except for column positions. Because Ventura lets you base one tag on another, a complete style sheet can be generated fairly quickly.

The text file is created simply by typing the column name followed by the text or call for graphic that that column is to contain.

Once a system like this is created, it can be altered for different configurations, including different page sizes. A more detailed description of the system appeared in *Step-By-Step Electronic Design* (May, 1989), reviewed in the Resource section in this book.

The type design combines the Helvetica Condensed family with Times Roman.

The digitized photos were taken using Aldus Snapshot with a video camera plugged into the computer. They were saved as TIFF files and imported in to Ventura.

Design (above left): Andrew Faulkner (Boston, MA)

Flyer for the WGBH Brown Bag Lunches. Trim size: 8-1/2 by 11

Design (above right): Michael Sullivan (Cambridge, MA)

Corporate résumé for DesignSystems. Trim size: 8-1/2 by 11

This poster for a lecture by two pioneers of electronic art speaks in the language of their subject: the new technology and its impact on graphic design.

A digitized image of the two lecturers is printed almost life-size. The reduction on this page does not do justice to the impact of the 17- by 22-inch poster. This bold enlargement of a digitized image gives the feeling of a glimpse into the future. At a time when we are seeing more and more bit-mapped art (much of it bad), the raw power of the form is particularly evident in this large size.

The text is handled in three panels that jut into the picture plane. A second color (orange) highlights the first name of each speaker and the date and sponsor of the event.

Folded twice, the poster also serves as a self-mailer.

Quoting from the poster: "New electronic formats, including the personal computer, CDs, and video imaging systems, have opened up vast new visual possibilities and have inexorably drawn our profession into a communications environment which is multi-media and interactive. The formerly separate disciplines of writing, visualization, and sound making are joined through these tools. ¶Eric predicts a return to the designer as generalist—fluent in more than one discipline—and feels we need to readjust our notion of what constitutes adequate training for this broader role."

Design: Chris Pullman, WGBH Design (Boston, MA)

Poster for AIGA/Boston lecture by April Greiman and Eric Martin.
Trim size: 17 by 22

10 YEARS OF GREAT RADIO!

RHYTHMIC WARRIOR + YARDBIRD SWEETS + TURNER'S ARENA + SIMPLY JAZZ + THE ARTS CALENDAR + FIRST LIGHT + CAN YOU IMAGINE + G-STRINGS + SMALL TALK + CHILDREN'S RADIO THEATRE + BERIMBAU + YOUR PSYCHIC TOMORROW + VOIGT'S VOICES + PUENTES + PUBLIC NOTICE + CITYSCAPE + BUYER BEWARE-BUYER BE WISE + THE BAMA HOUR + THE ARTS SHOW + EVIDENCE IN THE AFTERNOON + FREEDOM OF SPEECH + GOLD MOUNTAIN + MUSICA DE LOS AMERICAS + BLACK, BEIGE AND BROWN QUINTET + THE WAY WE WERE + THE OTHER SIDE OF THE BAMA + JAZZ CORNUCOPIA + GREEN DOLPHIN STREET + NEW DIRECTIONS + HEALING FORCE + LEGENDARY PROFILES + OUT OF THE AFTERNOON + THE PUBLIC AWARENESS CALENDAR + CARIBBEANA + DIALOGUE WITH DOROTHY HEALEY + AUDIO EVIDENCE + BANBOCH KREYOL + AFRICAN RHYTHMS AND EXTENSIONS + A SUNDAY KIND OF LOVE + BLUE MONDAY + THE JAZZ CALENDAR +

JAZZ

and much, much more...

SOPHIE'S PARLOR + HARVEST TIME + SOUNDS OF SURPRISE + PEOPLE OF THE WORLD + OLD AND NEW DREAMS + THE POET AND THE POEM + CORN BETWEEN YOUR TEETH + NATURAL PROGRESSIONS + I'VE KNOWN RIVERS + SHOCKWAVES + FOOTPRINTS + FIRE IN THE MIDDLE + STOLEN MOMENTS + MIDNITE TRACKS + 2000 BLACK + BRIGHT AND EARLY + BACK STREET JAZZ + GOSPEL EXPERIENCE + SPIRAL + SOFT AND EASY + LET 'EM PLAY

WPFW 89.3 fm

1977

1987

Pacifica Radio
700 H Street, NW
Washington, DC 20001
202-783-3100

Design: Richard Steele, Steele & Co. (Washington, DC)

Poster produced for a radio station's tenth anniversary.
Trim size: 11 by 17

To print oversize pages such as this, you'll need to respond to Ventura's Overlap prompt after you okay the other print specifications. You can print the page actual size on several sheets of paper and manually paste them together. Or for quick proofing, you can "shrink" the output to fit an 8.5- by 11-inch page.

Well-designed type and a two-color scheme can deliver the message and the graphic impact at the same time. The word JAZZ (printed off center in large red type) catches the eye immediately; "10 YEARS OF GREAT RADIO" (reverse type against a gray panel) defines the occasion; and the call numbers 89.3 (off center in large red type) tell you where to tune in. The three horizontal panels toward the bottom of the poster are red, the main body of the text prints gray, and the station's call letters and logo are reverse type on a gray panel.

Two-color printing need not be limited to black and a second color. A screen of black is just a neutral gray, and although this is desireable for publications that include halftones, many more shades of gray are available as PMS colors. The cool blue-gray used in this poster plays off well against the red.

The type is Futura Light and Futura Book, with Futura Bold Condensed for the station's call letters. The designer played with the letterspacing and tracking to get the open effect he wanted for the show listings and the tight spacing for the station's numbers. The .3 in the call number is a superscript. The superscript option provides a useful way to adjust the baseline of type, but you will generally need to play with the size of the superscript to visually proportion it to the adjacent type, as the designer has done here.

When you run on lists of items as a solid text block, both readability and visual appeal are improved by using a type element such as the plus sign in this poster. Extra word space without a type sort (as these elements are traditionally called) would create rivers of white throughout the text.

Rotation of type in Ventura is limited to 90, 180, and 270 degrees. To get the angles used for JAZZ and 89.3, the designer created each of those pieces of type to the desired size and spacing, printed them out, positioned them on the desired angles, and had them scanned at a service bureau. Then he imported each of the digitized images into the Ventura page as art.

FOLDERS

Folders provide a convenient format for promoting products, services, and events. The folded piece can be racked or mailed (either in a standard business envelope or as a self-mailer), and the fully open piece can be used as a poster. The folder format also works well for a series—educational literature and programs, for example; once you have a format worked out, you can make a template and reuse it for each piece in the series.

The mechanics of a folded piece present unique conceptual and design opportunities. Try to use the panels to organize and build on a message, to visually lead readers from the cover through the inside flaps to the fully open piece. A folder, especially a large one, requires more effort on the reader's part than a booklet or brochure, so you need to motivate the reader to begin unfolding the piece to get to the message.

The most common sizes for folders are 8.5 by 11 inches (generally folded in half to create four panels or folded twice to create six panels), 8.5 by 14 inches (generally folded into eight panels), and 11 by 17 inches (generally folded in half twice, or in half and then twice again). When planning the concept and layout, work at full size (you can tape together two or more sheets of paper if necessary) so that you can actually fold the piece and see it as the reader will. Once you have a pencil sketch in this form, you'll need to figure out the most efficient way to assemble the elements in Ventura. For example, if you are doing an 8.5- by-14-inch folder, you might set it up as four 8.5- by 7-inch pages. Keep in mind, also, that flaps that fold in should be a half pica or so narrower than the other panels.

The mechanics of certain folds require that the type in some panels be oriented on a right angle or upside down. Ventura's ability to rotate type 90, 180, or 270 degrees is very useful in these situations, though larger folders will still require some manual pasteup. You will need, also, to indicate fold marks for the printer; use dotted lines outside the image area on the camera-ready art.

Folders in this section

- *World Trade Institute*—a large-format program announcement
- *Holiday Inn System Conference*—a little pizzazz from a triangle border
- *Drugs & Alcohol*—a strong, consistent format for a series of educational folders
- *34 Yerba Buena Avenue*—a model realty promotion
- *Colligan's Stockton Inn*—warm, friendly, and as suitable for mailing as it is for posting
- *Royce Investment Group*—ruled subheads, effective and easy
- *InFractions*—the spotlight on fashion
- *Family Programs*—a poster format for three months of museum events
- *Historic Hudson Valley*—tourist attractions in an 11-by-17 format

World Trade Institute 1988-89 Program

Developing New Markets Through Exporting

This is the first is a series of educational programs organized by the World Trade Institute designed to develop and sharpen the export skills of managers of Atlantic Canadian companies.

The program takes a *highly interactive approach* to the delivery of practical information so that course attendees can put their new skills to work immediately. The program also allows for exporters and those seriously considering export trade to meet and discuss issues of mutual interest.

Each session of the program incorporates case materials from Atlantic Canadian companies whenever possible. Classes will focus on group discussion and group work. Participants will learn directly from guest resource people in various industries, and will make use of computer-assisted instruction, videos, simulations and role playing. This innovative program promises to provide participants with a stimulating and effective method of gaining sound knowledge of the requirements for successful export trade.

Opening Reception
September 11, 1988

1. What you need to know to be a successful exporter
September 12 & 13, 1988
Faculty: Dr. Mary Brooks, Dr. T.S. Chan

This first session of the program will teach you *how to carry out an effective information search.* You will learn what information sources are most useful, their cost, how to access them, and how to decide on your best markets.

2. Creating an Export Strategy
October 17 & 18, 1988
Faculty: Dr. Norman McGuinness, Dr. Donald J. Patton

Strategic thinking allows you to plan for – and create – export opportunities. This session investigates *exporting as a prime business philosophy* as opposed to an afterthought of domestic operations. Subjects include using exports as a way to grow and spread risk; the issue of long term commitment; and how to develop a practical export game plan.

5. Promoting Your Export Product
February 13, 1989
Faculty: Dr. Donald J. Patton, Dr. Philip Rosson

In *Promoting your Export Product you will learn how effective sales and marketing communications programs are created, what services and materials are required, and how much they will cost.* This session will also teach you how to prepare for differing trade customs that affect language, currency, packaging and advertising. *Special emphasis will be placed on using trade fairs and sources of promotional assistance.*

4. Making the Export Deal
January 9 & 10, 1989
Faculty: Dr. Mary Brooks, Dr. Norman McGuinness

Making the Export Deal will teach you what you need to know in order to make the export quote. This session defines the fundamentals of exporting: *Pricing, Documentation, Transportation and Foreign Exchange.* Topics to be explored include negotiating tactics, coping with cultural differences when securing an export contract, transportation alternatives, and the effect of efficient distribution on long-term price competitiveness.

Awards Dinner
February 13, 1989 at the World Trade Club

For further information see the back of this poster, or contact the World Trade Institute for a brochure and registration form.

World Trade
INSTITUTE

3. Decisions, Decisions! Entering and Expanding Export Markets
November 21 & 22, 1988
Faculty: Dr. T.S. Chan, Dr. Philip Rosson

This session looks at the pros and cons of using agents, distributors, and selling direct. The first day highlights *the importance of choosing the right distribution system – and then making it work.* Day two focuses on living with your decisions: establishing, managing and ending the relationship.

PO Box 955
1800 Argyle Street
Halifax, Nova Scotia
B3J 2V9
Telephone: (902) 428-7233
Fax: (902) 422-2922

The World Trade Institute is a partnership of the World Trade Centre Halifax, Nova Scotia; the Centre for International Business Studies at Dalhousie University; and the Nova Scotia Department of Industry, Trade and Technology.

Please Post

Developing New Markets Through Exporting

A program designed
to develop and sharpen
the export skills of
managers of Atlantic
Canadian companies.

World Trade
INSTITUTE

1988-89 Program

The primary function of the cover of a folder is to get you to unfold it. And art that continues from one panel to another uses the physical properties of the format to achieve that purpose. In this sample, art bleeding off both sides of the cover leads the reader to the next panel (not shown), where the loops of the arms are completed. The fully open folder repeats the art.

The logo incorporates a subtly playful effect by transposing the sans serif d in "World" with the serif d in "Trade." Note also the spacing of the word "Institute" to match the length of the words above it.

The type is organized so that each panel contains a different text unit. This works particularly well for a program or series in which each event can be featured, as they are here. Numbering each event reinforces the organization.

The "Please Post" tab in the lower right is also visible in the half-folded position because of the cropped upper-right corner.

Design: Paul Hazell,
Communication Design Group Limited
(Halifax, Nova Scotia)

Folder for the World Trade Institute training programs.
Trim Size: 11 by 17, folded in half and then folded twice accordion style

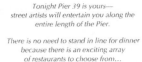

Tonight Pier 39 is yours—
street artists will entertain you along the
entire length of the Pier.

There is no need to stand in line for dinner
because there is an exciting array
of restaurants to choose from…
and they will all be pulling out the "stops"
to make you feel welcome this evening!

So don't linger too long in one spot
or you will miss many colorful
moments along the way
in this "night to remember".

☆ ☆ SCHEDULE OF EVENTS ☆ ☆
6:15 PM
Shuttle transportation to begin from all hotels to Pier 39.
6:30-8:00 PM
"A TASTE OF THE WINE COUNTRY" --- Northern California is known as one of the world's premier wine producing regions. Tonight several of our foremost wineries will be offering some of their best vintages for a true California wine tasting. Hors d'oeuvres will be served to compliment these fine wines.
6:30-9:30 PM
BLUE AND GOLD FLEET
From 6:30 to 9:30 we will have 1/2 hour bay cruises for those of you who want to see the beautiful San Francisco skyline from the Bay.
8:00 PM
Enjoy panoramic views at each of the restaurants which will be hosting you this evening. Restaurants will be ready to host you starting at 6:30 pm. Please feel free to dine at your leisure.
9:00-10:00 PM
Shuttle transportation to hotels from Pier 39 will begin at 9:00 p.m. Last motorcoaches will depart at 10:00 p.m.

The triangle border (far left) is actually a column of Zapf Dingbat diamonds positioned with their centers at the trim so that half of the diamonds would be cropped off, thus creating the triangles. The folder itself is a 9 by 11-3/4 landscape page (the cover shown is the right third of one page). But in order to bleed the diamonds as described, the designer worked on an 11 by 17 page and created the actual page size as a frame within that. To create this border effect, you need to play with the leading until the characters are flush; the ones here are 32/23.

A boxed schedule (left) uses tinted banners to organize the events of the evening. This highly structured approach quickly delivers a clear sense of the program. The other two panels of the open folder fill out the picture with a list of restaurants and wineries participating in the event.

Design (left): Carol D. Finkelstein (San Francisco, CA)

Folder from Holiday Inn Conference. Trim size: 9 by 11-7/8, folded twice

Design (below): Jim Parker (Phoenix, AZ)

Drugs & Alcohol folder published by the Do It Now Foundation. Trim size: 14 by 8-1/2, folded in half twice to create four panels

Organization and continuity for a series of pamphlets (below) are created through the use of rules, banners, geometric shapes, and intial caps .

The display type is Avant Garde; the body text is Helvetica. The type prints in purple, and the rules and shapes print in rose.

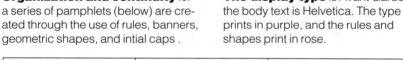

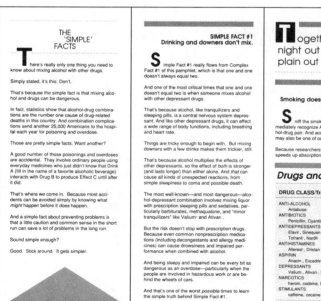

34 Yerba Buena Avenue

St. Francis Wood Traditional

Address: 34 Yerba Buena Avenue

Price: $529,000

Abstract:
LOT SIZE: 60' x 75' HEATING: Central gas
FLOORS: Hardwood YEAR BUILT: 1923
PLUMBING: Copper ZONING: R1-D
ELECTRICITY: 220 V

Main Level: Living Room with fireplace, formal dining room, kitchen, sunroom, and one half bath.

Upper Level: Three bedrooms, one bath.

Lower Level: Full basement, laundry area, one car garage.

St. Francis Wood Dues: Approx. $340/year

Description: This two story traditional home is located in prestigious St. Francis Wood. Behind its distinguished facade this residence offers all the character and craftsmanship of a vintage 1920's home while offering all the modern conveniences available today.

The main level of the home features a large living room with a picture window overlooking the park-like backyard towards the ocean. This room has a large wood burning fireplace. The dining room adjoins the center entry hall and is generously proportioned for entertaining. Mayta Jensen remodeled the sunny kitchen which includes a dishwasher, garbage disposal, instant hot water tap, tile counters, fine cabinetry and all the built-ins. There is a breakfast area and a sun room adjoining the kitchen. All three rooms overlook the garden. A guest half bath completes this floor.

The second floor has three separate bedrooms and one full remodeled split bath featuring Corian counter tops and tub enclosure. The grand sized master bedroom along with a second bedroom have views to the ocean and walk-in closets.

The lower level contains a full basement with a laundry area, storage, and a one car garage with an automatic door. This level has access to the large landscaped backyard perfect for children at play.

For further information call:

Greg Germano Century 21 Fox & Fox Realtors
(415) 665-0330 100 West Portal Avenue
San Francisco, CA 94127

Design: Donna Kelly, Zetatype (San Francisco, CA)

Folder for Century 21 Fox & Fox Realtors.
Trim size: 8-1/2 by 11, folded in half

Real estate promotions are well-suited to desktop publishing. Once you create templates and style sheets for different formats, you can very quickly plug in the specifics for each new property.

The art used on the cover and inside of the folder is a pen-and-ink drawing that was manually stripped in to the electronically-composed pages. For less expensive properties, you could scan a black-and-white photo, or paste in a photostat or even a good quality photocopy.

Gray speckled textured paper suggests the high quality of the property being sold.

The contrasting typefaces— Helvetica Black, Helvetica Light, and Garamond—make the information easy to read and attractive.

The right aligned Helvetica heads create a clean gutter for the flush left information that follows. This is a good example of how the choice of typeface and alignment interact. In addition to defining the relationship of one piece of type to another, the alignment of elements also defines the white space on the page. In this particular page, if you visualize the headlines flush left, you will see a very raggedy space between the two kinds of information; either the gutter between them would be uneven, or the left margin of the Garamond type would be uneven.

Designed for multiple use, this folder can be tacked up on bulletin boards fully open, while the folded piece functions as a self-mailer.

A warm, friendly, cheerful image is conveyed through the art style, typography, and newspaper-like composition. The flavor is just what you'd want from a country inn during the holiday season.

The typeface is New Century Schoolbook. It prints in green on a gray textured paper.

Borders and rules help organize the small items, which are set to different measures.

The art was created by hand and pasted onto camera-ready pages.

Each panel of this accordion-fold design (facing page, bottom) features a different clothes style. The panels were assembed on-screen, two to a page, and two pages were pasted together for each four-panel side of the camera-ready art.

Silhouette photos work well for fashion because they highlight the shape of the clothes. The contrast between dark and light, front and back, and large and small adds to the casual liveliness of the composition. Although the larger photos share a common ground, the smaller ones bounce playfully around the page without regard for perspective. The interaction of the image with the background in a context that defies logic brings a fresh spatial energy to the page. Three additional styles, similarly formatted, are printed on the reverse side of the sheet.

The pattern through the center was created in the page layout and echoes the subtler pattern behind the logo. It's a decorative motif especially well suited for fashion literature.

The typeface is Goudy Old Style. Labeling is minimized to keep the spotlight on the clothes. The type and pattern print in teal blue with black accents.

Design (left):
Carla Bond Coutts
(Lahaska, PA)
Folder for
Colligan's
Stockton Inn.
Size: 8-1/2 by 14,
folded in half
twice

Design (facing
page, top):
Beverly Kay
Rubman
(Westbury, NY)
Folder from Royce
Investment Group,
Inc.
Trim size:
8-1/2 by 11,
folded twice,
accordion style

Design (facing
page, bottom):
Edward Hughes
(Evanston, IL)
Folder from
InFractions, Inc.
Trim size:
17-3/6 by 10-1/8,
folded three times,
accordion style

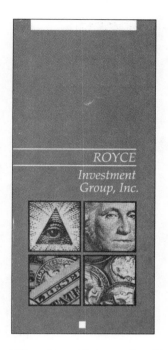

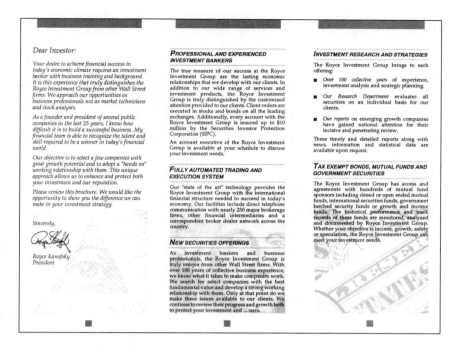

The art on the cover, which was produced as a conventional halftone, is repeated inside in very light gray. You have to be extremely careful surprinting type over art in this way. If it compromises readability at all, you'll loose the reader for sure.

The cover type is Palatino, which has a very elegant and readable italic.

Ruled subheads are easy to create and work with using Ventura's style sheets. The tag for each head incorporates the following specs: the paragraph is 11-point Helvetica bold

italic; the "Big First Letter" (Ventura's endearing label for an initial cap) is 14 points; the Ruling Line Above is 0.5, column width, with 2 points above; the Ruling Line Below is 0.5, column width, with 3 points below. Add a line or two to any section and all the rules move with their respective subheads.

A quarterly program of events is designed as a poster, with different styles of art interspersed throughout the listings. Folded, the piece is suitable for self-mailing and is also easily racked in the museum lobby and bookstore.

The headline and names of months are Franklin Gothic Demi. The listings are in the Helvetica family.

The use of color and the space around each listing make it very easy to check out the programs on any given date.The main headline, banners at the top of each column, highlighted events, and dates print in red.

All elements—art, borders, and computer-generated type—were manually pasted onto artboard to create the two oversize pages for the camera-ready art.

Design: Ann Wassmann Gross (Chicago, IL)
Program from The Art Institute of Chicago. Trim size: 10-7/8 by 22-5/8, folded four times to create five panels

---

Family Programs · Fall '87

September

Sanat Şöleni: A Summer Festival of Turkish Arts
daily through September 7
12:00-3:00 Miniature Painting

Turkish Craft Demonstrations
through September 5
Tuesday, Thursday, Friday, and Saturday
12:30-2:30 Uğur Derman, Calligraphy
F. Çiçek Derman, Embroidery

Gallery Walks and Art Activities

Saturdays and Sundays, 2:00-4:00
Theme: Hispanic Arts in conjunction with the exhibition "Recent Developments in Latin American Drawing"
Saturday, September 12, 19, & 26
Sunday, September 13, 20, & 27

Artist Demonstration

Every Saturday and Sunday from 12:30-2:30
September: Carlos Cortez, Woodcut and linoleum-block printmaking

Arty Animals

Saturday, September 26   Age: 6 and older
Visit the Art Institute's galleries in the morning followed by a lunch break and tour of the Lincoln Park Zoo.

10:30-11:45	Gallery Walk: Animals in Art
11:45-1:00	Lunch on your own Provide your own transportation to zoo
1:00-2:30	Animal Walk: Lincoln Park Zoo
Cost:	$2.00 Member (adult or child) $3.00 Non-member (adult or child)

Name	# of children
Address	# of adults
City	State Zip Code
Telephone number	
Member	Non-member

$
Amount enclosed
Send check payable to *Museum Education*
Mail to: The Art Institute of Chicago
Department of Museum Education
Family Programs
Michigan Avenue at Adams Street
Chicago, IL 60603

October

Saturday, October 3
10:30-11:30 Early Birds: Once Upon a Time
1:00-2:00 Gallery Walk: American Art
2:00-4:00 Family Workshop: A Story in a Picture

Sunday, October 4
12:30-1:30 Early Birds: Once Upon a Time
12:30-1:30 Drawing in the Galleries
2:00-4:00 Family Workshop: A Story in a Picture

Saturday, October 10
10:30-11:30 Early Birds: Over and Under
1:00-2:00 Gallery Walk: That's What They Wore
2:00-4:00 Family Workshop: Weaving

Sunday, October 11
12:30-1:30 Early Birds: Over and Under
12:30-1:30 Drawing in the Galleries
2:00-4:00 Family Workshop: Weaving

Monday, October 12
1:00-3:00 Columbus Day Special: Family Workshop

Saturday, October 17
10:30-11:30 Early Birds: Animal Kingdom
1:00-2:00 Gallery Walk: Vase to Vase
2:00-4:00 Family Workshop: Symbolic Animals

Sunday, October 18
12:30-1:30 Early Birds: Animal Kingdom
12:30-1:30 Drawing in the Galleries
2:00-4:00 Family Workshop: Symbolic Animals

Saturday, October 24
10:30-11:30 Early Birds: Pablo's Palette
1:00-2:00 Gallery Walk: French Art
2:00-4:00 Family Workshop: The Eye of Picasso

Sunday, October 25
12:30-1:30 Early Birds: Pablo's Palette
12:30-1:30 Drawing in the Galleries
2:00-4:00 Family Workshop: The Eye of Picasso

Saturday, October 31
10:30-11:30 Early Birds: Tricks or Treats
1:00-2:00 Gallery Walk: Masks and Cover-ups
2:00-4:00 Family Workshop: 'Day of the Dead' Celebration

Artist Demonstration
Every Saturday and Sunday from 12:30-2:30
October: Noreen Czosnyka, The art of wall stenciling

Storytelling
Every Sunday from 2:00-3:00
October: Carmen Aguilar, Latin American folk tales

November

Sunday, November 1
12:30-1:30 Early Birds: Tricks or Treats
12:30-1:30 Drawing in the Galleries
2:00-4:00 Family Workshop: 'Day of the Dead' Celebration

Saturday, November 7
10:30-11:30 Early Birds: A Taste for Art
1:00-2:00 Gallery Walk: Portraits and Pictures
2:00-4:00 Family Workshop: The Delicious Still Life

Sunday, November 8
12:30-1:30 Early Birds: A Taste for Art
12:30-1:30 Drawing in the Galleries
2:00-4:00 Family Workshop: The Delicious Still Life

Saturday, November 14
10:30-11:30 Early Birds: Funny Food
1:00-2:00 Gallery Walk: Travel Plans
2:00-4:00 Family Workshop: Soft Sculpture

Sunday, November 15
12:30-1:30 Early Birds: Funny Food
12:30-1:30 Drawing in the Galleries
2:00-4:00 Family Workshop: Soft Sculpture

Saturday, November 21
10:30-11:30 Early Birds: Blue Plate Special
1:00-2:00 Gallery Walk: Art of Italy
2:00-4:00 Family Workshop: Designing Dishes

Sunday, November 22
12:30-1:30 Early Birds: Blue Plate Special
12:30-1:30 Drawing in the Galleries
2:00-4:00 Family Workshop: Designing Dishes

Friday, November 27
1:00-3:00 Special: "Day After Thanksgiving" Workshop

Saturday, November 28
10:30-11:30 Early Birds: Incredible Edibles
1:00-2:00 Gallery Walk: Animal Kingdom
2:00-4:00 Family Workshop: Edible Art

Sunday, November 29
12:30-1:30 Early Birds: Incredible Edibles
12:30-1:30 Drawing in the Galleries
2:00-4:00 Family Workshop: Edible Art

Artist Demonstration

Every Saturday and Sunday from 12:30-2:30
November: Lorraine Peltz, Still Life painting

Storytelling

Every Sunday from 2:00-3:00
November: Assorted tales by assorted tellers

Historic Hudson Valley

Kitchen at Van Cortlandt Manor

View of West Point from the Highlands

Miniatures at Montgomery Place

S ettled largely by ambi-
tious and adventure-
some immigrants from
Europe, the Hudson Valley
saw great tracts of land held
by single families and culti-
vated by tenant farmers.
Frederick Philipse came to
New Amsterdam from Hol-

*Matisse Window, Union Church of
Pocantico Hills*

land as a carpenter and soon
owned better than 50,000
acres of land. From the wharf
at Philipsburg Manor, Upper
Mills, flour and other goods
were shipped to ports all
over the world. Today,
young visitors enjoy the
antics of spring lambs on the

farm, while watching early
American technology at work
in the water-powered grist
mill.
Owners of the vast Van
Cortlandt Manor were among
the most influential families
in New York as the new
American nation emerged.
Pierre Van Cortlandt was the
state's first Lieutenant Gov-
ernor and his son Philip
served both as an army officer under General Wash-
ington and as a United
States Congressman. Visi-
tors to the Manor today
find elegant antiques and
beautifully restored gar-
dens which capture the
spirit of this leading Hudson
River Valley family.
Washington Irving, famed
author of "Rip Van Winkle"
and "The Legend of Sleepy
Hollow," often said that in
all his European travels he
had seen nothing to com-
pare with the view of the
Hudson from the porch at
Sunnyside. Irving trans-
formed what had been a
small, Dutch farm cottage on
the Philipse Manor into a
picturesque country home he

called his "snuggery."
Winding pathways along the
river, hillsides of daffodils in
the spring and the cozy, hos-
pitable atmosphere of Sunnyside combine to make
today's visitors feel they have
been the guests of this em-
inent Hudson Valley squire.

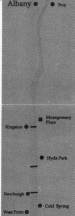

Albany

Troy

Kingston

Montgomery
Place

Hyde Park

Newburgh

Cold Spring

West Point

Bear
Mountain

Van Cortlandt
Manor

Philipsburg
Manor

Union
Church

Tarrytown

Sunnyside

New York City

Montgomery Place, one of
the ancestral homes of the
Hudson Valley's prominent
Livingston family, will open
to the public in June, 1988.
The 23-room mansion was
built by Janet Livingston
Montgomery, widow of
Revolutionary War hero
General Richard Montgom-
ery, and later remodeled by
America's leading 19th-
century architect, Alexander
Jackson Davis. Visitors will
want to linger on the more
than 400 acres of land at
Montgomery Place, savoring
the beauty of the woods,
streams and gardens, taking
in the views of the river
and the Catskill
Mountains, and
picking fall apples
in the estate's
orchards.

*Montgomery Place, Annandale-
on-Hudson*

A unique complement to
the other properties of **Historic Hudson Valley** is
the Union Church of
Pocantico Hills, where
light is transformed
into vivid color
through stained glass
windows created by
modern masters Henri
Matisse and Marc Cha-
gall. The modest stone
sanctuary contains the
only cycle of church
windows by Chagall in
the United States.

The collections of **Historic
Hudson Valley** represent in
every detail the people who
have lived on the banks of the
river. At each of the four
historic properties, original
family and authentic period
furnishings, objects and
works of art are on display.
Paintings by many important
American artists are apparent, as are children's toys,
handwoven textiles and
looms, simple kitchen uten-
sils and farm implements,
fine porcelains and silver.

*Van Cortlandt Manor (right)
Philipsburg Manor (below)*

*Philipsburg Manor (above)
Christmas at Sunnyside (left)*

Discover
Historic
Hudson
Valley

Sunnyside
Philipsburg Manor
Van Cortlandt Manor
Union Church of Pocantico Hills
Montgomery Place

**The elements needed to pro-
mote tourism** work well in this 11-
by 17-inch sheet, folded first in half
and then in thirds.

The front cover, with its oval-
shaped detail of an old engraving
and centered format, suggests that
this is the official guide to the region.

The tall orientation of the fully
open sheet works well for a stylized
map of the river valley. The river
prints in blue, the surrounding valley
in green. A detailed road map appears on the back cover (not shown).

A five-column format accommodates photos of different sizes and
shapes to break up the text.

The photographs, all in color,
were stripped in by the printer. Picture frames were positioned during
electronic pasteup to facilitate the
text wrap.

Design: Wadlin & Erber (New Paltz, NY)

*Folder published by
Historic Hudson Valley.
Trim size: 11 by 17, folded in half and
then twice again*

BROCHURES

Brochures provide a broader creative challenge than many other kinds of publications. Because they are generally one-shot efforts, intended for use over a relatively long period, more time, effort, planning, and money is often allocated to their development. The challenge, for writers and designers, is to come up with a theme or concept that is unique to the needs of that message for that audience at that particular time. The solution should *look* obvious once it is executed, although of course the conception and development of that absolutely right idea may have taken months of research, analysis, brainstorming, and rethinking of hypotheses, as well as many rounds of rough sketches and format changes along the way.

As the samples in this section demonstrate, there is considerable variety from one brochure to another and even within the pages of a single brochure. The styles are as diverse as the messages they convey; they range from straightforward simplicity to complex persuasion, from the stylishly new wave to the classically elegant, from the quietly dignified to the boisterously bold.

Even the size and shape of the page varies more in brochures than in other kinds of publications. This is partly because brochures are often produced in small press runs where the cost of paper isn't so critical, and partly because brochures often have generous budgets that can absorb the increased cost of a nonstandard paper size. As you'll see in some of the samples, an unusual size or an odd shape feels fresh to the eye just because it's different. Of course nonstandard sizes also give designers an opportunity to create unusual solutions to familiar problems and to play with the shape itself as part of the design motif. But unless the solution is a good one, the shape alone won't carry the message.

Brochures in this section

- *inFidelity: Keith Yates Audio*—stylishly active design
- *Clackamas Community College*—a strong, simple concept
- *Pitney Bowes Mail Management*—a lesson in variety
- *Success Encyclopedia*—well organized and accessible
- *Washington, DC Convention & Visitors Association*—graceful typography and generous white space
- *Why Design?*—a five-column grid with punch
- *European Terracotta Sculpture*—quiet sophistication
- *Arthur D. Little*—a map metaphor for the future
- *ML Technology Ventures*—a conservative style with a little animation
- *ML Media Partners*—a dynamic, narrow-column format
- *Subscription Programs*—compact information in an elegant format
- *Islam and the West*—the photographic story of a TV series
- *Sacramento Regional Foundation*—bit-mapped art and mug shots
- *Alaska Vacation Planner*—a magazine format for an official state guide

A sales brochure that calls itself a newsletter borrows editorial techniques from the newsletter format.

Each product is treated as a self-contained unit with its own design, and each spread has a different composition. The contrast and varied texture make each spread feel like a collage.

Two unifying elements balance the seemingly dominant diversity: an underlying four-column grid and a stylishly high-tech design that provides its own continuity.

Silhouette photos focus attention on and dramatize the product.

Computer-assembled gray tones of different values, such as the light gray of the first two letters of the logo against the darker gray of the banner, register perfectly. In traditional pasteup it would be virtually impossible to achieve a clean edge with overlapping gray tones.

Design:
John McWade,
PageLab
(Sacramento, CA)

Brochure published by Keith Yates Audio.
Size: 8-3/8 by 10-3/4

A simple concept, well executed, makes for a very effective four-color recruitment brochure for a small college.

The cover borrows techniques from advertising design, with large, centered display type expressing a single bold statement. When you use this technique, the statement had better be right on target for your audience.The inside pages answer the question implied on the cover.

Each spread follows an identical layout, creating a strong sense of continuity that orients readers very quickly to the information on the page. This would become monotonous in a longer publication. (Two additional spreads, not shown, do vary from this format, and a bind-in card provides a checklist of additonal information the prospective student can request.)

The strong concept and controlled continuity of the layout require considerable planning. Creating and refining pencil sketches before you begin work on the computer can save a lot of time in this sort of project.

Each spread uses a different color scheme keyed to the box in the upper left corner. (The number in that box prints in reverse type.) The color is used in the banner above the student quote and as a tone behind the boxed copy on the right-hand page.

The bleed photos on the inside spreads heighten the strong horizontal axis created by the rule above them. Actually, there are elements that bleed on all four sides of the spread, setting up a visual tug of war that makes the pages very dynamic.

The principle of contrast is used very effectively here. The angled photos on the right-hand pages contrast with the crisp, clean rectangles that dominate the rest of the layout. These photos are also black and white, whereas the others are in color. And the two small photos play off against the one large one on each spread.

The typeface is Garamond throughout.
Body text:12/20
Captions: 9/11 italic
Numbers: 96 point
Headline: 60 point condensed

Condensed Garamond is currently very "hot" in display typography. Few readers are aware on a conscious level that a particular font is in fashion, but there are subliminal effects to seeing a typeface that has a lot of media penetration. As is true with any kind of fashion, trends in typography change quickly.

Design:
Ralph Rawson
(Oregon City, OR)

A student recruit-
ment brochure for
Clackamas
Community
College.
Trim: 8-1/2 by 11

3. A price you can afford.

Tuition at CCC is $23 per credit hour, or $230 per term for a full-time student.* That's less than half the cost of tuition at a state university, and a fraction of what you'd pay at many private colleges. It adds up to a sensible, economical solution to the rising cost of a college education.

"Can I get financial aid?"
Last year, nearly half of CCC's full-time students received some kind of financial aid — an average of ___ per student! The chances are good that ___ work study pro-

Chrissy Pagh
Freshman, Gladstone
"I chose Clackamas because I knew the quality of the classes was equal to a four-year school, without having to pay the money. I haven't had a teacher yet who hasn't been great. And because the classes are small, there's a lot more inter-action and a lot more learning."

2. Courses that count.

Planning to transfer to a four-year institution?
All lower division college transfer courses at Clackamas Community College are fully accredited and transferable to any college or university in Oregon, and to public and private institutions throughout the country. ___ can take your freshman and soph-___ a junior to

Neale Frothingham
Sophomore, Oregon City
"Having been here for a year, and realiz-ing how good the instruction is, I realize I made the best choice educationally that I ever could have made. The size of CCC definitely enhances the quality of educa-tion. It's very personal."

1. Teachers who care.

*In class and ___
students get ___
Opportunities ___
theatre, spo___
instrument___
student go___
student ne___
mural spo___
20 specia___
ranging ___
mountain___*

Clackamas Community College is a public two-year college with an annual enrollment of 2400 full-time and 8600 part-time students. The campus is located on 175 acres of forest and farm-land in the foothills of the Oregon Cascades, 20 miles southeast of downtown Portland.

Personal attention to your learning needs comes first at Clackamas Community College. Our classes are small (average size: 21 students). Our teachers can take the time to get to know you, to find out where you're going, and to help you get there. Our total commitment is to make your college experience a success.

At Clackamas, you can explore creative writing with an award-winning novelist, learn algebra with the man who wrote the textbook, or play in the band with some of Oregon's most sought after musicians. CCC's faculty includes nationally recognized experts on sub-jects ranging from computer-aided drafting to Middle Eastern history.

But our most important recognition comes from former CCC students. In surveys, letters, and inter-views, they consistently say that the personal attention they got at Clackamas was a major reason for their success — in college and beyond.

CCC graduate Laura Onstott
(with chemistry instructor Margi Arighi)
"Margi made the class interesting, and fun, and always challenging. She always made me feel that I could succeed. By the end of that year, I knew I wanted to get a degree in chemistry." (Laura, now a senior at Reed College, was recently awarded a scholarship by the American Chemical Society.)

Everything you need to succeed.
CCC backs up your classroom experience with first-rate student support services, including:

☐ Program planning with CCC's expert team of counselors and advisors.

☐ Career planning and job placement assistance with the resources of CCC's Career & Job Development Center.

☐ Personal tutoring by CCC instructors and advanced students.

☐ The Computer Lab, with tutors on hand to help you build vital math and computer skills.

☐ And, if you're not yet ready for college level course-work, individualized instruction in basic reading, writing, math, and study skills (including high school completion programs).

Clackamas Community College is an equal opportunity, affirmative action institution.

An ambitious, high-budget production gives both the company and the designer an opportunity to dramatize their message. Although the resources to execute a brochure like this may be beyond your budget, the publication has elements you can incorporate in more a modest undertaking.

The story in this brochure is that managing mail is a complex business. The opening page (not shown) contains a single small photo of a row of rural mailboxes and begins, "There was a time when getting the mail out was pretty simple...." When you turn to the page shown below, the helter-skelter array symbolizes the choices, the pace, and the complexities of today's mail.

The words put the pictures into context, and the pictures dramatize the words. The story, as it unfolds on the next spread (not shown), is that increasingly complex mail systems require increasingly complex paperwork. But "Whatever you're sending, no matter where, we can show you how to get it there, how to prepare it for going, how to account for it after it's gone."

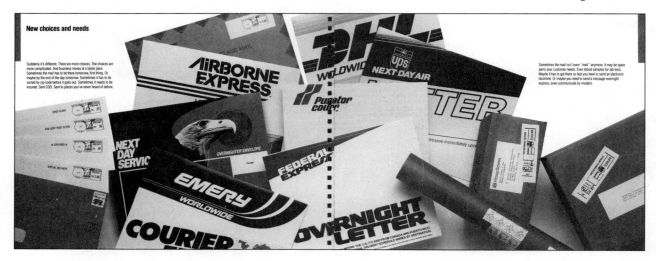

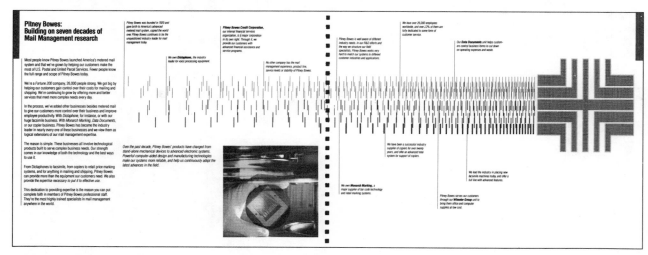

The direct statement of what Pitney Bowes is and what products it offers is presented as time-line-style captions to a piece of art that suggests the speed and intelligence of today's technology. The symbol on the far right is the company logo.

The information is broken down into accessible pieces. The very direct, well-written statement in the left column is only about 250 words long, with very short paragraphs. Each captionlike statement describes a different service or division of the company.

The strong, three-column grid is apparent when you compare the spread shown above to the one at right. The horizontal structure that runs across both is maintained throughout the 34 pages. This grid brings a feeling of order and control to pages that contain a wide variety of photos, charts, diagrams, documents, and other visuals.

The large photo in the spread below introduces a new service and adds yet another texture as you turn the pages.

Subtle graphic humor is seen throughout the brochure. A tortoise-and-hare metaphor is used in the diagram on this spread to compare the old and new meter refill service.

The typeface throughout the brochure is Helvetica Condensed for body text, Helvetica Condensed Black for headlines, and Helvetica Condensed Oblique for captions and for contrast with the opening text. The type treatment is kept simple to balance the diversity of the art and layout, with a crisp, modern, efficient look that is obviously appropriate to the subject.

Design: Weisz Yang Dunkelberger Inc. (Westport, CT)

Pitney Bowes brochure entitled Building on Seven Decades of Mail Management Expertise. *Trim size: 11-1/4 by 8-1/2*

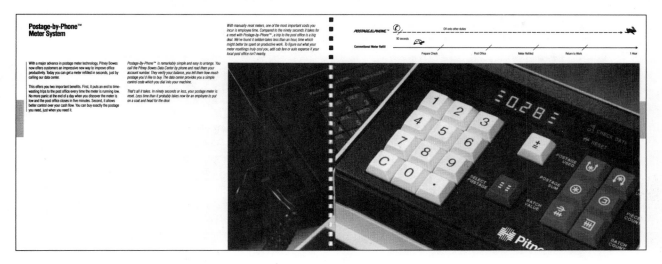

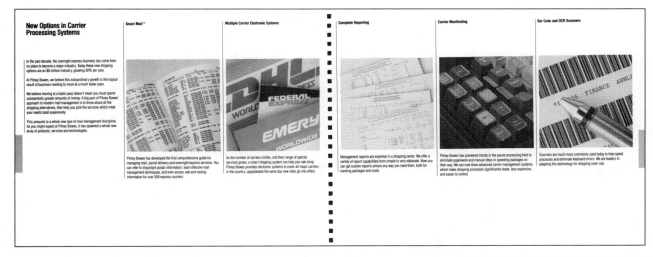

The structure of the grid is most apparent in the spread shown above. The sequence of photos with headings above and text below suggests a series of pigeonholes that echo the partitioning inherent in sorting mail. The grid reinforces an image in which nothing is accidental, everything is tightly choreographed.

The nine-unit grid used in this brochure is diagrammed at right. It provides a useful structure for organizing a horizontal page.

168 Mentors

This anthology series contains 168 chapters—each one by a different person. (It's like having 168 *mentors* on call whenever you need their help or advice.) Contributors include Dorothy Jongeward, author of the 2,000,000 copy bestseller, *Born to Win*; Jim Tunney, the well-known National Football League official—a highly popular motivational speaker; and Cavett Robert, founder of the 4,000 member National Speakers Association—someone who's inspired audiences totalling millions in a dozen countries around the world.

Everything You Could Possibly Want—And More!

The content of this series is as rich as you'll find in self-help book collections costing many times this price. Here, you'll discover inspiring chapters by people who've overcome severe financial, physical and medical handicaps. You'll learn success techniques from experts on self-image psychology, creativity, stress management, negotiating, interpersonal skills, goal setting, time management, body language, active listening, self-motivation, and much more. Just about every single topic of interest to a public speaker is addressed in this series.

Learn From The Best!

There are close to three thousand pages in this SUCCESS ENCYCLOPEDIA. *Anyone* who desires a more fulfilling life will benefit from chapters by psychologists, career and business consultants, psychiatrists, sales professionals, and even successful artists. As we said, most of these authors are enormously popular national and international public speakers—people paid thousands of dollars for each talk they deliver at conventions, seminars, success rallies, company meetings and intensive training sessions.

Professional Production Standards—Start To Finish

Once these success experts agreed to participate in the project, most of them provided recordings of their best live presentations. (A small number of contributors submitted manuscripts—as is more customary in the publishing industry.) The tapes were transcribed into manuscript form. Next, all of the information was painstakingly crafted into chapters by a small team of professional authors and editors. As an added touch, it was decided that each chapter would feature a biographical sketch and photograph of the author. Today, the completed SUCCESS ENCYCLOPEDIA is a unique collection of twelve numbered volumes, each containing fourteen digest-style condensed chapters.

> *"I have really enjoyed the convenience of dipping into the series anywhere I like.*
> *It's great to review a single chapter without feeling the need to read the preceding chapter*
> *or the one following. It's a great resource and a terrific, time-saving concept."*
> Barbara W. Emery, President, "Looking Terrific"

Digest-Style Convenience!

The digest-style, stand-alone feature of each chapter is enormously popular with our readers. They love being able to pick and choose from among the 168 chapters without losing the slightest continuity. It's like feasting at a lavish smorgasbord of motivational, inspirational and self-help ideas. With *Build A Better You—Starting Now!*, you don't have to struggle chapter-to-chapter, cover-to-cover through a cumbersome text just to get a few key ideas. Every single chapter is a distillation of ideas—the *essence* of the material each speaker/author covers in his or her most popular live presentations.

> *"An extremely varied resource. ...Excellent!"*
> Stephen Ash, PhD

First Time Available As A Complete Series!

Since the first book in this SUCCESS ENCYCLOPEDIA series was published, hundreds of thousands of copies have been sold—but not in stores. Up until now, these volumes have been available almost exclusively from the speakers themselves—and never before as a full set.

Each volume in this series has been sold at the list price of $12.95—and well worth it! (That's $155.40 for the set.) Now, we are able to offer this unique SUCCESS ENCYCLOPEDIA at less than half price.

That's Right—Less Than Half Price!

For just $69.95, a limited number of people (first come—first served) can enjoy the entire series and experience the combined expertise of 168 motivational and self-help professionals. You can benefit from this SUCCESS ENCYCLOPEDIA at less than $6 for each idea-packed, hardcover volume! (To make you purchase an even easier decision, we've arranged to accept your bank credit card.)

With an opportunity like this, we know you'll understand when we explain that this is a limited time offer. Order early to avoid disappointment! (Please include $4.85 for shipping plus California sales tax—where applicable—with your order.) Act now—you'll be glad you did.

VOLUME 10	VOLUME 11	VOLUME 12
Whole-Person Excellence: The Wellness Lifestyle by Donald B. Ardell, Ph.D.	**The Three Imperatives** by Harry N. Peelor	**Success Has Its Price** by Rose Lane
Becoming "Becoming" by Orv Owens, Ph.D.	**I Want To Change, But I Don't Know How** by Tom Rusk, M.D. and Randy Read, M.D.	**This Is Your Life, Not A Dress Rehearsal** by J. Steven Cates
Love, K.I.S.S., And Quassilassitude by Alys Swan	**Write On!** by Nancy Lyle Bennett	**Spotlight On Achievement** by Terrence J. McCann
How To Acquire And Manage Information by Dennis R. Briscoe, Ph.D.	**Women Feeling Good, Working Good** by Patricia A. Mitchell, Ph.D.	**Design Your Destiny: Be The Architect Of Your Future** by Ralph M. Ford
The Power Of Silent Signals by Maxine McIntyre, CSP	**Attitudes And Opportunity** by Ronald G. Zinnemeister	**Managing Your Life And Your Job** by Michael F. "Mike" Baber, P.E.
Make Your Own Magic by John H. Edwards	**Visualization Training: Programming Yourself For Success** by Sharon Fleming	**A Message To Parents From A Grown-Up Kid** by Mark Rhode
You Are What You Think by Doug Hooper	**It's O.K.** by Wally Minto	**Risk-Taking: Why Are You So Afraid?** by Beverly Kievman
Moving Through The Corporate Crowd by Robert L. Bailey	**The Cookie Jar Caper** by David L. Ward, Ph.D.	**Leadership And Mangement** by Clifford B. Bertram, C.L.U.
A Strategy For Success: Setting Career Goals by Louis Olivas, Ph.D.	**How Public Relations Can Earn You A Doctorate In Living** by Mort Stein	**Happiness Is Balanced Growth** by Wayne W. Cotton, C.L.U.
Living With Stress by Dr. Joyce and Dr. Robert Brockhaus	**The S.T.P. Syndrome** by Mary Lee Williams, M.A.	**How To Cheat And Stay Healthy** by Gary L. Couture, Ph.D.
Overcoming Organizational Barriers by Johanna S. Hunsaker, Ph.D.	**Cobwebs Of The Mind** by J. Paul Boyer	**Wise Seamen Don't Cross Shoalwaters** by Robert Kausen
The Real Key To Motivation by Paul J. Micali	**Happyrich Secrets To Success And Wealth** by "Positive Paul" Stanyard	**Living Life On Purpose—Not By Accident** by J. Terryl Bechtol
The Ultimate Partnership by Robert C. Spaan	**A Personal Flight Plan** by Bob Miller	**Managing Stress For Success** by Rosalind Newton, CSP
A Winner Never Quits by Lonnie C. Johnson	**Total Perspective** by Douglas H. Tanner	**Reaching The Summit** by Gordon D. Hawkins
243 pages	242 pages	242 pages

The purpose here is to organize simple material in a clean, orderly way. Doing that well suggests that the product—in this case, a series of self-help books—is similarly well-organized.

The ruled subheads are created with Ventura's style sheets. The tag is 18/36 Palatino bold italic centered; the custom ruling line below is a 0,5 rule with 2 points above, a 1,10 pica indent, and a width of 34,02 picas. The rules are printed in red. The body text is 10/11 Palatino, and the inset quotes are 10/12 Palatino italic.

The volume numbers (left) are 16/18 Franklin Gothic Heavy. The article listings are 8/9 Palatino with 9 points between listings.

The rules between the volume boxes are also red. They can be generated automatically in Ventura by turning on the Inter-Column Rules option on the Vertical Rules menu.

Design:
Carol D. Finkelstein
(San Francisco, CA)

Brochure for a book series from the Showcase Publishing Company.
Size: 8-1/2 by 11

The gracefulness of Palatino italic, the organization provided by rules, and generous white space are the cornerstones of this design.

The header is 16-point Palatino italic. Note the differences between the headers on the pages shown. On the contents page, the ruling line above the type has a custom width of 14 picas to maintain the center alignment of that page. On the spread below, the rule is defined as column width to maintain the grid established by the vertical rules.

The contents type is 12/15 Palatino bold, centered. The page numbers are bold italic, with 5 points of space below.

The open leading on the inside spread balances the white space of the pages. The text is 12/18 Palatino italic. The initial cap is 36 points and is printed in burgundy.

Note the consistent space between the edges of the photos and the boxes around them.

Design:
Richard Steele,
Steele & Co.
(Washington, DC)

Annual Report for the Washington, DC Convention & Visitors Association.
Size: 8-1/2 by 11

National Cherry Blossom Parade

4

INDUSTRY OVERVIEW

*E*ach year the Washington area's hospitality industry contributes over $2 billion to the local economy through visitor spending on lodging, food, transportation, entertainment, gifts and other incidentals; this dynamic industry sustains more than 53,100 jobs for area residents.

During 1988, the total number of visitors to Washington continued a steady upward trend that has continued for the past decade. The Association's annual estimate of 19.6 million visitors to the nation's capital reflects a 3% increase over 1987.

As Washington's primary tourism and convention marketing organization, WCVA is pleased to present the following summary of 1988 programs which have contributed significantly to the continued growth of our city's second-largest industry.

5

The organization of complex, multitiered information is the fundamental challenge in many publications. This tutorial about the effective use of electronic design addresses that very issue and uses the techniques it espouses. Information is broken into manageable "chunks," and the importance of different elements is made readily apparent through the use of headlines, rules, numbers, and color.

The handwritten annotations are red; the 6-point rules above headlines, the highlighted quote, and the marginal copy are green. Red and green spot color is also used in the diagrams.

The format combines different kinds of editorial material—running text, charts and diagrams, numbered points, quotes offset from the main text, and even handwritten annotations of typeset words. The mix of techniques gives readers different ways to enter the page. It must be carefully organized in order not to backfire.

The five-column grid uses an 8-pica measure with 1 pica between columns. The wider columns in the top spread are 17 picas wide (two of the five-column units plus the space between).

The typography adheres to the principles of simplicity and familiarity—Helvetica and Times Roman are used throughout.

Design: Watzman + Keyes (Cambridge, MA)

Brochure entitled Why Design? *published by Watzman + Keyes Information Design.* Trim size: 8-1/2 by 11

Information Design

The *visual*
- *intuitive*
- *easier to remember*
- *less effort by the reader*
- *pre-processed*

Automation and Communication
Most users of electronic publishing focus on automation and assume that communication will take care of itself. They are mismanaging the technology and missing rare opportunities to achieve three things simultaneously:
- **Increase impact and effectiveness** by ensuring that information gets noticed, understood, used and remembered.
- **Develop proprietary, customized systems of graphic standards** to ensure quality and consistency, increase market visibility and streamline the production of communication materials.
- **Leverage the value and competitive advantage that EP technology promises** by encoding standards in software and systems as proprietary templates or style sheets.

Critical Trends

The following trends affect you and your organization's bottom line:

Growing demand for customer services | Diminishing labor supply | Growing demand for publishing services | Information overload

1987 — 1990 | 1987 — 1990 | 1987 — 1990 | amount of information

Growing Demand for Customer Services
The profusion of "smart" products has led to demand for materials which explain them. Clearly, products a customer does not understand, serve neither the customers nor the maker. Careful attention to passive...

Diminishing Labor Supply
The U.S. faces a severe labor shortage at a time when communication skills are at a premium. Since electronic publishing requires skilled professionals, the gap is widening. Design cannot be automated any more than writing can be... serious loss of...

Growing Internal Demand for Publishing Services
When customers demand service, managers demand more support – and control and faster turnaround. Electronic publishing creates demand, accelerates production, and decentralizes a process which, because it used to be slow,...technical and...

Information Overload
There really is such a thing as "too much information." When people are bombarded with more information than they need or can use, their performance actually suffers. Too much information *increases* error-making, *reduces* attentiveness, and *induces* boredom and dissatisfaction. This is a clinical fact which surging docu... ...tion will ...In the ...th informa- ...r business.

The Need for Corporate-Wide Graphic Standards Systems (CoGSS)©
The current emphasis of electronic publishing vendor marketing is on the *freedom* and *flexibility* which their systems provide to individual users. But the "Sorcerer's Apprentice Problem" makes clear that *decentralization* and *loss of corporate control* in the visible area of communications is not good for business. The result is *decreasing quality, decreasing effectiveness, loss of corporate image* and *poor product recognition*.

But electronic publishing technology has another capability which has yet to be developed: it can set consistent, well-defined, customized default standards for published materials (CoGSS). Such standards eliminate much of the time-consuming activity that goes into publishing. At the same time, standards enforce quality and consistency by providing a matrix of solutions to a broad range of communication needs.

The Information Design Perspective: Cognitive Human Factors as a Basis for Design
CoGS Systems produce two outcomes: **First**, they provide dramatic managerial control over staff use of money, time and materials. They do this by providing a matrix of predetermined solutions to communication problems. Typical problems are solved in advance, or solved the first time they occur. After that, producers of communication materials are guided by clear procedures which ensure consistency and quality.

Second, CoGS Systems significantly enhance the value of printed materials by using human factors techniques to improve the usefulness of information to readers. With "smart" products which require extensive documentation or complex sales messages, improving reader response has a significant impact on sales, marketing efforts, customer satisfaction, customer service and training costs.

As a growing number of leading companies are discovering, arriving at a performance-oriented CoGS System makes good business sense. Approaching the problem requires skill and knowledge in four areas:

Sensitivity to the importance of careful, informative, writing;

Background in the relatively new field of cognitive human factors;

Education and experience in design and the development of Corporate Graphic Standards Systems;

Familiarity with the proliferating range of EP technologies.

"Information is easier to remember when it is in an orderly state, rich in pattern and structure, highly interconnected, containing a good deal of redundancy.
Disordered information that lacks structure is easy to forget."
Jeremy Campbell
Grammatical Man

Developing a CoGS System
Because of the range of disciplines required to develop a CoGS System (and the short-term nature of the projects), companies often turn to outside firms for assistance–and do so before they buy electronic publishing equipment.

Based on experience with Fortune 500 companies, threshold companies and high technology start-ups, Watzman+Keyes has developed a six-stage process for developing a CoGS Systems. The process insures that the system uses *both* capabilities of electronic publishing: it *improves* staff productivity and *enhances* user satisfaction and performance. This six-stage process incorporates research, design, testing and training into an efficient cycle that gives clients cost-effective solutions prior to automation.

The Information Design Process: Six Steps to a Graphic Standards System

Analysis → Development → Production

1 | 2 | 3 | 4 | 5 | 6
Define | Examine | Design | Test | Codify | Monitor

What is Information Design?
Information design is a truly professional process which integrates technology, design and cognitive science to achieve three ends:

1 *Streamline* the process of creating documents and communication materials;

2 *Improve* the impact, effectiveness and quality of communication programs and materials;

3 *Manage* the transition to high technology-based print communication programs.

Phase 1: Define
Define the business problem. Who is sending the message? for what purpose? using what technologies? What constraints exist (budgets or staffing, etc.)? What degree of control or decentralization is advisable or realistic? This phase ends in a *compilation and review*.

Phase 2: Examine
Understand the users. Who are they? How do they use information ? What are their backgrounds and educational levels? Do they have unusual constraints? This and Phase 1, are a complete *communication audit*.

Phase 3: Develop
Brief the design team so they can develop design alternatives (several alternatives are necessary for valid testing). This results in a *presentation of alternatives* to the staff who will use the CoGS System.

Phase 4: Test
According to Nobel Laureate and A.I. expert, Herbert Simon, "Design is both the *development* and *testing* of alternatives." In this phase, alternatives are subjected to cognitive testing. The results are used to *refine* the CoGS System.

Phase 5: Codify
Once the CoGS System is developed it can be codified in software or in a manual. These products are used to train staff about the CoGSS System. Electronic publishing *fundamentally alters* the way documents are produced and the way people work, so this phase includes training in teamwork as well as system familiarity.

Phase 6: Monitor
This phase ensures that the system does the two things it is supposed to do: helps *staff* be productive and helps *users* learn complex equipment and tasks easily.

10   11

9

European Terracotta Sculpture
from the Arthur M. Sackler Collections

The Art Institute of Chicago / December 9, 1987 - March 6, 1988

end of the eighteenth century. Clodion's ex-
quisite terracotta statuettes (nos. 19 and 20)
captivated Rococo collectors. In his suite,
Neoclassical sculptors, such as Simon Louis
Boizot (no. 22) and Joseph Chinard (no. 23),
perfected his smooth, sensuous surfaces.
French artists also adopted the medium for
the portrait bust, enlivening this formal type
with the vivacity of touch possible in terracotta. Pajou, in his Bust of Corbin de Cordet
de Florensac (no. 24), achieves a sense of
motion and captures the sitter's alert gaze
with the flicker of a modeling tool through the
hair and incisions in the pupils. Such Rococo
portrait conventions were revived in the nine-
teenth century by Carrier-Belleuse (no. 29).
Nineteenth- and twentieth-century sculptors
flaunted the rugged surfaces of worked clay.
The brooding power of Rodin's Titans (no.
31) is emphasized by the retention of the
scumbled surfaces and blocky musculature
of the figures in their adaptation to the form
of a vase. Jagged, seemingly random gouges
in Vallmitjana's Wounded Bullfighter (no.
30) underline the violence of the subject. The
deliberate roughness of Martini's figural
studies expresses barely containable energy
(no. 33).
Changing attitudes toward terracotta over
the six centuries represented in this exhibition
are representative of similar developments
throughout the visual arts. One is the shift in
attitude toward the medium; it is less important to us today what materials are used by the
artist than how they are manipulated. Another
is our desire to see the traces of the artist's
encounter with the medium—our interest in
the process of creation as well as the finished
product. These beautiful studies and finished
works amply demonstrate the role of terracotta in the development of sculpture from the
Renaissance to the twentieth century.
This exhibition has been selected from over
one hundred examples in the Arthur M.

Sackler collections. In 1981-82 a larger exhibition of these holdings circulated to The
National Gallery of Art, Washington, D. C.,
The Metropolitan Museum of Art, New York,
and the Fogg Museum, Boston. It is a great
pity that Dr. Sackler's death last May pre-
vented him from the pleasure of seeing his
objects in this and other exhibitions from his
collections presented this year. We are most
grateful to the Sackler Foundation for continuing with plans for this show at such a difficult time and for its generous support for this
project. Dr. Lois Katz, Administrator of the
Sackler Foundation, has provided invaluable
advice and assistance.

Ian Wardropper
Associate Curator
European Decorative Arts and Sculpture

This exhibition was funded by The AMS Founda-
tion for the Arts, Sciences and Humanities,
Washington, D.C. and the Arthur M. Sackler
Foundation, Washington, D.C.
The Chicago exhibition was partially supported
by the John D. and Catherine T. MacArthur
Foundation Special Exhibitions Grant.

Jan Baptiste Van der Hoegen
Flemish, 1688-c. 1740
Saint Joseph Holding the Christ Child, c. 1723
Terracotta statuette

Giuseppe Maria Mazza
Italian, 1653-1741
David Triumphant over Goliath, c. 1675/1725
Terracotta statuette

**The quiet, elegant sophisti-
cation** of this brochure projects an
image that is completely different
from any of the other documents in
this section. The style is entirely
appropriate for the subject of 17th-
and 18th-century terracotta
sculpture.

**The brochure is an 8-1/2- by
25-1/2-inch sheet folded twice**
to make six 8-1/2- by 11-inch pages.
Shown are the cover and the right-
hand page of the fully open
brochure.

**Contrast is an effective
element** in this design. The
saturation of the full bleed, sepia-
toned cover plays off against the
generous white space of the open
text pages as well as the silhouetted
shapes inside the brochure. The
reverse type in the cover banner is
set off like a plaque from the cover
art. Note the open letter spacing in
the brochure title, which improves
legibility of reverse type in relatively
small sizes.

The text is 9/14 Times Roman
italic in a 14-pica column. The use of
italic for running text is unusual
because it is generally difficult to
read. Here it adds to the traditional
elegance; the open leading and
surrounding white space compensate to improve readability.

The justified text is in keeping
with the formality of the design. The
hard edge of the right margin works
better with silhouette photos than a
ragged right margin would.

The silhouettes are enhanced
by other elements in the design. The
rules at the top of the page, from
which the text seems to hang, create
a free but defined space for the
shapes. The captions are set on a
half-column grid so as not to
interrupt that space.

*Design: Joseph Cochand,
The Art Institute of Chicago*

*Brochure for a show of European
terracotta sculpture at
The Art Institute of Chicago.
Trim size: 11 by 25-1/2, folded twice*

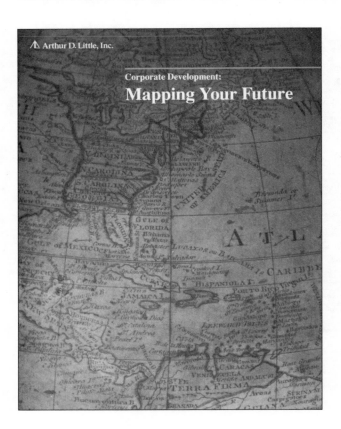

The theme of this campaign—guiding corporate clients through the future—suggested the map metaphor. Hence the title, Mapping Your Future, and the graphic direction.

The globe on the cover was found in an old museum and photographed for use in the brochure. The full bleed image on the cover (left) opens to reveal the contour of the globe on the inside cover (below left). The photograph of Earth from outer space provides a visual contrast to the globe, reinforcing the message that "The world has changed." As you examine the elements of the pages here, you can see how the selection and layout of the graphic elements are inextricably tied to the message in this well-designed piece.

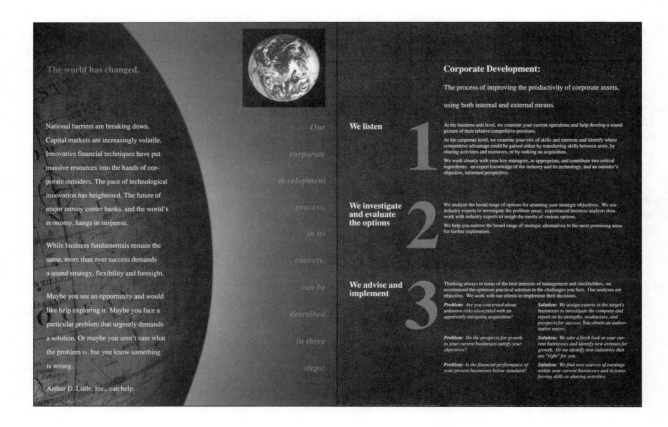

The typefaces are Times Roman and Helvetica. Resident on most laser printers, these are probably the most frequently (and blandly) used of all typefaces in desktop publishing. They were required in this brochure to conform to the company's design standards, yet they don't limit the layout or the type style at all. Reverse type, varied column widths and leading, and large numbers are among the elements that lend diversity to the most familiar faces.

The wide image area needed for the page below is made possible by a gatefold—an 11- by 25-1/2-inch sheet, folded twice. The gatefold is bound in to the center of an 11- by 17-inch sheet, folded once. You don't start with the idea of using a page configuration such as this; it evolves out of the elements created to deliver your message.

The contrast between old and new continues on the open gatefold, where old black-and-white engravings are juxtaposed with color photos representing contemporary products and new technologies.

The illusion of depth is created through a variety of techniques. Overlapping images will in themselves almost always create a sense of depth. Here, the map recedes in the background, the engravings float in the middle ground, and the color photos push into the foreground. Cool colors recede (the map is printed in cool shades of blue and gray), warm colors advance (the photos have lots of red and orange and are framed by 3-point orange rules). The amount of detail in an image also determines its relative perspective, with simpler, softer images receding and more detailed ones advancing. You can see that the designer has worked not only with the height and width of the page but also with the depth.

Design: Art director, Michael Sullivan; Designer, Kris Busa (Cambridge, MA)

Brochure for Arthur D. Little, Inc.
Trim size: 8-1/2 by 11

Gen-Probe, Inc.

Gen-Probe is a leader in medical products based on genetic probe technology. Clinical laboratories use the Company's products to diagnose infectious diseases in humans. Most current infectious disease testing relies upon slow culture techniques which require days or weeks to get a test result. Gen-Probe's tests provide more accurate results within hours, allowing physicians to treat infectious diseases more quickly and effectively.

To date, the Food and Drug Administration (FDA) has approved ten of the Company's genetic probe products, more than all other companies combined. This includes a recently approved test for chlamydia, an infectious disease which has traditionally been difficult to accurately diagnose. Gen-Probe is also in the early stages of applying its genetic probe technology to cancer diagnostic and therapeutic products. Chugai Pharmaceutical Company, Ltd. of Tokyo has signed a letter of intent to market some of Gen-Probe's products in Japan and other selected Asia/Pacific countries and to fund Gen-Probe's development of cancer and viral diagnostic products. Gen-Probe raised $16.3 million in an initial public offering in September 1987 managed by Merrill Lynch Capital Markets.

Gen-Probe and ML Technology Ventures are developing genetic probe test systems to diagnose urinary tract infections (UTI). Through the end of 1987, the Company has spent 81% of the Partnership's $5.75 million commitment. An estimated 60 million UTI tests are performed annually in the United States, more than any other microbiology diagnostic test. Gen-Probe's first UTI system is being submitted to the FDA in mid-1988.

Interleaf, Inc.

Interleaf is a leader in high performance computer-aided publishing systems sold primarily to business, government and universities. Interleaf's systems integrate text processing and graphics at the desktop to create a full range of documents on a customer's in-house computers. These include executive presentations, reports, proposals, forms, manuals and viewgraphs.

ML Technology Ventures and Interleaf aim to expand the market for Interleaf's software by adapting it to several widely used computer systems in the United States and in Europe. Through the end of 1987, the Company has spent 57% of the Partnership's $3.5 million commitment. Interleaf is beginning to sell the first of the Partnership's new products, a high performance desktop publishing system designed to run on Apple's Macintosh II™ computer system. The Company has also adapted the product to work in 13 different languages, including French and German, and expects to begin shipping in Europe during 1988.

Photon Technology International, Inc.

Photon Technology International, Inc. (PTI) is a pioneer in developing electro-optical systems which use the properties of light as advanced analytical or therapeutic tools. The Company also supplies proprietary components to other manufacturers who use them as building blocks in a wide range of electro-optical systems. This building block approach allows PTI to rapidly and cost effectively develop its own complex systems for customers in medicine, environmental science, industrial process control and at prestigious research centers around the world.

During 1987, Photon Technology completed an initial public offering of stock and grew rapidly with employees increasing from 18 to 60. In November, the Company established a Canadian subsidiary which produces nitrogen and dye lasers used in both medical and industrial applications.

ML Technology Ventures and PTI are developing one major new product and several product line extensions for existing systems. Through 1987, PTI has spent 27% of the Partnership's $3.2 million commitment. The first of the product line extensions is expected to be ready for installation by mid-1988. Development work on the major new product and the other product line extensions continues on schedule and under budget.

7

Plant Genetics, Inc.

Plant Genetics, Inc. (PGI) uses biotechnology to make agricultural products including early generation seed potato tubers, proprietary alfalfa and proprietary tomato seed. PGI's proprietary Nu-Spud™ system allows the seed potato farmer to produce commercial quantities of potato tubers twice as fast as in traditional systems. Nu-Spud products address a U.S. market for potato tubers estimated to be $160 million per year and international markets which are estimated to be larger. During 1987, PGI made arrangements to tap these markets in the future by way of a joint venture in Europe, a licensing agreement in Japan and a marketing agreement in Argentina. In alfalfa, PGI introduced five more proprietary varieties during the year; its sixteen total varieties now address 70% of the U.S. alfalfa market. PGI completed an initial public offering in June 1987.

ML Technology Ventures and PGI are aiming to improve the four most common varieties of PGI's Nu-Spud products. These improvements are particularly important for processed potato markets and use PGI's expertise in somatic cell genetics and somaclonal variation. In addition, the R&D venture aims to improve disease resistance using proprietary molecular biology techniques. Through the end of 1987, the Company has spent 42% of the Partnership's $2.5 million commitment. The R&D program is currently on plan and under budget.

United AgriSeeds, Inc.

United AgriSeeds, Inc. (UA) is an agricultural biotechnology company which develops and sells new corn hybrids and soybean varieties. The Company uses both conventional plant breeding and genetic engineering techniques to develop proprietary products. UA is one of the 10 largest domestic seed corn producers with about $30 million in sales last year. Sales of corn seed account for the majority of the Company's revenue. During December 1987, The Dow Chemical Company (Dow) of Midland, Michigan purchased the stock of this privately-held company for $44.5 million. This gives Dow a presence in the seed corn industry which compliments its presence in agricultural pesticides. As a result of the Dow acquisition, the Partnership received approximately $750,000 for its warrant position in UA and the Partnership is exploring ways to adjust the R&D program to mutually benefit all parties.

ML Technology Ventures and UA set out to develop new corn hybrids over a three-year period. UA has spent 28% of the Partnership's $5.7 million commitment. Over 3,000 new corn hybrids will be tested by UA for the first time this spring. The development work to date has proceeded on schedule and under budget.

Wyse Technology

Wyse Technology develops, manufactures, and markets a family of display-based computer products. The Company's strategy is to provide terminals, personal computers and application workstations with superior price-performance features. Wyse continued to expand its broad product line in 1987 with the announcement of a new family of IBM-compatible personal computers based on Intel 80386™ and 80286™ microprocessors.

In its seven-year history, Wyse has achieved an impressive financial record of growth with current sales in excess of $100 million per quarter. Management has kept the Company poised for further growth by building a new manufacturing facility, achieving record profitability and maintaining a strong financial condition. Wyse Technology employs approximately 3,600 people worldwide.

ML Technology Ventures meets bi-monthly with Wyse's technical and corporate staff to review progress on the R&D venture. Through the end of 1987, the Company has spent 62% of the Partnership's $2.4 million commitment. Wyse is meeting its performance and budgetary goals for the new computer products under development. The Company is scheduled to begin shipping test models of the initial family of products in the second half of 1988.

8

Television abc

Nationally syndicated game and talk shows, hit movies, soap operas and coverage of the 1988 Winter Olympics all contribute to the improved ratings of the Partnership's two ABC affiliated television stations.

KATC-TV
Lafayette, Louisiana

KATC-TV is an ABC affiliate broadcasting on Channel 3 from Lafayette to south-central Louisiana. Since the acquisition was completed on February 2, 1987, the Partnership has:

- Increased operating margins and cash flow and reduced operating expenses.
- Installed new top management, including a General Manager and Business Manager.
- Showed substantial gains in ratings, particularly among households with viewers in the 25-to-54 age range, the most desirable demographic grouping.
- Purchased new syndicated programming, including Oprah Winfrey, Wheel of Fortune and Jeopardy, under favorable long-term contracts.
- Launched a promotional campaign on new programming and station services to viewers.

KATC-TV Market: Serving the 113th ranked television market (referred to by advertisers as the Area of Dominant Influence, or ADI), KATC-TV is one of three stations in its 195,000 television household ADI and one of five stations (three VHF and two UHF) in south-central Louisiana, comprising the highest per capita income market in the state. The station was previously operated by a not-for-profit educational institution and was considered, at the time of acquisition, to be undermanaged by professional broadcast standards. The market served by the station had experienced an economic downturn because of its heavy dependence on oil production. Recently, efforts for economic diversification have shown results and a recovery is underway. An indication of the attractiveness of this market was the sale of the CBS affiliate, also a VHF station, in January 1988, for $51 million. Eleven months earlier, the Partnership acquired KATC-TV for approximately $26.8 million.

KATC-TV Programming: The broadcast schedule was revamped to increase revenues from advertisers on local and syndicated programs. The addition of new syndicated shows, particularly Oprah Winfrey, is strengthening ratings and improving audience carry over into ABC network programming. In addition, a new News Director was hired and local news coverage was expanded with more in-depth and investigative reporting, strengthening KATC-TV's position as the number-two rated TV news station. Strong sports programming is also offered, including preseason New Orleans Saints NFL games and the local University of Southern Louisiana football games.

6

WREX-TV
Rockford, Illinois

WREX-TV is an ABC affiliate broadcasting on Channel 13 to Rockford, Illinois and to the border counties in southern Wisconsin. Since the acquisition was completed on August 31, 1987, the Partnership has:

- Increased operating margins and cash flow and reduced operating expenses in the first four months of operations.
- Purchased rights to the Bill Cosby Show for its syndication debut in the fall of 1988 and initiated negotiations for favorable, long-term commitments for other highly rated syndicated programs.
- Improved overall Arbitron ratings from a weak third place (May 1987) to a solid second ranking (February, 1988) in terms of ADI share of viewing.
- Hired a new General Manager and is in the process of recruiting other top level management.
- Developed promotional and marketing strategies to increase advertising sales by taking better advantage of the station's superior signal strength.

WREX-TV Market: Serving the 115th largest ADI television marketing area, WREX-TV is one of four stations (one VHF and three UHF) in its 447,000 household ADI and its signal covers Rockford, the second largest city in Illinois, and border counties in southern Wisconsin. WREX-TV, the area's only VHF station, has a signal that is stronger than the three other competing UHF channels. That competitive advantage was not fully exploited by the prior owners but the Partnership immediately capitalized on WREX-TV's clear, far-reaching signal superiority by instituting new broad advertising promotions. The viewing area is largely rural, with Rockford serving as its transportation, manufacturing, retailing and medical center.

WREX-TV Programming: The program schedule is undergoing evaluation and reformatting to accommodate a stronger line-up of syndicated shows. In addition, local news and sports coverage has been expanded and more aggressively packaged. The WREX Eye Witness News at 5 p.m. is now rated number one in its time period. Basketball is avidly followed by the viewing audience and WREX-TV has instituted live broadcasts of high school and college games, including the sale of its telecasts to other stations. Advertising revenues should increase due to the favorable ratings impact the Bill Cosby Show is expected to have on its time period and on the programming preceding and following the show.

7

The narrative sections of the two annual reports on the facing page illustrate how similar approaches can be executed for rather different effects.

A conservative image for a technology partnership (top) is created through three 14-pica columns with their headlines aligned under bleed photos. A geometric grid over the photos playfully obscures their boundaries and softens the formality of the design. This adaptation of the video technique of blending is especially appropriate for the subject of technology. And instead of six static product shots, it creates an animated photo mural. The uneven bottoms of the text columns also loosen up the page and allow flexibility in copy length for each item. The text is Helvetica Condensed Light with Helvetica Condensed Bold subheads.

A more dynamic style is created for a media partnership (facing page, bottom). The narrow, 10-pica columns have uneven tops and bottoms, and text can continue from the bottom of one column to the top of the next. The running text is a condensed Cheltenham with Helvetica Bold for contrast. The rather extreme condensing of the body text works in these narrow columns, where the page is designed with a strong vertical emphasis.

Design (facing page, top and bottom): Emil Marin, Mayo-Infurna Design, Inc. (New York, NY)

Annual Reports for Merrill Lynch Technology Ventures (top) and Merrill Lynch Media Partners (bottom). Trim size: 8-1/2 by 11

Design (this page): Mary Grace Quinlan

Subscription programs brochure from The Art Institute of Chicago. Trim size: 4-1/2 by 10-3/4

Subscription Series

John Singer Sargent

Kent Lydecker, Executive Director, Department of Museum Education

Tuesday evenings, February 10, 17, 24, and March 3, 6:00-7:00, repeated on Wednesday afternoons, February 11, 18, 25, and March 4, 1:00-2:00

This series complements the *John Singer Sargent* exhibition, on view at the Art Institute February 7 to April 19. Kent Lydecker will present lecture I, II, and IV. Laurel Bradley, Director of Gallery 400, University of Illinois, Chicago, will present lecture III.
I *American Artists Abroad: Sargent in the Expatriate Tradition*
II *The Contemporary Scene: Sargent's Europe*
III *Sargent as a Portraitist*
IV *The Unsung Sargent: The Boston Murals*

John Singer Sargent. *The Fountain, Villa Torlonia, Frascati,* 1907. Oil on canvas. Friends of American Art Collection.

Four 1-hour sessions. Member: $30. Public: $40 Student (with ID) $20. Single tickets sold only at the door on the day of the lecture. Member: $9.50. Public $12. Student (with ID): $5. Meet in Morton Hall.

From Mice to Magic: Film Animation

Moderator: Richard Peña, Director, Film Center, School of the Art Institute

Sunday afternoons, 2:00-3:30, March 15, 22, 29, and April 5

Screen animation is one of the oldest and most popular cinematic traditions — Mickey Mouse is at least as well known internationally as Charlie Chaplin or John Wayne — yet the history and development of the art of animation is usually treated at best as a footnote to film history. In this series, issues in the history of animation, along with exciting new developments in the field,

Betty Boop

will be discussed in lectures featuring the screening of relevant films.

I *Animation in the Silent Cinema: The Pioneers — Emile Cohl, Windsor MacKay, and Lotte Reiniger* Donald Crafton, Professor, University of Wisconsin, Madison, and author of *Before Mickey*
II *Animation in the Studio Era: Mickey Mouse, Betty Boop, and Popeye and Their Creators such as Tex Avery, Chuck Jones, Max Fleischer, and Walt Disney* Maryann Oshana, Northwestern University
III *The Techniques of Screen Animation: cels, pin-screen, sand, clay, puppets, and*

"direct animation." Stephanie Maxwell, Visiting Artist, School of the Art Institute, and prize-winning animator
IV *Animation in the Eighties and Future Possibilities* Stephanie Maxwell

Four 1-1/2 hour sessions. Member: $45. Public: $60. Student (with ID) $30. Single tickets sold only at the door on the day of the lecture. Member: $14. Public: $18. Student (with ID): $7.50. Meet in Fullerton Hall.

Baroque and Rococo Art and Architecture in Austria and Bavaria

Robert Eskridge, Lecturer, Department of Museum Education

Monday afternoons, April 6, 13, 20, and 27, 1:00-2:00 repeated on Tuesday evenings, April 7, 14, 21, and 28, 6:00-7:00
Throughout the 18th century a spring-like efflorescence of building and decoration shaped the cities and country villages of Austria and Bavaria. Situated between Italy and France, the region absorbed the best qualities of both to create the distinctive

J.M. Fischer and J.M. Feichtmayr. *Gilded Stucco Cartouche, Priory Church, Diessen, Bavaria.* 1732-34.

monuments of the age. The series traces the Baroque and Rococo from its birth in Rome and Paris to its transformation in Central Europe.

I *The Origins of Baroque and Rococo in Rome and Paris*
II *The Baroque and Rococo in Austria*
III *The Bavarian Rococo Church*
IV *Munich and Würzburg*

Four 1-hour sessions. Member: $30. Public: $40. Student (with ID): $20. Single tickets sold only at the door on the day of the lecture. Member: $9.50 Public: $12. Student (with ID): $5. Meet in Morton Hall.

Johann Bernhard and Joseph Emmanuel Fischer von Erlach. *Karlskirche, Vienna, Austria.* 1716-33.

The long, vertical page of the brochure shown above is typical of museum programs. The shape fulfills two very different needs: In its vertical orientation, it is easily racked at information desks and museum stores; in its horizontal orientation, it's a self-mailer.

The two-column grid accommodates several self-contained items on a spread, with headlines in a second color (green here) for easy scanning. Variety on each spread increases the chance of getting the reader's interest.

The body text is 10/11 Garamond. The headlines are 11/13 Garamond bold italic.

Even though the photographs are small, the combination of the narrow page and narrow column width (11 picas) keeps them from looking like postage stamps. Art can also be sized to a two-column width.

This program guide for a TV series, *Islam and the West*, relies heavily on four-color photos to tell its story. The page composition varies considerably from spread to spread, depending on the size and placement of the pictures.

When selecting and placing several photos on a page or spread, keep in mind how they play against one another. When a visually literate eye is at work, as it is here, the photos work together to make a dynamic composition.

Contrast in subject, scale, direction, and color all contribute to the composition. It shows travel by land, travel by sea, and the gold coin that was the very reason for these century-old trade routes. The caravan moves back into the picture plane, the ship moves in a plane perpendicular to the caravan, and the movement of both contrasts with the still life of the coins. The vastness of the mountains makes the caravan seem small, and the coins smaller still. Consider also the visual forms themselves—the jagged mountains, the linear caravan, the circular coins, and the rickety lines of the ship.

The headline treatment at the top of each spread provides a strong unifying element given this varied compositon. The 3-point rule runs from one outer margin to the gutter, bleeding across the gutter (unless there is a full-bleed picture on one page of the spread).

The type is New Baskerville.

Design: Ira Friedlander (New York, NY)
Program guide for Islam and the West, *a television film series.*
Trim Size: 6 by 9

---

5. TRADE AND COMMERCE

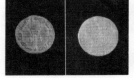

To this day caravans of camels still travel the Silk Route, long the only land link between East and West.
Left, Omani dhow.
Right, Islamic coins.

Islam seeks never to separate everyday life from religion. A person's livelihood and his beliefs are linked and he is taught that social and economic justice—and charity—are worthy matters. Thus Islam has always supplied trade and commerce with a formidable religious base.

After the death of the Prophet, both the religion of Islam and Muslim political and economic domination spread with amazing rapidity. So, outward from the heartland of Islam they came—Muslims traders travelling up and down the coast of Africa, across the Sahara, over the Silk Route to China, through the Indian Ocean to the Orient.

The sea routes, which the Muslims controlled, were crucial for the economic life of the Islamic world, as well as for trade between the Far East and Europe. Accounts of travel by sea to distant lands captured the imagination of Islamic peoples and entered into their literature in stories such as 'Sinbad the Sailor' in The Thousand and One Nights.

Over the land routes, traders carried ideas along with spices, silk and paper from the East to the Islamic world and through it to the West. Traders also played a role in the transmission of technology, for example in bringing paper and papermaking from China.

The importance of travel in their lives led Muslims to develop geography on a global scale. Always in their journeys, they relied on a singularly important instrument, the astrolabe. The astrolabe gave these traders their bearings, and gave the West the tool with which to reach the New World. Columbus would have been lost without his astrolabe and maps plotted by Muslim traders. Prince Henry the Navigator depended not only on that device, he also had a Muslim pilot.

Everywhere they went, the Muslim traders brought the Quran, their book of guidance, as well as their science, their art, and their culture.

The cover art was derived from a piece of clip art that was digitized and enlarged in the electronic page layout. The effective, bit-mapped result bears little resemblance to the fine-line style of the original art. It prints burgundy on a tan background. The same art was reduced for use as a decorative element at the bottom of each page.

The "border within a border" page frame provides a space for the organization's name letterspaced across the top of each inside page. This open spacing creates an effective and delicate treatment for a running head; you'll see it used in many different ways throughout this book (including in our own running heads). Note that the page frame is asymmetrical at the top and bottom, which keeps the design from being too rigid.

An underlying three-column grid used on pages not shown here is carried through on the cover (where one column is used for the title and the other two combine to provide a wide column for art) and on the spread of photos (where the two inner columns on each page have been divided in half to accommodate small mug shots).

The photos were sized and cropped so that all the heads appear approximately the same size and with the same eye level. This technique, which is particularly important when you group mug shots in a linear fashion, gives equal importance to all of the photos and helps minimize their varying reproduction quality. Imagine what a hodgepodge this page would be if all the heads were different sizes.

Design: John McWade, PageLab (Sacramento, CA)

Pages from the Sacramento Regional Foundation Yearbook.
Trim size: 11 by 8-1/2

A **magazine format** is used for this vacation guide to Alaska.

The table of contents is easy to follow, with secondary heads indented in smaller type under the main heads. Note that upsized folios accompany the main heads. Even if your publication does not break quite so neatly into different levels of headlines, it may be worth the effort to devise a two-tiered structure to lead the reader into the material.

For large photographs, you can maximize the space available by either surprinting or reversing small bits of text (facing page, top), and by running longer text blocks in tinted panels that drop in over the art (facing page, bottom). When using these techniques, look for open spaces in the photo so that the type treatment doesn't conflict with the composition of the image. Also, take note of the relative color of the photo and type: to be legible, white type must reverse out of a sufficiently dark background, and black type must print over relatively light areas.

The four-column grid is ideal for publications with lots of pictures and sidebars. Art and boxed material can be sized from one to four columns wide. Introductory copy can be set larger than the body text, in a two-column measure, as on the page shown above. This technique helps invite readers into a page that would otherwise be dense with columns of running text. Note also that the tinted panel that prints over the photo (facing page, bottom) is the same width as a one-column photo. Following the grid in this way helps to maintain a feeling of order within the most varied pages; it also helps you decide where and in what size to put items that vary a little from the straightforward interpretation of your format.

Rules between columns can help improve legibility in a narrow measure with relatively small type, such as used here. Ventura will generate these rules automatically if you turn on the Inter-Column Rules option on the Vertical Rules dialog box. When you don't want the rules to print (as in the introduction on the page above), you can mask them by drawing a white rectangle with the Line specified as none.

Wrapping text around irregularly shaped objects (above) is not one of Ventura's strong points. In order to do it, you need to create a series of frames that simulate the contour of the object.

Design: Drawing Conclusions

Pages from Alaska Official State Vacation Planner.
Trim size: 8-1/4 by 10-3/4

CHAPTER 6

PERIODICALS: NEWSLETTERS, JOURNALS, AND MAGAZINES

Regardless of subject, style, or frequency, the challenge common to all periodicals is to establish a strong identity that remains both familiar and fresh issue after issue. The subject, the tone, and the overall package and format should be unmistakably one's own, clearly established and consistently maintained over time. But within that familiar package it's the fresh ideas, the unexpected images, the new ways of presenting recurring themes that keep readers interested.

Once audience and editorial focus of a periodical is established, the foundation for the balancing act between the familiar and the new is the graphic format. This includes everything from logo and cover design to the treatment of feature stories and housekeeping details (mastheads, letters, calendars, and so on). Items that appear in every issue, such as contents listings, review columns, and news sections, should have a recognizable style and a relatively constant page position from one issue to the next. If there is advertising, the format must take into consideration where in the publication ads will appear, how to handle fractional ads, and how to distinguish clearly between ads and editorial items, especially when they appear on the same spread.

A format that works not only defines your image, it also determines how hard you'll work to produce each issue. A format consistent with your resources spells the difference between efficient and chaotic production. Desktop technology can streamline production tremendously, eliminating the days it used to take to turn manuscript into typeset galleys and to correct galleys as deadlines approached. The technology also gives editors and designers much greater control over the material through every step of the production cycle, allowing more refinement later in the process than was previously possible.

But established periodicals have established production systems. Converting to desktop publishing means that many functions previously performed by outside vendors are brought in-house to staffs that may already feel overworked. The technology is changing the roles of editors, designers, production managers, and layout artists in ways that are too new to be fully understood or predictable and that vary from one organization to another. If you are contemplating or are in the process of making the transition to desktop publishing, expect to spend six to twelve months evolving systems and roles. Talk with other people who have made the transition, and evaluate their experience within the context of your own product and the strengths and weaknesses of your staff. The benefits are ultimately everything they're alleged to be, but the transition can be quite a roller coaster.

NEWSLETTERS

Thousands and thousands of newsletters are published in this country. Whether for internal circulation or public relations, for marketing products or services, for raising money or raising consciousness, most newsletters exist to communicate specialized information to a targeted audience on a regular basis. It's essential to really understand your audience and what you hope to accomplish through the newsletter. You should be able to define not just a general purpose but very specific benefits that your organization can measure as a result of publishing the newsletter.

Unlike magazines, which usually have a staff dedicated to creating and producing the publication, newsletters are often produced by people who perform other functions for an organization. It's very important to match the newsletter format to the time and resources you'll have to produce it. If you're starting a new newsletter or making the transition from traditional to electronic production, you might consider using a free-lance designer, experienced in electronic publishing, to create a format and electronic templates consistent with your needs and resources. This may give you a much smarter look than you could achieve with an in-house design and still yield the cost savings of in-house production.

Newsletters in this section

- *Water Rights*—two equal columns for a quickly produced format
- *Application Success Stories*—a distinctive style using ruled heads
- *Housing Insights*—a wide and narrow column format
- *Inside Qualified Plans*—yet another two-column approach
- *Nooz*—playful mug shots in a five-column tabloid
- *Consumer Markets Abroad*—a format for charts and graphs
- *Perspectives*—a more open version of the two-and-a-half column grid
- *National Gallery of Art*—a narrow column for silhouetted art
- *ThePage*—the impact of strong cover concepts
- *Newservice*—the appeal and accessibility of a modular format
- *Friends of Omega*—on composing photos on the page
- *Indications*—marketing analysis with dimensional art
- *O'Connor Quarterly*—a friendly and sophisticated people-publication
- *The Freeze Beacon*—a strong identity from carefully styled details
- *Strategy: Resources for Retirement*—a five-column grid for quick scanning
- *Dear Nipper*—a bold and loud approach to marketing music
- *AmeriNews*—one approach to a tabloid format
- *RE:*—another approach to a tabloid format
- *Litigation News*—typographic variety for all-text pages

For hands-on instructions for creating newsletters, see Projects 3 and 4 in Section 3.

WATER RIGHTS

A MONTHLY NEWSLETTER PUBLISHED BY THE AMERICAN SOCIETY OF CIVIL ENGINEERS • VOL. 2 NO. 9 SEPTEMBER 1989

CONFIDENTIAL COLORADO STUDY SHOWS KANSAS MAY BE RIGHT

Colorado has long protested its innocence in the lawsuit Kansas filed against it in the U.S. Supreme Court over the flows of the Arkansas River. But a confidential Colorado study says that Kansas may indeed be right. WATER RIGHTS has obtained a letter written by a lawyer on the Colorado side of the dispute, in which he summarizes the study's results. The figures cited in the letter come very close to confirming Kansas' allegations.

Disputes over the Arkansas are nothing new. Colorado and Kansas have been suing each other over the river since about the turn of the century. Then, in 1936, Congress authorized the U.S. Army Corps of Engineers to build the John Martin Reservoir near Caddoa, Colo. The Supreme Court apportioned the water in it under the Arkansas River Compact of 1948. The compact provides no specific award of water to either state. Instead, it splits maximum releases from the John Martin Reservoir 60% to Colorado, 40% to Kansas.

Skimming Alleged

In late 1985, Kansas filed a complaint with the U.S. Supreme Court, claiming that Colorado has violated the compact. A major part of Kansas' allegations stems from the fact that Colorado water users have drilled hundreds of wells in the basin since the compact was enacted. Kansas says that these wells siphoned off 50,000 to 100,000 acre-ft of water a year that otherwise would have flowed into the John Martin, and become part of Kansas' share of the river.

Colorado hired Boyle Engineering Corp. to study water usage in the basin from 1940 through 1985. Colorado has refused WATER RIGHTS' requests for a copy of the study. However, on March 30, 1989 a number of participants on the Colorado side of the suit met to discuss its results. One of the participants, attorney Carl M. Shinn, wrote to his client, the District 67 Water Association, detailing the meeting and results of the study. WATER RIGHTS has obtained a copy of this letter.

In his letter, Shinn says that the study shows, "...there is a tremendous decrease in the river flow at the Colorado-Kansas state line and they have based it upon a great increase in the use of ground water in District 67 along the 'valley fill aquifer' (the area along the Arkansas with a direct connection to the surface flow)." The study identifies about 1,250 irrigation wells built from 1950 to 1985, between the city of Pueblo and the state line. These wells, according to statistics cited by Shinn, use a total of about 275,000 acre-ft of water a year.

Get Ready to Lose

Though Shinn writes he is skeptical about the accuracy of the study, he also notes, "I keep telling the lawyers that if they use this kind of figure in the lawsuit, they may as well get ready to lose."

Neither Shinn nor David Robbins, Colorado's attorney in the suit, returned repeated calls from WATER RIGHTS. However, Hal Simpson, Colorado's deputy state engineer, whose office ordered the study, was willing to comment on it.

Simpson stresses that the report contains preliminary figures; firmer figures, he says, will be out later this year. He says that many wells may indeed exist. But until a new report comes out he says of their effect, "We just don't know yet." Simpson says, for instance, the wells may just be a replacement for surface water diversions.

In This Issue

Sales Note #456
Form No. GU10-0025-00
5/23/88
Page 1 of 4

Application Success Stories

How Innovative Marketing Teams Sell Business Communications Systems

DISCOVER:

- *Why a customer requesting only a token-ring network installed a CBX-based switched data network as well.*
- *How one marketing team creatively leveraged an IBM account relationship.*
- *Why CBX data switching is a most attractive choice for networking PCs to S/36 and S/38 departmental systems.*

Application Selling At Its Best

The following scenario spelled "*Sales Opportunity*" for a marketing team from ROLM Systems in Lenexa, Kansas and IBM in Wichita, Kansas:

- Rapidly growing company
- Pending move to new location
- Expanding voice and data communications

The team took this opportunity, identified major data and voice applications key to the customer's business and proposed a system solution which combined a significant 9751 CBX data sale with a System/38 and Token Ring sale.

About The Customer

Company business: Appliance and audio/video equipment rental at very low daily and weekly rates. Currently about 200 storefront outlets nationwide. Local store managers maintain inventory and point-of-sale information, and send this into headquarters on a daily basis.

Company size and location: Approximately 400 employees at new headquarters in Wichita, Kansas. Recently purchased by major British music conglomerate for nearly $700 million.

IBM/ROLM Systems Relationship: Customer was an existing IBM account with two System/38s installed.

Competition: Both AT&T Direct and NTI, through the Regional Bell Operating Co., were proposing PBXs and Type 2 wiring to support Token Ring.

Customer Data Needs

There are two groups of System/38 users at headquarters. One group needs to access the inventory and point-of-sales information sent in by the local storefront managers. In the other group are programmers who needed uninterrupted system access. Both user groups had been accessing the System/38s through direct connections, from either native 525X terminals or PCs equipped with terminal emulation capabilities.

With the growth of the business, even more users would be given access to the System/38s via PCs. The move to the new headquarters created the perfect opportunity to take advantage of a new wiring plan to provide more flexible PC access. Type 2 cabling would be used to support the PBX and a Local Area Network. Early in the sales cycle, both the IBM Token Ring and Ethernet were the primary solutions being considered for PC connectivity and future network requirements.

Two system considerations drove the customer to evaluate alternatives to the existing PC-to-computer network implementation:

1. *Difficulty with the existing method for user access to the System/38s.* Often users required access to multiple System/38s to complete their work. This required the user to disconnect from one system and re-establish a physical connection to another, or to use multiple terminals.

2. *Rapid growth in the number of PC users.* As the PC user community grew, it became more difficult to meet and support the variety of software, print capabilities and configurations requested by *individual* PC users. Also the company needed to ensure other PC users did not block programmer access to the System/38.

IBM Internal Use Only 1

HOUSING INSIGHTS

DHCR HOLDS OWNER SEMINAR

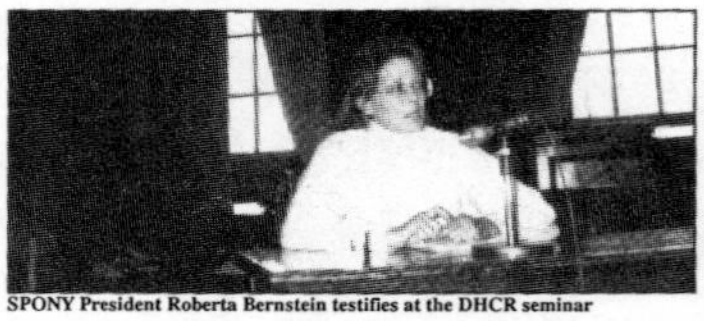

SPONY President Roberta Bernstein testifies at the DHCR seminar

The DHCR held its first Small Building Owners Seminar on May 4th. About 300 confused and unhappy small owners showed up in the hopes of obtaining help in dealing with the State's byzantine rental regulations.

State Housing Commissioner Richard L. Higgins did not show up, as was promised, but his deputy, Elliot G. Sander was there. Topics covered included Annual Registration, Major Capital Improvements (MCIs), Fuel Passalongs and Maximum Base Rents (MBRs).

The seminar reinforced the small owners feeling that the system is impossible to cope with. The speakers included the heads of the various departments of the DHCR and they were unaware of many of the policies and actions of their own staffs. One department head was often unaware of how another department operated.

Questions from the audience were limited and often answered with, "We'll look into the matter," and the festivities were topped off by a bomb threat.

PRELIMINARY RENT GUIDELINES ANNOUNCED, BUT MAY BE REDUCED

The Rent Guidelines Board has announced preliminary guidelines under which rents will be increased next year. However, the guidelines are by no means fixed, and a number of forces could drive them lower before the board approves permanent increases.

The board has set the preliminary guidelines at:

- 6.5% for one-year renewal leases;
- 9.5% for two-year renewal leases;
- an additional $5 for apartments renting for $325 or less per month;
- a vacancy allowance of 10%;
- initial stabilized rents would be an MBR plus 25% or an MCR plus 45%, whichever is greater.

Tenant activists are boycotting the rent guidelines hearings but are still

continued on page 4

OPINION

SYMPTOMS OF A PROBLEM

The recycling of trash is long overdue in New York City. The responsibility to solve the city's waste disposal problem will, one hopes, be placed on everybody's shoulders, as it rightfully should be. But if the New York City Department of Sanitation (DOS) could have its way, trash separation would be the responsibility of building owners alone. Fortunately, at this time, it appears that the more reasonable minds in the City Council who wanted to see a workable solution have prevailed. So why complain?

The problem is that the approach DOS was taking is typical of the contempt for owners that has permeated City Hall in the last 10 years. The Finance Department has raised assessments on multiple dwellings to levels that have put many buildings on the brink of default. This comes at a time when some were beginning to build cash reserves that could be used for major capitol improvements. These

continued on page 6

Volume 5 Number2
July/ August 1989

January 1990 *Vol. 3 Issue 1*

INSIDE QUALIFIED PLANS

Inside This Issue

The 401(k) Opportunity

Recent surveys indicate that 90% of Fortune 100 and 60% of all mid-sized companies now offer 401(k) plans as an employee benefit. More than $24 billion was contributed to 401(k) plans in 1988 alone. Nationwide, 401(k) assets now stand at nearly $150 billion.

New Plans

Generally, new 401(k) plans are established in the first quarter of the year. Because these plans are primarily funded through salary reduction contributions, new plans are more successful if they are set up earlier in the year.

A new 401(k) plan may be an employer's primary retirement benefit for employees, or it might be added to other programs already being offered. In either case, employers want simplicity. In order to sell the concept effectively, you should know a few basics about plan design, plan administration and funding.

Plan Design

The main plan design issue will be contributions—should the employer offer a matching contribution to entice plan participants to make contributions to the plan? Remember, highly compensated employees are limited to a multiple of the average percentage contribution made by the lower paid employees. It is critical that lower paid employees contribute to the plan. For this reason, many employers will make a matching contribution equal to $0.25 or $0.50 on the dollar for the first 6% that an employee contributes. *Lower paid employees are usually the only recipients of matching contributions.*

As an alternative, an employer might choose to make a *discretionary* contribution to the lower paid employees. Again, this contribution would be used to increase the average contribution for the lower paid so that the higher paid group could contribute the 1990 maximum estimated to be $7,993 (up from $7,627 in 1989). The new SLH 401(k) Flexible Prototype Plan offers an employer a first-rate plan and trust document which permits each of these options.

Plan Administration

401(k) plans, regardless of size, should use a plan administrator. The plan administrator will provide:

- nondiscrimination testing
- participant recordkeeping
- annual reporting to the government
- disclosure to participants

Participant statements can be provided as frequently as monthly. However, most employers choose to limit plan expenses by providing participants' statements semi-annually and certainly not more frequently than quarterly. 401(k) plans are funded primarily with salary reduction contributions. Therefore, timely accurate reporting to participants is crucial. The Trust Services department can suggest local or

SHEARSON LEHMAN HUTTON
An American Express company

Internal Use Only

A two-column newsletter is relatively easy to produce and, as the samples on the facing page illustrate, can take many forms. (See the Two-Column Grids section in Chapter 3 for other variations.)

Two 20-pica columns (*Water Rights*, far left, top) create a straightforward and efficient format. It satisfies the editor's need to pack a lot of information in every page. The 2-pica gutter between the columns has a 2-point vertical rule. The body text is Times Roman; the headlines are Helvetica.

More detailed headline styling (*Application Success Stories*) adds graphic punch to another two-column format. Note that the lengths of the 6-point rules above the headlines vary with the lengths of their respective headlines but that the 1-point rules at the top of each unit are always column width. This provides a good balance between the strong definition of each headline and the structure of the grid. Note also in the tease line ("Discover") at the top of the page how the rule treatment is reversed. The body text is Helvetica, the headlines are Helvetica bold, and the bulleted blurbs for inside stories are Helvetica Light Oblique.

A wide and narrow column format (*Housing Insights*) requires more decisions in layout but also provides more flexibility, especially in sizing art. The columns in the sample are 28 and 13 picas, with 2 picas between. The body text is Times Roman; the headlines are Helvetica.

A wide left margin (*Inside Qualified Plans*) results in two 17-pica columns. You don't fit as many words per page, but the pages are easier to read than those with wider columns. The text face is Bodoni, and the major heads are Helvetica Black.

Bulleted lists, used in three of the four newsletters, are easy to produce with Ventura's style tags. (You can choose from 15 default bullet types, or you can define any character in any font as a bullet.) Be careful of overusing this device, and don't be surprised if you run into an editor or art director or manager who says "No more bullets."

*Design (facing page, top and bottom left):
Howard Smallowitz, Braintrust Publishing Co. (Austin, TX)*

Cover of Water Rights, *published monthly by the American Society of Civil Engineers.
Size: 8-1/2 by 11*

Cover of Housing Insights, *published bimonthly by the Small Building Owners Association.
Size: 8-1/2 by 11*

*Design (facing page, top right):
Donna Kelly, ZetaType (San Francisco, CA)*

Cover of Application Success Stories, *published weekly by BCS Applications Product Marketing.
Size: 8-1/2 by 11*

*Design (facing page, bottom right):
David Russell, Graphic and Print Communications, Shearson Lehman Hutton (New York, NY)*

Cover of Inside Qualified Plans, *published monthly.
Size: 8-1/2 by 11*

Playfulness is the signature of this tabloid monthly newsletter (above). In both size and tone, it's at the opposite end of the spectrum from the straightforward newsletters on the facing page. The typewriter look of Courier sets the casual tone, and every design element follows through in kind.

Mug shots don't have to be boring. The shapes used here only begin to suggest some ingenious ways to treat both casual and posed snapshots. The circle, ovals, and rectangles were drawn in the page layout but the stars had to be created in a drawing program. Photos were stripped in as halftones by the printer.

For all the spontaneity in the treatment of graphic elements, the five-column grid provides the necessary understructure.

*Design:
Paul Souza (Boston, MA)*

Cover of Nooz, *published quarterly by WGBH radio.
Size: 11 by 17*

A two-and-a-half-column format is ideal for accommodating charts, graphs, and tables of different sizes. The narrow column works well for headlines and pull quotes, too. The running text always begins at the top of the page, and the charts are positioned flush with the bottom margin. Occasionally, the graphics are positioned one above the other. Given the diversity of the visuals, this consistent placement brings order to pages that might otherwise look haphazard.

Hairline rules create a half-page frame; a second half-frame brackets the main text block. This motif is adapted for the charts, where the headline and the half-frame are inside a box and alternate from the left to right side. This device might appear contrived in some publications, but it is both functional and subtly decorative here.

Design: Carol Terrizzi (Ithaca, NY)

Pages from Consumer Markets Abroad, *published monthly by American Demographics.*
Trim size: 8-1/2 by 11

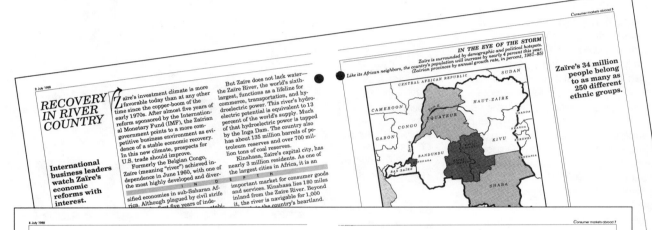

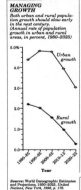

Design:
Partners by Design
(N. Hollywood, CA);
Agency: Jonisch
Communications
(Los Angeles, CA)

Pages from
Perspectives,
published quarterly
by the Transamerica
Life Companies.
Size: 8-1/2 by 11

The two-and-a-half-column format has a very different look when the text is broken up with banners, boxed copy, and illustrations.

Note the absence of rules to separate columns and define the image area. With the wide margin and generous space around headlines, the text block provides sufficient definition. A format with more tightly packed pages would need rules to delineate the elements.

The wide margin is used for quotes, a contents listing, and photos (not shown) that extend an additional 2-1/2 picas into the first text column.

Crimson banners with reverse Garamond type are used for department-style headlines.

The headlines and marginal quotes are Helvetica. The running text is Garamond.

The type prints in blue on bone-colored stock. Boxed copy prints over lavender or light blue tints. A blue tone prints over photos as well.

National Gallery of Art

NGA Chooses Executive Librarian

Neal Turtell

By Melanie B. Ness
In May of this year Neal Turtell became executive librarian of the National Gallery of Art. This major art research center comprises 150,000 books and bound periodicals, 75,000 vertical file pieces, and 60,000 auction catalogues. Also under Turtell's direction are the rapidly growing photographic

archives, headed by Ruth Philbrick, and the staff who tend to the library's many important activities.

Although founded in 1941 when the National Gallery opened its doors, most of the library holdings have been acquired within the past fifteen years, through either purchase or donation. Begun by gifts from the Gallery's principal benefactors, the library has burgeoned with the acquisition of the libraries of such noted scholars and collectors as Rudolph Wittkower, Huntington Cairns, Lessing J. Rosenwald, and John Rewald. The library is also the designated national repository—
(continued on page 2)

Nasher Sculpture Collection on View

By Nan Rosenthal
My recent telephone calls to Mary Sweet have been greeted with the wry question, "How many this time?" Our well-shod registrar was getting used to the idea that the size of the exhibition *A Century of Modern Sculpture: The Patsy and Raymond Nasher Collection* was about to expand again. Not, of course, on account of curatorial indecision, but because the Nashers had purchased yet another masterpiece.

Since Gill Ravenel, Mark Leithauser, and I made our first reconnaissance trip to the Nashers' Dallas home more than a year ago, a number of real landmarks in twentieth-century sculpture have entered the collection. Among them: Medardo Rosso's *The Concierge*, 1883; Matisse's *Reclining Nude*, 1907; Picasso's *Head of a Woman*, 1909; Brancusi's *Portrait of Nancy Cunard*, 1925-1927; Lachaise's *Elevation*, 1927; Giacometti's

No More Plays, 1932; and David Smith's *House in a Landscape*, 1945.

The exhibition contains 74 works by 39 artists, installed on three levels of the East Building: figurative and surrealist sculpture on the Mezzanine; cubist, constructivist, and minimal objects on the Main Floor; and a sampling of very recent sculpture on the Concourse.

The Nasher collection ranges in date from a life-size Alexis Rudier cast of Rodin's famous *Gates of Hell* figure, *Eve*, 1881, to several witty representatives of 1980s post—
(continued on page 6)

Barry Flanagan, Large Leaping Hare, 1982, Collection of Mr. and Mrs. Raymond D. Nasher

JULY–AUGUST 1987

The narrow column of this two-and-a-half-column format creates an ideal space for silhouetted art and captions. You can see on the pages shown how easily the art breaks the grid that is firmly established by vertical rules. The designer admits to having had to protect the white space created by the narrow column from text-hungry editors, who were always wanting to fill it with copy.

Rectangular photos can run one-half column, as seen on the cover. Note how the photo shares the left margin with the vertical rule. Occasionally, a photo or tinted panel runs the width of a text column plus the narrow column.

The typeface is Goudy Old Style throughout. The generous leading of the 11/14 body text adds to the openness of the page. The headlines are 24 point and the captions are 10/11 italic.

Design: Richard Steele, Steele & Co. (Washington, DC)

Pages from a bimonthly newsletter published by the National Gallery of Art. Trim size: 25-1/2 by 11, folded twice to create a six-panel piece

---

Alexander M. Laughlin Elected to Board of Trustees

Alexander M. Laughlin was elected May 8 to the Board of Trustees of the National Gallery of Art. Mr. Laughlin replaces Carlisle H. Humelsine who retired from the Board of Trustees in June. Mr. Laughlin also serves as Chairman of the Trustees' Council. Mr. Humelsine was voted Trustee Emeritus of the Gallery and is the first person ever to receive this honor.

"Alexander Laughlin and Carlisle Humelsine have served the National Gallery, and their country, with distinction," said J. Carter Brown, director. "We shall miss the wisdom and guidance that Mr. Humelsine has provided us down through the years. We also look forward with great anticipation to having the benefit of

Mr. Laughlin as a member of the Board of Trustees."

Mr. Laughlin is an Associate Director of Tucker, Anthony & R.L. Day, Inc. New York, a position he has held since 1977. He was Vice Chairman and Chairman of Jesup & Lamont (1970-1977), prior to serving as General Partner.

The National Gallery of Art is governed by a board of trustees composed of five private trustees and the Secretary of State, the Secretary of the Treasury, the Chief Justice of the Supreme Court and the Secretary of the Smithsonian Institution. The Trustees' Council advises the trustees on a wide range of program and policy issues affecting the Gallery.

NGA Chooses Executive Librarian

(continued from page 1)

instead of the Library of Congress—for materials such as dealers' catalogues, gallery announcements, and other ephemera. Much of Turtell's energies are devoted to buying more books and enticing owners of fine-art libraries to consider the Gallery as their collections' final and best resting place.

According to Neal Turtell, the library must be regarded as a very young one, but one that will grow substantially. Enough shelf space exists to accommodate twenty years of vigorous collecting. The library's present goals are to continue enhancing areas of current strength (western art and architecture), to meet in-house needs of curators and CASVA members, and to improve services. A major step toward "user friendliness" will be an automated information system that can be accessed from NGA offices. A library advisory group is also being established to help review collecting policy and services.

A dapper man with a quick wit, Neal Turtell was born in New York. He

completed his undergraduate work at Fordham University and undertook his master of library science degree at this country's oldest continuously operating library school, Pratt Institute in Brooklyn. Coming to Washington in 1975 he spent the next eight years in various positions at the Smithsonian Institution Libraries. As chief of the Catalogue Record Department, he coordinated activities of the three cataloging departments for the Smithsonian. From there, Turtell's career took him to the University of Wisconsin as assistant director for technical services and then back to Washington to the National Gallery as assistant librarian to Mel Edelstein.

When Mel Edelstein left the Gallery in 1986 for the Getty Museum in California to become senior bibliographer and resource coordinator, Turtell took over as acting chief librarian. It was not long before he was offered the position and new title of executive librarian of the National Gallery.

Curatorial Colloquy I

The Mellon *Venus*

This summer the Center for Advanced Study initiated a new program within its series of special meetings. This annual gathering, known as a curatorial colloquy, is intended to consider some aspect of the collections of the National Gallery of Art. One of its purposes is to encourage fruitful exchange between art historians teaching in universities and those in curatorial posts at museums.

The first curatorial colloquy, held in early June, focused on the Gallery's Mellon *Venus*, a life-size Renaissance bronze formerly ascribed to Jacopo Sansovino and more recently to an artist working in Italy, France, or Flanders in the late 16th century. The central issue

. . . the Gallery's Bacchus may perhaps have originated at the same time as Venus.

of the meeting was to identify a more precise location and attribution for the sculpture and related works of art, including the Mellon *Bacchus*, a pendant sculpture also in the Gallery's collection. In addition to these two monumental bronzes, the colloquy discussions involved a group of smaller works from the period 1570-1640, borrowed for the occasion from private and public collections in the United States and Great Britain.

The sessions, designed as round-table discussions, were led by Douglas Lewis, curator of sculpture, with the assistance of Alison Luchs, assistant curator, and Shelley Sturman, head of object conservation. The other participants, all specialists in Renaissance sculpture selected earlier this year from a pool of applicants, were: Sergey Androssov

(The State Hermitage Museum), Bruce Boucher (University College London), Charles Davis (Florence), Giancarlo Gentilini (Museo Nazionale del Bargello, Florence), Herbert Keutner (Kunsthistorisches Institut, Florence), Anthony Radcliffe (Victoria and Albert Museum), and Patricia Wengraf (London).

In seeking a more secure attribution for the Mellon *Venus*, the colloquy participants considered the sculpture's provenance in detail. Perhaps the most exciting discovery, presented to the colloquy by Professor Gentilini, is that by the early 19th century the Mellon *Venus* and *Bacchus* were both installed (with other life-size bronzes) in the garden of the Villa Litta-Visconti-Arese at Lainate, outside Milan. The dates when these sculptures were commissioned and when they entered the possession of the family of the Visconti-Borromeo (later Litta) family remain uncertain. During the course of the week's discussion, Jacopo Sansovino was ruled out as the sculptor of the *Venus* and *Bacchus*, as were artists in the circle of Giambologna. The colloquy reached a preliminary hypothesis, however, that the Mellon *Venus* was created by an artist, possibly a northern Italian or a Fleming, at work in Rome around 1600. Technical evidence, along with the new information on provenance, suggest that, despite stylistic differences attributable to separate artists, the Gallery's *Bacchus* may perhaps have originated at the same time as the *Venus*.

The second curatorial colloquy, scheduled for early summer 1988, will consider the Gallery's *Feast of the Gods* by Bellini and Titian. The discussion sessions will be led by David Brown, curator of Renaissance painting, and David Bull, head of painting conservation.

Venus Anadyomene, Bronze, Andrew W. Mellon Collection, 1937.1.132

Design: David Doty,
PageWorks (Chicago, IL)

Pages from ThePage,
published monthly by
PageWorks.
Trim size: 7 by 11

The cover-story concept, seen frequently in magazines, has unusual impact when used effectively in a newsletter. At their best, newsletters have an intimacy with their readers (the result of a shared special interest) and a timeliness that even magazines lack in today's fast-paced communications. So a newsletter cover story implicitly announces, "Here's a problem that many of you are grappling with, and here's what we know about it."

The visual continuity in these covers also seems closer to the world of magazines than to that of newsletters. Newsletters typically achieve their cover identity through a familiar grid and typographic treatment. Here, the cover design varies quite a bit from one issue to the next, depending on the subject. But the strong nameplate treatment, the unsual shape of the page, and the always-on-target theme provide their own very effective and unmistakable identity. Even though the pages were created in PageMaker for a Macintosh audience, the design lesson is universal.

A highly organized, modular format takes editorial planning and attention to detail when you assemble the pages but is very appealing and easy to read.

The cover uses multiple "sell" devices to get the reader's attention: a strong bit-mapped photo and caption with boldface lead-in, a headline for a related story inset in the cover story, and a contents box.

The bold rules are printed in a second color that changes with each issue. The 15-point rules allow ample room for reverse type (Avant Garde, with extra letterspacing).

Art breaks the grid at the top of the page (below). Pull quotes can also be used to break the highly structured grid and are also printed in the second color. (See additional pages from this newsletter in the section on Three-Column Grids in Chapter 3.)

Design: Jim Parker (Phoenix, AZ)

Pages from Newservice, published bimonthly by the Do It Now Foundation. Size: 8-1/2 by 11

The photographs available for most newsletters lack both the impact and the reproduction quality that would allow them to stand alone on the page. But when you group photos with an eye both to editorial content and the visual relationship that will be created between them, the whole can be greater than the sum of its parts.

Three photos often form an ideal combination. Two alone form only a one-on-one, back-and-forth relationship. Add a third, and you have a new and more dynamic chemistry. Four together will often start to pair off, and you're back with twos again. And visually, three photos can create an interesting triangular path for the reader's eye to follow.

In the example shown here, the photos promote summer workshops at a holistic learning center. The selection balances a single, silhouetted musician, a group seated casually at an outdoor seminar, and a third photo suggesting both the quiet time away from workshops and the recently improved wheelchair access on the campus.

When positioning photos on the page, consider where each picture will take the reader's eye, the relative size of the subjects, the lights and darks, and the horizon lines.

Three strong directions in these photos create visual energy that moves your eye from one picture to another. The silhouetted photo is looking away from the page; the lecturers standing in the group picture are looking into the page; and the figures shown from behind take your eye back into the page.

The people are captured in front views, back views, and profiles, and they are scaled differently in their individual environments. The uniformity of size generally recommended for head-and-shoulder portraits would make a group of casual photos such as this seem too static.

Silhouetting a photo, as in the top picture, can improve it by removing extraneous background images. The original photo in this instance included a group of people seated behind the subject; removing them focuses attention on the subject and also provides an interesting shape to work with. The freeform shape can be considerably larger than the other pictures without being out of balance. And you can rag the copy along the edge of the silhouette, which integrates the type and the photos. In this case, the photo was scanned in to produce a working on-screen image to help define the rag. But for better reproduction in print, a halftone was shot from the original photo and stripped in by the printer.

Visual illusions can be part of the unseen structure in a group of images. In the bottom two pictures, the horizon lines seem to meet, so that for a moment they appear to create a single panorama; the space between them creates the effect of a window on the scene. Opening up the picture plane in this way creates a sense of perspective and gives dimension to the page.

Design: Don Wright (Woodstock, NY)

Pages from Friends of Omega Newsletter, *published by the Omega Institute. Trim size: 8-1/2 by 11*

A serious, analytical image appropriate for a marketing newsletter is established through the continuous running text and the dimensional, diagrammatic art.

The narrow side margins (2 picas 6 points) allow for wide, 14-pica text columns, about the maximum width in a three-column grid. The density of the text is balanced by white space from a deep, 12-pica top margin, the floating art, and the open leading in the breakouts.

The dimensional "Market Power Grid," abstracted from the cover illustration (not shown), is picked up also as a design motif at the start of each section. The tinted square in each icon is keyed either to the larger grid on the page shown or to a similar grid on another page. The grid was created in Illustrator.

A second color is used for the art, headlines, and breakouts. This helps to break up the text and allows for downsized subheads without loss of emphasis.

The leaders and the narrow-measure callouts emphasize the vertical structure of the grid and keep the page clean and crisp. The small Helvetica type for callouts contrasts with the larger Times Roman used for running text and breakouts.

The bold initial cap, floating above a gray tinted box, draws the reader's eye to the beginning of the text. This is particularly effective in a page that otherwise lacks any dramatic contrasts.

Design: Marla Schay and Micah Zimring, Watzman + Keyes (Cambridge, MA)

Pages from Indications, *published bimonthly by Index Group, Inc. Trim size: 25-1/2 by 11, folded twice*

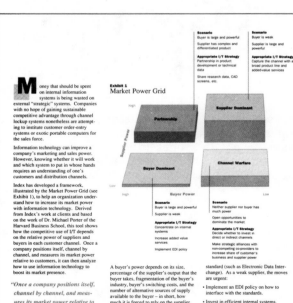

This newsletter achieves a completely different style within the three-column format than does the publication on the facing page. Here, rules and banners separating stories provide a clearly visible page structure, whereas the continuous narrative in the preceding publication is designed with a less apparent, though equally tight, framework. Compare also the justified text of this publication with the ragged right of the preceding one, and the paragraph indents here with the flush left first lines and open paragraph spacing shown on the facing page. Note, too, that the photos here are angled to break out of the grid, while the dimensional art on the facing page is positioned to emphasize the grid.

The angled snapshots over blue shadows loosen up the tightly structured page and also convey a warm, people-oriented image.

Goudy Old Style, used throughout, is a delicate typeface that is handled here with considerable sophistication. Note the open spacing of the all-caps category heads, which set elegantly against the gray banners above each story; the graceful initial caps, which print blue; and the alignment of text in adjacent columns, which adds to the crispness of the justified text. The delicacy of this typeface also makes it relatively forgiving of the uneven spacing often found in justified type.

Design: Kimberly Mancebo,
Castro Benson Bryant Mancebo
(Campbell, CA)

Pages from the
O'Connor Foundation Quarterly.
Trim size: 8-1/2 by 11

COMMUNITY OUTREACH

O'Connor Reaches Out to Kids as it Co-Sponsors Children's Discovery Museum Groundbreaking

Why did dozens of O'Connor Hospital employees spend an entire Saturday of their own free time volunteering at the Children's Discovery Museum Groundbreaking!

To help kids learn about health care. They manned interactive learning centers where they showed kids how to splint arms, listen through stethoscopes, navigate wheelchairs, read x-rays, and walk on crutches.

Not only did O'Connor employees participate in the Groundbreaking activities, but they also hope to establish long-term involvement after the Museum opens next year.

ADMINISTRATIVE DIRECTOR of Radiology Carol Yanz explains how x-rays give an "inside out" view of people.

PATIENT CARE

Monte Villa's Self Discovery Helps Troubled Youths

Located in a serene setting in Morgan Hill, O'Connor's Monte Villa Hospital (MVH) offers confidential adolescent psychiatric programs and chemical dependency services.

The Self Discovery program is committed to affirming life and respecting the dignity of adolescents and their families. The program offers troubled youths a chance to feel better about themselves, to understand their feelings and needs, to discover that they are likeable, and to feel accepted.

When a person comes to Monte Villa Hospital for care, he or she undergoes full medical and neuropsychological evaluations. Group and individual counseling promotes healing of specific physical, spiritual, familial, social, educational and emotional problems. Follow-up care is an integral part of the program. Accredited schooling is also available. For details, call Susan Titus at 408/779-4151.

NOBODY SAID ADOLESCENCE WOULD BE EASY, but for some teens it is absolutely overwhelming. Compassionate counselors help these youths find their way. The symbol was created by the teenagers at MVH and is used on T-shirts and binders as a reminder of the importance of their efforts in Self Discovery.

PHYSICIAN PROFILE

Golden Gloves Champion Dr. Calcagno Practices 50 Years at O'Connor

Imagine combining the slam bang vigor of a Golden Gloves boxing champion, the gentle sensitivity of a community volunteer, and the sophisticated intelligence of a physician. Put them all together and you've got the fascinating Dr. Joseph Calcagno, general practitioner at O'Connor for nearly half a century.

From the time Dr. Calcagno was old enough to walk, he gleefully tagged along with his dad to local boxing competitions, dreaming of the day when he, too, would win a title. The day came during pre-med school at Santa Clara University when he "left-and-right-hooked" his way through eliminations to win a 1934 Golden Gloves award in the Lightweight Division. That victory still remains one of the special moments in his life.

When he graduated from medical school in 1939, he joined World War II's War in the Pacific. "I spent the whole six years on the islands in field hospital MASH units," he says. "We were the envy of the soldiers, not only because we got Coca-Cola and fresh milk and meat from Army pilots as fringe benefits, but because we had 30 nurses to work with!"

By 1946, he was home again and opened a medical practice on Race Street. Soon after, his passion for boxing came back into focus, this time not as a participant, but as a licensed ringside physician for the California State Athletic Commission. As such, he has been the

> **"In** 1946, he opened a medical practice on Race Street, across from the O'Connor Sanitarium. He's been there ever since."

attending doctor at boxing and wrestling matches on the average of every other weekend for 46 years, with as many as 3-4 dozen matches in a single weekend. He examines all competing boxers and wrestlers—both amateur and professional—about an hour before each match and treats them immediately after they compete.

"Most injuries are minor face, eye and lip cuts," he explains, "but occasionally the officials or I will stop a fight if we see someone taking a beating, and submit a record to the California Athletic Commission."

As the only boxing/wrestling attending physician in the Santa Clara Valley, he ends up performing annual physicals on at least five professional boxers, wrestlers, officials or judges on any given weekday. They all need Dr. Calcagno's "stamp of approval" to retain their state licences.

A 20-year Volunteer for PAL
As a firm believer in community service, Dr. Calcagno extends his passion for these sports into volunteer work, having regularly donated his time to the boxers and wrestlers of the Police Athletic League (PAL) since the organization was founded in 1968.

Dr. Calcagno is one of those rare individuals who has been able to integrate his professional skills in the healing arts into a hobby which he adores.

"I feel very lucky," he says, "My hobby has become my work. What more could a person ask for!"

DR. CALCAGNO (photo left) now works beneath a wall filled with awards from his four decades of volunteerism. (Right) Barely into his twenties, Santa Clara University student Dr. Calcagno wins a Golden Gloves title.

VOLUME II NO.4 FALL 1987

NAVY WHISTLEBLOWER SPEAKS OUT
See Page 6

THE BEACON

Quarterly Newsletter of SANE/FREEZE of San Diego

INF TREATY

An Open Letter to Reagan and Gorbachev

Our organization congratulates both of you for your leadership and courage in bringing about a tentative agreement to eliminate all intermediate nuclear missiles in Europe and Asia. For many years we have been campaigning vigorously to reduce the threat of nuclear war. Now you have heard us!

We look to you, Mr. Reagan, to use your considerable influence with those members of the Senate who oppose arms control to help bring about the ratification of the INF Treaty. We further urge you to do your utmost to oppose any amendments that might defeat its purpose.

We look to you, Mr. Gorbachev, to continue your initiatives to improve the relations between our countries. Allay the fears that your large military forces create in Western Europe by bringing about balanced reductions in offensive conventional weapons. Help to avert a conventional arms buildup to offset the loss of nuclear weapons.

And we ask that neither of you lose sight of the fact that, while an agreement to reduce one particularly provocative and dangerous type of nuclear weapon is greatly welcomed, it will not in itself end the arms race. Nor will it repair the damage done by the scuttling of other arms limitation treaties. Significant though the agreement may be, it will reduce the total world nuclear arsenal only by a slight amount.

Finally, since it is the stated goal of both nations to reduce all nuclear weapons by at least 50%, let us call an immediate bilateral halt to the testing, production and deployment of any further nuclear weapons systems. It makes no sense to eliminate some weapons with one hand while creating many more with the other.

Signed, San Diego SANE/FREEZE

MEET THE PRESIDENT

Rev Coffin's Vision for SANE/FREEZE

The following is an edited version of the article by Kathleen Hendrix of the Los Angeles Times which appeared in that paper October 15, 1987. Our Executive Director, David Carpenter, attended the meeting with Rev. Coffin who, when he saw the Beacon, raved about its content and professionalism.

It was a hot night, ending one of several days in which the air refused to budge, and the meeting of the (Southern California regional) chapter of SANE/Freeze was slow to come to order. The 20 or so wilted people gathered in the community room of an apartment building in Hollywood, mixed themselves instant coffee, spread out notices of other meetings ... and waited for the Rev. William Sloane Coffin, Jr., to arrive.

In he came, looking rumpled and slightly paunchy, shirt open at the throat and sleeves rolled up. He appeared undaunted by the heat ... and with a friendly grin in place, strode across the room relaxed and affable, clapping back at the people who stood to applaud him. "It's neat," he told the group, "to get a chance to see what's going on." For many in that room, it was, in return, a chance to meet the legend, and their new national president.

Coffin became a household word during the '60's, when as chaplain at Yale he became a civil rights and anti-Vietnam War activist, joining freedom rides, marching in the South, collecting draft cards with Dr. Benjamin Spock, speaking out and getting arrested over and over again.

Coffin did not start his life this way. Born to wealth, his family founded the W. & J. Sloane furniture business. He first considered a career as a concert pianist, and then a diplomat. He was an Army liaison officer to the French and Soviet armies during World War II, and a CIA officer in West Germany during the Korean War, training anti-communist Russians for work within the Soviet Union. Finally, he said only half-jokingly ..., he lost the battle to stay out of the ministry. World War II had raised too many of the right questions.

Last July, saying the timing in history was right, Coffin announced he would step down as senior minister of New York City's Riverside Church at the end of 1987 to become the first president of SANE/Freeze. In creating the position of President, over that of the co-directors of the newly merged groups, the SANE/Freeze ... board announced it was looking for someone to "articulate the vision." If there is one thing Bill Coffin can do, it is articulate the vision. And shape it. It is not without reason that he calls his new job with the secular organization "a full-time peace and justice ministry." ... As he defines it, the SANE/Freeze (people) join him in a "disarmament and development" organization, concerned with

Continued on page 10

1

STRATEGY

Resources For Retirement

June 1989

Performance Plus
Consider Equities For Your Retirement Portfolio

At Shearson Lehman Hutton, we believe that Serious Investors who take the long view and seek fundamental values in markets throughout the world will reap the greatest long-term rewards.

Stocks have historically proven their value over the long term by outperforming most investments. Over more than 60 years, the stock market has shown an average compounded growth of 10% compared to 3.1% for inflation.

Stocks have historically outperformed most investments

No matter what kind of investor you are—conservative, moderate or aggressive—equities should be a part of your retirement investing plan. Your retirement portfolio, by nature, should be structured for the long term to produce the most attractive returns.

The stocks on our Recommended List have consistently outperformed the market averages. Your Financial Consultant can help you select equity issues from our currently recommended industry sectors. Watch for a special equity seminar coming to major cities beginning the week of June 19. Members of the SLH equity research department will discuss selected industries and stock recommendations. Also, ask your FC if your branch will be conducting a local seminar. ■

SHEARSON LEHMAN HUTTON
An American Express company

Is Your Retirement Agenda Set?

Now is the time to chart your future financial plans. With your Shearson Lehman Hutton FC at the helm, you can both periodically review and strengthen your retirement plans. These mid-course corrections will help safeguard your investments through various market climates and allow you to realize your financial objectives. An investment plan that is organized today will make for a more comfortable retirement tomorrow.

Turn to the PRO[sm]

The Personal Review Outline[sm] (PRO) is a customized analysis of your assets and investments in the context of your current needs and long-range goals. Based on information you supply in a structured, easy-to-complete questionnaire, the free PRO Analysis[sm] is prepared by your FC along with a team of Shearson Lehman Hutton professionals to devise investment strategies to meet your specific objectives.

Another tool available to your FC is the Retirement Planning Analysis (RPA). This personalized program establishes a plan to help you achieve your future retirement income goals based on an analysis of your projected retirement age, inflation and investment performance. ■

Understanding Your 401(k) Plan

A 401 (k) plan is a profit-sharing plan that permits employees to save for their retirement by making contributions to a savings plan. A 401(k) plan allows employees and employers to share in the cost and benefits of saving for retirement. There are several advantages to a 401(k).

Tax Savings and Tax-Deferred Compounding

By contributing a portion of your salary to the plan, you can reduce your current tax burden since contributions are not included as part of your taxable income.*

Second, all 401(k) contributions benefit from tax-deferred compounding as long as you remain in the plan. Even modest contributions can become a sizeable nest egg when invested regularly on a tax-deferred basis.

100% Vesting of Your Contributions

You are always 100% vested in any contributions you make to the plan. If you leave the company before retirement, you are entitled to take your contributions with you.

Distributions, however, may be subject to a 10% premature distribution penalty if they are not rolled into an IRA within 60 days of receipt.

Hardship Withdrawal and Loan Privileges

You may be able to withdraw money from your account prior to retirement due to a financial hardship. "Hardship withdrawals" are usually permitted for buying a primary residence or paying for

continued on reverse, last column

IRS Annual Report Alert

The IRS requires all pension and profit sharing plans to file annual reports (IRS Form 5500-EZ for plans that cover only owners, partners and spouses). Even frozen Keogh plans and Keogh plans with no employees must file this report. If you maintain more than one plan, you must file a Form 5500 annual report for each plan you maintain. Plans with participating employees should file a 5500-C or 5500-R.

Calendar year plans must file the 1988 annual report no later than July 31, 1989. Non-calendar year plans will have until seven months after the close of their respective plan years to file the report. The IRS will assess a $25 per day late filing penalty for each failure to make a timely filing. Consult your tax advisor. ■

A tightly structured nameplate, along with the headline and folio treatments, creates a strong identity for this newsletter. The lighthouse incorporated into the logo is a recognizable local landmark. The banner with reverse type at the top of the cover highlights a magazine-style feature article inside the issue.

A scanned photo on the cover is treated as a posterlike portrait of the subject, producing a more effective result than trying to make a bit-mapped image look like a halftone.

The wide-and-narrow-column format on the cover is adapted to a three-column format on some inside pages.

The typeface is Palatino. Varying the size and measure of individual headlines creates emphasis without the need to change the typeface.

Design:
John Odam
(San Diego, CA)
Pages from The Freeze Beacon, *published quarterly by San Diegans for a Bilateral Nuclear Weapons Freeze.*
Size: 8-1/2 by 11

A five-column grid, with one column left mostly open, works well for scanning short items.

Visual interest is provided by dotted rules, tints, and a second color for major headlines and breakouts. Boxed copy can run across two or three columns where needed.

The body text is 9/11 Helvetica with a 5-point Inter-Paragraph space. This space between paragraphs improves the readability of narrow columns and keeps the page from becoming too dense. The breakouts are 11/12 Helvetica, centered, with 1-point ruling lines above and below.

The headlines are 14/17 Futura Extra Bold. The subheads are 10/12 New Century Schoolbook bold italic. The choice of an italic serif for the subheads makes them stand out particularly well in a page of sans serif type.

Design:
Diane Layton,
Graphic and Print Communications,
Shearson Lehman Hutton (New York, NY)
Pages from Strategy: Resources for Retirement, *published monthly.*
Size: 8-1/2 by 11

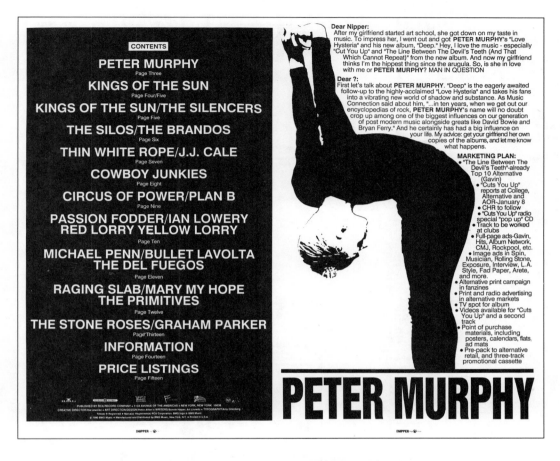

*Design:
Art direction,
Pietro Alfieri;
Typography,
Amy Ortenberg
(New York, NY)*

*Pages from
Dear Nipper, published quarterly by RCA Records.
Trim size:
14 by 22-3/4*

This in-house newsletter for a record company is appropriately designed like a music rag. It delivers marketing and promotion information much more effectively than a marketing plan would.

The oversize pages are created on an 8.5- by 14-inch page and then enlarged on a photocopy machine. The smaller page is easier and faster to work with on the computer than the actual size would be, and it eliminates the need for manually pasting together sections of oversize pages.

The type on both pages is Helvetica and Helvetica bold, which hold up well in large sizes on newsprint.

The Peter Murphy image and logo were scanned and saved as a PCX image. Scanning the logo as part of the artwork enabled the designer to use a larger type size than she had in her system. But the jagged edges of the digitized type had to be cleaned up in PC Paintbrush.

Wrapping text around an irregular object is difficult in Ventura, but it can be done by creating a series of empty frames that effectively force the text away from the image. In this instance, the designer started with the basic page frame for the text and then created a picture frame with the Flow Text Around option off. This would enable her to flow text over the picture. After

placing the picture, she created a series of about 15 smaller frames over it. Each of these frames extended from the left margin of the page to just past the curve in the silhouette where the type would begin, and for these the Flow Text Around option was on. When the text was placed in the page frame, these smaller frames forced it around the picture. When using this technique, the small frames have to butt perfectly or they will create uneven leading in the text around them. Another tip: Temporarily removing the image while placing and refining the position of the text speeds up the screen redraw during the process.

The two true tabloids on this page use the 11-by-17 page in similar ways but to different effect. Both rely heavily on white space and display type to make the oversize page accessible.

The three + one-column format (above) creates a half-frame of white space around the image area.

Photos, captions, and a statement of goals break into the white space without filling it.

The logo prints in red ("Ameri") and blue ("News"). The red is picked up in the banners with reverse type and in the rule at the bottom of the page. The blue is picked up in the initial cap, the two-column inset text, and the tint in the contents box. Red and blue are crisp, bold colors that liven up a mostly text page.

The two-column format (above right) is unusual for a tabloid, but the wide margin, used only for pull quotes and blurbs, and the space around the bold headlines make it work.

The nameplate banner is repeated in a smaller size on inside pages, providing strong identity.

A second color, crimson, is used for the alternating thick and thin rules, initial caps, display text inset in the running text, and company identification in the lower left.

The type is Helvetica Black for headlines and blurbs inset in running text, and Bookman for running text, captions, and marginal quotes.

Design (above left): Kate Dore, Dore Davis Design (Sacramento, CA)

Cover of AmeriNews, the inhouse newsletter of AmeriGas–Cal Gas. Trim size: 11 by 17

Design (above right): Mary Reed, ImageSet Design (Portland, ME)

Cover of RE:, a commercial/industrial real estate newsletter published by The MacBride Dunham Group. Trim size: 11 by 17

An all-text, newspaper-style page can be made engaging and attractive. Rules, initial caps, white space, and a second color all support the structural device of using story headlines to divide the page into text units with varying sizes and shapes. The effect is infinitely more appealing to readers than columns of type that simply march down the page. The approach here is conservative—and appropriately so for a bar association newsletter; the same devices, however, can be used to create many other styles.

The top of the image area is dropped so as not to crowd the page. The resulting white space creates a strong horizon line.

The body text is Times Roman, and the subheads are Times Roman bold italic.

The headlines and folios are a Caslon Extra Bold display face. The logo and the initial caps are set in Novarese. These faces were not yet available for desktop publishing when the issue shown was produced, but they have been part of the newsletter format for many years and were added by hand to the electronically composed pages.

The headlines are centered between brown rules, with a 2-point rule above and a 1-point rule below.

The initial caps print over a box with a horizontal-line fill and no outside rule (this fill also prints brown). Note the careful alignment of the baseline of the initial cap with the bottom rule in the box and the even spacing between the thin-line rule of the fill with the 1-point rule above. This particular fill is not available in Ventura, but the point to remember is that when you rely on typographic devices for the look of a page, the details are critical.

Design: Michael Waitsman, Synthesis Concepts (Chicago, IL)

Pages from Litigation News, *published by the American Bar Association. Trim Size: 10-3/4 by 13-7/8*

JOURNALS & MAGAZINES

The complexity of the magazine format, with its variety of editorial material in any given issue and the need to juggle several issues at once, makes the collaborative effort between editors and graphic designers one of the key elements of success. Editors who think visually and designers who get involved in the content of the material produce stories that are dynamic and attention-getting, with innovative approaches to even the most familiar ideas. The editor's job isn't over when the manuscript moves from word processor to page layout, and the designer doesn't wait for the manuscript to begin his or her work. Both work together to develop, shape, present, and refine each idea throughout the production cycle. Although desktop publishing is changing the nature of that collaboration, in some ways it presents the greatest opportunities for those editors and designers who don't see their functions as limited to either words or pictures.

Another unique challenge in producing magazines is the opportunity to use the dimension of time that is implicit in the magazine format. Each department and feature story is developed as a self-contained unit, but when you bind them together they become pieces of a whole. Play with that dimension as you make up the order of items in the magazine. Move from a picture story to an article with sustained reading text, from a story with black-and-white photographs to one that uses color illustration, from an idea that is light and accessible to one that is provocative and demanding. Even though few people read magazines from front to back, offering contrast from one story to the next creates an interesting texture and an attention-getting pace. Besides, using that dimension is fun and keeps your job interesting. The more you work with the flow and the pacing, the more they become a useful guide both in early planning and last-minute problem solving.

One of the great dangers in magazine publishing is that your approach will become stale. Don't confuse a consistent format with overreliance on formula. The degree to which you are inspired in producing each issue is probably a good measure of how that issue will be received by readers.

Journals and magazines in this section

- *Washington College Magazine*—a good format for feature articles in an alumni magazine
- *Back Talk Journal*—sophisticated type and photography in a small-format journal
- *American Demographics*—a format designed to introduce data, and some good filler ideas
- *Business North Carolina*—lessons learned from the redesign of a regional business magazine
- *Science Digest*—tricks from a technologically savvy editor
- *HeartCorps*—a stylish, upbeat design for an audience of heart patients
- *Mother Earth News*—low-resolution scans for high-efficiency production
- *Trips*—devices to break up running text

ABOUT TOWN

Karl And Irma Miller: Tillers Of Good Will

by Sue De Pasquale '87
Photographs by J.M. Fragomeni '88

Karl and Irma Miller are matter-of-fact when it ... about their gardening projects in ...

At 84 and 81, they see nothing unusual about a workload that keeps them bending, hoeing, digging and watering for hours upon hours nearly every day of the week. But ask people half their ... a quarter—who know ... a respect

K arl and Irma Miller nurture the College's students as lovingly as the Hynson-Ringgold gardens. Young adults who know the elderly couple say they have an uncanny ability to bridge the generation gap.

PIECES OF THE PAST

Colonel Brown And The Dancing Duo

by P.J. Wingate '33

Although Washington College has been promoting the arts and sciences for over 200 years, it is not well known for its contributions to the performing arts. Nevertheless, a Washington College graduate played a vital role in creating the most celebrated dance team in the history of the theatre—Fred Astaire and Ginger Rogers.

This alumnus was Hiram S. Brown, Class of 1900, and later president of the movie firm RKO, which produced the first Astaire-Rogers film, "Flying Down to Rio," and subsequently made millions of dollars from a series of movies by this most gifted pair of dancers. Colonel Brown, as he was known throughout most of his adult life, was no longer president of RKO when most of those later movies were produced, but it took no great foresight for Brown's successors to see that they had an artistic diamond necklace and a financial gold mine in the dance team of Ginger Rogers and Fred Astaire.

Both Rogers and Astaire had played in Broadway shows before they made their first movie together, and had also played minor roles in the movies, but neither was even close to being called a movie star when Hiram Brown brought them together in 1933. The best that could be said for them then was that they were featured players. The listed stars for "Flying Down to Rio" were Gene Raymond and Dolores Del Rio, both of whom have long since vanished into the mists of obscurity along with the plot of the movie itself.

Not so for Rogers and Astaire. They shot up into the theatrical sky like rockets, propelled by their own incomparable talents and the enchanting tunes by Vincent Youmans who provided the music they danced to: "The Carioca," "Orchids in the Moonlight," "Music Makes Me," and the title song, "Flying Down to Rio." In all subsequent movies which they made together, Ginger Rogers and Fred Astaire were the stars, and their dancing became artistic treasures which will be preserved for centuries to come.

The story of this famous dance team is too well known to be repeated here,

PHOTO: CULVER PICTURES

18   19   21

This alumni publication used to be a tabloid. After converting to desktop production, they saved enough money on typesetting and pasteup to upgrade the tabloid to the glossy magazine format shown on this page.

The style of feature articles defines a magazine's personality as much as any other element. Here, good photos given lots of space, graceful Palatino italic headlines, upsized introductions set on a two-column measure, and plenty of white space define an accessible style that opens every feature article. Subsequent pages of features follow the three-column format with photographs sized one, two, or three columns wide. This consistent style greatly speeds up layout and production time because so many decisions are already made.

The understated style works fine for a captive audience, which an alumni magazine such as this enjoys. A magazine with paid circulation has to work harder at varying its style and using catchy headlines to sell readers on each story.

Design: Meredith Davies (Chestertown, MD)

Pages from Washington College Magazine, *published quarterly. Trim size: 8-1/2 by 11*

Full-bleed photos, used frequently in this journal, have power and impact that you just don't get with photos that are contained on the page. The cover image provides a silhouette that is enviably appropriate for a clinic specializing in back pain.

Good printing on a heavy, coated paper stock brings out the best in the design and photos. The rich blacks contrast with the warm gray/brown used as a second color in the cover type, running heads, bold rules, pull quotes, and boxes for reverse-type initial caps.

The type selection contrasts the clean lines of Helvetica Black with the tall, thin shape of Garamond. The banner centered under the running head works because the two words above it have the same number of letters. The initial cap/small cap style of the subhead and running foot adds additional detail to the sophisticated typography.

Design: Bob Reznik (Plano, TX)

Pages from Back Talk Journal, *published annually by the Texas Back Institute. Trim size: 7-1/2 by 11*

WHAT IS A WORKING WOMAN?

If you think only half of women work, think again.

◆

by Horst H. Stipp

Whether a woman works outside the home or not is a vital piece of information for marketers who target women. Most rely on the standard published figures—52 percent of women aged 16 and older were working in 1986, for example.

New research indicates that this figure may be way off the mark. In fact, among a target group dear to the hearts of marketers—women aged 18 to 49—about 90 percent can be considered part of the labor force. The "typical housewife" has become rare indeed.

How can the standard statistics understate women's work patterns so dramatically? They overlook the fact that women enter and exit the labor force frequently. Both men and women occasionally change jobs, get laid off, or go to school. But many women also

Horst H. Stipp is the director of Social Research at NBC.

stop working for a while after they have a baby, when they get married, and for other reasons. Overall, women enter and exit the labor force much more frequently than men. As a result, a large percentage of women are both working and not working over a relatively short period of time. Many of today's nonworking women will be tomorrow's working women and vice versa. Most important, the attitudes of women with discontinuous work patterns are similar to those of women who are in the work force continuously.

THE PATTERN

The frequency with which women exit and reenter the labor force today is much less than it was 10 or 20 years ago. Nevertheless, demographers Suzanne Bianchi and Daphne Spain find that "women's participation in the labor force over the life course still remains more discontinuous than men's as women continue to exit and reenter the

A magazine that is chock-full of charts, graphs, tables, and just about every other form of statistical data works doubly hard to open each story as a general-interest feature. Bold headlines, hand-tinted photographs framed by heavy rules, and lots of white space provide lively hooks and a respite from the data prevalent elsewhere. The upsized introductory blurbs explain or provide context for the headline.

Effective fillers are the hot spots of many magazines. Fillers are simply standing items of varying length that you can plug in wherever space allows (or requires). A good concept for a filler is a fresh, timely, fascinating, or quirky angle on the magazine's subject matter. It's right on target even when it seems to come out of left field. A good filler is generally a quick read and may well be the first thing some readers look for when they pick up the magazine. The Demo Memo filler (above right) runs several times in each issue of *American Demographics*. It's easy to recognize and, for less than a minute of your time, is almost guaranteed to deliver some fascinating fact. The Lincoln Sample (below right) is, by definition, a limited-run filler: It follows a photographer's route from the Atlantic to the Pacific coast, with a picture of the road ahead taken every nine miles, exactly. Editorial techniques such as these keep magazines lively and changing and also provide flexibility in production.

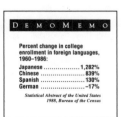

DEMO MEMO

Percent change in college enrollment in foreign languages, 1960–1986:

Japanese 1,282%
Chinese 839%
Spanish 130%
German .... –17%

Statistical Abstract of the United States 1988, Bureau of the Census

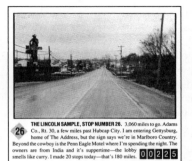

26 **THE LINCOLN SAMPLE, STOP NUMBER 26.** 3,060 miles to go. Adams Co., Rt. 30, a few miles past Hubcap City. I am entering Gettysburg, home of The Address, but the sign says we're in Marlboro Country. Beyond the cowboy is the Penn Eagle Motel where I'm spending the night. The owners are from India and it's suppertime—the lobby smells like curry. I made 20 stops today—that's 180 miles. 00225

Design: Michael Rider (Ithaca, NY)
Pages from American Demographics, *published monthly.*
Trim size: 8-3/8 by 11

When this regional business magazine approached a redesign, the staff focused on four goals: to capture the contrast of old and new that typified the audience; to sharpen the spotlight on people; to create a simple format that would free the small staff to focus on content rather than layout; and to convert the magazine to desktop publishing.

The audience combined the deep-rooted traditions of the North Carolina mountains and agricultural areas with the high tech innovations of businesses and universities in the state's Golden Triangle. Understanding the unique character of one's audience enables a magazine to use that character as a building block in the publication's design.

The typography in the logo captures the contrast inherent in the audience. The word "Business," set in Futura Extra Bold Oblique, is bold, contemporary, and aggressive. The words "North Carolina," set in the genteel, soft, and almost lyrical Palatino, add a quiet, reserved, and sophisticated counterpoint.

The spotlight on people was part of the magazine's editorial image all along. But the redesign process gives you the opportunity to look with fresh eyes at what you are already doing, as well as the opportunity to redefine your goals and determine how best to reach them. In this case, the new understanding led to a change from covers that varied in their subjects and art styles to photographic covers featuring a single business leader in his or her natural enviroment.

The emphasis on good, interesting photographs continues on the inside pages. Concentrating on a consistent visual approach and finding a small group of photographers who understand and can deliver the magazine's photographic style frees the art director from having to start at square one with every story.

A table of contents should be highly organized, graphically interesting, and uncompromisingly utilitarian—all at the same time.

The numbers in the contents listings are 24-point Futura Extra Bold Oblique. They are graphic as well as functional elements on the page. As is the case with headline type, numbers set in large sizes require careful kerning to achieve the even spacing seen here.

The rules are 18 point with 9-point Futura Extra Bold reverse type in all caps.

The descriptive lines are the 10/13 Palatino used for body text inside the magazine.

Art picked up from inside the magazine makes the contents page visually interesting and is selected both to highlight important stories and to arouse curiosity. If you use the art at the same size as it appears elsewhere in the magazine (even if it's just a detail from a larger picture), you avoid the cost of additional color separations.

FEATURE

BUSINESS IS LOOKING UP FOR GENERAL AVIATION

When it comes to flying for business or pleasure, the sky's not the limit.

By J.A.C. Dunn

he little plane circles the airport once, a tiny moving X in the cloudless eastern Carolina sky. Its single engine makes a barely audible hum. It disappears briefly beyond the woods, then suddenly reappears just over the trees surrounding the airport and lands on the longer of Warren Field's two runways. Taxiing to the front of the low, brick terminal building, it swings around to face the broad expanse of rough grass between the tarmac. The pilot cuts the engine, steps out of the cockpit and strolls across the apron and through the double glass doors of the terminal lobby.

"Morning," he says, genially, at large. Salesman, you think. He has a little sandy mustache and very alert eyes. Pointing at a tired-looking, twin-engine plane at one side of the apron, he asks, "That airplane out there. What is it? Does it fly?"

"That's an old DC-4," says Joe Leggitt, the airport manager. He's a stocky, muscular young man with a smiling, sunburned face. He used to be a commercial fisherman. He wears a khaki jumpsuit befitting the all-purpose manager of an all-purpose rural airport, but behind the counter he is barefoot: Warren Field is not a stuffy establishment. Authorities, he tells the pilot, impounded the plane after a drug raid last spring. It has been grounded ever since.

"You don't see many of those around any

more," the visitor says reverently. He leans against a counter and lights a cigarette. "I was flying over and noticed it, and I thought, 'I have to find out about *that*.' I'm just flying around, looking at the country. I have an appointment in Baltimore this afternoon. I don't want to get there too soon."

He introduces himself: Richard Leachman of Cessna Finance Corp. in Raleigh. Aircraft finance. It fit with the blue blazer, gray slacks, white button-down shirt, necktie and polished loafers. An airplane nowadays is often a corporate asset, not a Sunday toy, and its pilot, rather than a flying playboy nicknamed Ace, is likely to wear a business suit with a briefcase as his co-pilot. The Aircraft Owners and Pilots Association describes the average general aviator as 44 years old, the owner of a house and two cars, married with two children, a licensed, instrument-rated pilot who flies a single-engine, fixed-gear aircraft 116 hours a year and likes to fish.

Despite its apparent imprecision, the term "general aviation" is very specific. It embraces all flight except commercial airlines and the military. It doesn't grab the headlines, the way Piedmont's recent merger with USAir or the opening of a regional airline hub does, but its statistics are astonishing. The nation's general

Charles (left) and Winfield Causey were farming with their father in 1963. But they got bitten by the flying bug and turned from furrows to runways.

FEATURE

Phyllis Gallup replaced one plane wrecked by a student, who walked away from the crash. "All she said was, 'Oh, my hair must be a mess,'" Gallup says.

was a licensed pilot before he was 21. In 1921, he flew from London to China solo. The Winston-Salem airport bears his name. But it was only after World War II that airports, and aircraft to use them, began to take off in North Carolina. The stimulus was a liberal sprinkling of leftover military airfields, most of them in the eastern part of the state. The airports at Wilson, Rocky Mount (now closed), Lumberton, Kinston, New Bern, Beaufort-Morehead City, Washington, Manteo and Edenton were all originally military fields.

Most were used for training. Warren Field had T-6 trainers based on it, and the original runways are still in use, although their 45-year-old concrete pavement is showing signs of wear. The 82nd Airborne Division flew troop-carrying gliders at Maxton, and pilots took basic flight training at Horace Williams Field in Chapel Hill. When the present Raleigh-Durham Airport replaced Raleigh Municipal, it was called Raleigh-Durham Army Air Base until transferred to civilian hands after the war.

Several airports are still used by the military, such as McCall Field in Aberdeen and Oak Grove at New Bern. Thirty miles southeast of Elizabeth City is Harvey's Point, a small airfield deliberately kept small because the Central Intelligence Agency operates it. Some of the participants in the Bay of Pigs invasion were trained there.

During the 1950s, the economic value of general aviation began to take off. In 1958, the Federal Aviation Act provided the first federal funds for airport development. Nearly 20 North Carolina airports received improvement money until 1970.

In 1965, Gov. Dan Moore created the position of aviation specialist in what was then the Department of Conservation and Development to help communities attract

new business by providing a place for companies to park their planes. The state established an airport aid program with $127,000 in 1967, though this money could not be used to improve airports that had scheduled commercial service. The fund was increased to $150,000 a year in 1971.

The airport aid fund was increased to $2 million in 1973, when the reorganization of state government placed the aviation specialist in the Department of Transportation. Half the money went to airports with commercial service. The fund was increased to $3 million in 1974 and the distinction between commercial and general-aviation airports removed.

The federal deregulation of commercial airlines brought about this change. Before deregulation, airlines were subsidized, sometimes by as much as $60 per passenger per stop at an airport, to enable airlines to serve relatively low-traffic places, such as Elizabeth City. Airport managements charged the airlines for airport improvements, which the airlines paid for from their subsidies.

After deregulation, it became harder to maintain and improve airports because airline subsidy money was gone. But most communities found it worth their while to

A plane is a time machine, says the N.C. Division of Aviation's Willard Plentl. He wants every industrial area of the state to have an airport within a half-hour drive.

Design:
R. Kimble Walker
(Charlotte, NC)

Pages from
Business North
Carolina,
published monthly.
Trim size: 8-1/4 by
10-7/8

A strong, simple format enables the small staff to produce a quality magazine that competes for readers' time with big-budget national business magazines. By minimizing the choices for each story, the editor and art director can concentrate on substance rather than form.

The 72-point Futura Extra Bold initial cap with an 18-point bold rule continues the visual motif from the cover. Rules over photos print in a different color for each feature. This bold, crisp look helps tie together editorial pages in a magazine fractured by small-space ads.

The body text, 10/13 Palatino in two 16-pica ragged right columns, sets about one-third fewer words than the more typical 9/10 justified text found in many magazines. The open text was another result of the redesign, and the editors feel that less has proved to be more.

A well-thought-out format and a technologically savvy editor make this magazine a lesson in the marriage of good design and desktop ingenuity. It's the story of how dBASE, WordStar, Ventura, and a non-PostScript LaserJet Series II printer turned what could have been a nightmare of loose pieces into an efficient production system for a unique publication.

A true digest, all of the editorial material was culled from other publications. Each excerpt was keyboarded as a WordStar file and given an "SD" (the initials of the magazine) number. Each SD number was referenced in a dBASE file with a brief description of the item along with a line count, art availability, a source reference, and a code for as many of the magazine's 40 categories as were applicable. When compiling each issue, the editor would pick 12 to 15 categories, run the database to see which items were available, and make his selections. (The database file had a nonduplicate instruction built in.) Then he opened a WordStar file for each category and read the SD numbers into that file, and WordStar would string the individual items into one long manuscript for that section.

The Underlying Page is a two-column format with a 0.5-point vertical rule between the columns. By putting a frame over the narrow column, which was to be reserved for filler items and art, the single manuscript file for each section could be flowed automatically from page to page, filling only the wide columns. The reversed type headers were also part of the underlying page for each section; they were created as a repeating frame that was turned off for the section opener, where a larger reversed type banner printed below the 0.5-point horizontal rule. (See facing page, top left.)

Design: S. G. Design (New York, NY)

Pages from Science Digest. Trim size: 5 by 7-3/8

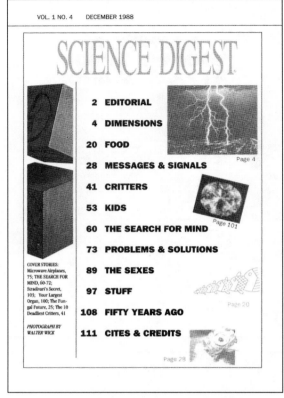

Well-designed type is the key ingredient in the appeal and accessibility of simple pages such as these. Only two typefaces were used— Garamond Condensed and Franklin Gothic Heavy—specified as follows:

Section Heads: 21-pt. Franklin Gothic reverse
Section Decks: 12/13 Garamond italic
Item Heads: 14-pt. Franklin Gothic
Body text: 12/13 Garamond
Filler Heads: 10-pt. Franklin Gothic; the 2-pt. ruling line below is 3 picas wide, lowered 2 points below the head
Filler text: 10/11 Garmond
Quote Marks: 36-pt. Frankllin Gothic
Headers: 14-pt. Franklin Gothic reverse

A tip about reverse type: Forget the cumbersome method, described in the early Ventura manuals, which uses the Ruling Line Above option. It is much easier just to make a frame with a black background and put white type in it.

Pages proofed in bit-mapped fonts were ultimately output in Post-Script on a Linotronic. The editor, who did the layout and production, didn't have a PostScript board for his printer. So he created two style sheets, one with a width table for bit-mapped fonts, the other with a width table for PostScript. For the Garamond body text (a BitStream font), he used the Fontware Installation Kit to generate identical bit-mapped and PostScript fonts. But for the Franklin Gothic display text (an Adobe font for which a bit-mapped version could not be generated), he had to substitute Helvetica for proofing. He used the bit-mapped style sheet for proofing pages on his LaserJet and then, before sending for Linotronic output, he switched to the PostScript style sheet. (Switching stylesheets converted all the tags automatically.) With this kind of workaround you have to carefully check all the line breaks on screen before sending for final output, but in this case there weren't any changes from the bit-mapped to the PostScript fonts.

FOOD

Exploring the edible universe

BONING UP

In one study of the bones of people who lived near the California coast before 1100 A.D., evidence indicated that the men ate mostly seafood while the women ate mainly plants. After that time, the difference disappears.

WHO ATE WHAT WHEN

WE ARE PARTICULARLY FOND of Jerold Lowenstein's "Landfall" column in *Oceans* magazine. Lowenstein, a professor of nuclear medicine, is a fine writer and a man of wide interests, including molecular evolution and a new subject called "paleo-diet," the study of what our ancestors ate. This last was the subject of a recent column, aptly titled "Who Ate What When."

For carnivores, creatures who eat other creatures, the the ratio of the animal's nitrogen-14 to nitrogen-15 levels is the number that scientists use to locate them on the food chain. Humans and other land carnivores rarely top nine on the scale. Sea carnivores, on the other hand, routinely have ratios of 20 or more. The highest ratio ever observed was 36, in a toothed whale. Says Lowenstein: "Twelve different sea creatures had to eat each other in sequence to achieve that concentration." *—Oceans*

CORE SOUNDINGS

AN APPLE COMPUTER invented far from Silicon Valley may lead to more bruise-free fruits and vegetables at your local greengrocer. No matter how carefully fresh produce is handled, some of each shipment is invariably damaged in transit. To cut this costly spoilage, the U.S. Department of Agriculture and Michigan State University have jointly

FOOD

developed a device to pinpoint rough handling. The apple-size, battery-powered gizmo, when placed in consignments of actual fruit, says Galen Brown of the USDA, "automatically records the bumps that real apples receive as they're moved from orchards to retail stores."

Cast in a protective sphere of beeswax, the artificial apple contains an accelerometer to measure the force and duration of bumps, a clock, and a computer to record the exact time of all bumps severe enough to cause damage. The data is then analyzed against plant and trip records. So far, researchers have found that apples best survive the trip from plant to store if individually wrapped in plastic foam packs. The team plans to adapt its sensor to study similarly fragile crops like citrus, melons, peaches, tomatoes, cucumbers, and potatoes.

—U.S. Department of Agriculture

❝

A short section of rough highway can take its toll on even carefully packed apples.

❞

—Galen Brown

Newcomer

THE ORANGE MUTANT

IT BEGAN IN CANADA, just north of Toronto, where a single dwarf orange mutant grew in the midst of a field of normal white cauliflowers. Scientists crossed the dwarf mutant with a standard cauliflower and the result was a full-size head that was bright orange—a new vegetable.

"Carotene, a hydrocarbon that converts to vitamin A when consumed by people, is the element that gives the vegetable its untraditional color," says Michael Dickson of Cornell's New York State Agricultural Experiment Station. The orange cauliflower has 100 times as much carotene as the white variety, and thus is a rich source of vitamin A. It tastes exactly like its white cousin, but some experts predict the bright orange color will boost its appeal. Says

---

STUFF

Shapely Sack

❝

The skin we actually see, then, no matter how glowingly supple the surface may appear to the poet, is in fact a shedding crust of dead and dying cells.

❞

—Albert Rosenfeld

THE SCOOP ON SKIN

THE HUMAN RIND is the body's largest organ, a wrapper that covers two square yards, weighs about nine pounds, and completely replaces itself about every 28 days. It fits firmly around the scalp, ears, hands, and feet, loosely around the abdomen, and is pleated for flexibility around the knuckles, knees, and elbows. Its nearly transparent outer layer, the epidermis, may be as thin as two thousandths of an inch (over the eyelids) or as thick as one sixteenth of an inch (on the soles of the feet). It contains glands that secrete a lubricant called sebum to keep it supple, and three million sweat glands to keep it cool. It is laced with nerves—1,300 receptors per square inch in sensitive parts of the hand—and at any one time holds 25 percent of the body's blood supply.

We learned all this and more from veteran science writer Albert Rosenfeld's excellent article on human skin. Once thought to be little more than a protective sack, scientists today view the skin as a complex, multi-purpose organ. Says Rosenfeld: "We now know that the skin is both a key element in the immune system and a chemical conversion factory that rivals the liver." *—Smithsonian*

DIAMONDS, PART ONE

WANT TO MAKE A DIAMOND? Nature does it with extreme temperature and pressure, deep in the earth. The most common way diamonds are made here on the surface is by cooling carbon at high pressure, but you also can do it by heating up carbon plasma to around $20,000^\circ$ C. and condensing it on a cooler surface, say around 700° C. Either way, the result will be a lot of little "industrial" diamonds.

STUFF

Nature's Own

❝

To use the product of high-pressure physics to pledge undying affection may not be entirely acceptable to the feminine psyche.

❞

—Anthony Butler

About the only other way to make a diamond is to use a technique developed by Russian chemists that requires neither high temperatures nor pressure. Simply spray an energetic beam of carbon ions on a surface and what you get is a new kind of diamond, one that is nowhere as dazzling as nature's creation but, according to two Australian physicists, at least as hard, perhaps harder. Applications for the new diamonds already are being considered—among them, machine tools, optical surfaces, diamond-coated metal for wrist watches, and a diamond-edged razor blade that would last for years. *—The Economist*

DIAMONDS, PART TWO

THE FIRST man-made diamonds were born in the high temperature press of a Swedish engineering company on February 15, 1953—unless you believe the tale of James Ballantyne Hannay, an eccentric Scotchman who lived from 1855 to 1931.

Hannay conducted a series of experiments in which various alkali metals and paraffin were heated in cast iron tubes welded shut. According to chemist Anthony Butler of the University of St. Andrews in Fife, Scotland, Hannay thought the reaction might crystallize carbon into diamonds, and on the 81st attempt, after countless explosions, he created what he thought were diamonds by heating a mixture of bone oil, paraffin, and lithium for 14 hours. He later wrote of his experiments: "The continued strain on the nerves, watching the temperature of the furnace, and in a state of tension in case of an explosion, induces a nervous state which is extremely weakening, and

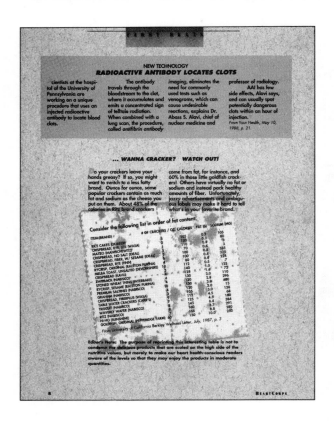

A stylish, varied, and active design gives a very upbeat image to this magazine for heart patients. The pages are full of tips, techniques, charts, and other information highlighted through a visual repertoire that includes initial caps, large numbers, and frequent use of sidebars.

Department pages such as the ones shown at left break from the traditional columnar format by having each item treated almost as if it were an index card. The shape of the text block, as well as the type size, leading, and column width, vary from item to item, but the single typeface (Futura) and the textured background unify these pages.

Dimensionality is another signature of this design. Note the use of the cracker as a self-referential background for a chart, with type surprinting at the top and bottom. And in the page shown below left, the first text block appears to be sandwiched between art in the foreground and background; while in the second item, the art is woven under the headline and over the text.

The headline type for feature stories (shown on the facing page) is Bodoni Poster, condensed to different degrees for each story depending on the length of the headline and the layout of the page. This provides the benefits of a unified typeface with many variations. Bodoni Poster works unusually well with this treatment because it maintains its distinctive relationship of thick and thin strokes. Many typefaces deviate too much from the original design when manipulated in this way.

The text wraparound (facing page, bottom) minimizes the copy lost to a fairly large illustration.

Design: Tom Lewis (San Diego, CA)

Pages from Heartcorps, *published bimonthly. Size: 8-1/4 by 10-3/4*

ROPE JUMPING
TOO GOOD TO PASS UP?
BY KEN SOLIS, MD

An often repeated adage states, "The best exercise is the exercise which you do." There are four essential questions which you must ask yourself to define if an exercise is one that you will likely do *on a regular basis and for an indefinite period of time*: 1) Is it right for your body? 2) Is it easily accessible? 3) Will it give the results you are looking for? and 4) Do you enjoy it?

Perhaps surprisingly, rope jumping is one form of aerobic exercise which nicely fits the bill for many people, even recovered heart patients. Now, even without the help of telepathy, I know that a good number of you readers have already been struck with the "but ... too" disease: "I'd love to try it, *but*

I'm *too* uncoordinated to jump rope" - or - "it sounds like fun, *but* it'd be *too* hard on my knees" - or - "it's *too* hard on my wind, and it's *too* boring." In fact, rope jumping is one of the most user-friendly, safe, versatile and productive exercises available. Unfortunately, it is also one of the most misunderstood. So before we write off rope jumping to highly-tuned pugilists and energetic school children, let's see if rope jumping is an exercise which you just might want to do.

ARE YOU READY FOR IT?

First ask your physician if your heart is ready for moderate to vigorous exercise. Rope jumping is not recommended for the early phases of cardiac rehabilitation since the heart rate response is less predictable

RATED PERCEIVED EXERTION (RPE) SCALE

0	Nothing at all
0.5	Extremely weak
1	Very Weak
2	Weak
3	Moderate
4	Somewhat strong
5	Strong
6	
7	Very strong
8	
9	
10	Extremely strong Maximal

FIGURE 1. On a scale of 1 to 10, exercise intensity is guided by using your own internal "sense" of how hard you are working. Exerting yourself in the range of 3 to 5 correlates well to the "target heart rate range."

Reference: Borg, G.V. *Medicine and Science in Sports and Exercise*, 14:377-87, 1982.

BY LEE LIPSKER, PH.D.

TIPS TO GET YOU THROUGH THE HOLIDAYS

Sugar plum fairies, chestnuts roasting on an open fire, colorful wrapping paper, friends and relatives gathered together, ... the holiday period of November through December evokes images which are nearly universal. It seems that most everyone is caught up in the spirit and mood of the season. Just think of the gusto with which we proclaim, "Happy Thanksgiving! ... Happy Hanukah! ... Merry Christmas! ... Happy New Year!" Unfortunately, this two or three month period of the year is often a time of anxiety, stress, and depression for persons with heart disease and their immediate family members.

Depression is a commonly reported problem for those who have experienced myocardial infarction (MI), coronary bypass surgery, angioplasty, or other heart-related illnesses. In fact, the research literature suggests that between 55% and 90% of all heart attack victims experience significant signs of depression as long as one year after the attack. In most cases, the depression and accompa-

1 TALK ABOUT IT. Part of the nature of depression is the tendency to believe that your difficulties are so unique that no one else could possibly understand. After all, you certainly wouldn't want to "burden" someone else with your problems! Nothing could be further from the truth. The many issues discussed here are so common that they are nearly as universal as are the mistletoe and colored lights. Surely everyone has experienced the disappointment felt when our expectations have not been met. Can any one of us honestly say that we have not been disillusioned by the over-commercialization of the holidays - at least for a little while? More significantly, most of your friends and family have had moments of depression. We all know what it is like to be "down."

Talking to someone about our problems can have many beneficial effects. First, by articulating our feelings we get to *hear* for ourselves just what is bothering us. Once the issues are on the table, we can call on many of our own resources to deal with them. With our thoughts laid out for us, we can identify the ones that are rational and have some basis in truth. Talking about what is bothering us also opens the door for help. It is often enough just to remind ourselves that someone will listen to us and care about how we feel. When we share our pain, discomfort, fear or sadness, we allow others to demonstrate their love and caring for us. In the sharing process, good ideas for solutions or understanding are generated by the parties involved.

Many of the issues that are involved in depression are of interest to the people that are closest to us. The variety of emotions that often accompany heart disease need attention. Your physician may be interested in your feelings for several reasons, not the least of which is the possibility of side-effects from prescribed medication. The holidays are often a period of increased spirituality - the perfect time to call on your pastor or rabbi. Or as described below, the holiday time might be the right time to get involved in a support group. The hardest part is to reach out initially and get beyond the reluctance that you will be "burdening" someone. It is a necessary step in overcoming depression and, once taken, can lead to happiness and long-lasting rewards.

2 GET INVOLVED. Few things contribute to our psychological well-being as greatly as knowing that we're important and needed. The holiday time presents us with a myriad of opportunities to become active in projects that can add immeasurably to our self-esteem. From volunteering on the children's ward at the local hospital to addressing and stuffing envelopes at the area American Heart Association or American Red Cross office - there are unlimited places and programs in which you can direct some energy. This form of involvement accomplishes

---

WALKING...
TAKING YOUR EXERCISE IN STRIDE
BY BILL BUSH, EDITOR-IN-CHIEF

A good brisk walk, several times a week, can strengthen the heart.

One of the most important steps in restoring heart health can be many steps taken in quick succession -- a brisk walk. The remarkable benefits of regular walking for cardiac rehabilitation have been acknowledged by virtually all cardiologists, who cite their own clinical experience and the growing body of long-term research.

Many heart patients wonder how something as easy as walking can have such a big impact on their physical condition. The simple truth is, a good brisk walk, several times a week can strengthen the heart. Adhering to a regular walking program may also have a favorable effect on blood pressure, serum cholesterol level, weight control, and psychological attitude. You may be thinking, "Can just simple walking regularly do all that?" and the answer is a resounding "Yes!"

While it is known and reported that high-intensity, "power" walking delivers great fitness benefits; low-intensity walking, "a brisk walk around the block" will return substantial health benefits as well, especially if done regularly and frequently. This is especially welcome news for the thousands who have come to believe that heart attack recovery and heart health can only be gained through heavy-duty exercise. The "no pain, no gain" body-building adage simply doesn't hold true for cardiac rehab.

Dr. Neil Gordon, at the Institute for Aerobics Research in Dallas, Texas, starts every patient with a walking program. According to Gordon, "Walking is the ideal exercise for heart attack patients." He recommends walking for cardiac patients because it tends not to promote the injuries common to jogging, like shin splints, muscle and tendon pulls and joint inflammation. "Often heart patients are older and ill-prepared to suffer the jarring and compression that go with other types of exercise," says Dr. Gordon. "Walking is a natural movement for the body and , therefore, it is very low impact but can be very aerobic if done properly."

Patients at Gordon's clinic are tested to determine optimum exertion levels for the course of their cardiac rehabilitation. Using a treadmill, Gordon gradually increases speed and elevation to a point where the patient is substantially taxed and approaching problems -- 70% to 85% of that level of exertion is determined to be the patient's "symptom-limited maximum heart rate." Gordon's exercise prescription, which all patients must have before undertaking any type of strenuous program, is typically a regimen calling for walking sessions lasting 20 to 40 minutes, three to five times a week at the rate determined by the stress test.

Dr. Gordon, in our interview, emphasized that the "symptom-limited maximum heart rate" is quite different from the "target heart rate" training guidelines that have thousands of fitness-devoted Americans regularly checking their pulses during and after exercise. (See page 24.)

The American Heart Association and American College of Sports Medicine recommend an exertion level measured at 60-75% of the maximum heart rate, sustained for 30 minutes at least three times a week. They assert that exercise above 75% may be too strenuous unless in excellent physical condition; and exercise below 60% gives the heart and lungs little physical conditioning.

Brisk walking - - about four to five miles per hour, can elevate heart rates into the ideal conditioning range. But even walking at three and one-half miles per hour may be too taxing for those on the mend from a heart attack.

Fortunately, there is an increasing body of knowledge through research that suggests substantial health benefits can be achieved at exercise levels far below the 60% to 75% target zone. "Walking for 45 minutes a day is wonderful, even without ever reaching your target heart rate zone," says Dr. Bob Hopper of the Cardiac Health & Diagnostic Center in Long Beach, California. Hopper, an exercise physiologist, makes a key distinction between *health* and *fitness* : the data suggests physical activity is related to lower heart disease risk, not necessarily fitness. A good physical fitness program will achieve heart healthy benefits, but walking and never achieving your target heart rate is also very good."

Hopper says moderate activity equal to expending about 2000 calories a week will reduce the risk of heart disease, but not necessarily improve fitness. He admits that his is a minority "but growing" opinion on the value of moderate exercise for heart health. However, he argues that nationally, adherence to more rigorous fitness programs have been dismal, especially in older age groups. "The fitness craze has been a failure," says Hopper. "Only a small percentage of Americans, one study says about 6.5%, reach the American College of Sports Medicine guidelines of 30 minutes at the target heart rate, three times a week."

Hopper strongly believes in the ACSM guidelines, but takes a more pragmatic view when dealing with cardiac rehab patients. "We talk with our cardiac patients and find out that they have not been able to stay with a fitness program. For the long term, its better to get heart patients on a

ILLUSTRATION: JOHN CARLYLE

Generally, the more deeply an exercise makes you breath, the more it burns calories and body fat...

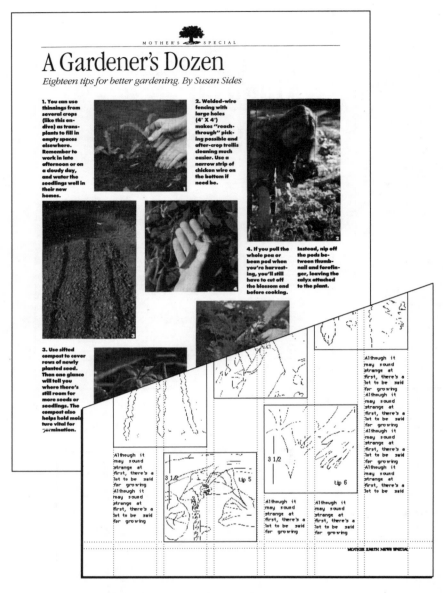

Scanning photographs for reproduction, in both black and white and color, pushes desktop publishing to its outer limits. It can be done, but for most people it requires too much time, skill, and memory to produce a satisfactory result. The cost of converting a photograph to a halftone for black and white reproduction is still one of the best bargains commercial printers offer. And the quality is far superior to what most people can achieve using desktop technology. Color scanning is even more difficult, and of course the hardware required is even more expensive.

Using a scanner as a production tool, on the other hand, provides a great deal of control and flexibility when you design pages with numerous photographs or illustrations. In the sample shown here, we used low-resolution scans to do very precise layouts, saving time (and money on photostat bills) for pages that would be commercially typeset and manually pasted up, with color art stripped in by the printer. The on-screen image is shown in front of the printed page.

Working from 35mm transparencies, we projected the slides on a wall to make rough tracings. (We simply put a piece of tracing paper over the projected image and literally traced it.) We scanned each tracing individually as simple line art at 150 dots per inch, saved it in MacPaint format, and placed and sized it in the electronic page layout.

Bogus copy was used to simulate the caption-style text. With all the elements in electronic form, we could manipulate their sizes and positions to develop the layout.

The laser proof served as the final layout guide for the pasteup artist as well as for the printer when stripping in the original art.

Design: Don Wright (Woodstock, NY)

Page from Mother Earth News, *published bimonthly.*

Trim size: 8-1/8 by 10-3/4

If you need more detail in your layout, you can scan black-and-white photos—or color laser copies—as low-resolution halftones, as we did with the sample shown at left. None of the scans described on this page are memory intensive. The scans of tracings ranged from 9 to 20 KB and took about 18 seconds each; the halftone scans ranged from 12 to 36 KB and took about 40 seconds each.

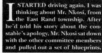

Running copy is the backbone of many magazine pages. But you don't have to present it as marching columns of text. The designer's palette contains a wide range of devices to break up the text and add graphic impact to the page.

An inset photo with wraparound text (far left) varies the shape of the columns on the page in addition to providing visual interest. Note the weight of the double-ruled border, which makes old (and in other cases inferior) photos pop.

Section breaks in a story (left) provide an opportunity for graphic treatment. Here, the first seven lines of each new section are upsized with an initial cap and reversed out against a black background.

Borders can dress up a page with a style appropriate to the story, even without the added interest provided by angled photos and wraparound text on the page below. There are numerous borders available in electronic and traditional clip art.

Design and Art Direction: Roger Black (New York, NY) and Margery Cantor (Menlo Park, CA)

Pages from Trips, *published by Banana Republic. Trim size: 7 by 10*

CHAPTER 7

DATA: CATALOGS, DATA SHEETS, FINANCIALS, AND FORMS

Publications with large amounts of data rely heavily on careful organization and deft styling of typography. Some require clear delineation and consistent handling of repetitive elements, such as product names, prices, and descriptive listings; others require formats that can accommodate different kinds of elements, such as continuous narrative interspersed with tables, charts, and graphs.

Before settling on an approach, you'll need to analyze the material and experiment with different typographic styles. The ability to experiment on the desktop is a decided advantage when you are designing these publications, and you can save time by testing small samples of data before styling the entire document. In testing the type style and tab positions for tables, be sure to include both the maximum and minimum number and length of elements you have to accommodate, so that you can see the balance of the two in any format.

CATALOGS & DATA SHEETS

When you have to pack a lot of text into a small space, you will generally enhance the appeal and overall readability if you choose a small, tightly leaded, condensed type style and maximize the space around the text. Larger sizes surrounded by less white space result in pages that are dark and unrelievedly dense. Use rules and borders to aid organization and to change the color of the page. Even in publications without a second color, rules with contrasting weights can add much-needed graphic variety as well as organizational clarity.

Catalogs and data sheets in this section

- *Tables Specification Guide* —diverse elements in a landscape format
- *Books on Black Culture*—art livens up straightforward catalog listings
- *Beverly Hills Motoring Accessories*—boxes, banners, and more boxes and banners
- *The Concept Technical Manual*—technical illustrations for ski clothes
- *Teaching Tools*—a highly structured catalog of educational software
- *School of Visual Arts*—a little style dresses up straightforward listings
- *Clackamas Community College catalog*—a format that accommodates many different kinds of listings

- *Portland State Quarterly*—adventurous typography in a newspaper format
- *MathCAD Manual*—a smart format uses Ventura's automated features
- *Fitzgerald, Abbott & Beardsley*—consistency in a presentation folder
- *Indelec*—a two-column format that fits the product
- *Infrared Optics Cleaning Kit*—handsome simplicity
- *Smith & Hawken product assembly sheets*—an easily implemented format consistent with the company look
- *Questor Inlets*—leadered callouts and a functional use of color

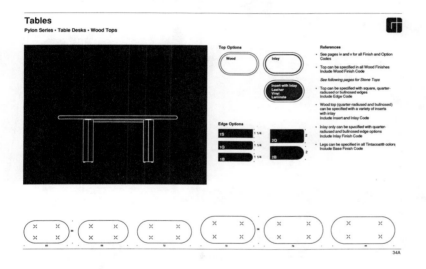

The horizontal format provides more flexibility than a vertical page in organizing the many options available for items in this catalog.

The rules, logo, headlines, and black box on the top page and the rules and bar coding on the bottom page are consistent throughout the catalog. In addition to simplifying electronic page assembly, this uniformity brings visual order to a complex document. It also makes it easy for readers to find information about any given product because similar information appears on the same place on every page.

The line drawing of each item prints as a white line in a black box. This technique dramatically highlights the subject of each page, making it the dominant item amid the many other kinds of information. The drawings were created in a drafting program, saved as PICT files, and sized proportionately in the electronic page layout.

Design: Manfred Petri (Atlanta, GA)

Pages from Tables Specification Guide and Price List, *from Geiger International Trim size: 11-7/8 by 8-3/8*

The bold banner across the top of each page and the striking silhouettes of the African art give this book catalog a distinctive personality that is obviously appropriate to the theme of black culture.

The two text columns are boxed in with rules. The outer column is consistently used for art, which is photocopied (with permission) from one of the books in the catalog and pasted into position on the camera-ready pages. When a category of books does not require the two text columns on a page, additional art is used as filler.

The typeface for the book listings is Helvetica. The use of boldface caps to set off the titles, regular caps for the authors, and space between this highlighted information and the descriptive listings is handled consistently throughout and makes the catalog easy to use. The type overall is relatively dark, a result of using laser printer output for camera-ready copy. That darkness works here with the art style and format.

The category heads are Times Roman, reversed out of the black banners at the top of each page.

Design: Lisa Menders (Royal Oak, MI)

Pages from Books on Black Culture, *a mail-order catalog published by the book end in Southfield, MI. Trim size: 8-3/8 by 11*

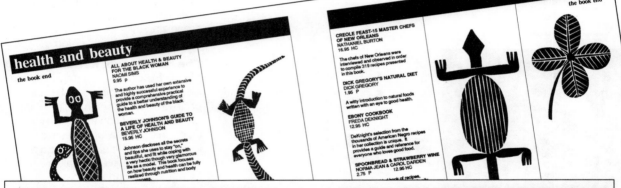

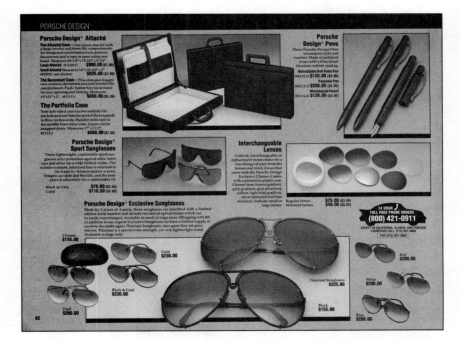

Boxes and banners are used throughout to organize the many elements on each page.

Black banners along the top function as tabs, with product categories in reverse type.

Photos are framed by 0.5-point rules on three sides; the 8-point rule at the bottom of each frame provides a solid base for each photo. This is particularly effective when the product is a car and also gives the catalog a distinctive style. Note the varied directions of the cars in the top row of photos.

Small objects are carefully arranged as still lifes to best display shape, texture, and different views and styles of the same product. The pattern of objects repeated on the page plays with color and shape to provide visual interest. Grouping small objects in one photo saves space as well as photo expenses.

Silhouette photos that extend beyond the picture frames have more dimensionality than photos that are contained. This technique provides variety within the basic format and maximizes the use of space where needed.

Text prints on a gray background. The boldface Helvetica headlines and prices are offset from the descriptive text, which is set smaller in Palatino.

Design: Bob Lee, Lee & Porter Design (Los Angeles, CA)

Pages from a catalog published by Beverly Hills Motoring Accessories. Trim size: 11 by 8-1/2

Simple technical diagrams
with leadered callouts tell the story in this wholesale catalog of ski clothes. Why diagrams? Because here the message is warmth, freedom of movement, and protection from impact and sliding hazards, rather than the fabric and fashion angle typically captured in photographs.

Careful alignment of elements
provides structure within a free-form design. A formal grid would have restricted the size of art and placement of callouts. The distinctive logo treatment, the art and callout style, and the typeface provide visual consistency from page to page.

The typeface is Bodoni, with Helvetica Black used for boldface emphasis in headlines. The ragged right margin suits the casual style and short line length of the callouts. As much as possible, leaders extend from the justified left margin, the top or the bottom, rather than the ragged right.

This highly structured format
positions the product in the same place on every page. The position of the headlines, lists of features, screen details from the programs, system requirements, and other elements also remain constant, making it very easy to find any piece of information for any product.

The headline and other boldface type is American Typewriter and matches the type on the packaging.

The row of triangles under each product name is a right-leadered tab. The leader is customized with a Zapf Dingbat (character number <116>) and a space. You can define a style for a customized leader; then, each time you want to add it to the document, simply position the cursor, apply the style, and insert the tab.

The triangles in the upper right of each page function as product category tabs. Each category uses a different color for that triangle, for the line of small triangles, and for the quote under each product.

Design (top):
Oscar Anderson,
Weingart/Anderson
(Chicago, IL)

Page from the
Concept Technical
Manual, *published*
by Apparel
Technology.
Size: 8-1/2 by 11

Design (bottom):
Partners by Design
(N. Hollywood, CA)

Pages from the
Davidson Educa-
tional Software
catalog.
Size: 5-1/2 by 8-1/2

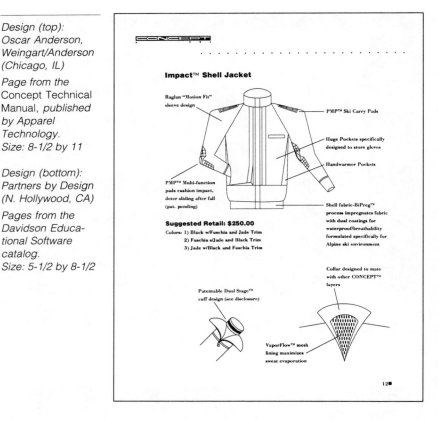

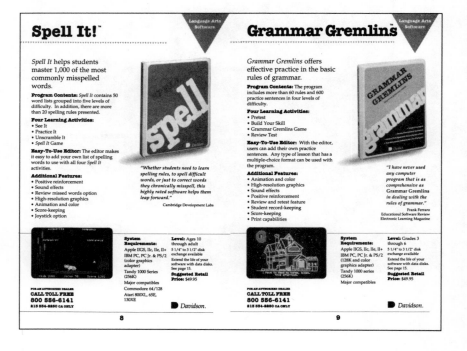

90 JOURNALISM AND PUBLIC RELATIONS

JOURNALISM AND PUBLIC RELATIONS

WRITING AND EDITING are the primary skills needed for a career in journalism and public relations. Learning to think and write clearly are skills that can be taught. And when the quality of thinking is drawn from intelligence, personal style follows.

Our society becomes increasingly complicated and with that awareness comes the need for skilled professionals who understand how to communicate creatively, to persuade and to present a point of view with clarity.

Journalism today no longer means working only for newspapers. Journalists work on staff and freelance for magazines, radio stations, television local stations, networks and cable stations.

Public relations experts also work on staff and freelance for individual corporations — almost every large company needs a public relations division — educational institutions, in all broadcast media, as well as with specialized public relations firms. As a writer learning or reacquainting yourself with the essentials of style can be the beginning of a new career with a focus. A working knowledge of the press, understanding how to write press releases or copy, and editing can be important regardless of where you focus your writing talent. The more skills and the more flexibility you have as a writer the more valuable you will be in applied writing in journalism and public relations.

Class hours: 7:00 pm to 9:40 pm unless otherwise indicated. Add registration fee (non-refundable) of $20.00 when registering for these courses.

TE109A
Freelance Magazine Writing: Making the Right Moves for Success
Mon - 2 Credits - $250.00
Creative careers need professional guidance. This is a course for writers who need to know how the marketplace operates. We will examine how to: query editors, make contacts, exploit research resources, gear an article to the appropriate magazine, negotiate fees and expenses. Drawing on your own editorial interests and enthusiams, you will learn how to produce winning story proposals, getting actual assignments from real magazines. Guest lecturers will include accomplished writers and editors. A certain passion for the printed word, rather than any publishing experience, is the course's only prerequisite.
David Abrahamson, Writer, Journalist. B.A., Johns Hopkins University; M. Journalism, University of California; Oxford University. Formerly, Managing Editor, "Car and Driver." Publications include: "The New York Times Magazine," "Science '86," "New York," "Playboy," "Backpacker."

TE205A
Editing Workshop
Thurs - 2 Credits - $250.00
Copy editors are the unsung heroes of the publishing world. Their work clears what was muddled, simplifies the complex, and imposes stylistic order. Good copy editors are in great demand for newspapers, magazines and book publishers. Learn how to handle the copy - the hard, sweaty part - and write headlines, the fun part.
Jack Robbins, Copy Editor, Business Week. Formerly, Editor, McGraw-Hill; Reporter, "The New York Post."

TE207A
How to Promote Practically Anything — Including Yourself
Thurs - 2 Credits - $250.00
This is a course in personal public relations. You will be shown how to put together your own press package for your company or yourself. Topics will include: working knowledge of the press; release writing; fundamentals of public speaking; projecting your own image.
Marilyn McCrudden, President, McCrudden and Sullivan Communications. B.A., University of Minnesota. Clients include: Grafton Street Irish Imports; Parke Bernet Galleries; Delmonico's Hotel; Carson, Lundin & Thorson, P.C., Architects; Scandinavian Airlines; Hearst Publications. Publications: "Who's Who in American Women."

Open leading and a two-column measure (left) add importance to the introduction for each section of this catalog without requiring the space of a full page.

Small pieces of art, which print in green, are sprinkled throughout the pages to help break up the text.

Quotes from instructors and experts (below right) are also used to break up the text. Although the type is smaller than that usually found in blurbs, the open leading, the border, and the green initial cap combine to make this a strong visual element.

The typography for course listings is simple and effective: a 2-point rule, a Futura Heavy course number, a Futura Bold course title, italic for schedule/credit/fee data, and Century Old Style for running text with the instructor's name in boldface.

The triangle borders use the same Zapf Dingbat technique as the educational catalog on the facing page but without a character space.

Design: School of Visual Arts Press (New York, NY)

Pages from the catalog for The School of Visual Arts. Trim size: 7-1/4 by 10-3/4

68 PHOTOGRAPHY

process their own film outside class.
William L. Broecker, Photographer. B.A., University of Michigan; M.A., Michigan State University. Editor: *ICP Encyclopedia of Photography; Leica Manual 15th ed.*; Associate Technical Director, *Encyclopedia of Practical Photography*. Publications: "Popular Photography," "Invitation To Photography," "35mm Photography," "Color Photography Annual," "Exposure," "Infinity."

PROFESSIONAL

The following courses are offered to advanced students of photography and working photographers who are able to maintain the pace of classes that take for granted basic technical skills and experience. These professional level courses focus on portfolio development in the different photographic specializations. Critical analysis of all aspects of the photograph from concept through to finished prints/chromes is offered. At this stage self-initiated work is essential and the personal aesthetic is further refined.

¶ If you are interested in learning new techniques or exploring unfamiliar advancements in technology, there are a number of courses for you to consider.
¶ If you are dissatisfied with the results your current portfolio is getting, a professional course offering critical analysis may be helpful.

PC300A
Advanced Printing
Tues - 2 Credits - $250.00
Lab Fee, $20.00
A course designed for the intermediate and advanced student who is interested in approaching printing as a fine art. Each print will be tailored to the photograph itself. Students should come to the first class session ready to print. Prerequisites: PC205, Basic Photography II, and PC256, Black and White Printing, or presentation of your portfolio at the first session.
Bob Brooks, Photographer, Printer. Has worked in many studios including those of Irving Penn and Bob Adelman. One-Person Exhibition: Plaza Caribe. Group Exhibitions: Floating Foundation of Photography; The People Yes Show, Central Park. Clients: Xerox Corporation, Playtex, Coca-Cola, Fischbach Gallery. Publications: "U.S. Camera," "The Visual Dialogue," "Art News."

PC307A
Photojournalism
Thurs - 2 Credits - $250.00
A survey of practical photojournalism as it exists at wire services and newspapers. The training of perception and the use of the camera as a reporting tool are stressed. Topics to be discussed include: journalism for the photographer; personal vision vs. professional credibility; new technology and how it will affect you; paying the rent as a freelancer; how words can make your camera lie; the use and abuse of photography in public relations; portfolio critique and preparation. Students must have access to their own or commercial darkroom.
Edward Hart, Picture Editor, United Press International, New York City Bureau. B.A., Long Island University. Formerly, Writer/Producer, UPI Television Service. Member: National Press Photographers Association, Society of Professional Journalists, Reporters Committee for Freedom of the Press.

PC316A
Advanced Studio Photography
Mon - 2 Credits - $250.00
Model and Equipment Fees, $35.00
(Limited to twenty students)
A course designed for the advanced student who has successfully completed PC221, Basic Studio Photography, or equivalent. The first two weeks will be devoted to still-life, shot with the 4" x 5" view camera using Polaroid film. (Students must supply their own Polaroid film Type 52). The remainder of the course will be devoted to 35mm or 2 1/4" x 2 1/4" format. Controlled lighting, using strobe to establish mood rather than just illuminate, will be the theme of all assignments. The student will shoot still-life, fashion, beauty and nudes.
Len DeLessio, Photographer. B.F.A., School of Visual Arts. Publications: "Business Week," "Cosmopolitan," "New York," "Parents," "People," "Penthouse," "Viva," "Time," "Elle," "Working Woman." Clients include: American Optical, Binney & Smith/Crayola, Chesebrough Ponds, Fujinon Optical, Andrew Geller Shoes, General Foods - Gaines Dog Food, Mercedes-Benz, Parke-Davis, Perry Ellis, Pierre Cardin Fragrances, P&G - Cascade, Tide, Highpoint, R.J. Reynolds -

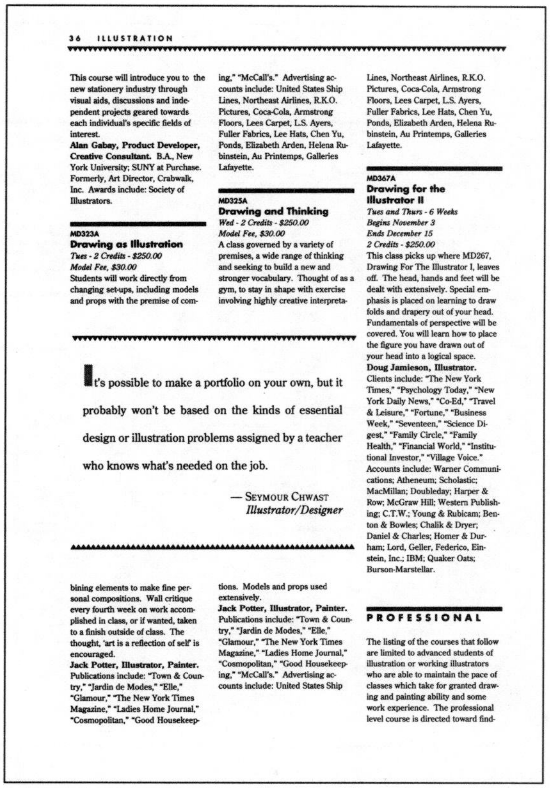

36 ILLUSTRATION

This course will introduce you to the new stationery industry through visual aids, discussions and independent projects geared towards each individual's specific fields of interest.
Alan Gabay, Product Developer, Creative Consultant. B.A., New York University; SUNY at Purchase. Formerly, Art Director, Crabwalk, Inc. Awards include: Society of Illustrators.

MD323A
Drawing as Illustration
Tues - 2 Credits - $250.00
Model Fee, $30.00
Students will work directly from changing set-ups, including models and props with the premise of combining elements to make fine personal compositions. Wall critique every fourth week on work accomplished in class, or if wanted, taken to a finish outside of class. The thought, 'art is a reflection of self' is encouraged.
Jack Potter, Illustrator, Painter. Publications include: "Town & Country," "Jardin de Modes," "Elle," "Glamour," "The New York Times Magazine," "Ladies Home Journal," "Cosmopolitan," "Good Housekeeping," "McCall's." Advertising accounts include: United States Ship Lines, Northeast Airlines, R.K.O. Pictures, Coca-Cola, Armstrong Floors, Lees Carpet, L.S. Ayers, Fuller Fabrics, Lee Hats, Chen Yu, Ponds, Elizabeth Arden, Helena Rubinstein, Au Printemps, Galleries Lafayette.

MD325A
Drawing and Thinking
Wed - 2 Credits - $250.00
Model Fee, $30.00
A class governed by a variety of premises, a wide range of thinking and seeking to build a new and stronger vocabulary. Thought of as a gym, to stay in shape with exercise involving highly creative interpretations. Models and props used extensively.
Jack Potter, Illustrator, Painter. Publications include: "Town & Country," "Jardin de Modes," "Elle," "Glamour," "The New York Times Magazine," "Ladies Home Journal," "Cosmopolitan," "Good Housekeeping," "McCall's." Advertising accounts include: United States Ship Lines, Northeast Airlines, R.K.O. Pictures, Coca-Cola, Armstrong Floors, Lees Carpet, L.S. Ayers, Fuller Fabrics, Lee Hats, Chen Yu, Ponds, Elizabeth Arden, Helena Rubinstein, Au Printemps, Galleries Lafayette.

It's possible to make a portfolio on your own, but it probably won't be based on the kinds of essential design or illustration problems assigned by a teacher who knows what's needed on the job.

— Seymour Chwast
Illustrator/Designer

MD367A
Drawing for the Illustrator II
Tues and Thurs - 6 Weeks
Begins November 3
Ends December 15
2 Credits - $250.00
This class picks up where MD267, Drawing For The Illustrator I, leaves off. The head, hands and feet will be dealt with extensively. Special emphasis is placed on learning to draw folds and drapery out of your head. Fundamentals of perspective will be covered. You will learn how to place the figure you have drawn out of your head into a logical space.
Doug Jamieson, Illustrator. Clients include: "The New York Times," "Psychology Today," "New York Daily News," "Co-Ed," "Travel & Leisure," "Fortune," "Business Week," "Seventeen," "Science Digest," "Family Circle," "Family Health," "Financial World," "Institutional Investor," "Village Voice." Accounts include: Warner Communications; Atheneum; Scholastic; MacMillan; Doubleday; Harper & Row; McGraw Hill; Western Publishing; C.T.W.; Young & Rubicam; Benton & Bowles; Chalik & Dryer; Daniel & Charles; Homer & Durham; Lord, Geller, Federico, Einstein, Inc.; IBM; Quaker Oats; Burson-Marstellar.

PROFESSIONAL

The listing of the courses that follow are limited to advanced students of illustration or working illustrators who are able to maintain the pace of classes which take for granted drawing and painting ability and some work experience. The professional level course is directed toward find-

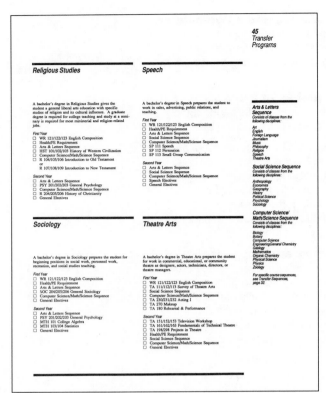

The format for this catalog accommodates several different kinds of listings, three of which are shown here. The distinctive treatment of the top and bottom margins and the consistency of the type style unify the different components of the catalog.

The heavy rules are 4 point.

The typeface makes good use of the contrast between Helvetica Narrow and Times Roman.

Design: Lisa Wilcox and Bill Symes (Oregon City, OR)

Pages from the Clackamas Community College catalog. Trim size: 8-3/8 by 10-3/4

A highly styled newspaper format (below) sets a dynamic tone for the "Course Highlights" section in the opening pages of this continuing education catalog.

The type styling in the spread below illustrates how you can achieve a great deal of variety through an adventurous use of the two most familiar typefaces. The Helvetica family is used for display and Times Roman for running text. Note, though, the contrasting leading and column widths, the letterspacing, reverse type, wrap-around text, type on tints, dotted rules, initial caps, and boxed copy. Each text block is treated as a pattern of type that is distinct from every other text block on the spread.

The same four-column grid ties together the opening pages and the course information (above left). In the course listings, the outer column is used to list the schedule, credit, and fees for the courses described on that page. Where needed, the outer two columns can be used for this purpose.

Design:
Jonathan Maier
(Portland, OR)

Pages from the Portland State University Quarterly Bulletin for Continuing Education.
Trim size:
11-1/4 by 13-9/16

2

QUARTERLY
BULLETIN

Portland State University Continuing Education Winter 1988

Courses listed in the Quarterly, whether for credit or noncredit, are scheduled for enrollment by all people. For your convenience, courses are arranged alphabetically by subject area and title. Browse the course descriptions and check the sidebar schedule for time, location and fees. Use this information to complete registration.

The Community/Campus courses are for people able to meet a regular classroom schedule. Independent Study provides university, college and high school courses outside the classroom setting. See the Independent Study insert for complete information.

Registration may be completed by mail, telephone or in person. Please see page 30 for instructions and forms (page 158 for Independent Study).

What you are seeking might appear in different subject areas. Please review all listings. Let us know if your class is missing and we will do our best to schedule it for future terms. Call the office of the Dean of Continuing Education, 464-4849.

PORTLAND STATE UNIVERSITY BULLETIN (1986-87) USPS 439-380; Vol. 22, No. 3, Winter 1988. Second class postage paid at Portland, Oregon. Published five times a year: quarterly (fall, winter, spring, and summer), and once in August at Portland State University, 1633 SW Park, Portland, OR. (POSTMASTER: Send address changes to Portland State University Bulletin, PO Box 751, Portland, OR 97207.) Copies of this quarterly may be obtained without charge by writing Portland State University Continuing Education Quarterly, PO 1491, Portland, OR 97207.

Portland State University supports equal opportunity in admission, education, and use of facilities by prohibiting discrimination in these areas based on race, color, creed, religion, sex, national origin, age, physical or mental handicap or veteran status. This policy implements state and federal law (including Title IX); inquiries about it should be directed to the Affirmative Action Office, 122 Cramer Hall. The University reserves the right to change or withdraw courses, to change the fees, rules and calendar for admission, registration, instruction and graduation, and to change other regulations affecting the student body at any time.

Published by the Oregon State System of Higher Education.

BURKE'S BRILLIANCE

PBS personality, James Burke presents public lecture; course offered concurrently through Portland State

James Burke presents a public lecture, "Mechanisms of Change: Do Lemons Whistle," in Portland, Monday, February 1, 1988, 7:30pm. Burke is a master at creating thought-provoking programs which make the complex subjects of science and society both understandable and entertaining as can be seen in his PBS series, "The Day the Universe Changed: A Personal View by James Burke." Written and produced by Burke, the series explores the critical moments in Western history when a major shift in knowledge caused people to see everything around them in a different way. Burke comments, "This series is based on the premise that you are what you know. As what you know changes, you change." "The Day the Universe Changed" follows the tremendous success of Burke's award-winning series of 1979, "Connections," which describes the unpredictable ways in which science and technology affect our lives. The book was a bestseller and the program attracted the largest U.S. audience ever for a documentary series.

Burke's brilliant capacity to bring knowledge of many disciplines— history, politics, economics, religion, education, psychology—to his audiences through humor, metaphor and drama makes him an extremely popular international speaker.

A special workshop, "James Burke: Interdisciplinary Journalist," is offered in association with Burke's local appearance. See the course description and schedule under General Studies.

For ticket information call Portland State University Box Office, 464-4440. To register for the workshop, which includes tickets for the public lecture, call 464-4832.

3
COURSE HIGHLIGHTS

James Burke,
British Television
Writer and Producer

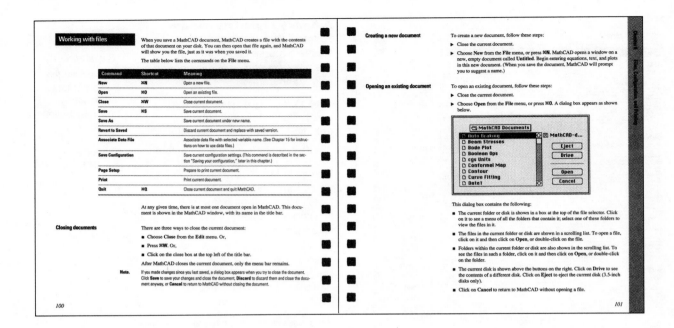

A wide and narrow column format is ideal for technical manuals. The wide column (28 picas in the sample shown) efficiently accommodates running text and art, and can be divided into two narrower columns when needed. The narrow column (12 picas in this sample) is reserved for subheads, captions, and, occasionally, small pieces of art, creating generous white space so that the sections are clearly identified and the pages are not unrelievedly dense.

The type combines the sans serif Univers Condensed (Light and Bold) with Times Roman.

The running heads are rotated 90 degrees and print black against a lavender tint.

The lavender tint also prints behind equations, giving uniformity to what would otherwise be a lot of loose little items. The same tint also prints behind screen images.

Revisions in both text and graphics are numerous in technical manuals, where beta versions of the documentation are developed hand in hand with beta versions of the software. Ventura's many automated features greatly facilitate the revision process. Ventura layouts are dynamically linked to the original source files, so changes made to the text in the Ventura layout are automatically saved back to the source file, and changes made in the source file are automatically incorporated in the Ventura page. Similarly, screen images that are updated with the evolving software can automatically be incorporated into the layout pages: Simply give each new screen image the same name as the earlier version and put it in the same subdirectory as the earlier version, and Ventura will automatically put the new image in place of the old one.

Ventura's frame anchoring feature lets you associate picture frames, such as those holding the equations at the top of the facing page, with text. If the text moves as a result of changes elsewhere in the document, the associated picture moves with it.

The table of contents generator will collect all instances of up to ten different paragraph tags and then organize them in a Ventura-generated text file. You can then import this file into a chapter that can be combined and printed with the rest of your document.

The index generator will collect and organize all your index citations into one Ventura-generated file. It has the capability to cross-reference entries as "See" or "See Also" items, and to incorporate user-defined sort priorities that put numerical terms in proper alphabetical sequence (for example, sorting 21st Street as Twenty-first). The index generator can automate a tedious process, but as with so many powerful electronic tools, the result relies more on the skill and care of the human being who defines the citations and designs the type than on the automatic organization of the items.

Design: Art Director, Michael Sullivan; Designer, Kris Busa (Cambridge, MA)

Pages from the MathCAD Manual. *Trim size: 8-1/2 by 8-1/2*

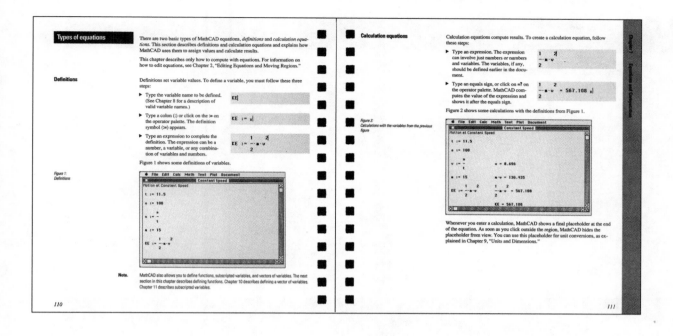

Types of equations

There are two basic types of MathCAD equations, *definitions* and *calculation equations*. This section describes definitions and calculation equations and explains how MathCAD uses them to assign values and calculate results.

This chapter describes only how to compute with equations. For information on how to edit equations, see Chapter 2, "Editing Equations and Moving Regions."

Definitions

Definitions set variable values. To define a variable, you must follow these three steps:

▶ Type the variable name to be defined. (See Chapter 8 for a description of valid variable names.)

▶ Type a colon (:) or click on the ≔ on the operator palette. The definition symbol (≔) appears.

▶ Type an expression to complete the definition. The expression can be a number, a variable, or any combination of variables and numbers.

Figure 1 shows some definitions of variables.

Figure 1: Definitions

Note MathCAD also allows you to define functions, subscripted variables, and vectors of variables. The next section in this chapter describes defining functions. Chapter 10 describes defining a vector of variables. Chapter 11 describes subscripted variables.

110

Calculation equations

Calculation equations compute results. To create a calculation equation, follow these steps:

▶ Type an expression. The expression can involve just numbers or numbers and variables. The variables, if any, should be defined earlier in the document.

▶ Type an equals sign, or click on ═ on the operator palette. MathCAD computes the value of the expression and shows it after the equals sign.

Figure 2 shows some calculations with the definitions from Figure 1.

Figure 2: Calculations with the variables from previous figure

Whenever you enter a calculation, MathCAD shows a final placeholder at the end of the equation. As soon as you click outside the region, MathCAD hides the placeholder from view. You can use this placeholder for unit conversions, as explained in Chapter 9, "Units and Dimensions."

111

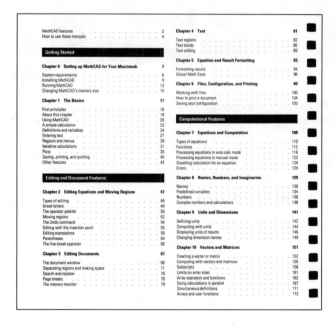

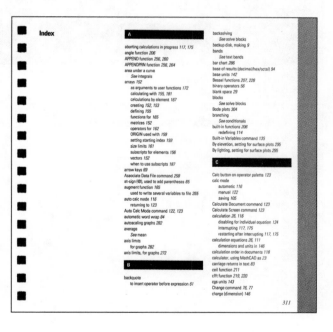

Index

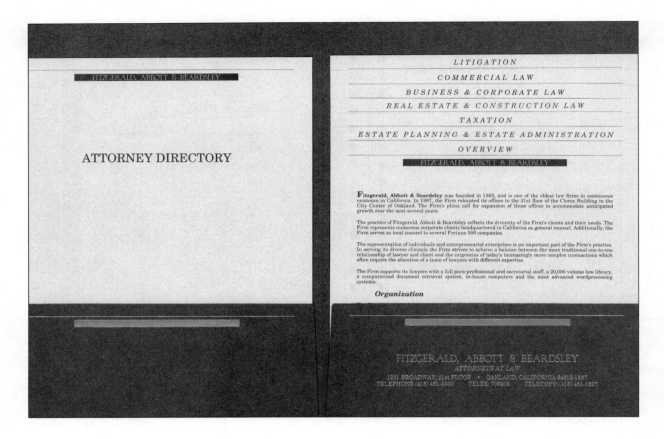

A smart-looking, conservative format for this law firm is enhanced by gray speckled textured paper. The directory and information sheets are inserted in a pocket folder with elegant silver printing.

Each information sheet is 2-1/2 picas taller than the one in front, creating a vertical index of headers when you first open the folder. All the sheets were created on 8.5- by 11-inch pages, and the crop marks were added manually.

The typeface is Palatino throughout, except the firm's logo, which is an engraver's face the printer stripped in to the 1-pica deep panels.

Design: William Tracy & Company (San Francisco, CA)

Presentation folder for Fitzgerald, Abbott & Beardsley.
Trim size: 18 by 12

The
**INDELEC
Family of
Industrial
Automation
Software
Products**

MICRO-VIEW

PLANT-VIEW

MULTI-VIEW

SPC-VIEW

A full bleed color photo sets a dramatic tone for a product sheet on a line of industrial-automation software. Helvetica Black type prints red on blue panels.

A straightforward two-column format with uneven bottoms affords a separate column for each of the company's four products. Bold Helvetica subheads make the key features of each product easy to scan.

The body text is New Baskerville. Its small x-height makes it set efficiently, yet it is very easy to read. It also has a gracefulness that contrasts nicely with the industrial nature of the product it describes here. Novice designers generally overlook the opportunity to select a typeface for this sort of contrast.

Design: Art Director, Michael Sullivan; Designer, Cynthia Delfino (Cambridge, MA)

Product information sheet from Indelec. Trim size: 25-1/2 by 11, folded twice to create a six-panel piece

---

MICRO-VIEW

A low-cost, Man-Machine Interface product which provides Graphics and Reporting environments for applications requiring fewer than 1000 I/O points.

A GRAPHICS ENVIRONMENT

The Graphics environment allows the user to integrate alarms, trending, and dynamic, high-resolution graphical displays to provide a user-friendly window into any process. With a mouse-driven editor, pull-down menus, on-line help, and symbol library, MICRO-VIEW provides the system configurator a set of tools to quickly develop and test the application.

A REPORTING ENVIRONMENT

The Reporting environment allows the user to completely customize reports, which can be generated based on time of day, time interval, and/or event. These reports can be a single line of data, or multiple screens cascaded together. The report generator allows several options for output (printer, disk, file server, and/or RAM) in an industry standard format.

USER-DEFINED FUNCTION KEYS

Each screen can define up to 30 function keys, and each key can be one of 25 properties. The benefit of this functionality includes being able to completely customize the package, regardless of your industry or application. These properties can be very simple (such as jumping from one screen to another) or complex (exiting to DOS and executing user-defined batch files).

All of these properties can be event-driven, as well as operator-driven. This provides complete hands-off capability to change screens, send files up to a host, and download values. The potential uses are unlimited.

When the system requirements demand a larger I/O point database, advanced supervisory control, and recipe management capabilities, PLANT-VIEW becomes the product choice.

PLANT-VIEW

PLANT-VIEW contains all of the features of MICRO-VIEW, and provides additional functionality as well as expansion capabilities. The new features include:

- *Enlarged database*
- *Powerful math algorithms*
- *Advanced control facilities*
- *Robust recipe/batching modules*

MATHSHEET

PLANT-VIEW adds the Mathsheet, a powerful module which provides users with a unique environment for implementing an array of functions.

Many of our customers have utilized the Mathsheet as an "internal database" from which other functions, such as Graphics and Reporting, pull their data for final display and output.

With the tools provided, customers can quickly configure the Mathsheet to perform both simple and complex tasks, including machine run/downtime timers, fault occurrence counters, report and recipe scheduling, inventory control (with automatic part re-ordering), averaging, work order generation, direct feedback to process, operator input accepted from Graphics, validation checks before downloading to process, plus much more.

RECIPE

With PLANT-VIEW's new recipe module, the simplest to the most complex type of recipes and scheduling algorithms can be easily implemented. With an unlimited number of recipes, and up to 7000 elements/steps per recipe, the user can adapt PLANT-VIEW to applications which previously required expensive PLC add-on modules, and minicomputer or even mainframe processing power.

PLANT-VIEW's Graphics interface can be customized to allow operators to easily call up recipes, make changes, and initiate the down-load. If automatic recipe handling is required, the Mathsheet can read and write recipes from disk, based on time or event. For example, a PLC as part of a batch system could send a signal indicating batch complete. MULTI-VIEW could then automatically read the next batch scheduled and download all associated parameters, without operator intervention. The same modules can be easily adapted to perform machine set-up data, part tracking, internal scheduling, and more.

This data can be stored on a central file server, and maintained by any software which can manipulate ASCII files. For example, this allows the production department to use its favorite word processor package to maintain/edit production data which can be automatically downloaded via PLANT-VIEW.

MULTI-VIEW

MULTI-VIEW, Indelec's most versatile product, combines all of the features of MICRO-VIEW, PLANT-VIEW, and provides for simultaneous communications with several communications links, powerful networking options, and enhanced data sharing. Only MULTI-VIEW allows the user complete flexibility, maximum power, and true ease-of-use to satisfy most every requirement from a basic Man/Machine Interface, to an Information Gateway, to fully networked cell control, *all* within the same computer!

COMMUNICATIONS

While the previous products offered a single communications link to PLCs and other devices, each MULTI-VIEW station allows up to *nine* independent communications links to *any* number of intelligent devices. You have the ability to window into your process with a single PC, and integrate up to nine links, with information transfer between dissimilar data highways easily implemented.

NETWORKING

For those systems which require a high-speed, fully functional network, MULTI-VIEW stations can be networked using virtually any Local Area Network (LAN) which emulates NETBIOS. There are many to choose from, including IBM's PCNET, DEC's ETHERNET, Novell, and Arcnet. Usually these LAN systems are researched and installed based upon business needs. Only MULTI-VIEW is designed to co-exist with these systems without causing any system degradation or interference to existing systems. If you haven't selected a LAN system, Indelec will recommend the most appropriate system based upon your existing and projected needs.

CONTROL

With definable execution rates and optimized communications, the users can off-load time-consuming tasks from the PLC. The control capabilities include implementing true on-line SPC/SQC functions, with direct feedback.

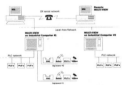

Integrate All Your Dissimilar Devices on a Common AT Platform

SPC-VIEW

The Indelec SPC-VIEW system is a comprehensive, interactive, yet easy-to-use family of statistical process control software for use on IBM or 100% IBM-compatible personal computers. SPC-VIEW meets the quality assurance needs of a wide range of industries including continuous, batch, and discrete processes.

The SPC-VIEW family consists of SPC-VIEW operating as an analytical tool for full statistical analysis of data, and Real-Time SPC Module, a dynamic control chart. Indelec's Real-Time SPC Module, available in MULTI-VIEW, offers dynamic real-time control charts including alarm monitoring. Control Charts, containing variable subgroup size, control limits, specification limits, and variable update rates, become an added component of the MULTI-VIEW system.

SPC-VIEW's up-to-the-second and historic capabilities are available through either MULTI-VIEW or SPC-VIEW. SPC-VIEW extends the statistical analysis capabilities of Real-Time Module past control charting to capability studies, histogram analysis, statistical estimation and Pareto analysis.

SPC-VIEW may also be used as a free-standing off-line product. The off-line process allows extensive analysis of historical data for the identification and analysis of quality control problems.

MAJOR FUNCTIONS

- *Real-time dynamic process monitoring, statistical analysis and control*
- *Real-time static and off-line analysis of archived (historical) data*
- *Concurrent Real-time Module — SPC-VIEW operation*
- *Discrete and analog input*

SYSTEM FEATURES

Descriptive statistics, control charts, statistical estimation, process capability studies, sampling plan studies, frequency curve comparisons, user-configurable analysis and output keystroke logging, full-screen text editor, data input from spreadsheets and databases.

NOTE: Combined SPC-VIEW/MULTI-VIEW or SPC-VIEW/PLANT-VIEW operation requires the use of Expanded Memory.

This data sheet is not as slick as the one on the preceeding page, but the handsome format, careful product display, and well-organized typography still evoke confidence in the product.

The three-column grid is given a strong horizontal structure through the use of horizontal rules.

The top rule and the company logo print in red, adding a spot of color that contrasts with the overall quietness of the page.

The contents of the kit are itemized in a bulleted list with hanging indents. The typography, Helvetica Black and Helvetica Light, is simple, nicely spaced, and easy to read.

A simple format with well-rendered line drawings (facing page, top left and bottom) is used for all the assembly and care sheets shipped with products from this large mail-order business.

The rules, logo, column guides, and footlines are standing items in the electronic templates, and a text placeholder is left in position for the product name. For each new product, the actual name is typed over the placeholder (maintaining the text specifications and placement), and text is placed in position. Hand-drawn illustrations are pasted manually onto camera-ready pages. The bottom sample is a half-page size, printed two to a sheet and then trimmed.

Before the conversion to desktop publishing, there was no standard format for these information sheets. According to one of the designers, it took only a few hours to go from no standards to an easy-to-implement design that was consistent with the corporate look.

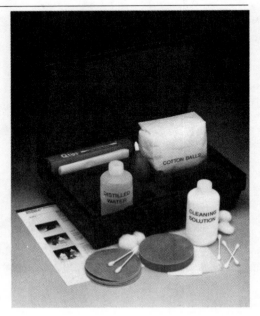

Infrared Optics Cleaning Kit

II-VI **Two-Six Incorporated**
Saxonburg Boulevard
Saxonburg, PA 16056
Telephone (412) 352-1504
Telex 469864

Description

Proper handling and cleaning procedures are critical to prolonging the life of infrared optics in high-power situations.

Infrared optical materials are very fragile. They are not as strong as glass and will not withstand procedures normally used on glass parts.

The Infrared Optics Cleaning Kit provides industrial users with the tools needed for proper optics maintenance. Included are:

- A complete instruction sheet detailing the correct use of the Kit's contents in order to maintain your infrared optics.

- An air bulb to blow away dust and debris from the optical surface.

- Special optical cleaning formula to remove harmful contamination from the optic.

- Supply of reusable cleaning/polishing pads to ensure even cleaning with no distortion of optical surface.

- Sturdy optical block for firm support of pads.

- Distilled water to wipe free any residual cleaning solution.

- Paper-bodied cotton swabs to use as an applicator with the cleaning solution.

- High-quality abrasive-free surgical cotton balls to use as an alternative to cotton swabs.

- Specially formulated, lint-free lens tissues to protect clean optics from airborne contaminants.

- A sturdy, customized carrying case for easy transportation of all tools and solutions.

- Refill Kits available to replace all consumable items.

Printed in USA   Publication 124

Design (above): Agnew Moyer Smith (Pittsburgh, PA)

Data sheet for an infrared optics cleaning kit from Two-Six Incorporated.
Trim size: 8-1/2 by 11

Design (facing page, top left and bottom): Kathy Tomyris and Deborah Paulson (Mill Valley, CA)

Product sheets from Smith & Hawken.
Trim size: (top) 8-1/2 by 11; (bottom) 5-1/2 by 8-1/2, printed two to a sheet

S M I T H & H A W K E N
Adirondack Chairs

#2093 Cedar Adirondack   #2090 Painted Chair
#2094 Cedar Footrest   #2091 Painted Footrest
#2095 Cedar Table   #2092 Painted Table

Your Adirondack Chair will arrive packed in one box. When you are ready to assemble it, unpack and carefully lay the Chair parts on a clean, flat, padded surface such as a carpeted floor or the cardboard box the Chair was shipped in. Carefully examine the contents.

ADIRONDACK CHAIR
CHAIR PARTS: Two Arms with front Legs attached, Seat, and Back
HARDWARE: Six sets of 1-1/4" carriage bolts with washers and nuts, Two cap nuts and washers for the hanger bolts attached to the seat.
TOOLS REQUIRED: Crescent wrench or 3/8" wrench

As you assemble the Chair, do not drive in the carriage bolts. Slide in the bolt, slip on the washer and then thread on the nut. As you tighten the nut, use the wrench to draw the bolts up tight. When each bolt is tight, the square end under the bolt head will seat and prevent the bolt from turning. You might also apply a small amount of beeswax or parafin to the bolts to ensure that it will be easy to disassemble the Chair.

CHAIR ASSEMBLY
1. With the seat lying flat on the floor, attach the Chair back onto the hanger bolts mounted at the back of the seat. Be sure that the back is pulled flush to the seat and the fit is smooth. Loosely secure with a washer and cap nut on each side. You should not tighten any of the hardware until the Chair has been completely assembled.

2. Turn the Chair on its side and line up the two holes drilled in the leg portion of the arm/leg assembly with the corresponding holes on the forward side of the seat. Placing the nut and washer on the inside, use two carriage bolts to loosely attach.

3. On the same side, line up the back of the arm with the hole drilled in the arm support attached across the back of the Chair. You may have to press down slightly on the arm in order to line up these holes, but as long as you have left the other carriage bolts loose, there will be enough flexibility in the Chair for the arm to fit.

4. Turn the Chair over and repeat the arm/leg assembly for the other side.

5. Now begin to tighten the carriage bolts. Tighten each a little bit at a time rather than tightening each all at once.

ADIRONDACK FOOTREST
FOOTREST PARTS: Footrest, two Legs, and four sets of 2" carriage bolts with nuts and washers.

ASSEMBLY: Attach the legs to the inside of the Footrest frame and use two carriage bolts on each side to secure. Tighten firmly.

ADIRONDACK TABLE
TABLE PARTS: Table top, four Legs and eight sets of 2" carriage bolts with nuts and washers.

ASSEMBLY: The four legs attach to the outside of the table top with two carriage bolts each. Tighten firmly.

CARE FOR YOUR ADIRONDACK
We recommend that you store your furniture indoors over the winter months, especially in harsh climates.

The Cedar Adirondack requires no specific care. The wood will gradually weather to a soft grey when placed outdoors. If you prefer a finished chair, a UV resistant exterior varnish can be applied on an annual basis.

The Painted Adirondack is finished with a durable Linear Polyurethane paint. If you should wish to repaint the Chair, we recommend that you use a high quality enamel paint.

25 Corte Madera, Mill Valley, California 94941   Customer Service (415) 383-6292

Questor Inlets

The Standard Questor Inlet

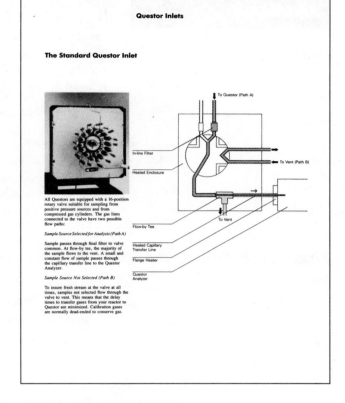

To Questor (Path A)
In-line Filter
Heated Enclosure
To Vent (Path B)
To Vent
Flow-by Tee
Heated Capillary Transfer Line
Flange Heater
Questor Analyzer

All Questors are equipped with a 16-position rotary valve suitable for sampling from positive pressure sources and from compressed gas cylinders. The gas lines connected to the valve have two possible flow paths:

Sample Source Selected for Analysis (Path A)

Sample passes through final filter to valve common. At flow-by tee, the majority of the sample flows to the vent. A small and constant flow of sample passes through the capillary transfer line to the Questor Analyzer.

Sample Source Not Selected (Path B)

To insure fresh stream at the valve at all times, samples not selected flow through the valve to vent. This means that the delay times to transfer gases from your reactor to Questor are minimized. Calibration gases are normally dead-ended to conserve gas.

S M I T H & H A W K E N
Caring for your Teak Planter

The Teak Planters and Window Boxes can be left exposed to the weather all year round. The wood will gradually weather to a soft, silver gray as the oil in the exposed wood dries. This is the preferred method of non-maintenance. If you prefer an unweathered appearance, you may choose to maintain the golden color of the teak by applying teak or tung oil every 6-8 months. When doing so, apply the oil sparingly and rub it in well, leaving no oil on the surface to soak in. The planter should be kept moisture free while the oil is drying, about two days.

As the wood weathers, checks may appear in the exposed ends and finials of the planters. This is the opening of the wood grain due to variations in the temperature and humidity.
Checking does not effect the structural
Integrity or strength of the planter.

Please call if you have any questions or need more information.

25 Corte Madera, Mill Valley, CA 94941   (415) 383-6292

Design (top right): Agnew Moyer Smith (Pittsburgh, PA)

Data sheet for the Questor Inlet system from the Extrel Corporation. Size: 8-1/2 by 11

A narrow column for the product photo and text (above) leaves plenty of space for the technical illustration and leadered callouts. The illustration was created in MacDraw.

All the leaders are parallel to one another and the callouts align left for a highly organized presentation.

Yellow is used as a functional second color to indicate the flow of gases; the light and bold horizontal rules at the top and bottom of the page also print in yellow.

Three typefaces are used for contrast: Futura Heavy for the boldface, Times Roman for the running text, and Univers Light for the callouts.

FINANCIALS

The financials in this section are from annual reports, where a narrative story, tabular data, and charts and graphs often must coexist between the same covers. In some reports the financials are quarantined in the back. The greater challenge—one that results in a more impressive presentation—is to devise a format that allows you to integrate the financial data into the body of the report.

Annual reports are very image-conscious documents. The style of presentation is obviously related to the size of the organization and the health of the bottom line. But whether yours is a growing company with increased earnings or a modest organization with a not-so-great year, the typographic organization discussed in the introduction to this chapter and in the introduction to the Catalog section is the first building block for financial presentations.

Financials in this section

- *MasterCard*—slick, dramatic photos with a life-sized twist
- *College Auxiliary Service*—mug shots that put a face on numbers
- *Regional Transportation Authority*—charts, tables, and bannered heads
- *Medic Alert*—elegant typography in an integrated format
- *Cutco Industries*—contrasting type for easy reading

A lavish annual report such as the one on the facing page reflects the bullishness of a good year. For modest or declining earnings, you'd expect a more conservative presentation.

A photo of the product itself is used to chart growth in comparison to the competition. The life-size photos dramatize the product, especially when juxtaposed against smaller-scale photos of the competition.

The financials in the bottom spread shown give the big picture—cards in circulation, merchant outlets, gross dollar volume—against a dramatic black background in which the earth revolves. The image of the earth reinforces the message of global growth set forth in the table at the top of the page.

Straightforward charts become dramatic when each bar prints in a different color, as they do here, against a black background.

Design: The Will Hopkins Group (New York, NY)

Pages from the annual report of MasterCard International, Inc. Trim size: 8-1/2 by 11

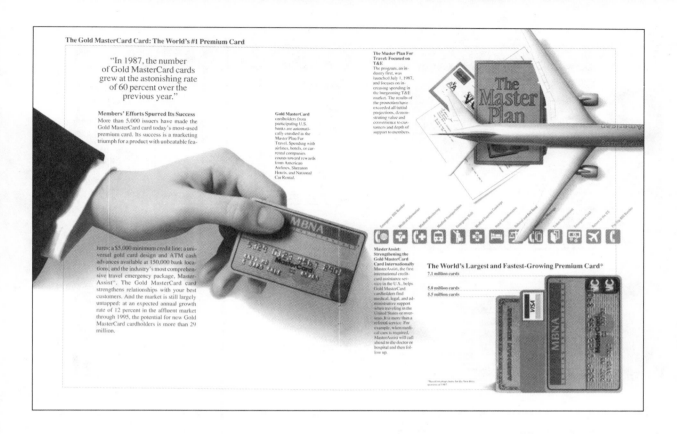

The Gold MasterCard Card: The World's #1 Premium Card

"In 1987, the number of Gold MasterCard cards grew at the astonishing rate of 60 percent over the previous year."

Members' Efforts Spurred Its Success
More than 5,000 issuers have made the Gold MasterCard card today's most-used premium card. Its success is a marketing triumph for a product with unbeatable features; a $5,000 minimum credit line; a universal gold card design and ATM cash advances available at 150,000 bank locations; and the industry's most comprehensive travel emergency package, MasterAssist™. The Gold MasterCard card strengthens relationships with your best customers. And the market is still largely untapped: at an expected annual growth rate of 12 percent in the affluent market through 1995, the potential for new Gold MasterCard cardholders is more than 29 million.

Gold MasterCard cardholders from participating U.S. banks are automatically enrolled in the Master Plan For Travel. Spending with airlines, hotels, or car rental companies counts toward rewards from American Airlines, Sheraton Hotels, and National Car Rental.

The Master Plan For Travel: Focused on T&E
The program, an industry first, was launched July 1, 1987, and focuses on increasing spending in the burgeoning T&E market. The results of the promotion have exceeded all initial projections, demonstrating value and convenience to customers and depth of support to members.

MasterAssist: Strengthening the Gold MasterCard Card Internationally
MasterAssist, the first international credit-card assistance service in the U.S., helps Gold MasterCard cardholders find medical, legal, and administrative support when traveling in the United States or overseas. It is more than a referral service. For example, when medical care is required, MasterAssist will call ahead to the doctor or hospital and then follow up.

The World's Largest and Fastest-Growing Premium Card*

7.1 million cards

5.8 million cards

5.5 million cards

*Based on average balance for the four-three quarters of 1987.

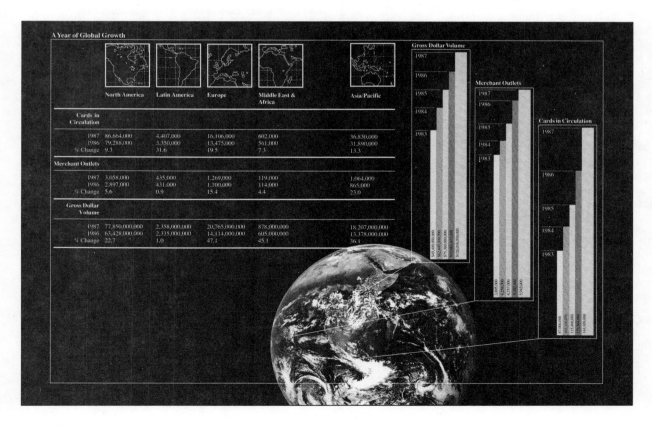

A Year of Global Growth

	North America	Latin America	Europe	Middle East & Africa	Asia/Pacific
Cards in Circulation					
1987	86,664,000	4,407,000	16,106,000	602,000	36,830,000
1986	79,288,000	3,350,000	13,475,000	561,000	31,890,000
% Change	9.3	31.6	19.5	7.3	13.3
Merchant Outlets					
1987	3,058,000	435,000	1,269,000	119,000	1,064,000
1986	2,897,000	431,000	1,100,000	114,000	865,000
% Change	5.6	0.9	15.4	4.4	23.0
Gross Dollar Volume					
1987	77,850,000,000	2,358,000,000	20,765,000,000	878,000,000	18,207,000,000
1986	63,428,000,000	2,335,000,000	14,114,000,000	605,000,000	13,378,000,000
% Change	22.7	1.0	47.1	45.1	36.1

Gross Dollar Volume
1987 / 1986 / 1985 / 1984 / 1983

Merchant Outlets
1987 / 1986 / 1985 / 1984 / 1983

Cards in Circulation
1987 / 1986 / 1985 / 1984 / 1983

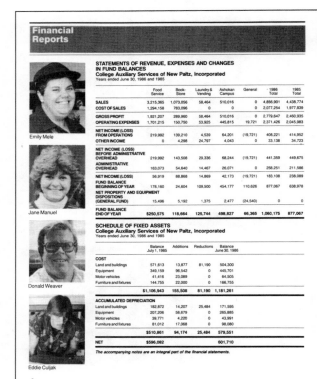

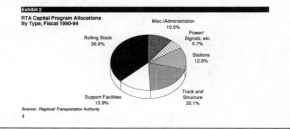

Photos in the narrow outer margins throughout the report above emphasize that this college auxiliary service is a people business. The mug-shot format enables the publication to serve three very different purposes—annual report, morale booster for current employees, and recruiting tool for managerial positions.

Contrasting bold and regular Helvetica with light and bold rules helps organize the tables. The crimson banner at the top of each page provides accent color.

The chart and labels (right) were created in Harvard Graphics. PostScript screens sometimes appear differently in the Ventura page than in the original art file.

The tabs for the table were set in Multimate and the decimal alignment specified in Ventura.

Design (above): Wadlin & Erber (New Paltz, NY)

Spread from a report for the College Auxiliary Services at The College of New Paltz, State University of New York. Size: 8-1/2 by 11

Design (right): Mary Beth Glascow and Mary Jo Nasko (Chicago, IL)

Page from the Northeastern Illinois Regional Transportation Authority Report. Size: 8-1/2 by 11

Sᴏᴜʀᴄᴇꜱ ᴏꜰ ʀᴇᴠᴇɴᴜᴇ ᴀɴᴅ ʜᴏᴡ ᴛʜᴇʏ ᴡᴇʀᴇ ꜱᴘᴇɴᴛ   19

Financial Highlights . . . The Medic Alert Foundation International accounts for all membership fees, contributions and other revenues with utmost care. These pages were prepared under the direction of Robert C. Johnson, Treasurer, to highlight the financial activity for the twelve month period ended September 30, 1987. A complete, audited financial statement is available on request.

Fund Balance Summary . . . All fund balances for this period increased $1,179,960 because support and revenue exceeded expenditures. All Foundation funds totaled $4,163,018, of which $2,206,916 is invested in the headquarters building. Fund balances are used for working funds and have been designated to cover the cost of updating the Foundation's membership services computer system.

Wʜᴀᴛ ᴡᴇ ʀᴇᴄᴇɪᴠᴇᴅ . . .

*T*otal support and revenue for the 12 months was derived from several sources:

Membership Fees - The number of new members was the same as the previous year. However, reorders increased 10% and updates increased by 14%. The volume of gold and silver emblems is also increasing. As a result, membership fees increased 6%.

Contributions - Contributions by our membership for the support of Medic Alert continued to increase. All solicitations were made by mail to members only. Contributions amounted to 42% of the Foundation's total support and revenue.

Other Revenue - Reimbursement from foreign affiliates for support of international membership expansion increased during the year. Earnings on investment increased because the Foundation had larger investment balances.

Sᴜᴘᴘᴏʀᴛ ᴀɴᴅ ʀᴇᴠᴇɴᴜᴇ

	For Twelve months 9/30/87	Compared to prior 12 month period
Member's Fees	$3,769,278	up 6%
Contributions	3,023,234	up 26%
Other Revenues	379,152	up 60%
Total Support and Revenue	7,171,664	up 13%

Exᴘᴇɴꜱᴇꜱ

	For Twelve months 9/30/87	Percent of Expenditures
Membership Services	$4,096,091	69%
Professional Education Volunteer Training & Public Information	447,860	7%
International Development	221,511	4%
Total Services	$4,765,462	80%
Management & General	546,505	9%
Fund Raising	652,487	11%
TOTAL EXPENSES	$5,964,454	100%

Fᴜɴᴅ ʙᴀʟᴀɴᴄᴇꜱ

Beginning of Period (10/1/86)	$3,328,254
Support & Revenue	7,171,664
Expenditure and Charges to Funds	<5,991,704>
End of Period (9/30/87)	$4,508,214

Wʜᴀᴛ ᴡᴇ ꜱᴘᴇɴᴛ . . .

Membership Services - The cost of establishing new members' medical records and maintaining and updating members' records.

Professional Education, Volunteer Training and Public Information - Costs of continuing education of professionals, volunteers and the public to the vital information and lifesaving potential of Medic Alert services.

Fund Raising - Fund raising expenses increased only 1%, while contributions increased by 26% and substantially increased the number of members and donors to the Foundation.

Management and General - These costs declined slightly, primarily due to one time costs charged in the previous year.

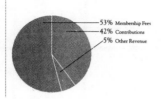

53% Membership Fees
42% Contributions
5% Other Revenue

69% Member Services
11% Fund Raising
9% Management & General
7% Professional Education & Training: Public Relations
4% International Development

Consolidated Balance Sheets
CutCo Industries, Inc. and Subsidiaries

Assets

	June 30 1988	1987
Current assets:		
Cash	$ 253,309	$ 269,395
Short-term investments, at cost which approximates market	1,432,832	526,435
Notes and accounts receivable, trade (net of allowances) (Note 2)	1,212,170	1,224,890
Merchandise inventory	366,646	463,892
Prepaid income taxes		58,060
Prepaid expenses and miscellaneous receivables	64,869	88,727
Investment in 50%-owned company		229,344
Total current assets	3,329,826	2,860,743
Property, plant and equipment, at cost:		
Furniture, fixtures and equipment	1,937,993	2,558,583
Leasehold improvements	975,228	1,552,987
	2,913,221	4,111,570
Less accumulated depreciation and amortization	1,564,683	2,151,044
	1,348,538	1,960,526
Other assets:		
Notes receivable, due after one year	668,976	354,098
Deferred charges and other (Note 4)	164,343	196,352
Deposits	262,091	233,510
	1,095,410	783,960
	$5,773,774	$5,605,229

See notes to consolidated financial statements.

Design (above):
Tom Lewis
(San Diego, CA)

Pages from the Medic Alert annual report.
Size: 8-1/2 by 11

Design (left):
Beverly Kay Rubman
(Westbury, NY)

Pages from Cutco Industries Annual Report.
Size: 8-1/2 by 11

Data for revenues and expenses in the report above is accompanied by sidebars with explanatory notes and comparisons to previous years' data.

The format throughout the report combines a single column of running text with one- or two-column sidebars. On pages without financials, sidebars focus on human interest stories, such as volunteer of the year, and special events, such as a video documentary about the foundation.

The elegantly styled typography, with its use of large and small caps, is Goudy Old Style. The running text and financial data print in gray-brown; the sidebar and running head print in black.

Contrasting color for the type helps make these numbers (left) easy to follow. The categories and current year's figures are printed in blue and stand out from the line items and previous year's figures, which are light gray. The typeface is Glypha. Not frequently used in annual reports, it gives this one a fresh look.

FORMS

The goal of a form is decidedly simple: It should be easy to read, easy to complete, and easy to retrieve data from, all of which is easier said than done. Once you think you've got it right, try testing your form on some typical subjects. Chances are they'll question something you thought was obvious or enter information in the wrong place. Of course, there's no way to account for the range of attention, or inattention, respondents will bring to the forms you create. But the goal of designing an effective form is to try to make it is simple as possible.

A company with a long tradition of graphic design excellence turns forms into a minimalist art. Intended for internal use, these forms assume more information on the user's part than would be appropriate in a form to be circulated outside the company.

The black panels with reverse type give the forms a dramatic and sophisticated style. The shadow in the company logo adds to the effect.

An unruled, 10% gray panel sets off the "needed" and "used" dates to be filled in for each item on the billing form. Gray should be used cautiously in spaces where the respondent must write.

Design: Mary Salvadore (Boston, MA)
Forms from WGBH Television.
Trim size: 8-1/2 by 11

Forms in this section

- *Billing and Traffic*—an artful style for internal use
- *Employee Information*—a lesson in good spacing
- *Bonus Interest!*—using Ventura's Form Function feature
- *Proposal Evaluation*—ruled space for narrative responses
- *Application for Admission*—adapting a publication's grid for a form
- *InFractions*—a triplicate sales receipt

Employee Information

Basic Information • *Required for all Actions*

Action (*circle*)	Hire	Separation	Personal	Pay Rate	LOA	Job Change	Other

Last Name	First Name	Middle Initial

Effective Date	Employee Number	Dept./Location

Personal

Street	City

State	Zip Code	Telephone

Birth Date	Social Security No.

Sex (*circle*)	Male	Female	Race (*circle*) White	Asian	Am. Indian	Black	Hispanic	Other

Salaried Personnel Only • Attach Voided Original Check for Direct Deposit Services

Insurance

Marital Status

Spouse Name	Birth Date

Dependent Name	Birth Date

Dependent Name	Birth Date

Dependent Name	Birth Date

Life Beneficiary	Relation

Leave of Absence

Start Date	Anticipated Return Date

Reason for Leave

Pay Rate • *Do Not Fax Pay Information*

Previous Pay Rate	New Pay Rate	Pay Type (*circle*) Hourly	Salary

Job Change

Previous Position/Level	New Position/Level

Previous Department	New Department

Separation of Employment

Type of Separation (*circle*)	Resignation	Discharge	Other

Vacation Pay Due	Severance Pay Due

Explanation • Comments

Authorization / Date

Originator	Senior Management

Human Resources	Payroll

A banner incorporating the company logo, used here and in the forms on the facing page, is a useful device for maintaining a consistent image in forms and other communications.

Ruled gray panels direct the eye to different categories of questions in this employee information form. The distance between the top and bottom of each panel is the same as the distance between all the other rules on the page.

The typeface is Helvetica bold and regular throughout, with italic used to distinguish special instructions (such as the word "circle" when two or more options are given).

Design: Manfred Petri (Atlanta, GA)
Employee Information form from Geiger International.
Trim size: 8-1/2 by 11

Join Us in Celebrating Our 125th Anniversary!

Bonus Interest! ENROLLMENT FORM

☐ *Yes!* I would like to take advantage of Bonus Interest on my new Money Market Account, and open the associated qualifying accounts indicated below. I have read and understand the Bonus Interest rules and conditions. I would like to open the following new Bank of California Accounts (*Please note – all accounts must be of the same category, either Personal or Business*):

THE CENTER FOR FIELD RESEARCH
PROPOSAL EVALUATION

copyright 1987 Earthwatch

Contrasting green and gray type, tints, and rules enhance the organization of information in the panels of the form above.

The elegant Bodoni typeface was part of a 125th anniversary promotion. The Bonus Interest logo for the campaign was created in GEM Artline from one of the program's generic typefaces.

The Form Function feature in Ventura's Professional Extension was used to create the "Bank Use" panel listing the various types of accounts. The designer specified a form 13 cells wide and 8 cells deep. This created a form of equal-size cells, which were then customized using the Table Edit Menu. In the title panel at the top, for example, all the cells were combined to create a single, column-width cell. In the "Account Number" panel below that, the nine small cells sized for the numbers were combined to create a single, wide cell.

The height of each cell is determined by the type in the cell; this simplifies form generation for novices, but it forces experienced designers to resort to trial and error to get the cell height they want. It also makes it difficult to create complicated forms that are computer or typewriter fed.

Rules between cells can be customized by selecting segments of lines and choosing attributes ranging from invisible to specified point sizes.

Control of overline and underline options further enhances Ventura's form-making capability. You can customize both the weight of the rule and its relationship to the baseline of the type. (The default values tend to be too tight to the type.) The rules in the "Client Signature" panel toward the bottom of the form were created as left-aligned tabs between center-aligned type; the left-aligned tabs were then specified as overlines.

When a form requires more than a few words for each answer (as in the one above), ruling the space generally improves the legibility of the responses.

The typeface is Times Roman throughout, but the styling of headlines as large and small caps makes it look distinctive and contrasts nicely with the italicized questions that follow. The type is blue on a gray background.

Design (above left):
William Tracy & Company
(San Francisco, CA)

Enrollment form for the Bank of California.
Trim size: 8-1/2 by 11

Design (above right):
Earthwatch (Watertown, MA)

Form used to evaluate field-research proposals by this nonprofit scientific research organization.
Trim size: 8-1/2 by 11

120
Application for
Admission

Application for Admission

Date / /

Applying for entrance in ❑ Summer ❑ Fall ❑ Winter ❑ Spring 19 ____

Social Security number

Name
Last First Initial

Date of birth / /
Month Day Year

Address
Street

City State Zip

Phone number
Day Evening

State resident
❑ Yes (living in Oregon currently and for preceding 90 days)
❑ No

District resident
❑ Yes (Clackamas County except for Sandy Union High and Lake Oswego School Districts)
❑ No

Course of study
Please include program title and code (see back of form).

High school last attended
Name State

Date of high school graduation or GED / /
Month Day Year

Sex ❑ Male ❑ Female

Ethnic data (optional)
❑ White, non-Hispanic ❑ Asian or Pacific Islander
❑ Black, non-Hispanic ❑ American Indian or Alaskan Native
❑ Hispanic ❑ Handicapped, needing special assistance*

*the Handicap Resource Center coordinates special assistance such as notetakers and sign language interpreters. If you need assistance, check this box and the NRC will contact you. Response is voluntary and will not influence admission to the college.

In case of emergency, please notify
Name Home phone Work phone

Direct application to
Office of Admissions
Clackamas Community College
19600 South Molalla Avenue
Oregon City, OR 97045

Clackamas Community College supports equal education opportunity regardless of sex, race, national origin, age, marital status, handicap or religion.

---

732 West Schubert
Chicago, IL 60614
312 477 5063

Sales Receipt

Sold to:
Name
Address Apt. No.
City State Zip
Day Telephone Evening Telephone

Ship to:
Name
Office Use Only/Order Number Address Apt. No.
Date City State Zip
Day Telephone Evening Telephone

101	Long Sleeve Boat Neck Top	❑ ❑ ❑	$35.00	
103	Long Sleeve Cowl Top	❑ ❑ ❑	45.00	
204	Pants	❑ ❑ ❑	35.00	
205	Full Skirt	❑ ❑ ❑	45.00	
206	Straight Skirt	❑ ❑ ❑	35.00	
308	Cowl Dress	❑ ❑ ❑	80.00	
309	Jumper	❑ ❑ ❑	75.00	
410	Jacket	❑ ❑ ❑	60.00	
511	Sash	❑ ❑ ❑	9.00	
	Shoulder Pads	❑ ❑	10.00	

Signed Date Sub-Total
Charge to my ❑ MasterCard ❑ Visa Exp. Date Tax
Shipping
❑ a check for the total amount is enclosed. No COD's accepted Total

Preprinted triplicate sales forms speed up order writing and help ensure completeness and clarity as well. If you compare this form to the sales promotion for the same company (included in the Folders section in Chapter 5), you'll see how the combination of a strong logo and consistent type styling create a distinct and consistent image for a company of any size.

Design: Edward Hughes (Evanston, IL)
Order form from InFractions Inc.
Trim size: 5-1/2 by 8-1/2

An application bound into a college catalog uses the catalog grid to create a clear and smart-looking form.

The running head, the 2-point rules at the top and bottom margins, the headline and text style, and the use of the narrow outer column are design elements from the catalog format, shown earlier in this section.

The shadowed ballot boxes for options to be checked by the respondent are Zapf Dingbats character number <111>.

Design: Lisa Wilcox and Bill Symes (Oregon City, OR)

Admission application from the Clackamas Community College catalog.
Trim size: 8-3/8 by 10-3/4

HANDS-ON PROJECTS

SECTION 3

INTRODUCTION TO THE PROJECTS

The projects in this section are structured so that beginners can start right in on Project 1 without any prior experience in creating Ventura Publisher documents. The instructions do assume, however, that your computer is up and running, that Ventura is installed and you know how to open it, that you can locate files on your hard disk, and that you know how to print on your workstation.

The purpose of these projects is to provide experience with Ventura Publisher's tools and techniques in the context of creating real publications. The difference between reading about a technique in a manual and using it in real life provides a stumbling block to many new Ventura users. Real publications move from one kind of tool or technique to another in a way that is fairly specific to that project. And there's a certain rhythm to using the tools, of Ventura or any other program, in the context of real work that manuals can't begin to capture. Each job you do with a program not only builds knowledge of specific techniques but, perhaps even more importantly, builds an understanding of the program's internal logic. It's this understanding that enables you, eventually, to figure out why the program responds in certain ways and how to work around apparent limitations.

These projects (with instructions by Ricardo Birmele) are therefore intended to supplement the Ventura Publisher manual by applying information covered there to some typical publications. The focus is on building a familiarity with and an understanding of the basic techniques and on developing a certain manual dexterity when you are using those techniques to achieve effects that require some precision.

The layouts of the publications themselves were designed to further this tutorial function. If you find that you can use one of the formats as a prototype for your own publication, that's fine. The point, however, is not so much to say, for example, that you should use racing stripes on a flyer (Project 5) but to take you through the steps involved in creating that kind of graphics effect and incorporating it into a real document. To take another example, you may have an existing format for a newsletter or report that you'd like to convert to desktop production. By working through Project 3 or 4, you should get a good understanding of how to create a style sheet template to your own specifications using the Base Page, Column Guides, and Paragraph Tags.

One of the wisest and most universally acknowledged pieces of advice in the world of computers is to learn a few programs and to learn them well. With that in mind, we've exploited Ventura Publisher's text and graphic tools as much as possible, more so than one might actually do in real-life work. Certain aspects of the projects could be done faster or more effectively in a graphics program. By doing them in Ventura, you'll master tools and techniques that undoubtedly will improve your Ventura skills. So you'll find, for example, instructions for creating some interesting graphics effects while you work with scanned

THE PROJECTS AT A GLANCE

The first three projects are arranged in order of difficulty. Each one assumes that you are familiar with techniques used in the previous project. The last four projects are all more complex than the first three, although it's difficult to say that any one of those last four is more complex or difficult than the others. They simply use different techniques. The earlier projects provide more detail about basic techniques; the later projects, while they still take you through each step needed to produce the sample document, assume that you know the basics covered in earlier projects. For example, an early project would tell you where and how to move the zero point, if that was required; a later project would simply tell you where to move it.

Project 1: A Simple Certificate for Ventura Publisher Novices

This project guides you through the basic procedures of setting up a new Ventura document, using the rulers, moving around the publication window, changing the page view, typing text in Ventura, and using Ventura's tools to create very simple graphics (circles, rectangles, lines).

Project 2: Two Invitations with Variations on Each

There are really two projects in this section. Project 2A, an all-text invitation, takes you through many of the same techniques used in Project 1 but with less detailed instructions. Project 2B introduces working with precise increments of space and creating a simple thematic graphic with Ventura's tools. It also teaches you how to print multiple copies of an undersized document on a single sheet.

Project 3: A Simple One-Column Format for Newsletters and Reports

This project introduces the use of base pages and templates with a simple format suitable for newsletters and reports. It also introduces placing text in Ventura that you've created in a word processor; for that purpose you can use any text file that you have. The project also includes an exercise using leadered tabs to create a rule; if you have a mental block against tabs (as many people seem to), this may help break through it. Finally, there are sidebars that focus on controlling text in Ventura.

Project 4: A Two-Column Newsletter

A basic, two-column format is used to create two versions of the newsletter in this project. Different typefaces and headline treatments give each version a unique look. But both use the same basic techniques: working with base pages and templates, defining and applying styles, creating and using a graphic placeholder, and styling hanging indents. The headline treatment used in Project 4B is more demanding than the one in 4A.

Project 5: A Flyer with a Coupon

This project lets you work with different column settings within the same page, use tabs in the traditional manner to set columnar material, and set up a coupon. You'll use Ventura graphics, which requires a certain precision.

Project 6: A Tabloid Ad with Photographs and Display Typography

This project demonstrates several Ventura bit-mapped graphic effects. The art includes importing a scanned photograph and a piece of clip art. The scanned photograph exercise is included to show how you can alter a bit-mapped graphic by cropping and how to use some interesting Ventura printing screen effects. The text gives you experience in refining display type.

Project 7: Using Ventura with a Database

With this project, you will combine the capabilities of a database program with those of Ventura to create an employee address directory. You'll also take a closer look at running headers and footers, as well as at paragraph breaks.

Ninety-five percent of the people will always use a program at the lowest level. They don't use even 30% of the features—they use 10%; and, next year, when more features come out, they'll use 5% of those.

—*Alan Kask,*
PC World

photographs. These include different printing screens, and duplicating and cropping graphic images.

The tutorials focus on tasks that beginning and intermediate Ventura users need to be in command of in order to use the program with some confidence in document production. Some advanced features, specifically the use of color, are not included because we feel their use is still fairly specialized at this time.

Inevitably, projects such as these do not address the very important early stages of publication work—developing the concept, planning the format, and massaging the individual elements to fit the format. For a detailed look at this process in one publication, see the case history in Chapter 4.

The structure of the projects

Each project begins with a brief introduction that describes the format and design elements. The actual document is reproduced full size (or, in the case of documents with a horizontal orientation, as large as is possible on these pages). Within the first few pages of each project, you'll also find a list of the Ventura techniques that you will learn in that project. Use these lists as a guide to help you select which projects you want to work through.

The projects are organized so that numbered, boldface instructions describe the general steps (specify the page setup, define the image area, draw the banner, and so on). Bulleted paragraphs within those numbered instructions detail the specific procedures and techniques required to execute that step. Generally, unbulleted paragraphs explain and amplify the techniques. By organizing the information in this way, we hope you'll be able to move as quickly, or as slowly, through the projects as suits your needs and level of experience.

Marginal tips highlight shortcuts as well as procedures that are important for a fundamental understanding and control of Ventura's personality. Most tips are placed adjacent to a step within the project to which that tip can be applied. You'll find additional tips in the margins of the Glossary in the back of the book. The glossary also includes key sequences for many Ventura commands so you can refer to that section when you can't remember how to crop a picture, type an em dash, place text or an image into a frame, and so on.

TIP

Familiarize yourself early on with Ventura Publisher's on-line help. You can access this by clicking on the question mark (?) in the upper right corner of many dialog boxes. You will be shown a list of that dialog box's options. Click on the one you have a question about, and Ventura will display another dialog box that contains a paragraph or two of explanation. After you have read the explanation, click on OK or press Return to continue your work.

Screen details with captions provide additional tips throughout the project section. Note, however, that the distortion in letter and word spacing that sometimes occurs on-screen in Ventura is exacerbated when screen images are reduced in size, which they generally are for reproduction in this book.

In addition, throughout the projects you'll find sidebars that focus on Ventura functions in a context that is both specific to the project at hand and more general as well. You can locate these through the index or by browsing through the project section. These sidebars are highlighted with a gray tint to make them easy to find.

For some projects, we've included variations on the basic design. The purpose of this, as in the grid chapter earlier in the book, is to show how the same underlying page structure can result in publications with rather different "looks," depending on the styling of type and the use of art. If any of the variations meet your own publication needs, you will need to extrapolate some of the details of creating them from the instructions for the basic design.

The projects are self-contained, and all the information you need to complete them is included as part of the instructions. But because the projects build on one another, later projects do not detail certain techniques that have already been covered. Also, some options—such as the page view you work at—vary depending on the size of the monitor you work on, and it would be cumbersome to cover all the possibilities.

Capitalization and italics

The names of all menu commands and dialog boxes are capitalized in these instructions; we have sometimes abbreviated the full name used in Ventura. For example, whereas the Ventura menu reads "Page Size & Layout," our instructions will tell you to choose the Page Size command; we might also tell you to specify information in the Page Size & Layout dialog box. On the other hand, if we are speaking generically about page layout, the phrase is not capitalized.

Specific words or values that you are instructed to type in dialog boxes are italicized. If the words should actually be italicized in the publication, that will be stated explicitly.

Menu commands

Ventura has a variety of menu commands. Some of them (such as Rulers and Column Guides) are like toggle switches that you click on and off. For example, the word "Hide" (as in the Hide Rulers command) indicates the command is active; the word "Show" (as in the Show Column Guides command) means it is inactive. Similar to these are commands (such as the page-view options and Ventura mode) that are on (and checked) until you choose another command in the same category.

Another set of commands (such as Copy and Paste) are either black or gray. When a command is gray, it currently does not apply to anything on the page and cannot be selected. For example, the Copy command will be gray unless some text or a graphic is selected.

Commands that are followed by an ellipsis on the screen, such as Edit Special Item… and Update Counters…, display dialog boxes through which you select options and type in specifications.

To select the mode you need, click on that icon in Ventura's mode selector box. The on-screen pointer turns into different shapes, depending on the mode selected.

▼ ▼ ▼

mode icon	name
+	*Frame mode*
▦	*Paragraph mode*
I	*Text mode*
➤	*Graphics mode*

▲ ▲ ▲

When you want to select a button surrounded by a heavy border, such as the OK button above, simply press the Return or Enter key instead of moving the cursor to the button and clicking it. This keyboard shortcut can be used in any Ventura dialog box, so it's a good one to remember.

Finally, some Ventura commands can be invoked through keyboard shortcuts—usually a key combination where you press and hold the control key while typing another key. Each shortcut appears next to a command's name on the various menus as a caret (^) and a letter. If the keyboard shortcut appears gray rather than black, the shortcut (and its associated command) is not currently available.

Defaults

Defaults are preset values or options that Ventura uses until you specify otherwise. You can change Ventura's defaults any time they appear in a dialog box, but it does save time to set them to the choices that you use most frequently. For example, Ventura's default unit of measure is inches, so until you specify otherwise, the ruler increments (for example) will be in inches. If you work in picas and points more frequently than in inches, you'll want to change the Ruler default to picas. To do this, choose Set Ruler from the Options menu and click on Inches next to Horizontal Units in the dialog box and drag the highlight down to Picas. The rulers will then use picas for their horizontal unit of measure.

Sometimes Ventura seems to have a mind of its own, insisting on one typeface when you select another. Usually, as in the case of the Zapf Dingbat or the Symbol font, this "condition" is because Ventura does not have a screen font (the one you see displayed on your computer's CRT) that corresponds to the printer font (the one that is actually used in printing). Because Ventura maintains a width table for each font, it "knows" how much room to allow on a line for each letter to be printed. For that reason, while it might not look correct on your screen, the final product will print out correctly—perhaps even as you intended.

The project instructions generally assume that you are working with Ventura's original defaults. If you've changed any of them, your screen might look different from the one that is described in a particular project. If you want to restore Ventura's original defaults, simply delete the default file named VP.INF in the \VENTURA subdirectory. The next time you open Ventura, the program will automatically create a new, default VP.INF file.

Measurements

Unit of measure

As was mentioned previously, the Set Ruler command on Ventura's Options menu lets you specify whether you want rulers in inches, picas, or centimeters. Most of us think of page size in inches, but picas generally provide a more convenient and flexible measurement system for margins and other page dimensions—such as the amount of space between a headline and a rule. Then again, we generally size art in inches, a tradition resulting from the fact that the proportion wheels used to size art give results in inches, not picas.

Ventura has an extremely useful feature that allows you to change the current unit of measure within dialog boxes such as Sizing & Scaling or Paragraph Alignment. You do so by simply clicking on the default unit when the dialog box is displayed. Each time you click on the unit, Ventura moves to the next among the four possible choices: inches, centimeters, picas and points, and fractional points. Ventura will remember your new unit of measurement from session to session until you change it.

In the project instructions, we freely mix measurement systems, using whichever is most useful for the space or object being measured. You can use our measurement unit choices, or you can change them according to your preferences.

Rulers

We almost always work with rulers turned on. To have them appear as a default for all publications, choose Show Rulers from Ventura's Options menu.

Fractional measurements

In keeping with Ventura Publisher's menus, fractions of inches are expressed as decimals, fractions of picas are expressed as points, and fractions of points are expressed as decimals. Thus, you'll find measurements such as these:

8.5 by 11 inches

07,06 (equivalent to 7 picas 6 points)

9.50 fractional points (equivalent to 9.5 points)

Ventura has one eccentricity when it comes to displaying its units of measurement. Normally, we separate numbers from their fractions by a decimal point. Ventura uses this convention for points and fractions of points—which it calls "Fractional Points." However, if a number is separated by a comma—as in "07,06"—it signifies picas and points. The "07" is seven picas. The "06" is six points, or one-half pica. If you were to enter a number like "7,12" Ventura would interpret it as being 8 picas.

Remember that there are 12 points in a pica. When calculating measurements, be careful not to confuse fractions of picas expressed as decimals with points. For example, if you used a calculator to divide 11 picas in half, you'd get 5.5 picas. Properly translated into points, that's 5 picas 6 points, or 05,06.

To convert a fraction of a pica into points, multiply the fraction by 12. Say you want to divide a 7-pica measure into three parts: $7/3 = 2.33$ picas; $0.33 \times 12 = 3.96$. So one-third of 7 picas is actually 2 picas and 3.96 points. Because Ventura allows measurements of this sort, in either picas and points or in fractional points only, you express this number as 27.96 fractional points. These small dimensional differences may seem insignificant, but if they are not accurately worked out, they can throw off your layout as they accumulate and leave you feeling incredibly frustrated.

Although you can use either inches or picas as the unit of measure in Ventura, fractions of inches must be specified as decimals. We find the following conversions useful to have on hand.

▼ ▼ ▼

Inches	Decimal	Points	Picas
1/32	.03125	2.25	00,02
1/16	.625	4.50	00,05
3/32	.09375	6.75	00,07
1/8	.125	9.00	00,09
5/32	.15625	11.25	00,11
3/16	.1875	13.50	01,02
7/32	.21875	15.75	01,04
1/4	.250	18.00	01,06
9/32	.28125	20.25	01,08
5/16	.3125	22.50	01,11
11/32	.34375	24.75	02,01
3/8	.375	27.00	02,03
13/32	.40625	29.25	02,05
7/16	.4375	31.50	02,08
15/32	.46875	33.75	02,10
1/2	.50	36.00	03,00
17/32	.53125	38.25	03,02
9/16	.5625	40.50	03,05
19/32	.59375	42.75	03,07
5/8	.625	45.00	03,09
21/32	.65625	47.25	03,11
11/16	.6875	49.50	04,02
23/32	.71875	51.75	04,04
3/4	.750	54.00	04,06
25/32	.78125	56.25	04,08
13/16	.8125	58.50	04,11
27/32	.83475	60.75	05,01
7/8	.875	63.00	05,03
29/32	.90625	65.25	05,05
15/16	.9375	67.50	05,08
31/32	.96875	69.75	05,10
1	1	72.00	06,00

For greatest accuracy when constructing grids, drawing rules at precise locations, and performing other procedures that require precise measurement, turn on Column Snap and Line Snap.

Snap commands

Line Snap and Column Snap are toggle switches on the Options menu. If these are on, when you add a new frame (or move an existing one) Ventura will cause its boundaries to snap to an invisible grid the software places on your on-screen workspace. Horizontally, the grid lines occur at the base line spacing of the current Body Text font; vertically, the lines occur at your column guide boundaries.

Turn on Line Snap when you
- draw Ventura graphics (squares and so on) that require precise measurements.

- want to place a frame in exact alignment with another frame.

Turn off Line Snap when you
- want to place a text or graphics frame out of strict alignment with other screen elements.

Turn on Column Snap when you
- place frames in exact alignment with column boundaries.

- want to align existing graphics with existing column boundaries.

Turn off Column Snap when you
- position graphics or text blocks near, but not directly on, the column boundaries.

- want to use Ventura's tools to draw graphics, such as squares or rectangles, and have them align exactly with text columns.

It's important to distinguish refinements that you should make early on in Ventura Publisher from details that you should postpone. The type specs of headlines and the size and placement of art contribute to the clarity of your message and affect line count and page breaks, so you should resolve these toward the beginning of your project. The exact placement of rules, on the other hand, is a detail that can be handled later. In this tip, for example, a small editorial change can alter the depth of this text block, and hence the length of the vertical rule at right. You can waste a lot of time refining graphic details too early on.

Page views

Four page views are available on the View menu. Larger page views enable you to see less of the page in greater detail than smaller page views. The view you choose depends on what you're doing, the size of your monitor, and the precision (and perfection) you require in your work. Generally, you edit text at Normal View or Enlarged View (200% of Normal View), depending on the legibility of the screen font. You check overall page composition at Reduced View or Facing Pages View, so you can see the entire page or spread at once. Because Enlarged View expands the objects on your screen to twice their normal size, it is often easiest to check critical alignments using this view. Because of the many variables in system configuration, we've generally left it to you to determine the page view as you work on the projects. We spend a lot of time toggling back and forth between page views and thus find the keyboard shortcuts for doing this among the most frequently used.

Keyboard shortcuts for changing page view

View size	Keyboard shortcut
Normal View	Ctrl-n
Reduced View	Ctrl-r
Enlarged View	Ctrl-e
Facing Pages View	(no shortcut available)

To move to the next page or spread at the view in which it was last seen:

Press PgDn (Page Down).

To move to the previous page:

Press PgUp (Page Up).

Saving your work

To save your work the first time you save a new Ventura chapter—or to save an already used chapter under a different name—click on Save As from the File menu. Otherwise, click on Save from the File menu or press Ctrl-s. Ventura will store your chapter file, any associated graphics files, and all associated text files.

A general rule of thumb is to save every 15 to 20 minutes or whenever you've done something you'd really hate to redo. With the exception of a Save and Print instruction at the completion of each project, we've left it to you to save according to your own habit. The keyboard shortcut for saving—Ctrl-s—is easy to remember and takes much less time than redoing lost work.

The Ventura Chapter

The fundamental unit of a document produced using Ventura Publisher is the *Chapter*. This is a text file in ASCII format that holds the names, types, and locations (within the document and on your computer's hard disk) of each text and graphics file that you import into your publication.

When you save your work on a project for the first time—using the Save As option on the File menu—Ventura automatically creates the Chapter file. With each subsequent save—using the Save option on the File menu—Ventura will update the Chapter file. At the same time, Ventura writes over each source text file you import into the chapter, incorporating any changes, and doing so in the format peculiar to the word-processing software you used. If you import a Microsoft Word document, it is saved in Microsoft Word format; if you use Word-Perfect or XYWrite, the document is saved in those formats.

The Ventura Publication

While each Ventura Chapter is a separate entity, several Ventura Chapters can be (although they don't have to be) combined into a Ventura *Publication*. The Ventura Publication makes it very easy to organize, produce, and then print a large document, such as a book. Page numbering (across the Publication and within Chapters), index citations, cross references (if you have Ventura Professional Extensions), and Table of Contents information are all tracked by the Publication file.

TIP

The term "template" has a number of meanings in electronic publishing. In this case, a "template" is a Ventura chapter file that contains paragraph tags and page layout dimensions, but no text or graphic files—yet. Templates are useful for publications that are redone from scratch periodically, such as a newsletter. Instead of laying out its pages and reformatting its paragraphs each issue, you can call up the template file, insert your text and graphic files, and then save the template as an individual chapter.

Because you can work with individual Ventura Chapters to the exclusion of Ventura Publications, it is as simple to produce smaller documents such as newsletters and brochures as it is to manage a large project such as a book.

The Ventura Style Sheet and Paragraph tags

Associated with each Ventura Chapter is a style sheet. The style sheet file stores the typographical information that is used to implement your design of the document's text—paragraph by paragraph. It does so by associating typographical attributes (font, type size, margin and line spacings) with paragraph tag names.

While many Chapters can share the same style sheet, each can use but one style sheet at a time. You can change style sheets at any time. However, if you do, remember that every paragraph's typographical attributes will change to reflect those of the new style sheet—a fact that could result in an unwanted ripple effect to your typography if you do not carefully control your modifications.

Most of the text you use in your designs will first be created using a commercial word-processing program. Ventura will accept input from most of the more popular programs, including Microsoft Word, Word-Perfect, Multimate, XYWrite, and WordStar. Ventura will also accept ASCII text files. As you bring text files into your chapters, the attributes of any paragraph tag names from the word processor that are not already listed in Ventura's style sheet will revert to those of the current Body Text paragraph tag.

Ventura paragraph tag names can be inserted directly into your word-processed file. Each paragraph tag name contains three parts: an "at" symbol (@), the tag name in capital letters followed by a space, and an equals sign (=) followed by a space.

@PARAGRAPH TAG =

A paragraph that doesn't have an explicit name associated with it is assigned the current Body Text typographical attributes.

Ventura Frames

As the Ventura Chapter is to your document's organization, the Frame is to its layout. Every design element having to do with layout is accomplished through frames that you create and position to conform with your design. The Base Page—the foundation of your Ventura workspace—is simply a frame of the same size as your entire work space. On it you place frames to hold text or graphics files, draw with Ventura's built-in graphics tools, and lay down column guides. Every manipulation that you can do with a frame—adjusting margins, creating backgrounds, and adjusting typography—you can do with the Base Page. In fact, you can think of the base page as being a kind of "master frame" that will hold your main text file and frames to contain its ancillary text and graphics files.

TIP

When editing text in Ventura, even at Normal Size, there are places where it's difficult to determine on-screen if you have the correct letter spacing and word spacing. Sometimes it looks like there's a space in the middle of a word, when in fact there isn't; sometimes it looks like there's no space between two words when in fact there is. A quick way to check is to use the cursor keys (the four keys with arrows pointing up, down, right, and left). With the text tool, set an insertion point in the text in question. Then press the right or the left cursor key (depending on the direction in which you're moving for your check). If one key press moves the cursor past the next letter, there's no space; if it takes two presses, there is a space.

WORKING WITH VENTURA PUBLISHER FRAMES

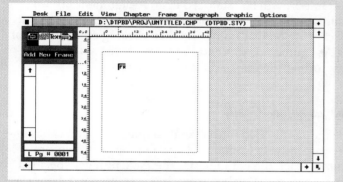

To insert a new frame, click on the Frame mode icon in the upper left corner of your main screen (or press Ctrl-u). Then click on Add New Frame immediately below the mode icons. As you do, the Frame mode cursor (a cross that moves as you move the mouse) changes to a corner with the letters "FR" in it.

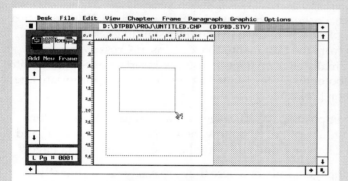

Put the apex of the corner at the point where you want the upper left corner of the frame to appear. Then click the mouse button and hold it down as you drag the lower right corner of the frame to the point where the frame is as large as you want.

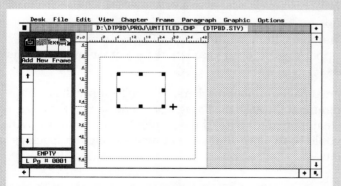

If you want to change the size of the frame later, "grab" one of the eight black "handles" and drag it with the mouse. The frame's handle (and associated boundary) will move with the mouse. This technique is especially useful if you're working with a frame that is larger than your computer screen. It is also useful when modifying the page layout.

TIP

Play is generally recognized as
an important component of learning and of creativity. Merely "playing around" in Ventura Publisher
can accelerate your learning
curve and sharpen your graphic
eye. When there's no end result
at stake, no fear of making a mis-
take, and no deadline to meet,
you might find it easier to experiment and to become comfortable
with the software's commands
and functions.

TIP

Ventura notes a page number at
the bottom left corner of its main
screen. This number is used by
Ventura internally; it might not correspond with the number that will
be printed as the publication folio.

Placing text or graphics files into Ventura frames is simplicity itself.
First you select Load Text/Picture on the File menu. You can then highlight the type of file you will be placing—whether it is a text, line-art,
or image file. When you click on OK, Ventura will display a further
dialog box with a list of files of the appropriate type from which you
choose those you want to import.

The file(s) you import will be cataloged in an Assignment List on
Ventura's main screen. To place a file, you select a frame in which it
should go by clicking on that frame and then clicking on the name of
the file in the Assignment List. Ventura places the file and automatically performs formatting translations if necessary.

Numbering pages automatically

If your publication is divided into several chapter files, you can number its pages consecutively from one chapter to the next. Ventura
begins numbering each file with the starting page number specified
in the Update Counters dialog box from the Chapter menu. For example, if you have a 200-page report divided into two files, and the first
file ends on page 109, the Restart Number on the second file would be
110, with the Chapter option box highlighted under Which Counter.

You can place a page number anywhere on your page. With your text
cursor at the place where the page number should go, select Insert
Special Item from the Edit menu. Click on Insert Cross Reference,
or press F6. Finally click on Page #. You can insert a page number into
a header or footer by placing your text cursor on the appropriate line
and clicking on [P#].

To create a composite page number, such as "Page 1" or "1-1" (for
chapter 1, page 1) or "1 of 7," follow the method outlined above, and
also click on Chapter #, and add a hyphen, before clicking on Page # .

Position your page numbers where they are easily seen, generally at
the top or bottom outside corners or centered at the bottom of the page.
It's best to keep them in the margins so that they won't interfere when
you flow text. Be sure, however, that they are within the printer
tolerance of your page trim.

You can choose among several styles in which to format page numbers: Arabic numbers, Roman numerals, or English words. You can
also specify upper-case or lower-case letters for Roman numerals and
English words.

For right-aligned page-number markers, be sure to apply the right
horizontal alignment through the Paragraph menu so that the alignment will be maintained for two-, three-, and four-digit numbers. An
alternative would be to place your page numbers using tab spacings
and alignments.

A few words of encouragement

Ventura is a very capable—and very complex—software product. For that reason, it can be somewhat daunting if you're new to computers or to desktop publishing. Remember, however, that you'll never ruin work you've created because you tried a new Ventura trick: If you ever get to the point where you want to "wad up the paper," you can always use the Abandon command—which lets you revert to the last saved version of your chapter. Saving your Ventura chapters *often* is your safety net.

As we said at the beginning of this introduction, you'll push Ventura pretty close to its limits by working through the projects in this section. One limit we noticed in particular is Ventura's sometimes quirky interaction between on-screen text and graphic objects. Occasionally, you may feel as though you can't do what we did in these projects. Well, you can—but, as with many of life's little problems, you might have to experiment a bit (trial and error) or simply print something to see how it comes out.

The best advice we can give you: Take your time as you work through the projects step by step. It's important to enjoy the learning process. Soon you'll be using your new-found Ventura skills and keener eye for design to express your own ideas visually. And that's where the real satisfaction lies.

PROJECT 1

A SIMPLE CERTIFICATE FOR VENTURA NOVICES

This project is intended for readers with very little experience using Ventura Publisher. The hands-on instructions will guide you through most of the basic procedures used to create and move around a page, with the exception of importing text and graphics from other applications. Because the document is so simple, it is created entirely in Ventura. The project also uses most of the tools in Ventura's repertoire.

If you want to produce a quick certificate without so much hands-on instruction, you should be able to move quickly through the boldface and bulleted instructions. Tips and paragraphs without bullets explain the techniques and Ventura basics in more detail than you will want if you already have a little experience with the program.

A similar diplomalike format could be used for business seminars, training programs, and workshops. It could be adapted to serve as an award—for employee or salesman of the month, for a good safety record, and so on. It could also be more personal—for a boss, a colleague, or an assistant—to recognize a job well done or a gesture appreciated, as a way to say thank you for going beyond the call of duty.

VENTURA TECHNIQUES YOU WILL LEARN

- Change the Page Size & Layout settings
- Display the rulers
- Change the page view
- Use Column Snap and Line Snap commands
- Select and change line weights
- Draw lines, rectangles, and circles with Ventura's graphics tools

- Use scroll bars to move around the screen
- Change type specifications
- Type text in Ventura
- Move text
- Move Ventura graphics
- Add shades to Ventura graphics

A horizontal, or landscape, page orientation with equal margins on all sides is typical of certificates and diplomas.

ENROLLMENT CERTIFICATE

THE DESKTOP PUBLISHING SCHOOL
ADMITS

TO
THE HANDS-ON DESIGN COURSE

Times Roman has a utilitarian elegance appropriate for a design course.

The ruling line around the certificate is very assertive and gives the certificate an official, bona fide look.

BLUEPRINT FOR THE CERTIFICATE

GETTING SET UP

If you haven't already done so, turn your computer on according to the manufacturer's instructions. After it has booted, type *VP* and press Return.

1. Specify the page size and layout.

- Move the pointer to the Chapter menu, drag to highlight the words Page Size & Layout, and click the mouse button.

- Make any necessary changes in the Page Setup dialog box so that it conforms to the following specifications:

  Orientation: Landscape

  Paper Type & Dimension: Letter, 8.5 by 11 inches

  Sides: Single

The Page Layout dialog box with specifications for this project. To change any parameter, place the cursor on it, press and hold the mouse button, and move the highlight over the new parameter selection. When you release the mouse button, Ventura accepts the new parameter.

▶ ▶ ▶

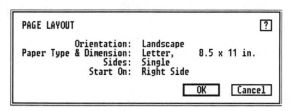

2. Specify the margins.

- Move the pointer to the Frame menu, drag to highlight the words Margins & Columns, and click the mouse button.

  Margin in inches: Specify 1 for all four margins.

  # of Columns: Click on 1.

- After you have specified your page setup, click OK.

The Margins & Columns dialog box with the specifications for this project. To change any dimension, place the cursor to the right of the dimension, use the keyboard to backspace, and type the number you want. To select an option within a box, click on that box to highlight the selection.

▶ ▶ ▶

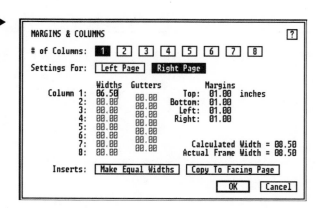

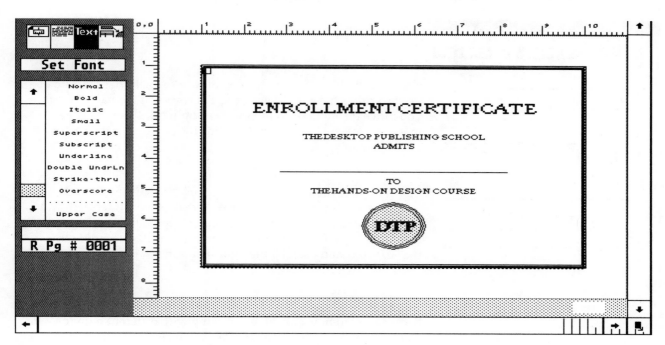

▲ ▲ ▲ *The certificate blueprint with title bar and rulers.*

3. Check your printer type.

- Check the printer by choosing the Set Printer Info dialog box from the File menu. Select the target printer from the list of devices, choose the port to which it is connected from the Output To list, and click OK.

4. Set up your on-screen work space.

- If the rulers and column guides are not visible, choose Show Rulers and Show Column Guides from the Options menu.

It is almost always useful to work with the rulers and column guides visible—they are indispensable for placing items where you want them on the page.

In this project, all measurements are in inches. This is Ventura's default setting for measurements, so unless you've changed your defaults you won't need to make any adjustments.

5. Select a page view (from the View menu) that enables you to see the entire document.

The View menu provides four page-view options. If you are not familiar with these options, take a moment to click on each one and observe how the publication window changes from one view to another. How much of your page you see at each view depends on the size of the page and the size of your monitor.

MOVING VENTURA'S RULER ZERO

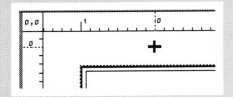

The default setting for the zero point, where the horizontal and vertical rulers meet, is at the upper left corner of the page. When you move the mouse around the Ventura work space, hairline markers move in both rulers to define the position of the cursor on the screen.

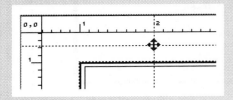

You can move the zero point by dragging the hairlines into the "0.0" box at the upper left corner (where the rulers intersect), and then out to where you want them on the page. You can reset them to their default position by placing your mouse cursor in the "0,0" box and clicking the mouse button.

Because different users will be working with different monitors, we generally will not specify an optimal page view. You'll undoubtedly need to change views as you work on this and any other document.

6. Save your Chapter.

- Choose Save As from the File menu.

- Type the name of your new chapter on the Selection line. You don't have to include a three-letter filename extension unless you want a designation other than the default CHP.

Each subsequent time you save a chapter, select Save on the File menu, or press Ctrl-s. Ventura updates changes you make to any text or graphics file in the chapter.

Get in the habit of saving your work every 15 minutes, or sooner if you've just done something to the layout that you'd hate to redo. The Save and Save As commands in Ventura are similar to commands of the same name in other applications.

7. Save this Ventura Style Sheet.

- Choose Save As New Style from the File menu.

- On the Selection line, type *PROJECT1* and press Return.

When you begin working on a new document, it's a good idea to load the DEFAULT.STY style sheet and then save it under a new name. That way, you'll always have a typographically familiar starting point that doesn't change from project to project, and yet allows you to accommodate the inevitable differences between projects.

TIP

One of the most useful keyboard commands is the one that saves your current document: Ctrl-s.

8. Turn on Column Guides.

- If your column guides are not displayed, select Show Column Guides from the Options menu.

CREATING THE CERTIFICATE

1. Create a frame.

- Move the cursor to the Frame mode icon and click.

- Move the cursor from the Frame mode icon down to the Add New Frame addition box and click once again.

- Move the cursor to about 1 inch from the left and upper margins (so that it is in line with the frame's column guides). Press and hold the mouse button while you drag the cursor down and to the right (to the lower right corner of the column guide, or as far as your screen will let you move it).

You will want the frame's borders to coincide with those of the column guides. The box below, "Specifying Precise Frame Dimensions," provides a convenient method that lets you easily create precisely placed and sized frames.

2. Create a border.

- With the frame highlighted, select the Ruling Box Around dialog box from the Frame menu.

SPECIFYING PRECISE FRAME DIMENSIONS

You can specify precise dimensions for any frame with a simple, two-step process. For instance, here is how to place the frame for the certificate in this project.

- Activate your frame by moving the cursor somewhere within the frame and clicking the mouse button.

- Select the Sizing & Scaling dialog box on the Frame menu. If the specifications shown do not conform to those listed below, make the necessary changes.

> Upper Left X: 1.00 inch
>
> Upper left Y: 1.00 inch
>
> Frame Width: 9.00 inches
>
> Frame Height: 6.50 inches

- If the specifications shown do not conform to those listed below, make the necessary changes.

  Width: Frame

  Color: Black

  Pattern: Solid

  Dashes: Off

  Space Above Rule 1: 0.00 fractional points

  Height of Rules 1 and 3: 0.25 fractional points

  Space Below Rules 1 and 2: 2.00 fractional points

  Height of Rule 2: 2.00 fractional points

The other rule space and height dimensions should be 0.00 fractional points. The overall height of the rules should work out to 4.97 fractional points.

Note: If you're working at a reduced page view, the border might look like a solid or double line. To see the line as it will print, choose Normal View (1x) from the View menu. At that size you may need to move around the screen to find the line. Use the scroll bars at the right and bottom of your screen to do so.

3. Add the certificate's text.

- Click on the Text mode icon.

- Move the I-beam text cursor to within the frame you created previously. Type *ENROLLMENT CERTIFICATE* and press Return.

- Click on the Paragraph mode icon. Move the cursor to the words "ENROLLMENT CERTIFICATE" that you just typed, and click.

- Click the mouse button on the box containing the words, "Add New Tag."

- When you see the Add New Tag dialog box, type *Headline* and press Return.

- From the Paragraph menu, select the Font dialog box. Choose these specifications:

  Font: Times Roman

  Size: 36.0 points

  Style: Normal

  Color: Black

Note: When you've chosen the specifications contained in this dialog box (as well as in any other dialog box), click on OK or press Return. When you do, Ventura accepts your changes (if any) and closes the dialog box, displaying your chapter once again.

TIP

Sometimes you will appreciate being able to see where you inserted blank lines (entered by pressing Return), double spaces, and tabs in text. Ventura provides the Show/Hide Tabs & Returns toggle command for this purpose. To display the extra spaces and tabs, select Show Tabs & Returns from the Options menu, or press Ctrl-t. When you don't want them displayed, select Hide Tabs & Returns from the Option menu, or press Ctrl-t once more.

- From the Paragraph menu, select the Alignment dialog box. Choose these specifications:

  Horizontal Alignment: Center

  Overall Width: Frame-Wide

- From the Paragraph menu, select the Spacing dialog box. Choose these specifications:

  Above: 6,03

  Below: 00,00

  Inter-Line: 3,00

  Inter-Paragraph: 00,00

  Add in Above: Always

4. Add the rest of the type.

- Click on the Text mode icon.

- Position the text cursor in the frame immediately to the left of the End-of-File box (❑), and type the following text:

  [press Return twice for spacing]

  THE DESKTOP PUBLISHING SCHOOL [Return]

  ADMITS [press Return four times for extra line spaces]

  TO [Return]

  THE HANDS-ON DESIGN COURSE [press Return two times for extra line spaces]

  DTP

Note: If you're working at a small page view, the text may appear on-screen as gray bars. This is called *greeked* text. To see the text, choose a larger page view.

- Click on the Paragraph mode icon.

- Highlight one of the five lines you just typed by clicking on it. The words "Body Text" should appear at the screen's lower left, at the bottom of the Assignment list box.

- Select Font from the Paragraph mode and make the following specification:

  Custom Size: 18.0 points

- From the Paragraph menu, select the Alignment dialog box. Indicate these specifications:

  Horizontal Alignment: Center

  Overall Width: Frame-Wide

TIP

You can change the formatting of text at any time. With the text tool active, drag the I-beam across the text you want to reformat. Then change the specifications through Ventura's Set Font facility or by clicking one of the attributes listed in the left side of the screen.

- Select Spacing from the Paragraph menu. Enter the following specifications:

  Above: 0.000 inches

  Below: 0.000 inches

  Inter-Line: 0.291 inch

- Click on the Text mode icon. Wipe the I-beam cursor over the letters "DTP." Click on Set Font, and change the letters to Times, 36 point, Bold.

5. Add the line for a signature.

No personal certificate is complete without a line to hold the bearer's name. One thing to keep in mind is that the certificate will look more balanced if the signature line is a little shorter than the headline. Also, this process is most easily completed if you are working in Reduced view.

- Move the cursor to the Graphics icon, and click the mouse button.

- Move the cursor to the 0,0 ruler intersection. Press and hold the mouse button as you move the mouse to the right until the vertical line bisects the middle frame handle.

- Select the line-drawing tool by clicking on the box containing a diagonal line from the six graphics tool boxes to the left of the screen.

- Move the cursor into the frame that holds the certificate's text until the left ruler hairline is at 4 inches and the upper ruler hairline is at 2 inches to the left of the upper ruler zero.

  Press and hold the mouse button as you draw a line to the right—until the upper ruler hairline is at 2 inches to the right of the upper ruler zero.

If you haven't drawn the line exactly horizontal (you can tell because it looks a bit jagged), you can straighten it easily. Simply select the line by clicking on it. Then "grab" a handle on one side or the other, and move that handle up or down until the line is straight.

Similarly, if you don't like the line's position, you can move it. To do so, select the line by clicking on it. Then put the graphic tool cursor somewhere along its length, press and hold the mouse button, and finally drag the line to where you want it placed.

6. Create a seal.

- Click on the Frame mode icon at the upper left corner of the screen, then move your cursor to just outside of the frame that holds the certificate's text and click.

- Click on the Graphic mode icon.

TIP

You'll find that drawing and positioning lines in this case is most easily done while using Reduced view. If you aren't already in Reduced view, press Ctrl-r.

WORKING WITH GRID SNAP

Ventura has a grid, like the intesecting lines on a piece of graph paper, that you can use to line up graphic objects more easily. You can turn the grid on and off as you find it convenient.

For this certificate project, we will turn on a grid of 0.1 inch.

- With Graphics mode active, select Grid Settings from the Graphics menu.

- Change the Horizontal and Vertical Spacing to 0.100 inch

- Turn Grid Snap on.

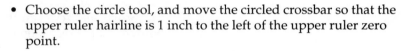

- Choose the circle tool, and move the circled crossbar so that the upper ruler hairline is 1 inch to the left of the upper ruler zero point.

- Hold down the Alt key and drag the crossbar on a diagonal to the 1-inch point to the right of the upper ruler zero. Release the mouse button before the Alt key. (It's the Alt key that restrains the graphic to a circular rather than an oval shape.)

▲ ▲ ▲

When you select a graphic with the pointer, the graphic is surrounded by eight small rectangles, or selection handles. To move a graphic drawn with one of Ventura's tools, point directly on the outline of the selected graphic; press the mouse button and, when you see a four-headed arrow, drag the graphic to the new position. If you point to a handle and drag, you will resize the graphic.

You are centering your first circle on the letters "DTP," which will appear at the center of your seal.

- Choose Line Attributes on the Graphic menu. Indicate the following specification:

    Thickness: Custom, 0.24 fractional points

- Select Fill Attributes on the Graphics menu. Choose the following specifications:

    Color: Black

    Pattern: 1

    Transparent

- Choose the circle tool, and create a second circle that is six points larger than the first, again centering the circle on the letters "DTP" as well as the circle you drew earlier.

- Choose Line Attributes on the Graphic menu. Indicate the following specification:

    Thickness: Custom, 2.00 fractional points

- Select Fill Attributes on the Graphics menu. Choose the following specifications:

    Color: White

    Pattern: Hollow

    Transparent

- Create a third circle in the same way you created the first two. It should be centered over them both, with a line thickness of 0.24

Note: When you move graphic objects with the pointer tool, press the mouse button until you see a four-headed arrow and the handles defining the graphic object block disappear.

FINISHING THE JOB

1. Save your work.

- Press Ctrl-s. It would be a shame to inadvertently lose what you've done and not be able to get it back. Besides, saving your work takes only a well-spent moment.

2. Review your work.

- Check to make sure everything is centered. Change the page view to Normal, and scroll around to check spelling, line weights (the border and the seal should be the same), and placements.

3. Choose To Print from the File menu.

- Take a moment to review the options in the Print dialog box. Make sure that you're printing only one copy. Because this is a one-page document, printing only the current page is okay; you don't have to set a print range.

- Your printer should be listed at the bottom of the dialog box. If it isn't, see step 3 under "Getting Set Up" earlier in this project.

- When all the printer specifications are correct, click OK.

4. Sign your name.

If the printed certificate looks as you expected, congratulations. Sign your name on the line and consider yourself enrolled.

HOW DID YOU DO?

If you had trouble completing this project... We recommend reviewing the tutorials provided with Ventura to help you become more comfortable with the tools and techniques that you'll use throughout the rest of this book.

If you completed the project but found it difficult... Try Project 2A or 2B. They will give you practice using many of these same tools and will introduce a few new techniques as well.

If you found it easy... You're not a novice after all.

TWO INVITATIONS WITH VARIATIONS ON EACH

Invitations and announcements are so easy to produce with a desktop publishing system that you may look for excuses to create them. Although they are simple, these design tasks still warrant your making a list of the copy points to be included and doing a thumbnail sketch on paper before you sit down at the computer. Once you've determined the basic approach, you can quickly enter and lay out the text directly in Ventura Publisher.

The Palatino italic, used for all the type, contrasts subtly with the rectilinearity of the border and rule.

The rule above the date helps the guests see at a glance the date, time, and location.

There is more space above and below the main text block than between the lines.

The company name is 14 point with 18-point initial caps, making simple typography look smart.

The 11/14 copy is centered and the lines kept short to contrast with the long company name.

NORTHERN LIGHT TEXTILES

Invites
you
for
champagne
and
hors d'oeuvres

January 22
5:00 p.m.
La Rondo Room
The Heraldry Hotel

The invitations in this chapter are really two separate projects. One is somewhat formal and straightforward, the other is informal and thematic. Both are 5.5 by 4.25 inches. We'll show you how to print four copies of the invitations on one sheet. Printing "four up" in this way is very efficient, whether you're doing the printing yourself or using a commercial printer.

If you're printing the invitations yourself, you'll want to get a 20-pound card stock with matching envelopes. Note that using this stock requires you to select the Manual option for Paper Tray in the Print dialog box; the paper will need to be hand-fed. When printing manually on card stock, we allow for about 15% waste due to poor alignment.

The crisp, structured organization is offset by playful, thematic art.

Avant Garde is a good contemporary face for an informal invitation, and its O's, being perfect circles, echo the sunset theme. The headline is 12/36, all caps. The body type is 10/36.

The text lines must be short enough not to intrude on the art. Maximum line length is about 42 characters.

The sunset motif is created using Ventura's circle graphic object with a white line masking the lower part of each circle. See the instructions in Project 2B.

CRUISE ON OVER TO RIVER'S END

The Western Travel Agents Association

invites you to a sunset buffet

on the patio of the River's End Restaurant

Sunday July 24

7:00 p.m.

$10 per person

door prize—Hawaiian vacation

AN EASY FORMAL INVITATION

A formal invitation sets the tone for an elegant event. The basic design for the invitation in this project uses an open banner at the top for the company's name and centered, calligraphic-style type throughout. All of the variations, shown on the pages following the instructions, maintain the formal rules and centered style even when more contemporary decorative elements are added.

As mentioned in the introduction on the previous page, the instructions for this project specify printing one invitation on a single 8.5- by 11-inch sheet. If you want to print four to a sheet, before beginning this project read the instructions for "How to Print Four Up" that appear at the end of Project 2B and adapt the instructions for a horizontal rather than a vertical orientation.

VENTURA TECHNIQUES YOU WILL LEARN

- Override the specified unit of measure
- Change the unit of measure
- Set the guides in back
- Create initial caps in display text
- Add a new frame to the base page
- Hide and display column guides
- Add hairline rules
- Select individual letters in italic type

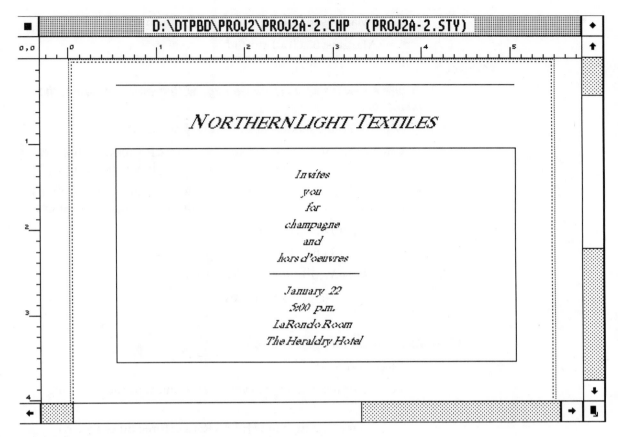

▲ ▲ ▲

The formal invitation is shown with ruler guides in place. Several variations follow the instructions for this basic blueprint.

BLUEPRINT FOR THE FORMAL INVITATION

1. Prepare your workspace for a new Ventura chapter.

- If you have a chapter already displayed on the workspace, select New from the File menu.

- Create a new stylesheet name for this project by selecting Load Diff. Style from the File menu, choosing DEFAULT.STY, and saving it as a new style named PROJ2A.STY.

2. Specify the page size and layout.

- Select Page Size & Layout... from the Chapter menu and choose the following options.

    Orientation: Landscape

    Paper Type & Dimension: Half, 5.5 by 4.25 inches

- Select Margins & Columns from the Frame menu.

    Margins: 03,00 all around

3. Create a new frame on the base page within which to format the invitation.

- While in Frame mode, click on Add New Frame.

- Move your cursor to the Ventura workspace, press and hold the left mouse button as you move the mouse down and to the right.

- Select Sizing & Scaling from the Frame menu and adjust options so that your new frame conforms to the following specifications:

    Upper Left X: 0.25 inch

    Upper Left Y: 0.25 inch

    Frame Width: 4.50 inches

    Frame Height: 3.50 inches

4. Add the text for the invitation.

- Select Text mode.

- Move your text cursor into your frame and type the following text:

    Your company name [press Return three times to leave room for a decorative rectangle]

    Invites [Return]

    you [Return]

    for [Return]

    champagne [Return]

    and [Return]

    hors d'oeuvres [press Return twice to leave room for a rule]

    5:00 p.m. [Return]

    La Rondo Room [Return]

    The Heraldry Hotel [Return]

5. Format the body text.

- Select Paragraph mode and click on one of the lines you have just typed to highlight it.

- Select Font from the Paragraph menu. Choose Palatino, italic, with a type size of 10 points.

- Select Alignment from the Paragraph menu and choose Center.

- Select Spacing from the Paragraph menu. Make any changes necessary in the dialog box so that its options conform to the following:

  Above: 0.000 inches

  Below: 0.000 inches

  Inter-line: 14.00 fractional points

*THERN**L**IGHT*

*THERN**L**IGHT*

▲ ▲ ▲

Selecting individual letters in italic is a little tricky. An individual letter is selected if, and only if, its lower left corner is highlighted. In the top screen detail shown here, only the L is actually selected; in the bottom detail, both the L and I are selected.

6. Format the headline.

- Click on the first line of the invitation to highlight it.

- Add a new tag named "Headline," formatted in 14-point Palatino italic.

- Select Ruling Line Above from the Paragraph menu, and incorporate the following options in the dialog box:

  Width: Custom

  Color: Black

  Pattern: Solid

  Dashes: Off

  Space Above Rule 1: 00,00

  Height of Rule 1: 00,01

  Space Below Rule 1: 01,06

  Custom Indent: 03,00

  Custom Width: 27,00

- Change the view to Enlarged View to make it easier to select individual letters, then click on the Text mode icon. Drag the text tool over the first letter of the company name to highlight that letter. Select Set Font and change the type size to 18 points. Repeat this for the first letter of each word in the company name.

TIP

Tab and return characters can give you landmarks by which you can quickly and evenly place graphic objects. If they're not already displayed and you want to use them for this purpose, press Ctrl-t to show them. When you press Ctrl-t again, they'll be removed from your display.

7. Add the hairline rule above the date.

- Select the frame containing the invitation by clicking on it while in Frame mode, and then click on the Graphics mode icon to activate that mode.

- Turn on the graphics grid snap by selecting Grid Settings from the Graphics menu, and set Grid Snap to On. At the same time, set the horizontal and vertical grid spacings to 00,01. This will give you a fine enough grid to easily position the hairline rule and border (to be described later).

- Click on the line drawing tool, move the pencil cursor to between the date and "hors d'oeuvres" and draw a horizontal line a bit longer than the length of the words that make up the date. You can use the paragraph return character between the two as a landmark to position the line evenly between the two lines of text.

  After you've drawn the line, you may have to adjust it up or down (by clicking on the line and moving it), or to straighten it horizontally (by dragging one of the handles on either end of the line). If you have not already specified Line Attributes as the default graphic object line thickness, you'll have to select it on the Graphics menu and adjust the line thickness to a Custom 00,01.

- In a similar way, use the rectangle-drawing graphic tool to draw a rectangle around the lower ten lines of the invitation. Be sure to set its fill attributes to hollow transparent white, and its line attributes to a Custom 00,01 thickness. You can use the ruling line above the headline to align your rectangle horizontally, and the paragraph return marks to align it vertically.

8. Review the other printing specifications and check to be sure your target printer is selected.

- To see the page on-screen as it will print, hide the column guides by clicking on that option from the Options menu, and then select Paragraph mode. (The Hide/Show Column Guides is one of several toggle switches on Ventura's menus: The feature is on when the option reads "Hide Column Guides" and off when it reads "Show Column Guides.") When you select Paragraph mode, Ventura turns off its display of frames, leaving only the text and graphic images that will be printed.

- After you check the page, print one copy to proof.

VARIATIONS

Even within this simple design, you can vary the graphic image considerably. The alternatives shown here use only Ventura's built-in graphics tools and Zapf Dingbats. When you use any of these devices to dress up a simple design, be playful but always err on the side of restraint. And be sure to put your result to the test of appropriateness.

For a short company name and for longer lines of text, use the same design in a vertical format, as shown here. The NLT logo is 31 points, the text is 11/20 Palatino italic, and the design above the date is a 14-point Zapf Dingbat (character number 118). The distance between the ruling line above the logo and the border below is 4,06. The margins are 3 picas all around, as they are in the basic design.

Northern Light Textiles

invites you for

champagne and hors d'oeuvres

when we present

our 1988 fabrics

featuring

new designs by Laurence Ralph

January 22, 5 - 7:30 p.m.

La Rondo Room

The Heraldry Hotel

Zapf Chancery, used here, is often recommended for invitations because it has a personalized, handwritten look. But it can also be a little fussy, especially in all caps, so we've changed the headline here to 14-point upper- and lowercase. The body text is 12/18; the decorative display is a 12-point Zapf Dingbat (character number 118) with 6 letterspaces between each unit.

The text position and line breaks have been altered from those specified in the blueprint in order to accommodate the decorative elements in this version.

❖

Northern Light Textiles

Invites you

for

champagne and hors d'oeuvres

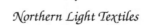

January 22, 5:00 p.m. La Rondo Room

The Heraldry Hotel

The decorative element here is a 1-pica-deep hairline-rule rectangle filled with diagonally-parallel lines. You can create this effect with Ventura's Graphics mode line tools, or you can import the filled boxes as graphic objects created using a drawing program. The text is 10/15 Palatino.

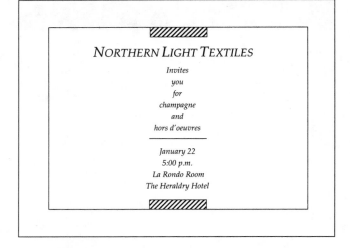

To personalize the invitation, you can type the guests' names one at a time using Ventura's built-in text editing tool, put the invitee's name in the banner, and rewrite the text to include the company name. This will take some extra time, of course, but might be a good choice for a limited number of guests and a very important event.

A modern decorative motif contrasts with the formality of the centered type. The corners are built out of rectangular modules (with black opaque solid fill) that decrease in width from 4 picas to 1 pica. The open stairstepping effect is created with a series of 1-pica hairline-rule squares, masked with a 12-point white opaque solid (and therefore invisible) diagonal line.

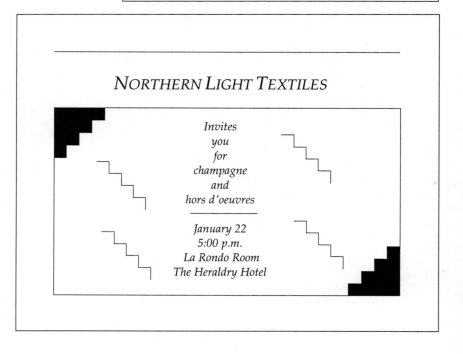

AN INFORMAL INVITATION WITH VENTURA GRAPHICS

This highly structured design could be used for a variety of informal events, with art suggestive of the theme of the party. The crisp organization suggests a shopping-list look, which is offset by playful art. The banner lends itself to different treatments, but the overall format works best with only one line of text occupying each space between the rules. For longer text, create additional spaces, as in the "Silvery Moon" version shown later; for shorter text, have fewer lines with more space between the rules. Several variations are shown following the blueprint instructions.

The invitation is designed so that four cards can be printed on a single 8.5- by 11-inch sheet. See the instructions for "How to Print Four Up," at the end of this project. Of course, you could easily vary the trim size to accommodate more text and print fewer cards on a sheet.

BLUEPRINT FOR THE INFORMAL INVITATION

TIP

Press the Tab key to move from one input line to another in Ventura dialog boxes. Press the Return key to OK a dialog box. Both of these keyboard shortcuts can be used so frequently that they are worth remembering early on.

1. Prepare your workspace for a new Ventura chapter.

- Select New from the File menu (if necessary).

- Create a new stylesheet name for this project by selecting Load Diff. Style from the File menu, choosing DEFAULT.STY, and saving it as a new style named PROJ2B.STY.

2. Specify the page size and margins.

- Select Page Size & Layout from the Chapter menu and choose the following options.

    Orientation: Portrait

    Paper Type & Dimension: Half, 8.5 by 5.5 inches

- Select Margins & Columns from the Frame menu and specify all four margins as 03,00.

3. Create a new frame on the base page within which to format the invitation.

- While in Frame mode, click on Add New Frame.

- Move your cursor to the Ventura workspace, press and hold the left mouse button as you move the mouse down and to the right.

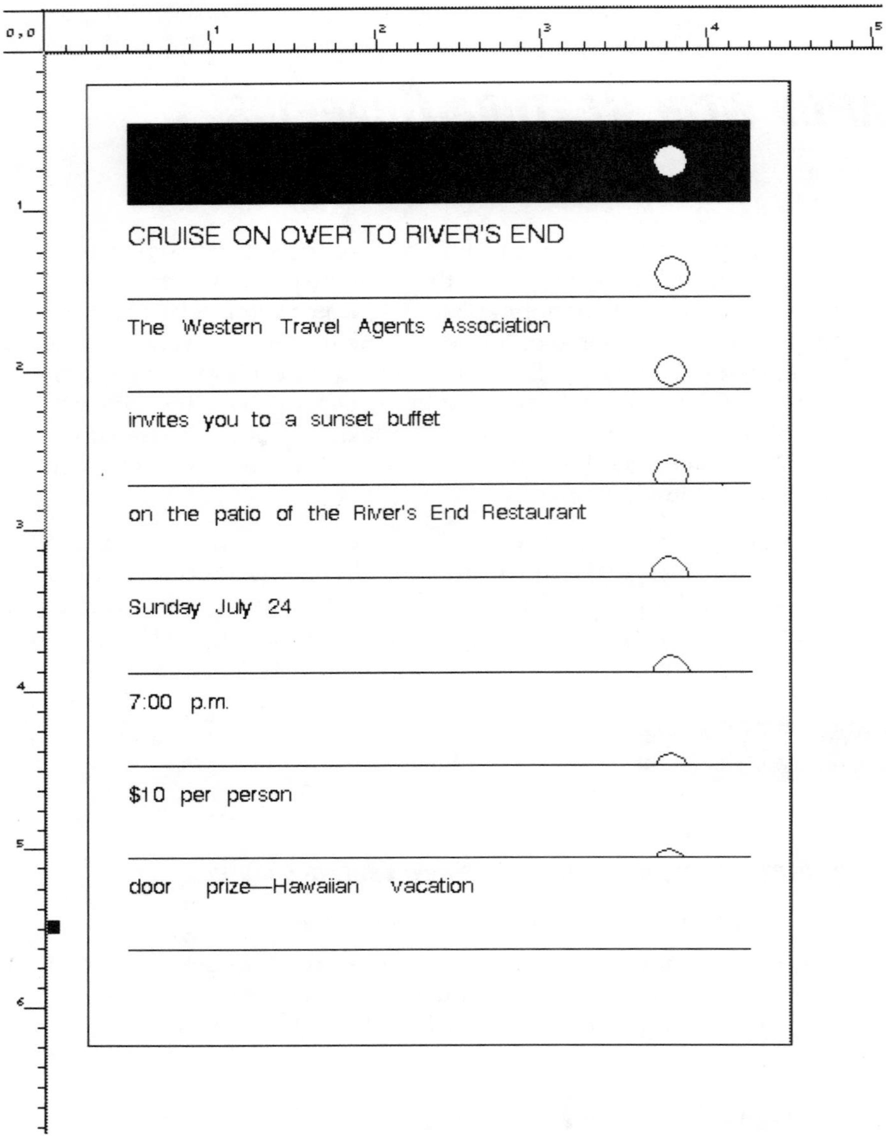

CRUISE ON OVER TO RIVER'S END

The Western Travel Agents Association

invites you to a sunset buffet

on the patio of the River's End Restaurant

Sunday July 24

7:00 p.m.

$10 per person

door prize—Hawaiian vacation

▲ ▲ ▲

The informal invitation is created in the upper left quadrant of an 8.5- by 11-inch sheet, and then copied and pasted three times to print four on a page. The graphics are created with Ventura's graphics tools.

VENTURA TECHNIQUES YOU WILL LEARN

- Create a solid banner
- Mask graphics with "invisible" lines
- Copy and paste Ventura graphics
- Use leading to space text between rules
- Use Ventura's Undo command
- Use the Select All command

- Select Sizing & Scaling from the Frame menu and adjust options so that your new frame conforms to the following specifications:

  Upper Left X: 0.25 inch

  Upper Left Y: 0.25 inch

  Frame Width: 4.50 inches

  Frame Height: 3.50 inches

4. Add the text for the invitation.

- While in Frame mode, select the new frame by clicking on it. Then select Text mode, move the vertical text cursor inside the new frame, and enter the following text:

  CRUISE ON OVER TO RIVER'S END [Return]

  The Western Travel Agents Association [Return]

  invites you to a sunset buffet [Return]

  on the patio of the River's End Restaurant [Return]

  Sunday July 24 [Return]

  7:00 p.m. [Return]

  $10 per person [Return]

  door prize—Hawaiian vacation [Return]

TIP

When you are working with part of a paragraph's text and want to edit that text, use the Text mode cursor to select it. Then you can change the type specifications of part of the text (font, size, style, and so on) or cut and paste it to a new location using Ventura's built-in editing facilities.

5. Set the font and spacing for the body text paragraphs.

- Select Paragraph mode; click on any line of text to highlight it.

- Use the Font, Alignment, and Spacing dialog boxes to adjust the text to the following specifications:

  Font: Avant Garde Gothic Book

  Size: 10 points

  Inter-Line Spacing: 36.00 fractional points

  Don't set spacings for above or below the body text paragraphs.

6. Add ruling lines above the lines of text.

- With one paragraph highlighted, select Ruling Lines Above from the Paragraph menu. Enter the following specifications:

  Width: Margin

  Color: Black

  Space Above Rule 1: 0.00 fractional points

  Height of Rule 1: 0.25 fractional points

  Space Below Rule 1: 6.00 fractional points

TIP

When you want to insert a graphic repeatedly in a document, such as the sun in this invitation, it is faster to copy and paste the graphic than to redraw it. Pasting also ensures consistency of size from one graphic to another of the same kind. You have to copy the graphic only once. It will remain on the graphics clipboard until you replace it with something else. You'll find the process very speedy when you use the keyboard shortcut for pasting (the Ins key).

7. Create the headline with a banner.

- Click on the first line to highlight it. Select Fonts from the Paragraph menu and make the following changes:

  Size: 12 points

  Note: The headline should be in all caps.

- Select Ruling Lines Above from the Paragraph menu. Enter the following specifications:

  Width: Margin

  Color: Black

  Space Above Rule 1: 0.00 fractional points

  Height of Rule 1: 36.00 fractional points

  Space Below Rule 1: 6.00 fractional points

8. Add the visual motif for the banner.

You can create the sunset using Ventura's graphics tools, as described below in the box "How to Create a Ventura Sunset."

9. Print your invitation.

HOW TO CREATE A VENTURA SUNSET

A hairline rule circle, partially covered by a frame, makes a setting sun.

You can create a sunset motif by using a white rectangle to mask more and more of each subsequent circle, thus suggesting the sun sinking below the horizon line.

1. With the frame containing the invitation selected, and while in Graphics mode, hold down the Alt key and use the circle tool to create the size sun you want.

2. Copy the circle once and paste it as many times as you want (say, seven). Position each copy a little lower on its horizon line than the one before, using the hairlines on the horizontal ruler to align the suns.

3. To cover the part of the circle below the horizontal line, create a frame and butt it to the ruling line above the text paragraphs. Then set its fill to solid white and create a ruling line above for the frame that matches the paragraph's. You'll have to adjust the position of this frame until the horizon line is unbroken and the portion of the circle below it is completely masked.

VARIATIONS

You can create a moonlight motif with a technique similar to the one used for the sunset. Select an opaque white fill for the circles from the Graphics menu to reverse the moons out of the black banner. You need five or six moons to convey the feeling of movement across the sky.

This variation has one more line of text than the basic design has, and the text has ruling lines below instead of above. The type specs are 12/33 Avant Garde for the headline and 10/33 for the body text.

A simple, all-text variation for this design uses the banner for the headline type instead of for art. To adapt the blueprint for this treatment, type the headline as two separate paragraphs in white 10-point type inside the black banner. One headline paragraph should be aligned flush left, and the other aligned flush right.

The body of the invitation uses the same interline spacing and ruling lines above as in the basic design.

SWOON BY THE SILVERY MOON

The Western Travel Agents Association

invites you to a moonlight cruise

on the good ship Pacifica

Broadway Pier

Sunday July 24, 9:00 p.m. anchors aweigh

$25 per person

dinner and dancing

Live music by the Streamers

CRUISE ON OVER TO

THE RIVER'S END

The Western Travel Agents Association

invites you to a sunset buffet

on the patio at River's End Restaurant

Sunday July 24

7:00 p.m.

$10 per person

door prize—Hawaiian vacation

Clip art is available to fit almost any party theme you could imagine. Here, the ship is a bit-mapped silhouette image. The palm trees are encapsulated PostScript art created from the image of a single tree, rotated and sized as desired to fit the layout.

The length of the ruling lines above varies depending on the length of the text and the position of the art. For the number of lines shown here, the top rule is 6 picas from the top trim.

The type is 10/48 Avant Garde.

CRUISE ON OVER TO RIVER'S END

Western Travel Agents Association

invites you to a sunset buffet

on the good ship Pacifica

Sunday, July 24 at 7 P.M.

door prize—Hawaiian vacation

Typographic details such as initial caps bring a touch of visual interest to an all-text invitation. Available from the Special Effects dialog box found on the Paragraph menu, the cap here is 72-point Zapf Chancery, partially overlapping a 40% black ruling line above.

The specifications for the text and rules are the same as those described in the blueprint, except that the text here is flush right.

*C*RUISE ON OVER TO RIVER'S END

The Western Travel Agents Association

invites you to a sunset barbeque

on the patio at River's End Restaurant

Sunday July 24

7:00 p.m.

$10 per person

door prize—Hawaiian vacation

How To Print Four Up

Invitations, business cards, name tags, and other documents with a small trim size can be printed efficiently with multiple copies of the document on one sheet of paper. Simply create a master of the document, copy it, and then repeatedly paste the copy to fill the page.

The following instructions for printing the invitation in these projects four to a page can be adapted easily for other dimensions.

1. Check all the alignments on your master.

Print a copy and proofread for spelling, accuracy of information, alignments, and so on.

2. Be sure Column and Line Snap are turned on.

If they are not on, select them from the Options menu, and click on them to toggle.

3. Copy the master frame.

- Click on the Frame mode icon, click on the frame to be copied, and select Copy Frame from the Edit menu (or press Shift-Del).

- Hold down the mouse button and slide the frame to the position its copy is to occupy.

4. Paste the master frame.

- Select Paste Frame from the Edit menu (or press Ins). Repeat this step for each additional copy of the original frame.

If you plan to print and trim the cards yourself, you may want to add little tick marks to guide your trim. It sounds ridiculous, but we've found that 8-point Helvetica periods, being 1 pixel high, provide a sufficient guide and virtually disappear in trimming. Place a period at the corner of the frames holding the card images. Another, manual, method is for you to use a ruler and pencil to mark the cuts and erase the pencil marks after trimming.

If you are printing the invitations on a laser printer, the 20-pound card stock must be hand-fed. Select the Paper Tray: Manual option in the Print dialog box (found on the File menu).

If your cards will be commercially printed, you will need to paste your camera-ready page onto a piece of art board and draw crop marks outside the live area to indicate the inside trim for each card.

PROJECT 3

A SIMPLE ONE-COLUMN FORMAT FOR NEWSLETTERS AND REPORTS

This project introduces two of the most important features of electronic pasteup: designing templates that you can use again and again and importing text created in a word processor. Templates enable you to have on file an electronic blueprint with page and type specifications, headline treatments, and other elements in documents that you produce repeatedly, such as newsletters and reports. They save you time (you don't have to reinvent the wheel on every page or in every issue) and help you to maintain consistency (you don't have to remember and re-create dozens of different specifications).

If you are unfamiliar with any of these features, this is a good project to do whether or not you need a format such as the one used in this report.

Because this is the first project that involves importing text files, we have also included some sidebar information about controlling text in Ventura Publisher.

Although the subhead for *Flash/Memo* labels it a newsletter, the same format could be used for a report. The format is a notch or two more complex and effective than what you could do on a typewriter. In fact, the typewriterlike face (Courier) and wide text column are intended to suggest the spontaneity of a typewritten document. That association may seem ironic given the slickness that desktop publishing offers, but it gives the page a feeling of hot news right off the press. You can't capture that feeling in a more highly formatted design.

The fact that the newsletter looks like it was quickly and easily put together in turn suggests that it can be read quickly and easily. Indeed, the generous white space around the headlines and the boldface leadins facilitates scanning. You would expect the writing style to be fast-paced—informal yet to the point. The format is designed to accommodate short items of about 150 to 200 words. If your editorial material doesn't lend itself to brief stories, this is not the design for you.

You should have at least six lines in a story that begins near the bottom of a page. If you don't, you can cut from and add to stories to adjust the position of headlines; or rearrange the order of stories; or stop the text short of the bottom margin and begin the new story on the next page. (The informal format allows for an uneven bottom.) Whether you make these changes in Ventura or in your word-processing program depends on the extent of the changes needed.

VENTURA TECHNIQUES

- Create and use a template
- Create unequal columns
- Change the default typeface
- Draw a dotted line using a paragraph tag
- Import text
- Export text to a word-processing application
- Translate file formats between different word-processing software
- Use paragraph breaks
- Mark up text

January 4, 1991

<table>
<tr><td>The Weekly
Newsmemo of
ACE
Marketing Co.</td><td># FLASH/Memo</td></tr>
</table>

Headline goes here on as many lines as needed

Loren ipsum dolor sit amet, consectetur adipscing elit, sed diam nonnumy eiusmod tempor incidumt ut labore et dolore magna aliquam erat vvolupat. Ut enim ad minimim veniame quis nostrud exercitation ullamcorpor suscipit laboris nisi ut aliquiip ex ea commodo consequat. Duis autem vel eum irure dolor consequat, vel illum dolorre eu fugi

At v
prae
cept
sunt
est
dit

• • • • • •

Headline goes here on as many lines as needed

Itaq
pref
tene
acco
etia
cess
toen
pecu
reli
pary
dode

Invi
aeug
est
noti
libe

• • • • • •

Headline goes here on as many lines as needed

Dabu
est
caus
faci
Sed

Page 2

January 4, 1991 FLASH/Memo The Weekly Newsmemo of ACE Marketing

Nos amice et nebevol, olestias access potest fierad augenas cum conscient to factor tum toen legum odioque civiuda. Et tamen in busdatd ne que pecun modut est neque nonor imper ned libiding genepular religuard on cupiditat, quas nulla priad im umdnat.

• • • • • • •

Headline goes here on as many lines as needed

Nos amice et nebevol, olestias access potest fierad augenas cum conscient to factor tum toen legum odioque civiuda. Et tamen in busdatd ne que pecun modut est neque nonor imper ned libiding genepular religuard on cupiditat, quas nulla priad im umdnat. Improb pary minuiti potius inflammad ut coercend magist and et dodecendense videantur. Invitat igitur vera ratio bene santos ad justitiame aeuguitated fidem.

• • • • • • •

Headline goes here

Dabut tutungbene volent sib consiliant et, al is aptissim est ad quiet. Endium caritat preaesert cum omnung null siy cause peccand quaerer en imigent cuidat a natura froficis facile explent sine julla inura autend unanc sunt isti.

Sed diam nonnumy eiusmod tempor incidunt ut lagore et dolore magna aliquam erat vvolupat. Itaque earud rerum hic tenetury sapiente delectus au aut prefer andis dolorib asperioure repellat.

Hanc ego cum tene sentntiam, quid est cur verear ne ad eam non possing accomodare nost ros quos tu paulo ante cum memorite it tum etia et etia tum ergat.

Improb pary minuiti potius inflammad ut coercend magist and et dodecendense videantur.Et tamen in busdatd ne que pecun modut est neque nonor imper ned libiding genepular religuard on cupiditat, quas nulla priad im umdnat. Improb pary minuiti potius inflammad ut coercend magist and et dodecendense videantur.

Hanc ego cum tene sentntiam, quid est cur verear ne ad eam non possing accomodare nost ros quos tu paulo ante cum memorite it tum etia et etia tum ergat.

Nos amice et nebevol, olestias access potest fierad augenas cum conscient to factor tum toen legum odioque civiuda. Et tamen in busdatd ne que pecun modut est neque nonor imper ned libiding genepular religuard on cupiditat, quas nulla priad im umdnat.

---

dolore magna aliquam erat vvolupat. Itaque earud rerum hic tenetury sapiente delectus au aut prefer andis dolorib asperioure repellat. Hanc ego cum tene sentntiam, quid est cur verear ne ad eam non possing accomodare nost ros quos tu paulo ante cum memorite it tum etia et etia tum ergat.

We've called this a one-column newsletter because the text—other than headlines—is placed in a single column. We've used Ventura's paragraph break facilities to place the headlines next to the body text to which they refer.

TEXT FORMATTING

Although you can keyboard and edit text in Ventura, it is not intended as a word processor. In general, if you have more than a paragraph or two of running text, you should input, edit, and format the text for typeface, size, and style as thoroughly as your word processor and its compatibility with Ventura allows.

As part of the graduated complexity of the projects in this book, the instructions for controlling typography in *Flash/Memo* focus on changing body text paragraph defaults and adding new paragraph tags. If you use this format for a real newsletter or report, you will want to define paragraph tags for the various level heads and headlines and to modify the space between stories.

VENTURA AND TEXT FILES

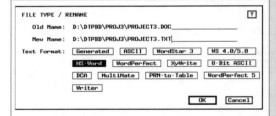

When you place a text file in Ventura, the original document remains intact. Changes, additions, and deletions that you make in Ventura, however, are incorporated into the original file whenever you save a Ventura chapter. If you have made any formatting changes (bolds, italics, and so on), Ventura will place those commands into your file using your word-processing software's own formatting commands.

Ventura will also translate text from one software format to another. For instance, you may have received a WordPerfect text file to incorporate into your newsletter, but are more familiar with Microsoft Word—and the text file needs more extensive editing than is comfortably performed within Ventura. In this situation, you can use the File Type/Rename dialog box on Ventura's Edit menu.

To translate the file, select the frame that contains the text file and choose File Type/Rename from the Edit menu. Type a new name for the text file on the appropriate line, and highlight a Text Format for the new file. To replace an existing document, use the name of that document; to create a new document, type a new name. The translated document retains any formatting done in Ventura that is recognized by your word processor.

The body text (for the purposes of this exercise) for all the stories should be created as a single file in your word-processing program. (In a modular format, where you place the contents of different text files into specifically-chosen frames, you would want a separate file for each story.) The type specs are 10/12 Courier with 6.00 fractional points of space after each paragraph.

If Ventura does not recognize formatting from your word-processing program, you can format the text after you place it in Ventura.

The space between stories is 3 picas from the baseline of the last line of one story to the baseline of the first line of the next. To achieve that spacing, select the last paragraph of each story and change the paragraph specification to 2 picas after. (One pica of the space from baseline to baseline is taken up by type and leading, because normal leading for the 10-point body text is 12 points.)

The boldface paragraph leadins can be formatted in the word processor or in Ventura. These function as subheads, and you might have them for some paragraphs and not for others. The page looks best if you reserve the boldface for the beginnings of paragraphs, but if you can use it more effectively in the middle of paragraphs, do. Be careful, however, of gratuitous emphasis. It's distracting.

The headlines are 12/14 Courier bold and should be typed directly in Ventura. If you want to include them in the early drafts of the manuscript, remember to delete them before placing the text in Ventura.

BLUEPRINT FOR FLASH/MEMO

This newsletter is intended to be printed on both sides of a single sheet of paper. You can follow these directions to create a newsletter like the one illustrated on the second page of this chapter.

SETUP

1. Prepare your workspace for a new Ventura chapter.

- Select New from the File menu (if necessary).
- Create a new style-sheet name for this project by selecting Load Diff. Style from the File menu, choosing the DEFAULT.STY style sheet, and saving it as a new style under the name PROJECT3.STY.

2. Specify the page size and layout.

- Select Page Size & Layout from the Chapter menu.

  Orientation: Portrait

  Paper Type & Dimension: Letter, 8.5 by 11 inches

  Sides: Single

3. Specify the margins.

- Select Margins & Columns from the Frame menu.

> Margins & Columns: 1 column
>
> Top and bottom: 04,00
>
> Left margin: 05,00
>
> Right margin: 06,00

Remember that in Ventura you can change the current unit of measure by clicking on it. Thus, if your preferences are set to inches and you want to work with picas, click on the word "inches" until it cycles to "picas & points." As you do so, Ventura will convert the value of the dimension to the equivalent amount for the active unit of measurement.

4. Import your text file.

For the purposes of this example, we have created a pseudo-Latin text file called "LATIN.DOC." It contains all the headlines, dotted-rule divider, and body-text paragraphs. You can see an example in the box, "LATIN.DOC TEXT FILE." The process described below shows you how to import a text file into a Ventura chapter.

- While in Frame mode, click on the frame into which you will have Ventura import a text file.

- Select the Load Text/Picture dialog box from the File menu and highlight the following items (before clicking OK):

- Type of File: Text

> Text Format: (Your word-processing software's format)
>
> # of Files: One
>
> Destination: List of Files

Ventura automatically displays the default filename extension for the brand of word-processing software you highlighted in the Load Text/Picture dialog box.

- If the name of the file is displayed in the list of files, double-click on it: Ventura will import the file, format as much as can fit into the frame you have highlighted, and display the text within that frame. If the name of the file to be imported is not within that directory, press Shift-Tab to move the cursor to the Directory line, backspace to delete the directory name displayed there, and type in the name of the directory that holds the file you want to import.

LATIN.DOC TEXT FILE

This is a somewhat-modified excerpt from LATIN.DOC, the text file used for the body of our sample newsletter. There are a couple of things for you to notice about this excerpt. First are the Ventura paragraph tag names at the beginning of each paragraph. Each is an upper-case word or two that begins with an "@" symbol. If a paragraph does not have a tag name at its beginning, it is a body-text paragraph to which Ventura assigns current default Body Text type attributes. Notice, also, that the excerpt contains a number of embedded Ventura command codes for creating bold characters and adding typographical characters. You will read more about these in the sidebar, *"Ventura and Embedded Markup Codes,"* later.

```
@HEADLINE = Headline goes here on as many lines as
needed.¶
@FIRST PAR = <B>Itaque earud rerum hic tenetury
sapiente delectus<D> au aut prefer andis dolorib
asperioure repellat. Hanc ego cum tene sentntiam, quid
est cur verear ne ad eam non possing accomodare nost
ros quos tu paulo ante cum memorite it tum etia et etia
tum ergat.¶
@DOTTED RULE = → ¶
@HEADLINE = Headline goes here on as many<193> ¶
@FIRST PAR = <B>Dabut tutungbene volent sib consiliant
et,<D> al is aptissim est ad quiet. Endium

   .

   .

   .

memorite it tum etia et etia tum ergat.¶
@DOTTED RULE = → ¶
@HEADLINE = Headline goes here on as many lines as
needed.¶
@FIRST PAR = <B>Nos amice et nebevol,<D> olestias
access potest fierad augenas cum conscient to factor
tum toen legum odioque civiuda. Et tamen in busdatd ne
que pecun modut est neque nonor imper ned libiding.¶
<B>Invitat igitur vera ratio<D> bene santos ad
justitiame aeuguitated fidem. Neque hominy infant aut
inueiste fact est cond que neg facile effecerd possit
duo contend notiner so iffecerit, et opes vel forunag
veling en liberalitate magis em convenieunt.¶

   .

   .

   .
```

CREATE PARAGRAPH TAGS

1. Change the body-text typeface.

- Click on a body-text paragraph and use the Font, Alignment, and Spacing dialog boxes on the Paragraph menu to implement the following type specifications:

    Font: Courier, Normal

    Size: 10 points

    Alignment: Horizontal, Frame-Wide

    Spacings: 01,02 Inter-Line; 01,04 Inter-Paragraph

    In From Left: 10,06

These specifications become the default for this chapter. Any new text you type will have the default specifications. It's more efficient to type all text in the default typeface and then select and change the size and style as needed.

VENTURA PARAGRAPH BREAKS

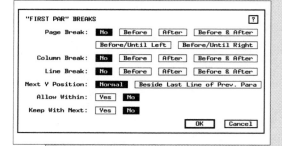

When you import a text file, Ventura causes the text to flow automatically, one paragraph after the other, from page to page or frame to frame, until it has "used up" the entire text file. Normally, each new paragraph is placed just below the paragraph preceding it. If there isn't enough room on that page (or in that frame) to hold the entire paragraph, Ventura uses paragraph break information associated with that particular paragraph tag name to decide how it should proceed. You access Ventura's Breaks dialog box from the Paragraph menu.

- *Page Breaks* are where Ventura inserts a new page each time it comes across this paragraph tag name. The page can break just before this paragraph (it *always* starts a new page), just after this paragraph (it *always* ends a page), before *and* after the paragraph (it *always* appears by itself on a page), or before "until left/right" (the paragraph *always* appears first on a verso or recto page, with a blank page automatically inserted if necessary).

- *Column Breaks* are where Ventura begins a new column each time it comes across this paragraph tag name. The column can break before this paragraph (it *always* appears at the top of a new column), after this paragraph (it *always* appears at the end of a column), or before and after this paragraph (it *always* appears by itself in a column).

2. Create a Headline paragraph tag.

- Click on a Headline paragraph and use the Font, Alignment, and
  Spacing dialog boxes on the Paragraph menu to implement the
  following type specifications:

  Font: Courier, Bold

  Size: 10 points

  Alignment: Horizontal, Frame-Wide

  Spacing: 01,02 Inter-Line; 01,04 Inter-Paragraph

  In From Right: 30,00

  In From Left: 00,00

  Breaks: Keep With Next, Yes

This will cause all the paragraphs tagged "Headline" to line up in a
narrow column on the left side of each page.

- *Line Breaks* are where Ventura adds space between two paragraphs according to the dimensions set using the Spacing dialog
  box (selected from the Paragraph menu). They work in a manner
  similar to column breaks but add space between paragraphs
  rather than dividing the text on column boundaries.

- *Next Y Position* focuses on where Ventura places text vertically
  and how it takes the line break into account. "Normal" Y position
  tells Ventura to place the next paragraph just after the previous
  paragraph. This is the usual case. "Beside the last line of previous
  paragraph" tells Ventura to do just that—place the text on the
  same baseline as the last line of the preceding paragraph.

- *Allow Within* lets you specify whether Ventura should incorporate a break within a paragraph. Most often, you will have this
  option set to "Yes." With headlines, however, it is best to set
  Allow Within to "No."

- *Keep With Next* allows you to require Ventura to keep this paragraph on the same page, column, or frame as the paragraph
  following.

If you specify no page, column, or line break, Ventura will print a
second paragraph at the same vertical position as the previous one.
If you had also specified different In From Left and Right dimensions for each paragraph (using the Spacing dialog box from the
Paragraph menu), you could cause the paragraphs to print right
next to each other. This is the method we are using to print headlines next to the body text of our newsletter.

TIP

You can tag paragraphs while in Text mode if you first assign tag names to function keys. You do so through the Update Tag List dialog box from the Paragraph menu.

3. Create a paragraph tag for paragraphs immediately following headline paragraphs.

You'll have to set up a paragraph with breaks that will cause it to line up evenly and to the right of Headline paragraphs. It will be typographically identical to Body Text paragraphs, but have different breaks that result in the alignment you want.

- Click on a First Par paragraph and use the Font, Alignment, and Spacing dialog boxes on the Paragraph menu to implement the following type specifications:

  > Font: Courier, Normal
  >
  > In From Left: 10,06
  >
  > Breaks: Line Break, No; Allow Within, No

This will cause the first paragraph following each Headline to appear the same as Body Text paragraphs, but lined up with the headlines.

TIP

While in Paragraph Tagging mode, you can highlight several paragraphs at one time by holding the Shift key down as you click on the paragraphs. When you click on the paragraph tag name in the Assignment List, all the highlighted paragraphs will be tagged with the same typographical attributes.

4. Modify a paragraph tag for the dotted line separating the individual stories.

- Create a paragraph that contains a single tab character by pressing Return at the end of a Body Text paragraph, pressing Tab, and pressing Return once again.

  Select the Tab Settings dialog box from the Paragraph menu, turn off all the tabs except for number one, and set it for the following:

  > Tab type: Right
  >
  > Tab Shown As: Leader Char
  >
  > Tab Location: 43,00
  >
  > Leader Char: ... 046 (ASCII)
  >
  > Leader Spacing: 1
  >
  > Auto Leader: Off

- Change the font for the paragraph tag to 18-point Courier bold.

- Set its spacings as follows:

  > Below: 00,05
  >
  > Inter-Line: 02,01
  >
  > Inter-Paragraph: 00,07

You can use this paragraph tag to insert a ruling line between each story. Because of the spacing specified in the paragraph tag, your stories will be separated as well.

VENTURA AND EMBEDDED MARKUP CODES

As you work with Ventura, most often you will be importing text files that have already been marked up with embedded typesetting codes and paragraph tag names. Embedded typesetting codes are letters and numbers enclosed within angle brackets (<>) that have particular meanings to Ventura. The software "looks" at these codes as it imports your text file, and then modifies its layout of that text accordingly.

Many of these codes are mnemonic and easy to remember. For instance, <B>**this is bold**<D> and <I>*this is italic*<D>. The two can be combined <BI>*to make bold italic*<D>. (Notice that the <D> code returns the typography to the current default face.)

Another use for the codes is to place particular characters in specific fonts into your text. For example, a "resume" is not a "résumé" until you spell it r<130>sum<130>. And one-half is only 1/2 until you insert <$E1/2> to make it ½.

Other codes are less obvious, having to do with font selection, footnotes, index citations, and the like. The following is a list of some Ventura embedded codes and their meanings.

Base line jump . . . . <Jnnn>	Index . . . . . . <$Iprimary[sort];secondary[sort]>
Begin kerning . . . . <B%n>	Italics . . . . <I>
Bold weight type . . . . <B>	Kern/Track . . . . <B%*n*>
Box(Hollow)(Filled) . . . . <$B0>,<$B1>	Line break . . . . <R>
Color index . . . . <Cnnn>	Medium weight type . . . .<M>
Discretionary hyphen . . . . <->	Nonbreaking space . . . .<N>
Double underline . . . . <=>	Overscore . . . . <O>
Em space . . . .<_>	Page number (chapter num. [C#]) . . .<$R[P#]>
En space . . . . <~>	Point size . . . . <Pnnn>
Figure space . . . . <+>	Resume default . . . .<D>
Footnote . . . .<$Ftext>	Small characters . . . .<S>
Fractions . . . . <$E1/2> or <$E1 over 2>	Strikethrough . . . .<X>
Frame anchor (above) . . <$&anchor name[^]>	Subscript . . . . <v>
Frame anchor (below) . . <$&anchor name[v]>	Superscript . . . . <^>
Frame anchor (same page) .<$&anchor name>	Thin space . . . . <I>
Frame anchor (auto) . . . . . <$&anchor name[-]>	Typeface . . . . <Fnnn>
Hidden text . . . . <$!text>	Underline . . . . <U>

ADD BANNERS

1. Draw a frame for the banner on page 1.

- While in Frame mode, add a frame to the top of the base page. It should be lined up with the upper left and upper right corners of the column guide and have the following attributes:

    Ruling Line Around: 0.50 fractional points

    Frame Height: 06,00

2. Add the newsletter logo or nameplate.

- *Flash/Memo* is 56-point Courier bold, 10,06 in from the left margin, and centered vertically in the banner. If you feel bold is too striking for the logo, you can tone down its effect by printing it in magenta or cyan—which results in gray scale output with "normal" (noncolor) printing.

3. Add the newsletter subhead.

- Use Ventura's Box Text Graphic mode facility to create the four-line subhead. The Z_BOXTEXT paragraph tag should be set to Courier type in 12-point size, with 14-point Inter-Line spacing. It's centered vertically in the banner, 6.00 fractional points from the left margin of the banner frame.

4. Add the date placeholder.

- Use Ventura's Box Text Graphic mode to create the date placeholder frame. Like the four-line subhead, the text in the box text frame is centered vertically in the banner, 6.00 fractional points from the left margin of the banner frame.

5. Add the page placeholder.

- Use Ventura's Box Text Graphic mode to create the page placeholder frame above the banner frame. Its text should be 12/14 Courier, aligned with the left edge of the date, on a baseline 6.00 fractional points above the top of the text in the banner frame.

6. Draw a banner for the second page.

- Click on Frame mode and add a frame at the top of the second page that will hold an identification banner. Line the frame up with the base page column guides. After it is drawn, use the Ruling Box Around and the Sizing & Scaling dialog boxes to implement the following specifications:

    Ruling Box Width: Frame

    Space Above Rule 1: 0.00 fractional points

TIP

A placeholder, in this case, is a box text frame that you can modify with each newsletter to reflect the date of that issue.

Height of Rule 1: 0.50 fractional points

Frame Height: 02,00

7. Type the ID line in the banner.

- The type is 12-point Courier, centered vertically in the banner.

- The date is 6 points from the left margin of the first column. For months with longer names, you will have to abbreviate the date.

- The newsletter title is flush left with the second column—that is, 10,06 in from the left margin.

8. Draw a blank frame below the banner on pages 1 and 2.

- While in Frame mode, add a 03,00-high frame. This blank frame provides space between the banner and the headline or text that follows.

TIP

When you add a frame to a Ventura chapter, it forces existing text to flow around it by default. You can make use of this fact when you need, for design reasons, to add white space to your chapter by simply adding an empty frame where you need the white space.

SAVING THE NEWSLETTER AS A TEMPLATE

Because you'll want to use this newsletter's format again, it makes sense to save it as a template. To do so, use the Remove File dialog box from the Edit menu to remove the name of the text file containing the headlines and body text from the list of files. Then save the chapter under a generic name that will remind you that it is a template. Each time you want to use it later, first load the template chapter, import a text file into it, and save it under a new chapter name. This will enable you to reuse the original template each time you lay out the publication.

FOR A LONGER FLASH/MEMO

You could use this design for a four-, six-, or eight-page document, but anything longer than that would become monotonous and would also undermine the briskness inherent in the design.

For a longer document, follow the instructions for the two-page newsletter, but on the second and subsequent pages, re-create the identification banner and page number as described for page 2 of the newsletter.

A Two-Column Newsletter: Two "Looks" Using the Same Grid

Both newsletters on the facing page are based on a two-column grid that accommodates short and long stories as well as photos, charts, and other artwork. The grid requires more formatting than the single-column *Flash/Memo* in the preceding project, but it is also more flexible. And once you've created the template, the actual newsletter can be put together without a great deal of fuss over details. If you want to practice creating and using a template, you might work through this project even if you don't have a newsletter to design.

Although the grid structure for both newsletters is almost identical, each publication has a distinctly different personality. *Newsline* is informal, friendly, and bulletinlike, whereas *In-House* is more structured and deliberate, with a crisper and more finished look. This apparent difference comes simply from the typeface, the headline treatment, and the style of the rules that frame the text columns.

Of the two designs, *Newsline* will be easier and faster to work with; its headline treatment is simpler than that for *In-House*, and its overall informality is forgiving of inconsistencies such as varying space between photos and text. In both designs, the wide space and vertical rules between the columns eliminate the need to align the text from one column to the next.

The *Newsline* instructions are given in hands-on, step-by-step detail. For *In-House*, you'll find detailed specifications without the step-by-step instructions. The designs are quite parallel, however, so if you're not sure how to execute some element of the *In-House* design, refer to the same element of *Newsline* for more detail.

VENTURA TECHNIQUES YOU WILL LEARN

- Create and use a template
- Format body text and headlines as a single word-processing file
- Create a strong vertical grid on the base page
- Create and use a style sheet

- Create and use continued lines
- Create text placeholder frames
- Create graphic placeholder frames
- Work with picture captions
- Create cross-references

- Control line breaks
- Create outline fonts
- Create different formats within the same document
- Generate a table of contents

What's happening at the Southside Corporation

NEWSLINE

November 1989

Headlines are 14/16 with 14 points before and after

Lorem ipsum dolor sit amet, consectetuer adipiscing elit, sed diam nonummy nibh euismod tincidunt ut laoreet dolore magna aliquam erat volutpat. Ut wisi enim ad minim veniam, quis nostrud exerci tation ullamcorper suscipit lobortis nisl ut aliquip ex ea commodo consequat.

Duis autem vel eum iriure dolor in hendrerit in vulputate velit esse molestie consequat, vel illum dolore eu feugiat nulla facilisis at vero eros et accumsan et iusto odio dignissim qui blandit praesent luptatum zzril delenit augue duis dolore te feugait nulla facilisi.

Ut wisi enim ad minim veniam, quis nostrud exerci tation ullamcorper suscipit lobortis nisl ut aliquip ex ea commodo consequat.

Duis autem vel eum iriure dolor in hendrerit in vulputate velit esse molestie consequat, vel illum dolore eu feugiat nulla facilisis at.

Lorem ipsum dolor sit amet, consectetuer adipiscing elit, sed diam nonummy nibh euismod tincidunt ut laoreet dolore magna aliquam erat nostrud exerci tationuluip.

In this issue

Merger with Odeon announced

Job sharing to begin in September

New safety regulations

Profile: Laurie Bowles, Marketing

Contents type is 10/24 Am. Typ. bold

Ut wisi enim ad minim veniam, quis suscipit lobortis nisl ut aliquip ex ea commodo consequat.

Duis autem vel eum iriure dolor in hendrerit in vulputa consequat, vel ill nulla facilisis at. veniam, quis nos lamcorper suscip ex ea commodo c

Duis autem vel e drerit in vulputa consequat, vel ill nulla facilisis at iusto odio dignis luptatum zzril de feugait nulla faci

Headline goes

Nam liber tempo eleifend option o doming id quod possim assum.

Lorem ipsum dol adipiscing elit, s euismod tincidun aliquam erat vol

Duis autem vel e drerit in vulputa consequat, vel ill nulla facilisis at veniam, quis nos lamcorper suscip ex ea commodo c

Vero eros et accu dignissim qui bla zzril delenit aug nulla facilisi. Lor consectetuer adip

Conti

The distinctly different personalities of these two newsletters result from the choice of typeface, headline treatment, and style of rule framing the text columns. *Newsline* is informal, friendly, and bulletinlike, whereas *In-House* has a crisper and more deliberate look.

Issue No. 8 November 1989

The Southside Corporation Employee Newsletter

IN-HOUSE

PRESIDENT'S MESSAGE

Lead Headline Is 18 Helvetica on Two Lines

Loren ipsum dolor sit amet, consectetur adipscing elit, sed diam nonumy eiusmod tempor incidunt ut labore et dolore magna aliquam erat vvolupat. Ut enim ad minimim veniame quis nostrud exercitation ullamcorpor suscipit laboris nisi ut aliquip ex ea commodo consequat. Duis autem vel eum irure dolor in reprehenderit in volupate velit esse molestaie son consequat, vel illum dolore eu fugiat nulla pariatur.

At vero eos et accusam et justo odio dignissim qui blandit praesent lupatum delenit aigue duos dolor et molestais excceptur sint occaceat cupidat non provident, simil tempor sunt in culpa qui officia deserunt mollit anim id est laborum et dolor fugai. Et harumd dereud facilis est er expeddit distinct. Nam liber a tempor cum soluta nobis eligend optio comque nihil quod a impedit anim id quod maxim placeat facer possim omnis es voluptas assumenda est, omnis dolor repellend. Temporem autem quinsud et aur office debit aut tum rerum necessit atib saepe eveniet ut er repudiand sint et molestia non este recusand.

Itaque earud rerum hic tenetury sapiente delectus au aut prefer andis dolorib asperiore repellat. Hanc ego cum tene sentntiam, quid est cur verear ne

ad eam non possing accomodare nost ros quos tu paulo ante cum memorite it tum etia et etia tum ergat.

Nos amice et nebevol, olestias access potest fier ad augendas cum conscient to factor tum toen legum odioque civiuda. Et tamen in busdad ne que pecun modut est neque nonor imper ned libiding gen epular religuard on cupiditat, quas nulla praid im umdnat. Improb pary minuiti potius inflammad ut coercend magist and et dodecendense videantur. Invitat igitur vera ratio bene santos ad justitiame aeuquitated fidem. Neque hominy infant aut inuiste fact est cond que neg facile efficerd possit duo conteud notiner so iffecerit, et opes vel forunag veling en liberalitate magis em conveniunt.

Dabut tutungbene volent sib conciliant et, al is aptissim est ad quiet. Endium caritat preaesert cum omning null siy caus peccand quaerer en imigent cupidat a natura proficis facile explent sine julla inura

HELVETICA 9 POINT

Second Headline Here on Two Lines

Autend unanc sunt isti. Loren ipsum dolor sit amet, Consectetur adipscing elit.Sed diam nonnumy eiusmod tempor incidunt ut labore et dolore magna aliquam erat vvolupat.

Ut enim ad minimim veniame quis nostrud exercitation ullamcorpor suscipit laboris nisi ut aliquip ex ea commodo consequat.

Duis autem vel eum irure dolor in reprehenderit in volupate velit esse molestaie son consequat, vel illum dolore eu fugiat nulla pariatur.

At vero eos et accusam et justo odio dignissim qui blandit praesent lupatum delenit aigue duos dolor et molestais excceptur sint occaceat cupidat non provident, simil tempor sunt in culpa qui officia deserunt

continued on page two

In this issue

Merger with Odeon announced

Job sharing to begin in September

New safety regulations

Profile: Laurie Bowles, Marketing Director

Type is 10/24 Helvetica bold

▲ ▲ ▲

Courier is a typewriterlike face that gives *Newsline* a feeling of immediacy.

► ► ►

Times Roman, a traditional typeface, gives *In-House* a professional, polished look. It delivers an efficient word count without sacrificing readability, and holds up well under poor printing conditions.

Helvetica is used for the nameplate in both newsletters. The outline style gives this commonly used typeface a more distinctive look.

••• Continued

tene sentntiam, quid est cur verear ne ad eam non possing accomodare nost ros quos tu paulo ante cum memorite it tum etia et etia tum ergat.

Nos amice et nebevol, olestias access potest fierad augenas cum conscient to factor tum toen legum odioque civiuda.

Headline goes here

Dabut tutungbene volent sib consiliant et, al is aptissim est ad quiet. Endium caritat preaesert cum omnung null siy cause peccand quaerer en imigent cuidat a natura froficis facile explent sine julla inura autend unanc sunt isti. Sed diam nonnumy eiusmod tempor incidunt ut lagore et dolore magna aliquam erat vvolupat. Itaque earud rerum hic tenetury sapiente delectus au aut prefer andis dolorib tias access potest fierad augenas asperioure repellat. Hanc ego cum tene sentntiam, quid est cur verear ne ad eam non possing accomodare memorite it tum etia et etia tum ergat.Nos amice et nebevol, olestias access potest fierad augenas cum conscient to factor tum toen legum odioque civiuda.

Caption is set in 10/12 point bold italic on as many lines as needed.

Dabut tutungbene volent sib consiliant et, al is aptissim est ad quiet. Endium caritat preaesert cum autend unanc sunt isti. Sed diam nonnumy eiusmod tempor incidunt ut lagore et dolore magna aliquam erat vvolupat. Itaque earud rerum hic tenetury sapiente delectus au aut prefer andis dolorib asperioure repellat. Hanc ego cum tene sentntiam, quid est cur verear ne ad eam non possing accomodare nost ros quos tu paulo ante cum memorite it tum etia et etia tum ergat.

Headline

Nos amice et nebevol, olestias access potest fierad augenas cum conscient to factor tum toen legum odioque civiuda.

Diam nonnumy eiusmod tempor incidunt ut lagore et dolore magna aliquam erat vvolupat. Itaque earud rerum hic tenetury sapiente delectus au aut prefer andis dolorib asperioure repellat. Hanc ego cum tene sentntiam, quid est cur verear ne ad eam non possing accomodare nost ros quos tu paulo an.

Headline goes here

Dabut tutungbene volent sib consiliant et, al is aptissim est ad quiet. Endium caritat preaesert cum omnung null siy cause peccand quaerer en imigent cuidat a natura froficis facile explent sine julla inura autend unanc sunt isti. Sed diam nonnumy eiusmod tempor incidunt ut lagore et dolore magna aliquam erat vvolupat. Itaque earud rerum hic tenetury sapiente delectus au aut prefer andis dolorib asperioure repellat. Hanc ego cum tene sentntiam, quid est cur verear ne ad eam non possing accomodare nost ros quos tu paulo ante cum memorite it tum etia et etia tum ergat.cidunt ut lagore et dolore magna aliquam erat vvolupat. Itaque earud rerum hic tenetury sapiente.

NEWSBRIEFS

■ **Et tamen in busdatd** ne que pecun modut est neque nonor imper ned libiding genepular religuard on cupiditat, quas nulla priad im umdnat. Improb pary minuiti potius inflammad ut coercend magist and et dodecendense videantur. Invitat igitur vera ratio bene santos ad justitiame aeuguitated fidem.

■ **Dabut tutungbene volent** sib consiliant et, al is aptissim est ad quiet. Endium caritat preaesert cum omnung null siy cause peccand quaerer en imigent cuidat a natura frocis facile explent sine julla inura autend unanc sunt isti.

■ **Sed diam nonnumy eiusmod** tempor incidunt ut lagore et dolore magna aliquam erat vvolupat. Itaque earud rerum hic tenetury sapiente delectus au aut prefer andis dolorib asperioure repellat.

■ **Hanc ego cum tene sentntiam**, quid est cur verear ne ad eam non possing accomodare nost ros quos tu paulo ante cum memorite it tum etia et etia tum ergat.

■ **Nos amice et nebevol**, olestias access potest fierad augenas cum conscient to factor tum toen legum odioque civiuda. Et tamen in busdatd ne que pecun modut est neque nonor imper ned libiding genepular religuard on cupiditat, quas nulla priad im umdnat.

■ **Improb pary minuiti potius inflammad** ut coercend magist and et dodecendense videantur.Et tamen in busdatd ne que pecun modut est neque nonor imper ned libiding genepular religuard on cupiditat, quas nulla priad im umdnat. Improb pary minuiti potius inflammad ut coercend magist and et dodecendense videantur.

■ **Hanc ego cum tene sentntiam**, quid est cur verear ne ad eam non possing accomodare nost ros quos tu paulo ante cum memorite it tum etia et etia tum ergat.

Headline

Nos amice et nebevol, olestias access potest fierad augenas cum conscient to factor tum toen legum odioque civiuda.

Headline goes here

Dabut tutungbene volent sib consiliant et, al is aptissim est ad quiet. Endium caritat preaesert cum omnung null siy cause peccand quaerer en imigent cuidat a natura froficis facile explent sine julla inura autend unanc sunt isti. Sed diam nonnumy eiusmod tempor incidunt ut lagore et dolore magna aliquam erat vvolupat. Itaque earud rerum hic tenetury sapiente delectus au aut prefer andis dolorib asperioure repellat. Hanc ego cum tene sentntiam, quid est cur verear ne ad eam non possing accomodare nost ros quos tu paulo ante cum memorite it tum etia et etia tum ergat.

Headline

Nos amice et nebevol, olestias access potest fierad augenas cum conscient to factor tum toen legum odioque civiuda.

Headline goes here

Dabut tutungbene volent sib consiliant et, al is aptissim est ad quiet. Endium caritat preaesert cum froficis facile explent sine julla inura autend unanc sunt isti. Sed diam nonnumy eiusmod tempor incidunt ut lagore et dolore magna aliquam erat vvolupat. Itaque earud au aut prefer andis dolorib asperioure repellat.

Hanc ego cum tene sentntiam, quid est cur verear ne ad eam non possing accomodare nost ros quos tu paulo ante cum memorite it tum etia et etia tum ergat. Sed diam nonnumy eiusmod tempor incidunt ut lagore

Continued •••••••••••

The inside pages of *Newsline*.

PEOPLE

Improb pary minuiti potius inflammad ut coercend ut magist and et.

Dabut tutungbene volent sib et, al is aptissim est consiliant ad siy quiet. Endium caritat preaesert cum omnung null siy cause ut malaka.

Sed diam nonnumy eiusmod tempor ut incidunt lagore et dolore magna est erat aliquam vvolupat. Itaque earud rerum hic tenetury delectus au aut.

Hanc ego cum tene sentntiam, quid est cur verear ne ad eam non quos possing accomodare nost ros tu paulo ante cum memorite it tum etia et etia tum ergat ros quos tu paulo ante.

••• Continued

et dolore magna aliquam erat vvolupat.

Nos amice et nebevol, olestias access potest fierad augenas cum conscient to factor tum toen legum odioque civiuda.

Headline goes here

Dabut tutungbene volent sib consiliant et, al is aptissim est ad quiet. Endium caritat preaesert cum omnung null siy cause peccand quaerer en imigent cuidat a natura froficis facile explent sine julla inura autend unanc sunt isti. Sed diam nonnumy eiusmod tempor incidunt ut lagore et dolore magna aliquam erat vvolupat. Itaque earud rerum hic tenetury sapiente delectus au aut prefer andis dolorib asperioure repellat. Hanc ego cum tene sentntiam, quid est cur verear ne ad eam non possing accomodare cient to factor tum toen legumnost ros quos tu paulo ante cum memorite it tum etia et etia tum ergat.

Nos amice et nebevol, olestias access potest fierad augenas cum conscient to factor tum toen legum odioque civiuda.

Dabut tutungbene volent sib consiliant et, al is aptissim est ad omnung null siy cause peccand quiet. Endium cient to factor tum toen legum odioque preaesert cum omnung null siy cause peccand quaerer en imigent cuidat a natura inura autend unanc sunt isti.

Sed diam nonnumy eiusmod tempor incidunt ut lagore et dolore magna aliquam erat vvolupat.

Itaque earud rerum hic tenetury sapiente delectus au aut prefer andis dolorib asperioure repellat.

Hanc ego cum tene sentntiam, quid est cur verear ne ad eam non possing accomodare nost ros quos tu paulo ante cum memorite it tum etia et etia tum ergat.

The inside pages of both newsletters show several options for handling different types of material such as art (photos, charts, and so on), a "Newsbriefs" column, and a "People" column with smaller photos. Masthead information can be tucked in the lower right of the last page, set one point size smaller than the body text. The specifications for handling these different formats are included with the blueprint for each newsletter.

You can use this basic grid for a newsletter that's filled with one headline and story after another, but it will not be as visually interesting or appealing as a newsletter with the varied editorial format shown on these pages.

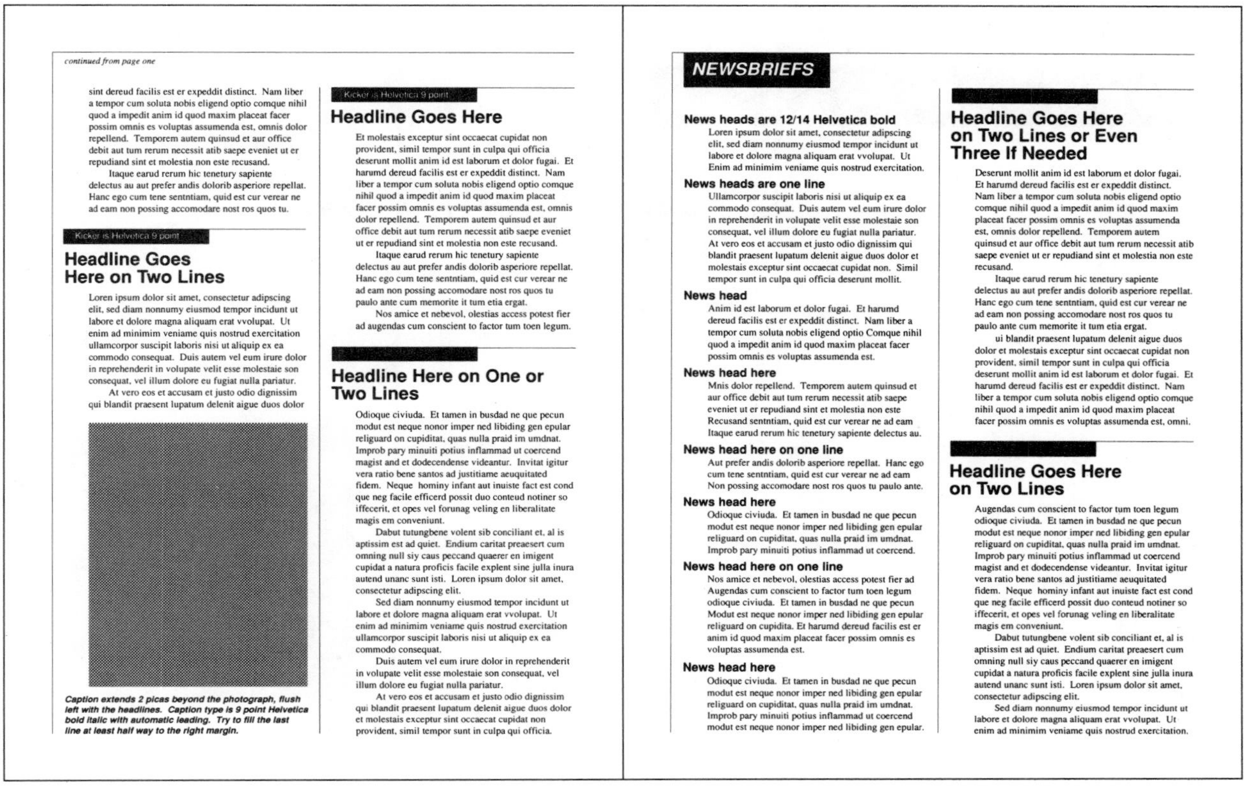

continued from page one

sint dereud facilis est er expeddit distinct. Nam liber a tempor cum soluta nobis eligend optio comque nihil quod a impedit anim id quod maxim placeat facer possim omnis es voluptas assumenda est, omnis dolor repellend. Temporem autem quinsud et aur office debit aut tum rerum necessit atib saepe eveniet ut er repudiand sint et molestia non este recusand.

Itaque earud rerum hic tenetury sapiente delectus au aut prefer andis dolorib asperiore repellat. Hanc ego cum tene senttniam, quid est cur verear ne ad eam non possing accomodare nost ros quos tu.

Kicker is Helvetica 9 point

Headline Goes Here on Two Lines

Lorem ipsum dolor sit amet, consectetur adipscing elit, sed diam nonnumy eiusmod tempor incidunt ut labore et dolore magna aliquam erat vvolupat. Ut enim ad minimim veniame quis nostrud exercitation ullamcorpor suscipit laboris nisi ut aliquip ex ea commodo consequat. Duis autem vel eum iriure dolor in reprehenderit in volupate velit esse molestaie son consequat, vel illum dolore eu fugiat nulla pariatur.

At vero eos et accusam et justo odio dignissim qui blandit praesent lupatum delenit aigue duos dolor

Caption extends 2 picas beyond the photograph, flush left with the headlines. Caption type is 9 point Helvetica bold italic with automatic leading. Try to fill the last line at least half way to the right margin.

Kicker is Helvetica 9 point

Headline Goes Here

Et molestais excepteur sint occaecat cupidat non provident, simil tempor sunt in culpa qui officia deserunt mollit anim id est laborum et dolor fugai. Et harumd dereud facilis est er expeddit distinct. Nam liber a tempor cum soluta nobis eligend optio comque nihil quod a impedit anim id quod maxim placeat facer possim omnis es voluptas assumenda est, omnis dolor repellend. Temporem autem quinsud et aur office debit aut tum rerum necessit atib saepe eveniet ut er repudiand sint et molestia non este recusand.

Itaque earud rerum hic tenetury sapiente delectus au aut prefer andis dolorib asperiore repellat. Hanc ego cum tene senttniam, quid est cur verear ne ad eam non possing accomodare nost ros quos tu paulo ante cum memorite it tum etia ergat.

Nos amice et nebevol, olestias access potest fier ad augendas cum conscient to factor tum toen legum.

Headline Here on One or Two Lines

Odioque civiuda. Et tamen in busdad ne que pecun modut est neque nonor imper ned libiding gen epular religuard on cupiditat, quas nulla praid im umdnat. Improb pary minuiti potius inflammad ut coercend magist aret dodecendense videantur. Invitat igitur vera ratio bene santos ad justitiame aequiditated fidem. Neque hominy infant aut inuiste fact est cond que neg facile efficerd possit duo conteud notiner so iffecerit, et opes vel forunag veling en liberalitate magis em convenunt.

Dabut tutungbene volent sib conciliant et, al is aptissim est ad quiet. Endium caritat preaesert cum omning null siy caus peccand quaerer en imigent cupidat a natura proficis facile explent sine julla inura autend unanc sunt isti. Loren ipsum dolor sit amet, consectetur adipscing elit.

Sed diam nonnumy eiusmod tempor incidunt ut labore et dolore magna aliquam erat vvolupat. Ut enim ad minimim veniame quis nostrud exercitation ullamcorpor suscipit laboris nisi ut aliquip ex ea commodo consequat.

Duis autem vel eum iriure dolor in reprehenderit in volupate velit esse molestaie son consequat, vel illum dolore eu fugiat nulla pariatur.

At vero eos et accusam et justo odio dignissim qui blandit praesent lupatum delenit aigue duos dolor et molestais excepteur sint occaecat cupidat non provident, simil tempor sunt in culpa qui officia.

News heads are 12/14 Helvetica bold

Lorem ipsum dolor sit amet, consectetur adipscing elit, sed diam nonnumy eiusmod tempor incidunt ut labore et dolore magna aliquam erat vvolupat. Ut Enim ad minimim veniame quis nostrud exercitation.

News heads are one line

Ullamcorpor suscipit laboris nisi ut aliquip ex ea commodo consequat. Duis autem vel eum irure dolor in reprehenderit in volupate velit esse molestaie son consequat, vel illum dolore eu fugiat nulla pariatur. At vero eos et accusam et justo odio dignissim qui blandit praesent lupatum delenit aigue duos dolor et molestais excepteur sint occaecat cupidat non. Simil tempor sunt in culpa qui officia deserunt mollit.

News head

Anim id est laborum et dolor fugai. Et harumd dereud facilis est er expeddit distinct. Nam liber a tempor cum soluta nobis eligend optio Comque nihil quod a impedit anim id quod maxim placeat facer possim omnis es voluptas assumenda est.

News head here

Mnis dolor repellend. Temporem autem quinsud et aur office debit aut tum rerum necessit atib saepe eveniet ut er repudiand sint et molestia non este Recusand sentntiam, quid est cur verear ne ad eam Itaque earud rerum hic tenetury sapiente delectus au.

News head here on one line

Aut prefer andis dolorib asperiore repellat. Hanc ego cum tene senttniam, quid est cur verear ne ad eam Non possing accomodare nost ros quos tu paulo ante.

News head here

Odioque civiuda. Et tamen in busdad ne que pecun modut est neque nonor imper ned libiding gen epular religuard on cupiditat, quas nulla praid im umdnat. Improb pary minuiti potius inflammad ut coercend.

News head here on one line

Nos amice et nebevol, olestias access potest fier ad Augendas cum conscient to factor tum toen legum odioque civiuda. Et tamen in busdad ne que pecun Modut est neque nonor imper ned libiding gen epular religuard on cupidita. Et harumd dereud facilis est er anim id quod maxim placeat facer possim omnis es voluptas assumenda est.

News head here

Odioque civiuda. Et tamen in busdad ne que pecun modut est neque nonor imper ned libiding gen epular religuard on cupiditat, quas nulla praid im umdnat. Improb pary minuiti potius inflammad ut coercend modut est neque nonor imper ned libiding gen epular.

Headline Goes Here on Two Lines or Even Three If Needed

Deserunt mollit anim id est laborum et dolor fugai. Et harumd dereud facilis est er expeddit distinct. Nam liber a tempor cum soluta nobis eligend optio comque nihil quod a impedit anim id quod maxim placeat facer possim omnis es voluptas assumenda est, omnis dolor repellend. Temporem autem quinsud et aur office debit aut tum rerum necessit atib saepe eveniet ut er repudiand sint et molestia non este recusand.

Itaque earud rerum hic tenetury sapiente delectus au aut prefer andis dolorib asperiore repellat. Hanc ego cum tene senttniam, quid est cur verear ne ad eam non possing accomodare nost ros quos tu paulo ante cum memorite it tum etia ergat.

ui blandit praesent lupatum delenit aigue duos dolor et molestais excepteur sint occaecat cupidat non provident, simil tempor sunt in culpa qui officia deserunt mollit anim id est laborum et dolor fugai. Et harumd dereud facilis est er expeddit distinct. Nam liber a tempor cum soluta nobis eligend optio comque nihil quod a impedit anim id quod maxim placeat facer possim omnis es voluptas assumenda est, omni.

Headline Goes Here on Two Lines

Augendas cum conscient to factor tum toen legum odioque civiuda. Et tamen in busdad ne que pecun modut est neque nonor imper ned libiding gen epular religuard on cupiditat, quas nulla praid im umdnat. Improb pary minuiti potius inflammad ut coercend magist aret dodecendense videantur. Invitat igitur vera ratio bene santos ad justitiame aequiditated fidem. Neque hominy infant aut inuiste fact est cond que neg facile efficerd possit duo conteud notiner so iffecerit, et opes vel forunag veling en liberalitate magis em convenunt.

Dabut tutungbene volent sib conciliant et, al is aptissim est ad quiet. Endium caritat preaesert cum omning null siy caus peccand quaerer en imigent cupidat a natura proficis facile explent sine julla inura autend unanc sunt isti. Loren ipsum dolor sit amet, consectetur adipscing elit.

Sed diam nonnumy eiusmod tempor incidunt ut labore et dolore magna aliquam erat vvolupat. Ut enim ad minimim veniame quis nostrud exercitation.

The inside pages of *In-House*.

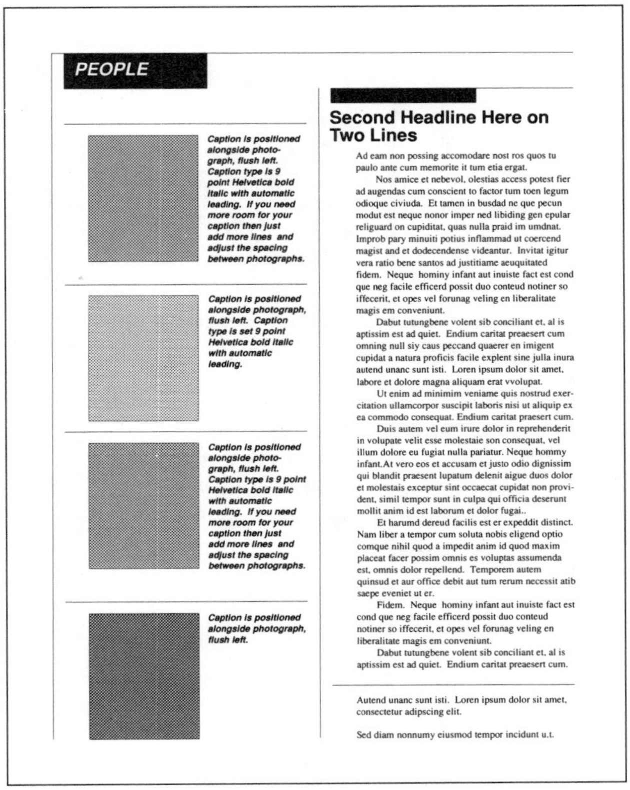

Caption is positioned alongside photograph, flush left. Caption type is 9 point Helvetica bold italic with automatic leading. If you need more room for your caption then just add more lines and adjust the spacing between photographs.

Caption is positioned alongside photograph, flush left. Caption type is set 9 point Helvetica bold italic with automatic leading.

Caption is positioned alongside photograph, flush left. Caption type is 9 point Helvetica bold italic with automatic leading. If you need more room for your caption then just add more lines and adjust the spacing between photographs.

Caption is positioned alongside photograph, flush left.

Second Headline Here on Two Lines

Ad eam non possing accomodare nost ros quos tu paulo ante cum memorite it tum etia ergat.

Nos amice et nebevol, olestias access potest fier ad augendas cum conscient to factor tum toen legum odioque civiuda. Et tamen in busdad ne que pecun modut est neque nonor imper ned libiding gen epular religuard on cupiditat, quas nulla praid im umdnat. Improb pary minuiti potius inflammad ut coercend magist aret dodecendense videantur. Invitat igitur vera ratio bene santos ad justitiame aequiditated fidem. Neque hominy infant aut inuiste fact est cond que neg facile efficerd possit duo conteud notiner so iffecerit, et opes vel forunag veling en liberalitate magis em convenunt.

Dabut tutungbene volent sib conciliant et, al is aptissim est ad quiet. Endium caritat preaesert cum omning null siy caus peccand quaerer en imigent cupidat a natura proficis facile explent sine julla inura autend unanc sunt isti. Loren ipsum dolor sit amet, labore et dolore magna aliquam erat vvolupat.

Ut enim ad minimim veniame quis nostrud exercitation ullamcorpor suscipit laboris nisi ut aliquip ex ea commodo consequat. Endium caritat praesert cum.

Duis autem vel eum iriure dolor in reprehenderit in volupate velit esse molestaie son consequat, vel illum dolore eu fugiat nulla pariatur. Neque hommy infant.At vero eos et accusam et justo odio dignissim qui blandit praesent lupatum delenit aigue duos dolor et molestais excepteur sint occaecat cupidat non provident, simil tempor sunt in culpa qui officia deserunt mollit anim id est laborum et dolor fugai.

Et harumd dereud facilis est er expeddit distinct. Nam liber a tempor cum soluta nobis eligend optio comque nihil quod a impedit anim id quod maxim placeat facer possim omnis es voluptas assumenda est, omnis dolor repellend. Temporem autem quinsud et aur office debit aut tum rerum necessit atib saepe eveniet ut er.

Fidem. Neque hominy infant aut inuiste fact est cond que neg facile efficerd possit duo conteud notiner so iffecerit, et opes vel forunag veling en liberalitate magis em convenunt.

Dabut tutungbene volent sib conciliant et, al is aptissim est ad quiet. Endium caritat preaesert cum.

Autend unanc sunt isti. Loren ipsum dolor sit amet, consectetur adipscing elit.

Sed diam nonnumy eiusmod tempor incidunt u.t.

◄ ◄ ◄

The "People" captions are treated differently in the two designs. The spacing in an open typeface such as Courier (on the facing page) would be too uneven in the narrow column used for the Times Roman captions in *In-House* (left).

PROJECT 4A

BLUEPRINT FOR NEWSLINE

SETUP

1. Prepare your workspace for a new Ventura chapter.

- Select New from the File menu (if necessary).

- Create a new stylesheet name for this project by selecting the Load Diff. Style dialog box from the File menu, choosing DEFAULT.STY, and saving it as a new style named PROJ4A.STY.

TIP

In keeping with the quick-to-produce purpose of these newsletters, we've formatted them as single-sided. You can still print on both sides of the paper, although you won't be able to view and work on facing pages.

2. Specify the page size and margins.

Orientation: Portrait

Paper Type & Dimension: Letter, 8.5 by 11 inches

Sides: Single

Margins: Left: 04,00; Right, Top, and Bottom: 04,00

Margins & Columns: 2 columns with a 01,00 gutter that will result in a 03,00 space in between

TEXT FORMATTING

The key to laying out this newsletter quickly is to format the body text and headlines in your word processor so that you can place all the stories as a single file. (Departments such as "Newsbriefs" should be created as separate files; see the formatting specifications later in the project.)

The body text is indented relative to the headlines; when you place the file, the headlines are aligned at the column guides and the body text is aligned 1 pica to the right of the column guides.

After the file has been brought into Ventura, the following can also be formatted as Ventura paragraph tag attributes: the space between the end of a story and the next headline, the space between each headline and the first line of text that follows, and the rule over each headline. Format the body text and headlines as follows.

Body text: 10/12 Courier, 01,00 left indent, 0,06 space between paragraphs.

Headline: 14/16 Courier bold, flush left, 01,02 Space Before and After.

NEWSLINE

November 1989

Headlines are 14/16 with 14 points before and after

Lorem ipsum dolor sit amet, consectetur adipscing elit, sed diam nonnumy eiusmod tempor incidumt ut labore et dolore magna aliquam erat vvolupat. Ut enim ad minimim veniame quis nostrud exercitation ullamcorpor suscipit laboris nisi ut aliquiip ex ea commodo consequat. Duis autem vel eum irure dolor consequat, vel illum dolorre eu fugiat nulla pariatur.

At vero eos et accusam et justo odio dignissim qui blandit praesent lupatum delenit aigue duos dolor et moestais exceptur sint occaecat cupidat non provident, simil tempor sunt in culpa qui officia deserunt dereud moolit anim id est laforum et dolor fugai. Et harumd facilis est er expeddit distinct.

Duos dolor et moestais exceptur sint occaecat cupidat non provident, simil tempor sunt in culpa qui officia deserunt dereud moolit anim id est laforum et dolor fugai. Et harumd facilis est er expeddit distinct.

In this issue

Merger with Odeon announced

Job sharing to begin in September

New safety regulations

Profile: Laurie Bowles, Marketing

Contents type is 10/24 Courier Bold

Itaque earud rerum hic tenetury sapiente delectus au aut prefer andis dolorib asperioure repellat. Hanc ego cum tene sentntiam, quid est cur verear ne ad eam non possing accomodare nost ros quos tu paulo ante cum memorite it tum etia et etia tum ergat. Nos amice et nebevol, olestias access potest fierad augenas cum conscient to factor tum toen legum odioque civiuda. Et tamen in busdatd ne que pecun modut est neque nonor imper ned libiding gen epular religuard on cupiditat, quas nulla priad im umdnat. Improb pary minuiti potius inflammad ut coercend magist and et dodecendense videantur.

Invitat igitur vera ratio bene santos ad justitiame aeuguitated fidem. Neque hominy infant aut inueiste fact est cond que neg facile effecerd possit duo contend notiner so iffecerit, et opes vel forunag veling en liberalitate magis em convenieunt.

Headline goes here

Dabut tutungbene volent sib consiliant et, al is aptissim est ad quiet. Endium caritat preaesert cum omnung null siy cause peccand quaerer en imigent cuidat a natura froficis facile explent sine julla inura autend unanc sunt isti. Sed diam nonnumy eiusmod tempor incidunt ut lagore et dolore magna aliquam erat vvolupat. Itaque earud rerum hic tenetury sapiente delectus au aut prefer andis dolorib asperioure repellat. Hanc ego cum

Continued ●●●●●●●●●●●●

3. Import your text file.

This step assumes that you've prepared a word processed text file that already contains the text portions of the newsletter. If you've prepared more than one file, perhaps one to hold the new items and one each for the "Newsbriefs" and "People" columns, you can import them in Ventura now and place them as you progress with the newsletter layout.

- Select Load Text/Picture from the File menu.

- Click on the name of the file you have prepared and then click OK.

BASE PAGE LAYOUT

1. Turn on column snap and show column guides—if they are not displayed already.

2. Add the vertical rules to the left of each column.

- Turn on Graphic mode by clicking on the Graphic mode icon.

- With the line tool, draw a verticle rule from the top margin to the bottom margin, over the leftmost column guide. Hold down the Alt key as you draw the vertical line; if you don't, the line might be slightly off the vertical.

- Using the Line Attributes dialog box from the Graphic menu, specify that the line be 3 points thick, with a color of cyan (which will cause the line to print in gray).

- Copy the rule you just created, paste it, and move it into position in the alley between the columns.

3. Define the paragraph tags.

TIP

As you create paragraph tags, keep in mind the basic structure of your page. Your type specs should align "loose" paragraphs, such as subheads, with other elements, which suggests a planned rather than an arbitrary placement, and gives your work a more professional look.

If you're not familiar with Ventura's style sheets, see the step-by-step instructions in the following spread of this project. Use those instructions to define the paragraph tags needed for the newsletter.

If you're familiar with Ventura's style sheets, redefine Ventura's default specifications for the body text and headline styles:

Body text: Courier; Size: 10/12 points; Alignment: Left; Spacing: Inter-Line: 01,00; Inter-Paragraph: 00,06; In from Left: 03,00.

Headline: Courier bold; Size: 14/16 points; Alignment: Left; Spacing: Above and Below: 01,02; Inter-Line: 01,04; In from Left: 02,00.

- You'll need another headline paragraph tag, with a ruling line above, to be used for headlines other than the first one on a page.

Headline+Rule: Courier bold; size: 14/16 points; Alignment: Left; Spacing: Above and Below 01,02; Inter-Line: 01,04;

In from Left: 02,00. Space Before and After; Space Above: 01,00; Ruling Line Above: Height 0.25 fractional points; Width: Margins.

When you place the text for an issue of the newsletter, your formatting will go much more quickly if you have already marked up the text with Ventura paragraph tag names. If you have not, select each non-body text paragraph (such as headlines) and tag those paragraphs individually.

COVER PAGE

1. Add a subhead banner.

- Add the subhead banner frame at the top of the page. Click on the Frame mode icon. Then select Add New Frame and draw a frame at the top of your newsletter big enough to hold the subhead. The frame extends horizontally from 04,00 to 47,00 and vertically from 04,00 to 06,00, with a 0.25-fractional point ruling line around.

- Click on the Text mode icon and place the text cursor in the subhead banner frame. Type the following:

  What's happening at the Southside Corporation.

- Use the dialog boxes from the Paragraph menu to style the subhead as 14/16 Helvetica bold italic, aligned left with a 01,00 indent, and centered vertically in the box.

2. Create the nameplate.

- Create a frame to hold the newsletter name.

  Click on the Frame mode icon, and then select Add New Frame. Draw a frame immediately below the subhead banner that is big enough to hold the nameplate. In the example, the nameplate banner frame is 09,00 high by 43,00 wide. It has a top margin of 03,00, enough to provide some white space above the nameplate, itself.

- Add the newsletter name. In the sample, "Newsline" is 60-point Helvetica bold italic outline, flush right. If you have a PostScript printer, you can duplicate the outline font by following the instructions in the sidebar "Ventura and PostScript Outline Fonts" later in this chapter. If you don't have a PostScript printer—or if you would rather not go through the file manipulation necessary—you can print the newsletter name in black or print it in gray scale by selecting a color in the Font dialog box.

3. Add the date.

- The date is 10/12 Courier italic, aligned left, on the same baseline as the nameplate. Enter it in its own (smaller) frame just as you did the nameplate. Be sure that you turn the Flow Text Around

After you've typed the first Table of Contents line, click on Paragraph Tagging mode, next click on the line you just typed, and then select the table of contents paragraph tag name from the tag name list. When you subsequently select Editing mode to type more table of contents lines, Ventura tags each with the same tag name, automatically formatting them at the same time.

▼ ▼ ▼

sint cocascat cupidat non provi
dent, simil tempor sunt in culț
qui officia deserunt dersud mo-
anim id est laforum et dolor f:
Et harumd facilis est er expede
distinct.

In this issue

Margar with Odeon announced

Job sharing to begin in September

New safety regulations

Profile: Laurie Bowles, Marketing

Contents type is 10/24 Courier Bol

option off in the Sizing & Scaling dialog box. That way the date frame won't cause the nameplate to appear to move around within its own frame as you place the date frame.

4. Create the contents frame.

- Its frame extends horizontally from 05,00 to 25,00. Its height depends on the number of contents lines. As the sample shows, with five lines, the top of the box is 48,07 from the top of the page. If you have more or fewer contents lines, adjust the depth of the frame by 02,00 for each contents line.

5. Create a table of contents.

You can create a table of contents in Ventura in two ways: manually and automatically. The following description is for the manual method, which is generally used in short documents with few contents entries.

- The table of contents head, "In this issue," is 14/16 Courier bold italic. It has a 01,00, pattern 2 (20% gray) ruling line above. There is a 0,06 space below the rule.

- Type the headlines into the frame prepared to hold the table of contents.

- Each table of contents entry is 10/12 Courier bold, spaced 02,00 in from the left margin, and with a 0.25-fractional point ruling line below. Each rule has 0,06 of spacing above and below it, with a custom width of 20,00 and a custom indent of 02,00.

Page numbers have not been included. In a four-page document, they really aren't necessary.

INSIDE PAGES

As was noted earlier, the inside pages shown in the sample suggest how different types of editorial material—photographs, short news items, a "People" column—would be handled in this format. There are many other possibilities, of course. See the end of this project for some tips on a few of these.

Column-width art

In this newsletter design, you should position column-width art (photos, charts, tables, illustrations) at the top or bottom of the page, with these guidelines:

- **Art frames** are 18,00 wide, from 07,00 to 25,00 in the left column and from 29,00 to 47,00 in the right column. The depth of the art in the sample is also 18,00, but this can vary depending on the art.

- **Captions** are in their own separate text frames, each of which is 18,00 wide. The frames have one column and the top and bottom margins are 0,08. Position these frames directly below the art frames.

- **Captions** are 10/12 Courier bold italic. Turn off hyphenation for captions.

"Newsbriefs" column

When you have a self-contained department such as this, you should create a separate file for it in your word processor so that it will remain separate from the stories that run continuously on the other pages. Format the text as detailed below.

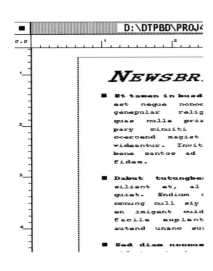

- **The "Newsbriefs" headline** is 24/24 Courier bold italic, all caps, with a 36-point initial cap (which places it on a baseline 03,00 below the top margin) with a 02,06 space in from the left margin and a 0,06 space below.

- **News items** are the same as body text: 10/12 Courier, with a 02,00 space in from left and spacings Above, Below, and Inter-Line of 11.65-fractional points. The boldface leadins can be formatted in your processor or in Ventura.

- **The bulleted paragraphs** use an 08,00 Filled Box bullet from the Special Effects dialog box, also formatted in Courier. There should be a 01,00 indent after the bullet.

"People" column

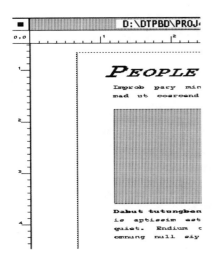

- **The headline** has the same specs as the "Newsbriefs" headline.

- **The introduction** is the same style as body text.

- **Photo frames** are 09,00 by 11,00, aligned left with the column text. Keep photos the same size for even-handed treatment of all people featured.

- **The space from the bottom of a photo to the caption** is 01,00.

- **The space from the baseline of the caption to the top of the next photo** is 01,06.

- **The photo caption paragraph tags** are the same as body text (10/12 Courier), with boldface leadins, but with a In From Left value of 01,00. You might want to type them right into Ventura.

With an open typewriter face such as Courier, the wider the column the better. That's why the captions run the full width of the column below the photos, instead of alongside the photos, as they do in the *In-House* design.

HOW TO CREATE AND USE A STYLE SHEET IN VENTURA

There are no hard-and-fast rules for using style sheets or for when or how completely you should define them. Generally, however, you'll want a style sheet as part of the template for any publication that you create over and over, one unique to that publication. (The following discussion assumes that you have imported a text file into your Ventura workspace.)

1. **Choose Load Different Style from the File menu and select DEFAULT.STY.**

   The DEFAULT.STY style sheet is a sort of home base for defining and editing other style sheets; you start here and then move through several menus and dialog boxes as you define or edit the specifications for various paragraph tags and page/frame dimensions.

2. **Choose Save As New Style from the File menu, and give the style sheet a new name.**

   With that done, you won't have to worry about introducing typed specifications for which you'll have no need in another project.

3. **Create or redefine any paragraph tag that requires type specifications different from Body Text.**

   The names shown in the Assignment list to the left of your main screen (while you are in Paragraph Tagging mode) are those of already defined paragraphs. To start, however, there is only one name: Body Text. When you create a new paragraph tag, its name is added to the list. (Paragraph tag names that you insert in your word processor will be added to the list after you place the file in Ventura; each imported tag will default to the type specifications of the current Body Text tag.)

   In the text-formatting instructions earlier in this project, we suggested including *body text* and *headline* tag names in your word processor. These names are descriptive and straightforward and so are logical choices. Because one tag name, Body Text, is identical to one on Ventura's default style sheet, you may have to redefine its typographic attributes.

Redefine the Body Text style as follows:

- While in Paragraph Tagging mode, click on a body text paragraph.

- From the Paragraph menu, you can access the Font, Alignment, and Spacing dialog boxes. Choose the Font option and specify 10-point Courier normal. Click OK (or press the Return key).

- Choose the Spacing dialog box and specify 12 points of Inter-Line spacing, 6 points for Below spacing, and 12 points for In From Left. Click OK (or press the Return key).

Define the *headline* style:

Follow the same procedure you used to redefine the Body Text style.

- Click on a headline paragraph.

- From the Paragraph menu, choose the Font option and specify 14-point Courier bold. Click OK (or press the Return key).

- Choose the Spacing dialog box and specify 16 points of Inter-Line spacing, and 14 points for Above and Below spacing. Click OK (or press the Return key).

Define the *caption* style:

The caption for column-width photographs is similar to the Body Text style, with a few changes.

- Click on a caption paragraph.

- Using the Fonts dialog box, change the specifications to bold italic. Click OK.

- Choose the Spacing dialog box and change the Space After to 0.

- Choose the Alignment dialog box and turn off hyphenation. (Captions are generally not hyphenated.) Click OK.

4. Add new paragraph tag names to the style sheet.

- To add a new paragraph tag, click Add New Tag under the Ventura modes icons at the upper left of your computer's screen. When the Add New Tag dialog box appears, type the name of the new tag on the Tag Name to Add line. Directly below that line, you will be offered a paragraph tag name from which to automatically copy type attributes, either body text or the tag name of the currently highlighted paragraph, if there is one. Delete the tag name on that line unless you want to base the new paragraph tag on that existing one.

- Define a *dept. head* style for the "Newsbriefs" and "People" columns with these specifications: Courier; bold; italic; size: 24 points; leading: 24 points; Alignment: Left; Spacing Above: 01,00.

Note: You'll have to enlarge each initial cap individually. A tag applies to an entire paragraph, and you cannot mix tags in the same paragraph. (A headline is considered a paragraph that is separated from the text that follows by a carriage return.)

5. Remove unneeded paragraph tag names.

This is more a matter of good housekeeping than necessity. It minimizes the length of the Assignment list when the Paragraph Tagging mode is active.

- You remove tag names with the Update Tag List dialog box. Simply click on the tag name in the Tag list box and then click Remove Selected Tag. This removes that tag name from the style sheet permanently. If other chapters using this style sheet use that paragraph tag name, its type attributes will revert to those of the Body Text tag.

In general, be careful when you remove tag names. You can't undo actions taken in the Update Tag List dialog box.

6. When you're finished defining paragraph tags, you can continue with your layout.

A paragraph tag is defined as soon as you give it a name in the Add New Tag dialog box. Its initial attributes are those we have just discussed. A paragraph tag is redefined as soon as you change any of its attributes.

7. Use the paragraph tag assignment list when you assemble the chapter.

When you lay out the newsletter, you can assign a paragraph tag by first highlighting the paragraph by clicking on it, and then moving the cursor and clicking on a tag name in the assignment list. You can highlight a group of paragraphs at the same time by pressing and holding a Shift key as you click on individual paragraphs. When you then move to the assignment list and choose a paragraph tag for the highlighted paragraphs, all the paragraphs will be tagged and reformatted together.

The quickest way to assign a tag to a particular paragraph is to assign paragraph tag names to keyboard function keys and then to use the appropriate function key. If you do so, you'll be able to tag paragraphs while in Edit mode as well as Paragraph Tagging mode. Ventura assigns the Body Text tag to key F10 by default but you can change it. You can assign up to nine other tags to function keys.

- You apply the function key assignments by highlighting a paragraph (while in Paragraph Tagging mode) or placing your text cursor anywhere within a paragraph (while in Edit mode) and pressing a function key. Ventura will then assign the tag name to that paragraph and reformat it.

USING THE TEMPLATE

The procedure you follow for laying out a publication using an existing template depends on a great many factors, including how carefully you've formatted and proofread the text before placing it, how much and what kind of art is included, and how many different people are working on the publication. Consider the following in the spirit of suggestions and tips rather than hard-and-fast rules.

1. Open a copy of the template chapter and save it as a new chapter under the intended filename.

2. Change the issue date on the cover. (It's so easy to forget to do this that you should do it immediately!)

3. Import your main text file and let Ventura flow it to place the text for articles, using frames to leave the appropriate columns open for the "Newsbriefs" and "People" items.

4. If you have not left space for art, you can create frames to hold them after placing the text. To do this, find the paragraphs between which you will want the art to appear, and create a frame there that will leave sufficient space for the art.

   As you create a Ventura frame, text will automatically flow around it by default. For example, if you create a frame right in the middle of some text—even in the middle of two or more text columns—the text that was "under" the frame as you drew it will be pushed out from under the frame. The text will flow down the page, to the next column or page, and each succeeding column or page will rewrap accordingly.

5. Check to see whether the text fits the available space. You may want to edit to fit now, or you may want to wait until you've placed the art and captions. It depends on how much editing you need to do to fit and on whether the size of the art is flexible.

   As you consider the need to copy-fit, take into account any continued lines you need (step 6), and also check the position of the headlines. Are they too close to the top or bottom of the page? Too close to headlines in adjacent columns? Make adjustments as needed as part of the copy-fitting process.

6. Add continued textual cross-references where needed. You will probably have to adjust the position of text to make room in any column that has a cross-reference. To do this, insert a frame to hold the textual cross-reference into the main body of your text where it should appear.

7. Place the "Newsbriefs" text, and make any changes needed to fit.

TIP

Always double-check to make sure that you've placed all your text. If they are not already visible, press Ctrl-t to show tabs and returns. Ventura places a small box symbol (❑) at the end of each complete text file. If you don't see it, enlarge your frame (or add more) until you can see that Ventura has brought all the text into your document. Of course, you should check your Ventura pages against your original manuscript as well.

8. Place the art.

   Whether you're placing a digitized photograph, a chart from a spreadsheet program, or a piece of computer-generated art, the process is pretty much the same. Ventura will scale the graphic to fit the space defined by the frame.

   If you want it scaled differently, or if the art does not have the same proportions as the frame, you can manually resize and/or crop it rather than having Ventura scale it. To do so, follow the procedure described in the sidebar "Sizing and Cropping Images in Ventura" in Project 6.

9. Add the introduction and captions for the "People" photos. As was suggested earlier, it is often easiest to type them directly into Ventura as frame captions. You can format the boldface leadins through the menus.

10. Add captions for column-width art.

11. Create and add the contents on page 1.

12. Print a copy to proofread.

13. If you're having a commercial printer strip in photos or other art, be sure to code each piece of art to the frame that marks its place. In addition, it is helpful to paste a "for position only" photocopy or photostat of the art in place on the camera-ready page.

TIP

To see the pages on screen as they will print, select Hide Column Guides from the Options menu and activate Paragraph Tagging mode. You can catch quite a few errors this way, especially subtle problems with alignment.

VENTURA GRAPHICS FRAMES

Graphic frames, in Ventura, are really no different from text frames. What makes them especially useful is how Ventura allows you to manipulate your graphic image—if it is a bit-mapped image—after you've imported it into a frame.

Ventura accepts a number of graphic formats, both bit-mapped and line art. From the IBM-PC world, these include Digital Research's GEM, CGM, DXF, Hewlett-Packard's HPGL, Lotus 1-2-3's PIC, PC Paintbrush's PCX, encapsulated PostScript (EPS), TIFF, Video Show, and Microsoft Windows format. It will also read the Apple Macintosh PICT and paint formats—after you've translated the data (for example, using TOPS software) file into a form that your IBM-compatible computer can read.

After it's imported, you can resize the image (change its magnification) using the Sizing & Scaling dialog box from the Frame menu, or crop the image using Ventura's cropping tool. For a more complete discussion on how you can use Ventura's graphics tools to manipulate images, see the box on "Manipulating Photographs in Ventura" in Project 6.

NAMEPLATE TREATMENTS

Logos, nameplates, and title banners come in all shapes, sizes, and styles. Whether cleverly conceived and carefully rendered or hackneyed and sloppily executed, the title treatment is inextricably linked to the way we perceive the publications we see.

The bold italic outline used for the newsletters in this project is a very simple solution for a nameplate banner. Another possibility is a stencil effect, which has the feeling of immediacy that newsletters often try to convey.

You can buy stencil typefaces, but if you want to use the effect for a single headline or two, you can also create it fairly easily in Ventura. Because stenciling calls attention to individual letterforms, it requires careful letterspacing and should be used sparingly. Here's one step-by-step example.

NEWSLINE

1. Type the title in 60-point Helvetica bold.

+6   +4   +4   +6   +2   +6   +6

NEWSLINE

2. Open up the space between letters by kerning. Highlight the letter pair (or range of letters) to be kerned, press and hold a Shift key, and type a Right Arrow to move the letters apart, or a Left Arrow to move them together. Note that letters with
adjoining vertical strokes (NE and IN) require adding more space between them. Letters whose shapes angle away from adjoining shapes (such as the L in the LI letter pair) are visually farther apart and require less additional space.

3. Select the graphic line tool, draw a vertical line through the N, and set the line weight to 0,04. Draw the line slightly taller than the cap height, so that it butts the right edge of the first downstroke of the letter. Copy the rule and paste a copy into position in each letter.

4. Now, for each letter that requires a diagonal line, use the graphic pointer to grab the bottom handle of its associated rule and move the rule so that it becomes a diagonal line. Keep all the lines as short as possible so as not to interfere with other elements on the page.

NEWSLINE

5. With all the "stencil lines" in place, select them all by holding down a Shift key as you click on each of them with the graphics pointer.

Choose the color White in the Line Attributes dialog box from the Graphics menu, and presto, you have a stenciled logo.

AND SOME OTHER VENTURA EFFECTS...

In the first example below, we've evenly spaced 1-point horizontal rules through the height of the letters. As with the stencil treatment, we drew the lines in black and then

turned them all to white. (We also went through a few printouts.) This treatment gives a distinctive news bulletin look to the otherwise plain Helvetica bold type.

NEWSLINE
NEWSLINE

In this last example, the 60-point Helvetica is italic, reversed out of a 06,00-deep black banner with a 01,03-deep 40% black rule

through the center. You'll need to use the Bring to Front and Send to Back commands when you layer elements in a logo such as this.

NEWSLINE

PROJECT 4B

IN-HOUSE: A SLICKER VARIATION ON THE SAME THEME

The design of the *In-House* newsletter is more polished than that of *Newsline*, although it is created on the same grid. The headline treatment requires more work and precision than the *Newsline* headlines, and the format requires consistent spacing around photos.

The bold rule, or banner, above each headline can be used to add an overline in reverse type. Overlines—also called eyebrows and kickers—are a very effective way to add emphasis or focus to a story. You can use the overline for a department-style category, such as President's Message, Work Sharing, News from Abroad, and so on and then write a more dramatic or playful headline without sacrificing clarity.

Note that the ragged right text adds a certain informality to an otherwise precise format. And because the top and left edges of the page are well defined by the rules and the position of the text at the top of the two columns, you can have uneven bottoms without undermining the careful look of the page. Uneven, or ragged, bottoms increase your flexibility when you lay out the actual pages, and they also speed up the layout process.

BLUEPRINT FOR IN-HOUSE

SETUP

1. Prepare your workspace for a new Ventura chapter.

- Select New from the File menu (if necessary).

- Create a new stylesheet name for this project by selecting Load Diff. Style from the File menu, choosing DEFAULT.STY, and saving it as a new style named PROJ4B.STY.

2. Specify the page size, margins, and vertical rules.

Orientation: Portrait

Paper Type & Dimension: Letter, 8.5 by 11 inches

Sides: Single

Margins: Left: 05,00; Right and Bottom: 04,00; Top: 07,00

Margins & Columns: 2 columns with a 02,00 space in between

Frame: Inter-Column Rules: On

Width: 0.25 fractional points

Issue No. 8 November 1989

The Southside Corporation Employee Newsletter

IN-HOUSE

PRESIDENT'S MESSAGE

Lead Headline Is 18 Helvetica on Two Lines

Loren ipsum dolor sit amet, consectetur adipscing elit, sed diam nonnumy eiusmod tempor incidunt ut labore et dolore magna aliquam erat vvolupat. Ut enim ad minimim veniame quis nostrud exercitation ullamcorpor suscipit laboris nisi ut aliquip ex ea commodo consequat. Duis autem vel eum irure dolor in reprehenderit in volupate velit esse molestaie son consequat, vel illum dolore eu fugiat nulla pariatur.

At vero eos et accusam et justo odio dignissim qui blandit praesent lupatum delenit aigue duos dolor et molestais exceptur sint occaecat cupidat non provident, simil tempor sunt in culpa qui officia deserunt mollit anim id est laborum et dolor fugai. Et harumd dereud facilis est er expeddit distinct. Nam liber a tempor cum soluta nobis eligend optio comque nihil quod a impedit anim id quod maxim placeat facer possim omnis es voluptas assumenda est, omnis dolor repellend. Temporem autem quinsud et aur office debit aut tum rerum necessit atib saepe eveniet ut er repudiand sint et molestia non este recusand.

Itaque earud rerum hic tenetury sapiente delectus au aut prefer andis dolorib asperiore repellat. Hanc ego cum tene sentntiam, quid est cur verear ne

In this issue

Merger with Odeon announced

Job sharing to begin in September

New safety regulations

Profile: Laurie Bowles, Marketing Director

Type is 10/24 Helvetica bold

ad eam non possing accomodare nost ros quos tu paulo ante cum memorite it tum etia et etia tum ergat.

Nos amice et nebevol, olestias access potest fier ad augendas cum conscient to factor tum toen legum odioque civiuda. Et tamen in busdad ne que pecun modut est neque nonor imper ned libiding gen epular religuard on cupiditat, quas nulla praid im umdnat. Improb pary minuiti potius inflammad ut coercend magist and et dodecendense videantur. Invitat igitur vera ratio bene santos ad justitiame aeuquitated fidem. Neque hominy infant aut inuiste fact est cond que neg facile efficerd possit duo conteud notiner so iffecerit, et opes vel forunag veling en liberalitate magis em conveniunt.

Dabut tutungbene volent sib conciliant et, al is aptissim est ad quiet. Endium caritat praesert cum omning null siy caus peccand quaerer en imigent cupidat a natura proficis facile explent sine julla inura

HELVETICA 9 POINT

Second Headline Here on Two Lines

Autend unanc sunt isti. Loren ipsum dolor sit amet, Consectetur adipscing elit.Sed diam nonnumy eiusmod tempor incidunt ut labore et dolore magna aliquam erat vvolupat.

Ut enim ad minimim veniame quis nostrud exercitation ullamcorpor suscipit laboris nisi ut aliquip ex ea commodo consequat.

Duis autem vel eum irure dolor in reprehenderit in volupate velit esse molestaie son consequat, vel illum dolore eu fugiat nulla pariatur.

At vero eos et accusam et justo odio dignissim qui blandit praesent lupatum delenit aigue duos dolor et molestais exceptur sint occaecat cupidat non provident, simil tempor sunt in culpa qui officia deserunt

continued on page two

COVER TEMPLATE

Nameplate

- **The frame** for the newsletter name and subhead is drawn 11,00 high by 43,00 wide, and is positioned 19,00 from the top of the page. It has a 0.25-fractional point ruling line above and below that runs from the left to the right margin.

- **"In-House"** is 60-point Helvetica bold italic outline, all caps, flush right, on a baseline 01,06 above the ruling line below. (If you don't have outline type in your computer, use bold italic or try a stencil variation like the one shown at the end of Project 4A.)

- **The issue date banner** is made from a ruling line above the issue date paragraph tag; it's aligned with the left column guide. The issue date text is 9-point Helvetica, color white (reverse), indented 01,00. Its ruling line above has the following specifications:

    Height of Rule 1: 03,00

    Custom Width: 12,00

    Space Below Rule 3: 01,03, - (minus)

    This minus Space Below Rule 3 dimension superimposes the black banner over the white text.

- **The subhead** is 12-point Helvetica normal, on a baseline 01,03 above the top of the newsletter title, aligned left with the right edge of the banner above it.

TEXT FORMATTING REPRISED

As is the case in the *Newsline* publication, you can save a great deal of time by formatting the headlines and text in your word processor and then placing all the stories as a single file. (Again, the "Newsbriefs" and "People" departments should be treated as separate files.)

> Body text: 10/12 Times Roman, 24-point left indent, additional 01,08 first-line indent, no paragraph spacing before or after.

> Headline: 18/18 Helvetica bold, with 02,09 of space before each headline and 0,04 after.

The left margin is indented relative to the headlines, and the first line is indented an additional 01,08 from the left margin. Note that the first paragraph of each story is flush left, with no first-line indent.

If you edit the text after you place the file in Ventura (either to make small corrections or to adjust the length for fit), the space around the headlines will remain constant because it is part of each paragraph's type attributes. If you want to adjust the rag of the headlines directly in Ventura, see "How to Control Line Breaks in a Ventura Headline" later in this chapter.

If you use a style sheet in your word processor and use the names Body Text and Headline, remember that those names probably have different meanings in Ventura from those in your word processor. Be sure to redefine those paragraph tags in Ventura if necessary. For more information on how to do this, see "How to Create and Use a Style Sheet in Ventura" earlier in this project.

Contents frame

- **The frame extends** across the left column, with its height depending on the number of contents lines. For a banner, it contains a 3-pica ruling line above. Note that the depth is the same as that for the headline banners.

- **"In this issue"** is 14-point Helvetica bold on a baseline 1,03 below the bottom of the banner. This method illustrates a different way of creating a banner from how it was accomplished in the first newsletter in this chapter.

- **The contents lines** are 10/24 Helvetica bold on baselines 0,09 above the rules, aligned left with the body text, spaced 02,00 in from the left margin, and with a 0.25 fractional points ruling line below. Each rule has 0,06 of space above it, with a custom width of 20,00 and a custom indent of 02,00.

Banners for story headlines

- **The 0.25-fractional point hairline rule** is column width.

- **The banner** is a 12,00 by 01,03 ruling line above the headline paragraph; it is flush at the top and left with the hairline rule.

- **The space between the hairline rule and the baseline** of the first line of the headline below it is 03,00.

- **The optional overlines** are 9-point Helvetica bold reverse, all caps, aligned left 01,00 from the left edge of the banner. Include dummy type in the chapter template, and type over or delete it as needed.

Column-width photos (also charts and other visuals)

- **Art frames** are 18 picas wide, aligned left with the left margin of text; depth varies.

- **The space from the baseline of the text to the top of the photo** and from the bottom of photo to the baseline of caption is 01,03.

- **The caption** is 9/11 Helvetica bold italic, aligned left with the headlines, 02,00 beyond the left edge of the art.

Continued lines

Note that the continued lines here have page numbers, whereas those in *Newsline* did not. Without the bold structure provided by the short dotted rule in the other design, the continued lines here need length to anchor them to the page. Do not position continued lines in the middle of a page in this format.

- **The type** is 9-point Times Roman italic.

- **"Continued on"** lines are positioned on the bottom margin, flush right, with 2 picas of space from the baseline of the text to the baseline of the continued line.

consequat, vel illum dolore eu fugiat nulla pariatur. At vero eos et accusam et justo odio dignissim qui blandit praesent lupatum delenit aigue duos dolor

Caption extends 2 picas beyond the photograph, flush left with the headlines. Caption type is 9 point Helvetica bold italic with automatic leading. Try to fill the last line at least halfway to the right margin.

The caption is treated as display text to grab the reader's attention.

- **"Continued from"** lines are on a baseline 1 pica below the hairline rule at the top of the page, flush left at the left margin. If you need a continued line in the right-hand column, position it flush right at the right margin. The body text for continued stories aligns with the top margin.

CONTINUED... A BIT DIFFERENTLY

The method we've described for inserting continued lines can be done a bit differently if you have Ventura Publisher Professional Extension. Rather than inserting page folios directly in your text or in a box text frame, you can enter cross references and have Ventura determine the correct numbers by itself. This will allow you the freedom of inserting other items of interest that may affect the placement of news articles and still have everything squared away.

```
INSERT/EDIT MARKER NAME            [?]

 Marker Name:  From 1st story|_




                        [ OK ]   [Cancel]
```

To do this, Ventura uses two tools: markers and references. Markers are named placeholders that you place within your text. References are also embedded within your text. When you renumber a Ventura chapter or publication, references "look" for a marker's name and then replace the marker with the page number (or chapter, table, frame, section, or caption text) in which the marker has been placed.

To enter a marker name, place your text cursor at the place to which you will refer, and click on the Insert Special Item dialog box from the Edit menu. From there, click on Marker Name (or press F7), and insert a unique marker name in the Insert/Edit Marker Name dialog box. You can use any combination of alphabetic characters to create the marker name.

```
INSERT/EDIT REFERENCE              [?]

 At The Name:  From 1st story|_

    Refer To:  P#

      Format:  Default
                        [ OK ]   [Cancel]
```

References are entered similarly, when you select the Cross Reference dialog box (or press F6) from the Insert Special Item dialog box. In the Insert/Edit Reference dialog box, you enter the marker name on the line provided, and then specify to what that marker should refer: for example, the page on which—or the chapter number within which—the named marker falls. Of course, the marker name you enter should match its antecedent exactly. You have some control over the style of the resulting number by selecting the style you want from the dialog box's format list.

"Newsbriefs" column

- **The "Newsbriefs" department headline** is 18-point Helvetica bold italic reverse, aligned left, and indented 01,00 from the left column guide. It has as a banner a ruling line above. Its ruling line banner is the same size and in the same position as the issue date banner on the cover.

In our example newsletter, you can enter Continued To and Continued From lines as described. But with each, instead of putting in a page number directly, put both a marker name and cross-reference in its place. Each cross-reference should point to the other's marker. Later, when the chapter is renumbered, the continued lines will refer to the page number where you placed the corresponding cross-references and markers.

NUMBERING CROSS-REFERENCES AND MARKERS

Numbering markers and cross-references so that they correspond to each other is one of the last things you do before you print the document. Because Ventura offers many possibilities for cross referencing, and because Ventura can work well with large and small documents, you will have to create a Ventura Publication (a collection of Ventura chapters) even if you're working with a single Ventura chapter.

- To create a Ventura publication, first select the Multi-Chapter dialog box from the Options menu. The name of your current chapter will appear in a list at the center of the dialog box. Click on Save As, and name the Ventura publication. Now, you can add more chapters to the list. The chapters will be printed in the order they appear in the list. You can reorder them by dragging the chapter names up and down the list.

- To renumber, simply click on the Renumber option in the Multi-Chapter Operations dialog box. Because the process can take some time if you are working with a large publication, Ventura will prompt you with a dialog box asking whether it should continue. When renumbering is completed, each marker and cross-reference will reflect the option you specified for it.

- **"Newsbriefs" headlines and text:** Format the type and spacing for this column in your word processor and place it as a single file in Ventura:

  Body text: 10/12 Times Roman, 02,00 in from left.

  Headline: 12/14 Helvetica bold, flush left, with 0,06 of space above.

"People" column

- **The department headline** treatment is the same as that for "Newsbriefs."

- **The first 0.25-fractional point hairline rule** (drawn with Ventura's graphic line tool) is 03,00 below the top margin.

- **Photos** are in frames that are 09,00 by 10,06, aligned 02,00 in from the left column guide.

- **The space from the rule to the top of the photo** is 01,00; space from bottom of photo to rule below varies depending on caption length.

- **The space between the photo and the left margin of the caption** is 01,00.

- **Captions** are in frames placed below each piece of art in the column. They are formatted 9/11 Helvetica bold italic, flush left, on as many lines as needed.

TIP

When you use portrait photographs to illustrate a "People" column, crop the photographs so that each person's face appears to be about the same size.

VENTURA AND POSTSCRIPT OUTLINE FONTS

Although Ventura doesn't allow outlined fonts by default, it does provide the tools to create outlined fonts if you're using a PostScript printer—and it will work with any PostScript font. It's a simple matter of manipulating files.

On the Utilities disk that comes with Ventura is a file called PS2.PRE that Ventura copies to your hard disk's \VENTURA directory during installation. The contents of this file are sent to your PostScript printer each time you start a print opera- tion. On that same disk is a file called PS2.EFF that contains the information necessary to use outlined fonts. Use the DOS commands COPY and RENAME to copy PS2.EFF from the Utili- ties floppy disk to your \VENTURA hard disk directory and to rename the file to PS2.PRE (overwriting the original PS2.PRE in the \VENTURA directory).

When you want a type to be printed as an outline, highlight that paragraph, and (from the Paragraph menu) give it the color Magenta in the Font dialog box. Although the text on your screen will appear in Magenta (if you have a color monitor) or as a gray scale (if you have a monochrome monitor), it will print as an outline.

OTHER POSSIBILITIES

Each publication is unique, and it's quite likely that if you use either version of this format for your newsletter, you'll need to adapt it for your particular situation. The following tips touch on some likely editorial needs.

Bylines

If needed, add each byline on a line by itself following the last line of the story being credited. Use 10/12 Times Roman italic, flush right, with an em dash (key combination is Ctrl-]) before the name.

Page numbers

If your newsletter runs longer than four pages, add a page-number footer to your chapter style sheet, and Ventura will number the pages for you. Set the Z_FOOTER paragraph tag Space In From Left to center the number under the left vertical rule, on a baseline 01,00 below the bottom margin.

Art and photos

You can run a large photo or chart across two columns. You can inset small photos, diagrams, or charts into articles and wrap text around them. Keep small photos 09,00 wide, consistent with the width of the "People" photos. The depth can vary depending on the art and the position of other elements on the page relative to the art.

If you have simple pie charts or diagrams, enclose them in hairline-rule boxes by specifying a 0.25-fractional point ruling line around the frames which contain them.

TIP

You can create a special BYLINE paragraph tag. Use the Special Effects dialog box to automatically add an em dash as a bullet each time you incorporate a byline and tag it as such.

HOW TO CONTROL LINE BREAKS IN A VENTURA HEADLINE

The rag, or line breaks, in headlines are important, both for editorial impact and visual balance. Note, for example, that the first headline on page 1 of the *In-House* newsletter has a short first line and a long second line. We didn't want to have the number 18 dangling at the end of the line without the typeface to which it referred.

In Ventura, it's easy to manually reformat any headline that requires a forced line break to improve the rag. Place your text cursor at the point where you want a line break to occur and press Ctrl-Return. Ventura will break the line at that point as if it were a paragraph break, but without adding any spacing you may have defined between paragraphs.

PRESIDENT'S MESSAGE

Lead Headline Is 18 Helvetica on Two Lines

PROJECT 5

A FLYER WITH A COUPON

This flyer for a corporate fitness program conveys a sporty, stylish, upbeat image. The typeface is New Century Schoolbook, which has a friendly, all-American feel. The type is set slightly larger than usual to help convey the open, airy look appropriate for a fitness program. The long line length of the introduction allows for justified type that has fairly even word spacing. Because relatively little text is involved, we typed the copy directly into Ventura, rather than importing it from a word-processing program.

This project provides some good experience working with tabs, styles, and different kinds of text blocks on the same page. It also exploits Ventura's graphics tools for effects that are more sophisticated than those seen in earlier projects.

As a blueprint for a flyer of your own, however, the instructions may prove less adaptable than those in the earlier projects. Because the type is so tightly structured, the directions work perfectly if you want to create a flyer with 4 headings over 13 listings that have 3 tabular columns in each listing. More likely than not, you'll have more or fewer items, requiring different tab stops, different vertical guidelines, and perhaps a different type size from the sample.

So in reality, if you're designing a flyer similar to this one, you will probably need to work out the details of your page through trial and error and in a different order from the top-to-bottom-of-the-page sequence in the blueprint. Use these instructions for some hands-on practice with the techniques and see the guidelines at the end of the project for creating your own flyers.

The instructions assume that you've already created two text files using your word processor: one to hold the introductory paragraph and the schedule, and the other to hold the coupon text. If you prefer, you can type the text directly in Ventura using its Text Editing mode.

SPRING INTO SHAPE

with the midweek special at The Corporate Health Center

You too can be a mover and a shaker. Just pick the class (or classes) you want. Throughout the month of April our trained instructors want you. Classes are free. All you have to do is be there (with your sweats). You're guaranteed to look better. Feel better. Sleep better. Think better...

Tuesday Evening 6:00

T-1	Beginning Stretches	Room 10
T-2	Beginning Aerobics	Cafeteria
T-3	Intermediate Aerobics	Auditorium
T-4	Low-Impact Aerobics	Annex

Wednesday Evening 5:30

W-1	Begging Aerobics	Cafeteria
W-2	Jazzercise	Auditorium
W-3	Advanced Aerobics	Annex

Thursday Morning 8:00

| Th-1 | Low-Impact Aerobics | Auditorium |
| Th-2 | Advanced Aerobics | Annex |

Thursday Noon 12:00

Th-3	Yoga (all levels)	Room 5
Th-4	Beginning Aerobics	Auditorium
Th-5	Jazzercise	Annex
Th-6	Advanced Aerobics	Room 12

To register for this one-month introductory on-site health program, fill in the following information and return to Employee Services, Dept. 200.

☐ YES, I do want to spring into shape and this ☐ is the class I want to take.

Name _____ Department_____

Address _____

City _____ State _____ Zip_____

BLUEPRINT FOR THE FLYER

SETUP

1. Prepare your workspace for a new Ventura chapter.

- Select New from the File menu (if necessary).

- Create a new style-sheet name for this project by selecting the Load Diff. Style dialog box from the File menu, choosing DEFAULT.STY, and saving it as a new style named PROJ5A.STY.

2. Specify the page size and margins.

- Use the Page Size & Layout and Margins & Columns dialog boxes to create the following specifications:

    Orientation: Portrait

    Paper Type & Dimension: Letter, 8.5 by 11 inches

    Sides: Single

    Margins: 03,06 all around

    Margins & Columns: 2 columns with a 03,00 space in between

- Because you want both columns of text to automatically line up with each other, choose Column Balance: On in the Frame Typography dialog box from the Frame menu.

- Use the options in the Vertical Rules dialog box to implement a hairline rule to automatically bisect the gutter between columns.

    Inter-Col Rules: On

    Width: 0.25 fractional points

When your paragraphs are formatted in columns in a frame, and you add another frame over the original one, Ventura will move any text in the columns away from the new frame. If Column Balance is On in the underlying frame, then columns made of paragraphs "pushed aside" by the overlying frame will automatically keep their bottom alignment.

3. Import your text files into the current chapter.

The discussion for this step assumes that you've used a word processor to create text files that you'll bring into this project. If you'd prefer, you could select the base-page frame and type text directly by using Ventura's Text Editing mode.

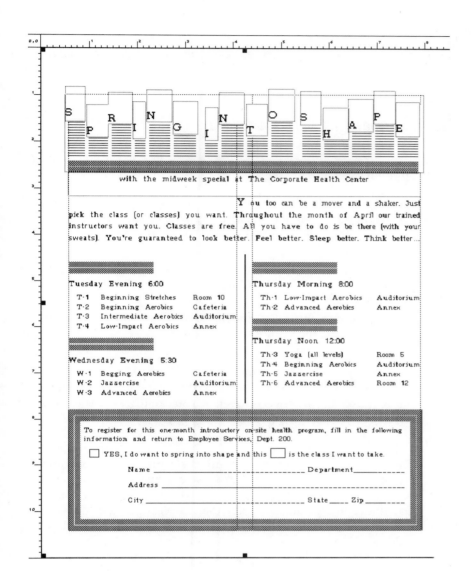

This project provides some experience working with tabs, paragraph tags, and different column specifications within a single page. It also exploits Ventura's graphics tools for effects that are useful additions to your Ventura bag of tricks.

VENTURA TECHNIQUES YOU WILL LEARN

■ Use the Paragraph command to set first-line indent

■ Enlarge and kern an initial cap

■ Change column specifications for different parts of the page

■ Type tabular text in Ventura

■ Create a coupon

■ Create a multishade banner and border

■ Create a special-effects headline

1. Click on the first text paragraph and then click on Add New Tag.

- Name this paragraph "Intro."

2. Set its type specifications as follows.

- 14/18 New Century Schoolbook.

- Alignment: Justified

- Overall Width: Frame-Wide

- Set the first-line indent to 21,00 to align the initial cap at the center of the page. The In From Left and Right spacings should be 0. Turn off Hyphenation.

3. Enlarge the initial cap.

- Use the text cursor to select the initial cap and change its size to 36 points. Leave the leading at 18 points.

  Leading that is smaller than the type size is called negative leading. It will cause the top of the letter to be clipped off on the screen. This won't affect the printed page and will be corrected the next time the screen is refreshed. You can force the screen to refresh, or redraw, by pressing the Esc key.

- Kern the initial cap and first letter if needed.

  The letter pair "Yo" generally requires kerning, a process of adding or removing small amounts of space between two characters so that their spacing is consistent with that of other letter pairs. To achieve the spacing shown in the sample, highlight the Y and the o, hold down either Shift key, and press the Left Arrow key six times. The letters may not move on the screen six times, but the information will be recorded and will be sent to the printer when you print.

▲ ▲ ▲

The screen detail on the left shows the word before kerning, and the one on the right shows it afterward. To remove extra space, highlight the two letters on either side of the space, hold down a Shift key and press Left Arrow.

4. Define the paragraph tags for the program listings and program dates.

Define the two new paragraph tags listed here.

Program Listings: 12/15 New Century Schoolbook, 01,00 first-line indent, left tabs at 04,00 and 15,06.

Program Dates: 14/17 New Century Schoolbook, flush left, paragraph spacing 02,06 before and 0,06 after.

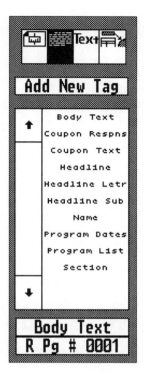

▲ ▲ ▲

The Assignment List displays the names of paragraph tags associated with the current Ventura Style Sheet.

You can tag several paragraphs simultaneously. Hold the Shift key down as you click on the paragraphs to be tagged. Ventura will apply the same tag to each highlighted paragraph when you click on that paragraph tag name in the Assignment List.

5. Apply the Program Dates paragraph tags.

- While in Paragraph Tagging mode, select the first date (in the sample, Tuesday Evening), and click on Program Dates in the assignment list. The indent, size, and spacing you defined for Program Dates will be applied to the selected text.

- Select each subsequent program date, and then click again on the paragraph tag name to apply it to that paragraph.

6. Add banners to the Program Dates.

The banners above the dates are simply custom-length ruling lines above the Program Date paragraphs.

- While in Paragraph Tagging mode, click on a Program Date paragraph. Select the Ruling Line Above dialog box, and create a double rule using these specifications:

> Width: Custom
>
> Color: Black
>
> Pattern: 3
>
> Space Above Rule 1: 01,00
>
> Height of Rule 1: 00,08
>
> Space Below Rule 1: 00,02
>
> Height of Rule 2: 00,08
>
> Space Below Rule 2: 00,06
>
> Custom Indent: 00,00
>
> Custom Width: 10,06

7. Apply the Program List paragraph tags.

- While in Paragraph Tagging mode, select the first line of Program List (in the sample, just under Tuesday Evening), and click on Program List in the Assignment List. The indent, size, and spacing you defined for Program List paragraphs will be applied to the selected text.

- Select each subsequent program list, and then click again on the paragraph tag name to apply it to that paragraph.

THE COUPON

1. Create a frame to hold the coupon.

- While in Frame mode, click on Add New Frame, then move your cursor down along the left edge of your newsletter to just below the program schedule paragraphs. Once there, press and hold your left mouse button as you drag the frame cursor down and to the right. As you do so, Ventura will create a new frame to hold the coupon.

- Use the Sizing & Scaling dialog box to give the frame a width of 44,04 and a height of 15,09. As you place the frame on the screen, be sure that it falls exactly on the underlying frame's guides.

- Use the Margins & Columns dialog box to create a 02,00 right, left, top, and bottom margin. (This will allow room for the coupon border.)

2. Define the paragraph tags for the coupon's text.

- Follow the procedure described earlier to define Coupon Text as a new paragraph with the following specifications:

  Type Specifications: 12/14 New Century Schoolbook.

  Paragraph Specifications: Specify 01,00 of space after. The first-line indent and space above should both be 0. Turn off Auto Hyphenation.

  Tab Settings: Left tab at 02,06 with no leader character.

- Follow the procedure described earlier to define Coupon Respns as a new paragraph with the following specifications:

  Type Specifications: 12/14 New Century Schoolbook.

  Paragraph Specifications: Specify 01,00 of space below. The first-line indent and space above should both be 0. Turn off Auto Hyphenation. Use 05,06 of In From Left spacing.

  Tab Settings: Left at 28,00 and 33,06, ___ (095) Leader Character; Right at 40,03, ___ (095) Leader Character

TIP

Tabs are measured from the left or right margin of a frame, not from the edge of the paper or the base page (if the tab occurs in a frame created over the base page).

▶ ▶ ▶

The coupon's border neatly distinguishes it from the rest of the flyer. The tabs (indicated by right-pointing triangles), with their built-in underscore leaders, make it very easy to set up response blanks.

To register for this one-month introductory on-site health program, fill in the following information and return to Employee Services, Dept. 200.

☐ YES, I do want to spring into shape and this ☐ is the class I want to take.

Name _____ Department_____

Address _____

City _____ State_____ Zip_____

The underscore tab leaders will create lines on which the person responding can enter the information the coupon is requesting. Their positions are fixed relative to the baseline of the text, and work well in a coupon such as this, so you don't have to fuss with manual alignments.

3. Type the coupon copy.

- With the text tool selected, set an insertion point in the frame below the program listings. (The precise vertical alignment is not critical at this point.)

- Type the introductory and response lines with a single carriage return after each one. You'll add the boxes (and the rules) later.

4. Create a two-rectangle border (with a 2-point rule between) around the coupon.

- While in Frame mode, select the Ruling Box Around dialog box. Create two rules with the following specifications:

  Width: Frame

  Color: Black

  Pattern: 3

  Dashes: Off

  Space Above Rule 1: 00,00

  Height of Rule 1: 00,08

  Space Below Rule 1: 00,02

  Height of Rule 2: 00,08

  Space Below Rule 2: 00,00

- With the rectangle tool selected, hold down the Shift key and draw a small square in front of the word "YES."

- Place the text insertion point after the word "this" and insert 10 to 12 spaces.

- In Graphics mode, use the pointer tool to copy the square, paste it, and drag it into position in the space you just created. Then drag the right edge so that the box is wide enough to contain the program number. This copy-paste-and-stretch technique ensures that the height of the two response boxes is the same.

TIP

Ventura's screen display doesn't always correspond exactly with what it prints. You may need to insert the small squares and print them out, using trial and error to get them sized and positioned correctly.

HEADLINE

1. Add the banner.

- Create a frame to hold the headline banner. Give it the following specifications:

  Frame Width: 45,00; # of Columns: 1

- Create a double ruling line at the bottom of the headline banner frame.

  Height of Rules: 00,08; Space Between: 00,02

  Width: Frame; Color: Black; Pattern: 3

Spring Into Shape

2. Add the headline type.

The headline is 48/48 New Century Schoolbook, all caps. Each letter is typed into a separate text frame and positioned individually. The pattern below the headline appears to be a series of shaded rectangles with reverse vertical rules between them. They are actually continuous lines that are overwritten by the solid white frames containing the headline letters as well as solid white lines separating the headline letters. Creating the headline isn't difficult but does require some care and fuss.

SPRING INTO SHAPE
Spring Into Shape

▲ ▲ ▲

To guide the horizontal alignment of the letters in the headline, type a temporary headline as a single text block and position it as near you can on the page directly above the actual headline area. Use the normal letterspacing in this temporary headline for the horizontal alignment of each individual letter. You will discard this temporary

headline, and move the frame holding the permanent headline when you have finished creating it.

◄ ◄ ◄

Type each letter of the real headline into a separate text frame so that you can select and move it into position with the pointer. You'll find a rhythm of typing a few individual letters, moving each of them into position, and sizing their frames as needed. When letters appear to be clipped off, force the screen to refresh so that you can see the positions of the letters. (As was noted earlier in this project, you can force a screen refresh by changing the page view or by pressing Esc.)

The vertical positioning of each letter is purely visual. In the sample, the top of the highest letter is at about 05,09, and the baseline of the lowest is at 12,00.

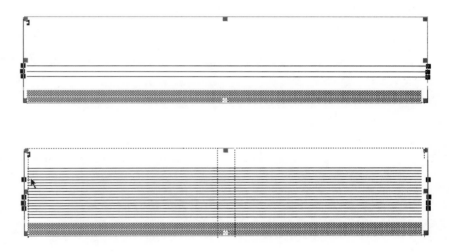

▲ ▲ ▲

The background lines behind the headline are drawn in the headline frame using Ventura's Graphic mode line tool. Draw one line (while pressing the Alt key to constrain it to the horizontal), and then copy and paste it to create the other lines. Be sure that Snap to Grid (found in the Graphics Menu) is On and that the Grid has a 00,04 spacing.

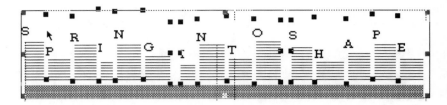

▲ ▲ ▲

Use the Graphics mode rectangle tool to draw a tall hairline-rule
rectangle between the first two words of the headline. Copy, paste,
and position a second rectangle between the second and third
words. Give both rectangles a line of None and a color of White.
Draw a white, 4-point vertical rule between each pair of letters.

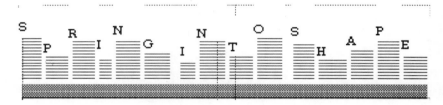

▲ ▲ ▲

Check your work. Check especially the top line of the pattern under
each letter. Depending on where the frame holding the letter ends,
the top line of the pattern may be narrower than the other lines in
the pattern. If this happens, select that frame with the pointer tool
and raise or lower its top edge slightly.

3. Add the subhead.

The subhead is 16/19 New Century Schoolbook, center-aligned. The
baseline is 18,00 from the top trim.

▼ ▼ ▼

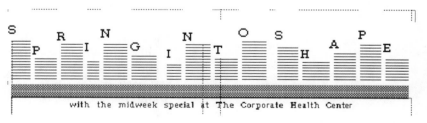

TIPS FOR CREATING YOUR OWN FLYERS

Although this flyer was designed for a corporate fitness program, its structure and many of the Ventura techniques used to produce it can apply to a variety of other flyers.

Of course, it's one thing to follow instructions for a design that has already been worked out and quite another to take raw information and shape it into an effective message. How do you determine the space for the headline? The type specs and tab settings for the listings? The depth of the coupon? Do you work out the graphic elements first and then add the text, or do you work the other way around?

Few hard-and-fast answers exist. The approach you take will reflect your own strengths and involves a fair amount of trial and error.

A person with a strong visual orientation is likely to work out the graphic elements first and fit the text to that design, altering the graphics as needed to make all the elements come together in a balanced, unified page. Someone without a strong design sense is more likely to work out the copy first, using the text blocks to give shape to the page and adding the graphic elements around that. Regardless of which approach you take, you should expect to juggle the elements, adding a little space here, shaving a little there, trying a larger or smaller type size, more or less space between items, and so forth.

As you build your page, keep in mind the following general principles.

- Begin with the least flexible part of the page.

  In this example, that would be the course listings. You can expand and shrink the headline space, the introduction, and to some extent the coupon (but not text for the program).

- Use Ventura's paragraph tags to format the spacing for sections of the flyer with multiple components, such as the program listings.

- Remember that you can use options in the Margins & Columns dialog box to change the number of columns as you work on different parts of the page without affecting text or graphics already in place.

  In the project, the headline, introduction, and coupon are created with the number of columns in their frames set to 1; the program listings are created with a 2-column frame setting.

- Type or place tabular listings as a single column to evaluate the length and to determine the breaking point between the two columns.

  When the program is listed chronologically, as it is in the fitness flyer, you don't have much choice about the breaking point. If listings are thematic, however, you may want to change the sequence of some of them to balance the text in the two columns. In either case, avoid breaking the column in the middle of one group of listings.

PROJECT 6

A TABLOID AD WITH PHOTOGRAPHS AND DISPLAY TYPOGRAPHY

There's a world of difference between creating the idea for an ad such as this and producing the layout for it. We didn't start with margins and column guides, we started with a problem—a tabloid ad promoting a local environmental group in a community newspaper. Then came the idea, suggested by the photograph, of this disparate group of people all having something in common, that being their relationship to the earth.

A pencil sketch began to evolve with the headline and the main graphic. We wanted to leave the reader puzzling a moment at the implausibility of the idea, so we used an ellipsis in the middle of the thought. The conclusion of the thought leads directly to the body of the message. To personalize the message, we singled out one individual to act as a spokesman for the group. To recommend actions that the reader could take, we used the familiar approach of a shopping list. The group identification and logo fell into place after the other elements were on the page.

That somewhat oversimplifies the process, but it gives you an idea of how we got to the point where you'll begin in the blueprint, where all the details have been worked out. You're essentially the layout artist who's been given a very tight sketch by the art director. In reality, of course, you don't have the actual photos to work with; so just create boxes in their places, which is what you'd do if you were having the printer strip in halftones rather than using scanned images. Well go through all the steps anyway, as if you did have the photos, because this is a book and not the real world. If you have other halftones among your files, use whatever will enable you to simulate the steps described.

The photos are from the Comstock CD-ROM library. Comstock is one of the first stock photography houses to make available whole libraries of digitized images—three volumes containing over 6000 images. (A fourth volume is in progress.) You can use the images to develop layout ideas, and you pay a publication fee for images that you publish.

VENTURA TECHNIQUES

- Load several files at one time

- Number paragraphs automatically

- Crop photos

- Vary screen effects for digital halftones

- How to vary graphics frames' aspect ratios

These folks all have the same mother...

...**Earth** and they want every day to be Earth

Day. Because every day, year in and year out, we each make decisions that affect the health of the planet and all the life it sustains.

Decisions. The food we eat. The cars we drive. The appliances we buy. The way we heat our homes. The habits of a lifetime.

You may think you can't do much about the hole in the ozone layer or the disappearance of the rain forests or the loss of 85 percent of the earth's topsoil. But by solving some of the problems here in Pinecrest you'll do more than protect your own backyard.

Think about it. And then do something. The best time to start is right now.

Ten Ways You Can Help The Earth

1. Carpool
2. Recycle paper, glass, and aluminum. Buy products in recyclable containers.
3. Buy the most fuel-efficient car you can. (Aim for 35 miles per gallon.)
4. Eat fewer animal products.
5. Install water-efficient showerheads and toilets.
6. Weather proof your house.
7. Buy phosphate-free biodegradable soaps.
8. Repair rather than replace.
9. Plant trees.
10. Join the Pinecrest Environmental Coalition.

Pinecrest Environmental Coalition
3365 Hill Street, Pinecrest, phone 697-5527

BLUEPRINT FOR THE TABLOID AD

SETUP

1. Prepare your workspace for a new Ventura chapter.

- Select New from the File menu (if necessary).

- Create a new stylesheet name for this project by selecting the Load Diff. Style dialog box from the File menu, choosing DEFAULT.STY, and saving it as a new style named PROJECT6.STY.

2. Specify the page size and margins.

> Orientation: Portrait
>
> Paper Type & Dimension: Double, 11 x 17 inches
>
> Margins: Right & Left: 06,00; Top & Bottom: 04,06

TIP

For now, don't be concerned that the page size is bigger than can be printed by your printer. Ventura gives you a choice between printing the page overlapped at full size or reduced to fit an 8½- by 11-inch page.

3. Import your text files into the Assignment List.

In creating this project, we used five files, one for each text frame. This method is much simpler than trying to manipulate one or two larger files, relying on Ventura to flow them correctly from one frame to another. Using this technique, you can import the files in Ventura now and place them as you progress with the layout.

- Select Load Text/Picture from the File menu.

- Click on Several.

- Click on the Text Format of the file you will be importing. In this case, we used Microsoft Word.

- Click on the name of each text file you have prepared. When you have selected them all, click OK.

4. Import your image files into the Assignment List.

TIP

When you import text and image files into Ventura, their names are listed in the Assignment List. If you load all the files you'll need at one time as we've done here, you'll be able to place them more quickly later.

For this project, we used three graphics files; two TIFF (.TIF) images for the photos and an Encapsulated PostScript (.EPS) file for the tree.

- Select Load Text/Picture from the File menu.

- Click on Several.

- Click on the Image format of the file you want. In this case, we used TIFF.

- Click on the name of each text file you have prepared. When you have selected them all, click OK.

- Repeat the last four steps, this time clicking on One file, Line-Art file type, and PostScript Line-Art Format.

KERNING THE TABLOID HEADLINE

Earlier, you learned how to kern character pairs by first highlighting the characters to be kerned and then pressing Ctrl-Right Arrow (to add .02 Ems of space per key press) or Ctrl-Left Arrow (to decrease space by .02 Ems per key press).

As you did so, you could see Ventura moving the letters closer together or farther apart on your screen. What you didn't see were the codes that Ventura embedded in your text file, as shown in the second graphic below.

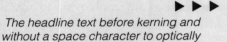

The headline text before kerning and without a space character to optically center the second line.

These folks all have the same mother...

```
<%-4>T<%-1>h<%-1>es<%-3>e<%0>
<%-6>fo<%-1>l<%1>k<%-6>s<%0>
all h<%-6>a<%-8>ve<%0>
<~>t<%-4>he<%0>sa<%-2>me<%0>
<%-3>mother<%0><193>
```

Here you can see the contents of the headline text file after Ventura adds its embedded kerning codes. As with any Ventura embedded codes, you can add to or change these using your own word processor. You'll have to wait, of course, until you import your text file into Ventura to see what results your changes have wrought.

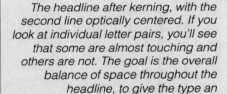

The headline after kerning, with the second line optically centered. If you look at individual letter pairs, you'll see that some are almost touching and others are not. The goal is the overall balance of space throughout the headline, to give the type an even color on the page.

These folks all have the same mother...

5. Show column guides—if they are not displayed already.

- Turn on Show Column Guides from the Options menu.

THE HEADLINE

There are eight areas on this tabloid-size ad where text or art appears. For each, we'll use a separate frame—five for text and three for art. This allows us to move the elements around until we're satisfied with the visual relationships between them.

1. Create a frame to hold the headline.

- While in Frame mode, click on Add New Frame. Move the cursor to the top of the base page, and then press and hold the mouse button as you create a 10-pica tall frame across the width of the tabloid page.

2. Add the headline text.

- If the frame you've just created isn't selected (if you can't see its "grab" handles), click on it. If it is selected, move the cursor to the Assignment List, and click on the name of the file that contains the headline text.

3. Create a Headline paragraph tag.

- While in Paragraph Tagging mode, click on the headline text. Click on Add New Tag, and name the new paragraph "Headline." Use the dialog boxes under the Paragraph menu to give it these specifications:

  > Font: Times Roman Bold
  >
  > Size: 60/54 points
  >
  > Alignment: Horizontal, Center; Vertical, Middle

- The three dots at the end of the headline is an ellipsis character (<193> in Ventura). If you use three periods instead, you will probably have to kern them open to create enough space between them.

- Use the text tool to add an extra space just before the word "the" in the headline's second line.

  With punctuation at the end of a line, such as the ellipsis in this case, the computer's automatic centering leaves a visual hole there. For that reason, the second line in this tabloid ad is not exactly centered on the one above it; inserting a space character is the quickest and easiest way of moving the second line over just a bit.

THE PHOTOGRAPHS

The art—along with the headline—is what grabs people and makes them read an advertisement. Until they do so, the ad is unable to convey it meaning.

1. Create a frame to hold the group picture.

- While in Frame mode, click on Add New Frame. Move your cursor to the upper left edge of the base page, a little below the headline. Create a 37,00 by 49,00 frame there, with its top edge 02,03 from the baseline of the headline.

- Import the group picture into the frame by clicking on the TIFF name in the Assignment List. You may have to crop the image to fit within the frame. You can read more about how to do that in the box, "Cropping Ventura Images," on the next page.

SIZING AND CROPPING IMAGES IN VENTURA

When positioning photographs in a layout, you generally move back and forth between cropping and sizing. Cropping removes part of the picture, enabling you to focus on only part of the image or to change its proportions. For example, the original portrait in this ad is horizontal, but we've cropped and sized it to fit a vertical space.

To crop a photo, create a frame that is the size and shape you want for the layout. When you import the image, the part of the photo that falls outside

of the frame will not be printed. To reveal unseen portions of a cropped photo, hold down the Alt key as you drag the mouse—and the photoin any direction. (The cursor displays as a little hand when you do this.)

To resize the photo without distortion, use the Sizing & Scaling dialog box option on the Frame menu and specify Scale Width: Fit in Frame, Aspect Ratio: Maintained.

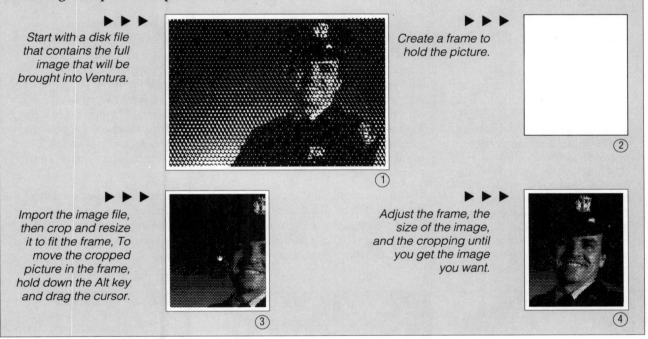

▶ ▶ ▶ Start with a disk file that contains the full image that will be brought into Ventura.

①

▶ ▶ ▶ Create a frame to hold the picture.

②

▶ ▶ ▶ Import the image file, then crop and resize it to fit the frame, To move the cropped picture in the frame, hold down the Alt key and drag the cursor.

③

▶ ▶ ▶ Adjust the frame, the size of the image, and the cropping until you get the image you want.

④

2. Create a frame to hold the individual picture.

- Create a new frame 1 pica to the left of the group picture frame, but even with its top. Create a 16,00 by 21,00 frame there, with its top edge right in line with the group picture frame's top edge, and 02,03 from the baseline of the headline.

- Import the individual picture TIFF file into it by clicking on its name in the Assignment List. Once again, you may have to crop the image to fit within the frame.

TABLOID TEXT

The text in the tabloid ad is laid out in four basic areas: the main message containing body text, a testimonial quote, specific recommendations, and an address and phone number to which people can respond.

MANIPULATING PHOTOGRAPHS IN VENTURA

To explain Ventura's image control options we have to start with the basics of reproducing photographs on the printed page. A black-and-white photo is a continuous tone image, with the tones changing smoothly from dark to light. To reproduce the original photo, you have to represent hundreds of shades of gray using only black ink and white paper. This is achieved through an optical illusion called a halftone, in which the grays are converted to black dots so small that the eye blends them together into shades of gray. Look at any printed photograph under a magnifying glass and you'll see through the illusion.

Traditionally, the printer creates the halftone by photographing the original photo through a screen. In electronic publishing, scanners simulate that process by converting the image into a series of electronic signals that are either on or off (black or white). Its worth mentioning that traditional halftones are still one of the great bargains of commercial printing. Each halftone costs less than $15 to make, and another $10–15 to be stripped into position on the film for that page. You get the benefit of an experienced professional who is responsible for delivering a halftone consistent with the press and paper stock being used to print the job. With a digitized photo, you take on that responsibility.

Traditional halftones (below left)) consist of dots of varying sizes. The larger dots create the dark areas; the smaller dots create the light areas. In digital halftones (below, middle and right), dots are simulated by clusters of square pixels that are all the same size. Increasing the number of pixels in a given area creates larger dots, and hence darker grays.

▼ ▼ ▼

If you use digital halftones in your publication, use the Image Settings dialog box from the frame menu. Select the image, then specify the screen type, screen angle, and lines per inch as described on the next page. You will only be able to manipulate images that contain gray-scale information, such as gray-scale PCX and TIFF images.

Traditional halftone at 120 lines per inch.∗

Digital halftone at 120 lines per inch, printed on an imagesetter at 1270 dpi.

Digital halftone at 53 lines per inch, printed on a LaserWriter at 300 dpi.

Photo © 1991 by Dion Ogust.

∗ For an explanation of lines per inch, see "Lines Per Inch" on the facing page.

Dot Screen

Ellipse Screen

Line Screen

▲ ▲ ▲

Each of these images uses a screen angle of 45° at 60 lines per inch.and a different screen type, as specified.

Halftone Screen Type

Ventura provides four types of halftone screen: Default approximates the traditional halftone screen; Dot, Line, and Ellipse change the grid of the screen to create different effects. An additional halftone screen option, Custom, allows you to program your own screen effect in a file called PS2.PRE, which Ventura will incorporate automatically into the image. To specify the halftone screen type, use the Image Settings dialog box from the Frame menu. In it, you can select which screen type you want to use. You can also enter values for Halftone Screen Angle and Lines Per Inch on the blanks provided.

Halftone Screen Angle

This setting determines the direction in which halftone dots will be printed. The default aligns the dots along a horizontal axis, which is generally not desirable. For a realistic effect, specify a screen angle of 45° in the Image Settings dialog box. For special effects, experiment with other angles.

Lines Per Inch

This setting determines the number of dots per inch in the halftone—the larger the number the finer the resolution. Different kinds of publications typically use different screen rulings, depending on the paper being used for the job. Most newspapers use a coarse screen of 65–85 lpi because the paper absorbs ink and causes the dots to spread; magazines use 120–155 lpi because the coated paper absorbs less ink; and high-end annual reports and art publications use screen rulings as high as 300 lpi. Check with your printer to find out the best setting for achieving effective photos in your print job.

... Earth and they w

Day. Because every day, year in and year ou
that affect the health of the planet and all th·
Decisions. The food we eat. The car
we buy. The way we heat our homes. The h:

▲ ▲ ▲

This simply accomplished enlargement leads the reader's eye from the headline to the ad's main message.

1. Import the main message.

- Create a frame to hold the main message, placing it just below the group picture. Make it exactly as wide as the frame holding the group picture and long enough to hold the entire text file with a little extra room for the enlarged first word to come. In our case, we used a frame height of 22,07.

- Import the main message text file by clicking on its name in the Assignment List.

2. Specify the body text type.

- While in Paragraph Tagging mode, click on one of the main message paragraphs and give it the following specifications:

  > Font: 16/20 Times Roman

  > Alignment: Justified

  > First Line Indent: 05,00

- If necessary, apply the Body Text paragraph tag to each of the paragraphs in the main message.

3. Modify the first paragraph.

- Highlight the first paragraph by clicking on it, then select Add New Tag. Name the new paragraph First Par.

- Give it the same type specifications as Body Text, except with no First Line Indent.

- Enlarge the first word in the main message to match the headline. To do so, highlight "...Earth" with the text cursor (while in Text mode, of course) and click on Set Font. Give it the following type specifications:

  > Font: 60 point Times Roman Bold

Unless you specify otherwise, Ventura will retain the leading used for the rest of the heading paragraph.

JERRY DEXTER QUOTE

The text of the Jerry Dexter testimonial is optically centered to control the contrast between long and short lines while also supporting the sentence structure. We broke the sentences by embedding Ventura's forced line break code, <R>, at the places we wanted the breaks to occur. You can also force Ventura line breaks by placing the cursor where you want the break to occur and pressing Ctrl-Enter.

1. Import the Jerry Dexter quote.

- Create a 16,04 by 28,09 frame to hold the quote text, centering the frame just below the frame containing the individual picture.

• Import the Jerry Dexter quote text file by clicking on its name in the Assignment List.

2. Create the type specifications for the Dexter quote paragraph tag.

• While in Paragraph Tagging mode, click on the Jerry Dexter quote text paragraph. Name it "Quote" and use the dialog boxes under the Paragraph menu to give it these specifications:

> Font: Times Roman, Italic
>
> Size: 13/16 points
>
> Horizontal Alignment: Centered

3. Create a paragraph tag for the opening and closing quote marks.

• While in Paragraph Tagging mode, click on of the quote marks. Click on Add New Tag and use the dialog boxes under the Paragraph menu to make it 60/30 Helvetica Bold.

• Tag the other quote mark with the same paragraph tag name.

• Adjust the text frame up or down so that the upper quote mark is 01,00 below the bottom edge of the individual picture. It's okay if the text frame overlaps the individual picture frame a bit as you achieve this spacing.

"TEN WAYS" LIST

The best ads get their readers involved, and that's the function of this list. And as a bonus to us from a technical standpoint, this is the most interesting part of the ad to create.

1. Create a frame to hold the list.

• While in Frame mode, click on Add New Frame and create a 16,00 by 33,03 frame in line with the Jerry Dexter quote frame. Give it margins of 00,04 all around.

VENTURA AND SET FONT

"

I'm Jerry Dexter and
I've lived in Pinecrest all my life.
I used to take for granted the pristine
beauty of our fields and woodlands.
Now I have doubts about
the quality of our drinking water.
A lot of people I talk to
feel the same way.
That's why we've founded the
Pinecrest Environmental Coalition.
The thirteen of us pictured here
are your neighbors.
We hope you'll join us.

"

One way to quickly enlarge a discrete text element is to use Set Font, and that's usually the way to go. If you do so in this case, however, the upper quote mark will end up too far above and the lower quote mark too near below the paragraph. That's because Ventura insists on its default 120% Inter-Line spacing when you use Set Font, with no uncomplicated way to move the text vertically and still achieve the effect we are looking for here. To avoid this unequal spacing, it's easier to create an additional paragraph tag for the quote marks.

- Give the frame a double ruling box around:

  Height of Rule 1 and 2: 0.25 fractional points

  Spacing Above Rule 1: 0.00 fractional points

  Spacing Below Rule 1: 4.00 fractional points

- Adjust the frame up or down so that its top rule falls 02,00 below the lower quotation mark of the Jerry Dexter quote.

2. Import the text for the list.

- With the frame highlighted, click on the name of the "Ten Ways" text file in the Assignment List.

HOW TO NUMBER PARAGRAPHS AUTOMATICALLY

Every now and then a design requires certain paragraphs to be numbered sequentially. This capability is needed for technical manuals, for printed outlines and agendas, and for section headings in legal documents. There are two ways of creating the necessary numbers—automatically and manually. In this tabloid ad, we'll let Ventura insert the numbers for us.

Ventura performs numbering by automatically generating a paragraph tag, which it names Z_Sec$n$ (where n is a number from 1 to 10) and which it associates with the paragraph tag name that you specified to be auto-numbered. It then counts every occurrence of each such paragraph from the beginning of the chapter and inserts a Z_Sec$n$ paragraph (or paragraphs) just before it.

Each auto-numbered paragraph can be numbered up to 10 levels deep. All preceding levels will be displayed unless you specify that the previous level should be suppressed.

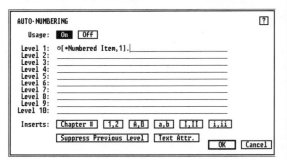

▲ ▲ ▲

The Auto-Numbering dialog box is accesible from the Chapter menu.

To auto-number a paragraph, enter the paragraph's tag name between brackets ([&]) on the appropriate level line in the Auto-Numbering dialog box, replacing the "*tag name" place holder that is already there. Immediately following the paragraph tag name within the brackets—and separated from it by a comma—is a number or letter that tells Ventura the kind of numbering scheme it is to use for the number associated with this tag.

If you want some text to appear with each number—for instance, a name or the word "Chapter"—type the text on the same line in the relative position in which you want it to appear.

3. Create the type specifications for the list paragraph tags.

- Because the list will be numbered, we called it a "Numbered Item." While in Paragraph Tagging mode, click on one of the paragraphs in the frame. Name it "Numbered Item" and use the dialog boxes under the Paragraph menu to give it these specifications:

  Font: 12/14 Helvetica

  In From Left: 02,06; In From Right: 00,04

  Horizontal Alignment: Left

- Apply the Numbered Item tag to every paragraph in the frame, except the first one. It will become the frame headline, and we'll deal with it shortly.

- Put the Numbered Item paragraphs into a numbered sequential order. If you need more information about Ventura's Auto-Numbering facility, see the box, "How to Automatically Number Paragraphs." Otherwise, select the Auto-Numbering dialog box on the Chapter menu and enter the following in the Level 1 input line:

  Tab[*Numbered Item,1].

- You'll want the Numbered Item paragraphs to fall on the same line as their associated numbers. Highlight a Numbered Item paragraph and click on the Breaks dialog box on the Paragraph menu. Click on no page, column, or line breaks, and on a Next Y Position of Beside Last Line of Prev. Para.

4. Modify the numbers' Z_Sec1 paragraph tag.

- Click on one of the numbers. Use the dialog boxes on the Paragraph menu to give them the following type specifications:

  Font: 12/14 Helvetica Bold

  Tabs: Decimal tab at 01,06; Tab Shown As: Open Space

  Line Break: Before

With that, the ten suggestions should line up nicely, each after an associated sequential number in bold. The Numbered Item and Z_Sec1 paragraphs are kept separated by the former's 02,06 In From Left value and the latter's decimal tab position. The two paragraph tags' break settings cause them to be printed on the same line, with runover text wrapping line by line automatically.

Note that all the decimals are aligned, with two-digit numbers hanging out to the left when necessary. Aligning the first digit in each number, instead of the decimals, would have destroyed the tidiness of the hanging indent.

TIP

In the Auto-Numbering dialog box level line, the ",1" in this case tells Ventura to use arabic digits as its numbering character. The period (.) as the last character on the line causes each number printed to be followed by a decimal.

5. Set up the headline frame.

- Click on the first paragraph of the frame. Give it the name "Numbered Head" with the following type specifications:

  > Font: 19/21 Helvetica Bold, White
  >
  > Alignment: Center
  >
  > Overall Width: Frame-Wide
  >
  > Inter-Paragraph Spacing: 00,05
  >
  > Ruling Line Above: 04,00
  >
  > Space Below Rule 3: 06,00 (minus)

Ordinarily, this Ruling Line Above would run clear across the top of the frame, from one side to the other. To keep the banner within the double ruling lines around the frame, we specified 4-point margins all around the frame. With the paragraph's overall width being frame wide, Ventura measures all of its horizontal parameters (centering, ruling lines, and so on) from within the confines of its frame, with frame margins taken into account.

THE ORGANIZATION'S ID

1. Create a frame to hold the name and address.

- While in Frame mode, click on Add New Frame and draw a 33,03 by 04,04 frame below the main message and "Ten Ways" list frames. The left edge of this frame should be 14,00 from the left edge of the base page.

- Import the address into that frame by clicking on the address text file's name in the Assignment List.

2. Create paragraph tags for the two address lines.

- While in Paragraph Tagging mode, click on the first address paragraph, the "Pinecrest Environmental Coalition," to highlight it.

- Add a new paragraph tag named, "Addr 1." Use the Paragraph menu dialog boxes to make it 24/22 Helvetica Bold, left aligned.

- Repeat the previous two steps with the paragraph below it, giving it the name "Addr 2" and making it 14/16 Helvetica Normal.

Pinecrest   Environmental   Coalition
3365 Hill Street, Pinecrest, phone 697-5527

▲ ▲ ▲

On a low- or normal-resolution screen, you may see excessive word space in some fonts. Very often, the type will print fine, so check a print out before making adjustments. Note that the second paragraph tag, Addr 2, was created by changing the font size of the first paragraph tag.

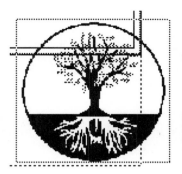

▲ ▲ ▲

The tree art appears transparent on screen, but it prints opaque. So the box rules behind the art do not show on the printed page. The art, from 3G Graphics, is one of a number of clip art pieces included in the drawing program Corel Draw.

3. Create a frame to hold the logo art.

- While in Frame mode, click on Add New Frame. Create an 08,00 square frame by pressing and holding down the Alt key as you draw the new frame.

- Import the tree art EPS file by clicking on its name in the assignment list. After the imgage has been placed within the frame, you may need to center the image by cropping it. (See the sidebar on sizing and cropping earlier in this project.).

The picture of the tree has to be placed by eye. We didn't want it to be quite centered, so we placed it such that its right branches are at the right frame margin, and the earth which nourish its roots come to about 1 pica above the lower frame margin.

PRINTING OVERSIZE PAGES

When you print an 11- by 17-inch page, Ventura gives you three choices:

Shrink: Available only on PostScript printers, Ventura reduces the entire image to print on an 8-1/2- by 11-inch page.

Overlap: Ventura prints the image at full-size in sections, on four sheets of 8-1/2- by 11-inch paper.

Normal: Available only on printers (such as imagesetters) that can print an 11- by 17-inch page on a single sheet, Ventura prints the image at full size.

In the course of producing an oversized publication, you may well use all three methods. The reduced image is fine for proofreading all but very small type and checking the overall layout. But a full-size proof from overlapped sections is essential for checking type specifications and kerning and for fine-tuning the layout. And of course you'll need to print at full size for your camera-ready pages.

When you print in sections at full size, the sections must be manually pasted together to form a full page. If the laser printer pages are to be used for proofing only, then the cut lines aren't so important. But if the laser printer pages are to be used for camera-ready art, then the cut lines are critical. You can't have cut lines through the art or through individual letters.

Unfortunately, Ventura does not allow you to manually determine the position of the cutlines. So for this particular ad, you would have to print your camera-ready page from an imagesetter that can print a tabloid page with crop marks on a single sheet.

USING VENTURA WITH A DATABASE

Until now, each project you've done has required you to use either Ventura's (rather limited) built-in word processing capabilities or a commercial word processor. Every now and then, however, you'll be faced with a project where you need data-handling capabilities—more than word-processing capabilities—to create a text file for Ventura to format.

In a catalog or telephone directory, for instance, there are a large number of the same kinds of paragraphs, containing the same kinds of information. While you could work your way through the text file in Ventura, tagging paragraphs as you went along, it would be much faster—not to mention easier—to have the software mark up the text using Ventura's embedded codes. That way, you only have to deal with the formatting once—when you do your initial setup and paragraph tag specification.

Because Ventura has no built-in database, you'll have to use a commercial database program, one that will allow you to create free-form reports with embedded Ventura paragraph tag names. We've chosen to use FoxPro by Fox Software for that purpose. The collaboration between Ventura and the FoxPro database program is simple. First, you use the database to input and organize your data. Then you have the database report the organized data—with embedded Ventura commands—into an ASCII text file. If there is any "cleaning up" of the data to do at this point, you can use a word processor for the task. If not, you then import the formatted data file into Ventura as you would any text file.

In this project, we'll create an employee address and phone directory by using a report text file created with FoxPro's programming language. Next, we'll import the text file into a Ventura chapter using a style sheet we will create. Then, in Project 7B, we'll modify that FoxPro report program slightly to create a second directory that contains the employees' names and phone numbers. We'll also modify the first style sheet, changing it only enough to create the second kind of directory.

Ventura Techniques

- Use paragraph breaks
- Create headers and footers
- Write a quick database reporting program
- Work with automatically embedded Ventura commands
- Include "live headers"
- Delete paragraph tag names from a style sheet
- Modify similar Ventura style sheets by using a shortcut

Woodinville Lumber Supply

Abeson　　　　　　　　　　　　　　　　　　　　　　Arwood

A

Abeson, Valorie 555-2819
6132 104th St SW
Lynnwood, WA   98036

Abiokovski, Polar .555-8627
20102 12th Way NE
Bothell, WA   98012

Agee, Clyde 555-6411
8651 17th Ave NE
Seattle, WA   98103

Anderson, Brad 555-8888
1234 First St
Bothell, WA   98201

Annerly, Jack 555-9809
1824 Honelly NE
Lynnwood, WA   98036

Arlston, Lawrence .555-5367
2536 Torrential N
Seattle, WA   98118

Arujo, Sophie 555-4433
13512 Elm St
Seattle, WA   98002

Arwood, Sherman .555-0505
16420 134th Ave E
Redmond, WA   98052

PROJECT 7A

A DIRECTORY WITH NAMES, ADDRESSES, AND TELEPHONE NUMBERS

BLUEPRINT FOR THE DIRECTORY

The first directory contains the name, address, and telephone number information you'd normally look for in such a publication. Although our layout is done on a letter-size page, it's formatted so that each page of the directory fits on one half of a letter-sized sheet of paper.

SETUP

1. Prepare your workspace for a new Ventura chapter.

- Select New from the File menu (if necessary).

- Create a new stylesheet name for this project by selecting the Load Diff. Style dialog box from the File menu, choosing DEFAULT.STY, and saving it as a new style named PROJ7A.STY.

2. Specify the page size and margins.

Orientation: Portrait

Paper Type & Dimension: Letter, 8.5 x 11 inches

Sides: Double

Margins, Top and Bottom: 14,00; Right and Left: 12,00

PARAGRAPH TAGS

The following steps assume that you've used a database program to create an importable text file. For more information about this, see the box, "From a Database to a Usable Text File," later in this chapter.

1. Import your data text file.

- While in Frame mode, click on the name of the text file in the Assignment List.

2. Save the chapter.

- Select Save As from the File menu, and give this project a name. Unless you specify otherwise, Ventura gives the chapter the same name as that of the first file you import into it.

TIP

After you've saved your chapter once, be sure to press Ctrl-s every now and again to resave your work.

A DATABASE PRIMER

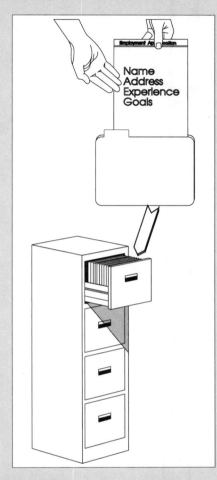

▲ ▲ ▲
You add to a database when you fill out a job application. The little blanks you fill in are fields, the entire form is a record, and a filing cabinet full of applications is a database.

If you haven't worked with a database, you'll need a while to acquire a feel for it—even if you've used word-processing programs. When using a database, you work with fields and records (rather than with words and sentences).

The first thing to understand is the difference between data and information. In this project, we're looking for information about individuals working in a company. We need to know their first and last names, where they live, and a phone number we can use to call them. Each individual item (formally called a "datum")— first name, last name, or phone number, for example—is a piece of the data. We orgranize the data in a meaningful way to derive information about a person.

Field

A field is the basic unit of a database. Each field must have a unique name and can hold only one piece of data. You may think of fields as being much like the questions on an employment application—each with its own prompt for an answer (the field's name) and a blank area to be filled in with data (the field itself). Until you fill in the blank, the field is empty—that is, it holds no data.

Record

A record is a collection of related fields. An example would be a completed application, which is a collection of fields containing data on a particular individual.

Using a database

You can derive meaningful information about a person or group of persons from data, by looking at a complete record or by looking at similar fields from a number of records. For example, by looking up all the employee records where the field named "State" contains "WA" and by noting the name in each, you can know which employees live in Washington. Or say you wanted to create a phone directory containing the names of all the people in a company. You would look through the data in all the employees' employment applications, "pulling out" names, the different parts of residence addresses, and phone numbers. You could also look at the first few letters of each record in the field named "Surname" to organize the names in the database alphabetically. And that's exactly what we've done in this project.

FROM A DATABASE TO A USABLE TEXT FILE

You can use FoxPro's internal report generator to create a quick report. If you need to create a report that includes embedded Ventura commands, you'll need to write a short FoxPro program.

Below, you can look over the program we wrote. Even if you're not a programmer, you can follow its progress by reading the comments (which are to the right of && on each line). The program is a series of instructions that begins with some identifying information, followed by its "working"

parts. You tell the computer the name of a file to use to hold the program's output and what output to include in that file.

A few bits of information will help you understand the report program: A question mark (?) or double question mark (??) is shorthand for "print this." An asterisk (*) as the first character on a line, or a double ampersand (&&) anywhere in a line, tells FoxPro to ignore the rest of that line and to treat it as a comment for the programmer.

```
***********************************************************
* PR_NAMES.PRG
*
*    Program to print names for catalog
*    with embedded Ventura Publisher commands.
*
*    Programmer: Ricardo Birmele
*
*    Variables: None
*
*    Uses: NAMES.DBF
*    Index: NAMES (on SURNAME)
*
***********************************************************
USE names INDEX names                         && file and index to use
set alternate to d:\dtpbd\proj7\nameaddr.txt  && where to send output
set alternate on                              && actually send output
set talk off                                  && turn off record numbers

GO TOP                                         && go to top of
                                               &&    the database file

DO WHILE .NOT. EOF()                           && start a loop
? "@SURNAME = " + TRIM(surname)                && print contents
                                               &&    of this field
? "@NAME = , " + TRIM(first_name)              &&    "    "    "
?? CHR(09)                                      && print a tab character
?? LEFT(phone,3) + "-" + RIGHT(phone,4)        && format and print
                                               &&    the phone number
? TRIM(street)                                 && print contents
                                               &&    of this field
? TRIM(city) + ", " + st + "    " + zip         &&    "    "    "
 SKIP                                          && skip to next record
ENDDO                                          && end the loop

* EOF pr_names.prg *******************
***********************************************************
```

▶ ▶ ▶

This program can be written by using FoxPro's built-in text editor or any editor that will produce an ASCII text file.

3. Modify the body text tag.

- While in Paragraph Tagging mode, click on any paragraph and use the dialog boxes found in the Paragraph menu to give this paragraph the following specifications:

  Font: 10/14 Helvetica

  Alignment: Left, Overall Width: Frame-Wide

4. Create a Surname paragraph tag.

- Highlight one of the last names in your file. They are distinguishable from first names in that they are each a single-word paragraph. Click on Add New Tag and designate it "Surname." Give it the following type specifications:

  Font: 10/14 Helvetica Bold

  Alignment: Left, Overall Width: Frame-Wide

  Spacing Above: 0,06

  Line Break: Before; Keep With Next: No

5. Create a Name paragraph tag.

- Click on a first name/phone number paragraph and call the new tag, "Name." Repeat the preceding steps to give Name these type specifications:

  Font: 10/14 Helvetica Normal

  Alignment: Left, Overall Width: Frame-Wide

  First Line: Indent; Relative Indent: On

  Spacing Above: 0,06

  Line Break: After

  Next Y Position: Beside Last Line of Prev. Para

  Tab Settings: 1 Right at 26,09, shown as ". . ."

We have set the breaks this way so that the first name and phone number will fall on the same line as the surname, and still leave the surname paragraph available to be used by the live headers that appear at the top of each page. (See the sidebar "A Word About Ventura Breaks" later in this chapter.)

6. Create a Head Letter paragraph tag.

- Before each group of names and addresses is a single-letter paragraph that sets each one apart. Because we wanted to keep the database report program simple, we had to add each of these letters manually to the data file output by FoxPro. Click on one of the letters and give it these type specifications:

  Font: 20/26 Times Roman, Bold Italic

  Spacing Below: 1,05

  Alignment: Center, Frame Wide

  Page Break: Before

If you want to minimize the numbers of pages, you can set Page Break to No for the Head Letter paragraph tag. With Page Break set to Before, each time Ventura sees a Head Letter paragraph, it will insert a page break, thus ensuring that a head letter is always at the top of a page.

• Add a double Ruling Line Below to the Head Letter paragraph
  tag.

>   Width: Margin
>
>   Color: Black, Solid
>
>   Space Above Rule 1: 4.00 fractional points
>
>   Height of Rule 1: 0.50 fractional points
>
>   Space Below Rule 1: 02.00 fractional points
>
>   Height of Rule 2: 2.00 fractional points

VENTURA HEADERS...

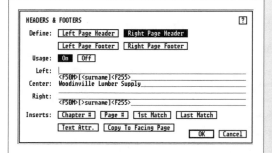

Headers and footers are created by using the same dialog box and
can be created at the same time. To create a Ventura header, click
on Left Page Header (or Right Page Header) and enter the information you want to be printed, and then highlight On in the
Usage selection box.

As you create a header, Ventura invokes its automatically generated Z_HEADER paragraph tag. In formatting the tag, Ventura
incorporates automatic left, center, and right tabs to arrange information on either (or both) of two lines for each type of tag. Anything you enter on the upper Left line, will print above what you
enter on the lower Left line—and both will be reproduced at the
left margin of the header (or footer) frame—unless you specify
otherwise. Information to be printed in the middle or at the right
is handled in a similar way, and you can change the horizontal
position of the tabs.

Ventura makes it easy for you to incorporate a "live head," like
you'll find in a dictionary or telephone book, making it easy for
your readers to orient themselves. You add these much as you do
page numbers—by selecting 1st Match or Last Match. As you do,
Ventura puts a place holder on the line at your cursor position. It's
up to you then to replace the words "tag name" with that of the
paragraph whose contents you want substituted in the live head (or
footer). Later, as Ventura formats each page of your chapter, it will
look for a tag with the same name and takes the contents of that
paragraph and copies it to the header (or footer) of that page only.

In our projects here, we've told Ventura to look for the first *and* last
occurrence of the Surname paragraph tag. With that, Ventura will
look for the first family name and the last family name (the contents
of the first and last Surname paragraph on a page) and place them
into the header on each page, in the correct order and position.

HEADERS AND FOOTERS

This directory uses a two-line header with a one-line footer, each in its own frame. The header frame contains the organization's name on the first line and a running "live header" on the second line (where the contents of the first and last Surname tag on each page are duplicated). The footer frame contains the publication title and a folio for each page; the folio is printed as a word rather than as a digit.

1. Implement your headers and footers.

- Click on the Headers & Footers dialog box in the Chapter menu.

- Define a Right Header by entering the following text on the lines indicated:

  Left (bottom): <F50M>[<SURNAME]<F255D>

  Center (top): Woodinville Lumber Supply

  Right (bottom): <F50M>[>SURNAME]<F255D>

The "<F50M>" before the live head tags cause them to be printed in Helvetica Narrow type. This makes them stand out, without their being too intrusive to the design. The "<F255>" returns the printer to the current default as defined by the Ventura generated Z_HEADER paragraph tag.

...AND FOOTERS

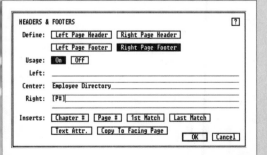

In Ventura, footers can be created at the same time as, or independently of, headers. To create a Ventura footer, click on Left Page Footer (or Right Page Footer) and enter the information in the same way as you do with Ventura headers.

As you are entering "normal" header/footer-type information to be printed, there are other items, such as the current chapter or page number, that you can include. To do so, place your cursor on the line at the position where you want the item to occur, and then click on its selection box at the bottom of the dialog box.

Ventura formats footer text using a built-in Z_FOOTER paragraph tag. Although its type specifications can be different from that of the Z_HEADER tag, the Z_FOOTER tag behaves exactly like its higher-on-the-page counterpart in every other respect.

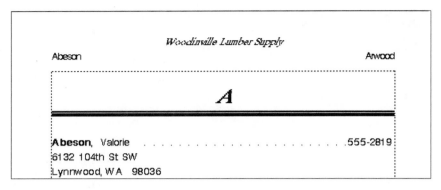

▶ ▶ ▶

The header with live running heads lets the reader know where he or she is within the directory's information.

▶ ▶ ▶

The footer, with its page number, lets the reader know where he or she is within the directory.

- Click on Left Page Header and enter the same information on the same lines as above. **Do not** simply click on Copy to Facing Page as a shortcut. If you do, Ventura will swap the Left and Right line(s), causing them to print the correct information on each page—but backwards.

- In the same way you created the headers for each right page, enter the following information to produce a right footer:

    Center (top): Employee Directory

    Right (top): [P#]

    Rather than typing in directly the page number, you can place your cursor on that line and click on the Page # selection box.

- Because having right- and left-page footers mirror each other is not a problem with this project, you can create a left footer by simply clicking on the Copy To Facing Page selection box.

TIP

Be careful, when you're adding "live headers" or footers, that you enter the correct character to accomplish what you intend. Ventura uses the less-than character (<) to denote first match and uses a greater-than character (>) to denote last match.

2. Size the header and footer frames.

- While in Frame mode, click on the header frame. Use the appropriate dialog boxes to give it the following size and margins.

    Margins, Top: 11,00; Left and Right: 12,00

    Frame Width: 51,00; Frame Height: 14,11

- Click on the footer frame and give it the following size and margins.

  Margins, Top: 3,06; Bottom: 10,00; Left & Right: 12,00

  Frame Width: 51,00; Frame Height: 14,09

3. Print the directory.

- Select the To Print dialog box from the File menu, and send the directory off to your printer.

A WORD ABOUT VENTURA BREAKS

As the reader uses this directory, he or she has no way of knowing the programming "sleight of hand" we used to hide how we achieved the live heads (guide words) while maintaining a smooth format for the names and addresses. The sleight of hand involves two of Ventura's capabilities: Next Y Position breaks and Relative Indent.

The Next Y Position is found in the Breaks dialog box of the Paragraph menu. Next Y Position refers to where the first line of a paragraph should be printed relative to the preceding paragraph. Normally, a paragraph starts on the line after its predecessor. (See graphic, below left.) With Ventura, however, we can specify that it is printed on the same line as that predecessor. (See graphic, below right.)

Relative Indent is an option found in the Alignment dialog box of the Paragraph menu. When it is on, Ventura looks at the last formatted line of a paragraph and notes how long it is. Ventura then indents the first line of the following paragraph an equal amount.

To create the directory, we start with the database report program, where we have it print each Surname as a paragraph on its own. That way, Ventura has a single-word paragraph to use in the live head. Each immediately succeeding line cum paragraph (tagged as a Name paragraph) begins with a comma and a space, followed by the first name and telephone number.

Because we specify the Relative Indent for the Name paragraph On and a Next Y Position beside the last line of the previous paragraph, Ventura formats Name paragraphs to print on the same lines as Surname paragraphs. For that reason, both paragraphs appear to have been initially input in that way—and we have a one-word Surname paragraph to use in our live heads.

```
Bartstown
  Craig . . . . . . . . . . . . . . . . . .555-4231
11546 NW 56th Ct.
Redmond, WA 98053
Bennett
  George . . . . . . . . . . . . . . . . .555-8533
2345 Charles Ave. W
Woodinville, WA 98072
Bietz
  Kathy . . . . . . . . . . . . . . . . . .555-8931
18124 112th Ave
Skykomish, WA 98000
```

```
Bartstown, Craig . . . . . . . . . . . . . . . . .555-4231
11546 NW 56th Ct.
Redmond, WA 98053
Bennett, George . . . . . . . . . . . . . . . . .555-8533
2345 Charles Ave. W
Woodinville, WA 98072
Bietz, Kathy . . . . . . . . . . . . . . . . . . .555-8931
18124 112th Ave
Skykomish, WA 98000
Boller, Donald . . . . . . . . . . . . . . . . . .555-4321
11400 North Tree Bvd
Bothell, WA 98022
```

PROJECT 7B

A Name and Telephone Number Directory

This project is very similar to Project 7A. If you've created the telephone directory with names *and* addresses, you can take a number of shortcuts as you do this name and telephone directory.

1. Start with the directory from Project 7A.

- Select Open Chapter from the File menu, and click on PROJ7A.CHP. Then immediately save it as PROJ7B.CHP.

- Because we're going to make a few changes, it would be best to retain the old style sheet. Create a new style sheet by saving PROJ7A.STY as PROJ7B.STY.

- Remove the Project 7A text file by selecting the Remove File dialog box from the Edit menu. Enter NAMEADDR.DOC on the File Name line and press return.

- Use the Load Text/Picture dialog box to load the name and phone text file, which we've called NAMEPHON.

- Save the new chapter under the name PROJ7B.CHP.

2. Modify two of the old paragraph tags.

- Click on a Surname paragraph. Use the Spacings dialog box to give it no space above. Otherwise, it can retain all its other type specifications.

- Click on a Head Letter paragraph, and give it a space Above of 01,10 and no space Below. Also, turn its double Ruling Line Below off, and its Page Break to No.

3. Print.

- Click on the To Print dialog box from the File menu, indicate which page(s) should be printed and click on OK.

TIP

You can use the Remove File dialog box to remove a file from a frame or from the list of files. The former causes the file's name to be retained in the Assignment List for later use, while the latter eliminates the file's name from the chapter entirely.

▶ ▶ ▶

For interoffice calls, a printed telephone directory is still faster to use than a computer database.

Woodinville Lumber Supply

Abeson   Christenson

A

Abeson, Valorie 555-2819
Abiokovski, Polar 555-8627
Agee, Clyde 555-6411
Anderson, Brad 555-8888
Annerly, Jack 555-9809
Arlston, Lawrence 555-5367
Arujo, Sophie 555-4433
Arwood, Sherman 555-0505

B

Bartstown, Craig 555-4231
Bennett, George 555-8533

THE DATABASE REPORT PROGRAM

Here is a part of the FoxPro program you saw earlier that we used to compile the data for the name and telephone number directory. You'll notice that we had to modify only three lines. The first was the "set alternate to" line, where we changed name of the output file. The second two were where we inserted asterisks on the street and city lines, which made FoxPro ignore the address fields in the database—and therefore those lines do not print. It would be just as quick to reverse the process and use the original program again—the next time we need to make a full name, address, and telephone number directory.

```
**********************************************************
* PR_NAMES.PRG
*
*    Program to print names for catalog
*    with embedded Ventura Publisher commands.
*
**********************************************************
USE names INDEX names                         && file and index to use
set alternate to d:\dtpbd\proj7\namephon.txt  && where to send output
set alternate on                              && actually send output
set talk off                                  && turn off record numbers

GO TOP                                         && go to top of
                                               &&   the database file

DO WHILE .NOT. EOF()                           && start a loop
? "@SURNAME = "  + TRIM(surname)               && print contents
                                               &&   of this field
? "@NAME = , " + TRIM(first_name)              && "    "     "
?? CHR(09)                                     && print a tab character
?? LEFT(phone,3) + "-" + RIGHT(phone,4)        && format and print
                                               &&   the phone number
* ? TRIM(street)                               && print contents
                                               &&   of this field
* ? TRIM(city) + ", " + st + "    " + zip      && "    "     "
 SKIP                                          && skip to next record
ENDDO                                          && end the loop
* EOF pr_names.prg ********************
**********************************
```

THE BACK OF THE BOOK

RESOURCES

Whenever you see an image [you like] in a magazine or newspaper or even on a packet of cereal..., cut it out and keep it in a scrapbook. My own method is to put whatever I find into the book in no particular order, just lightly taped so it can be removed if necessary.... When searching for an idea ..., all sorts of images can be viewed that will start the mind working—and perhaps along different lines from the preconceived.... The brain has a great capacity for putting odd images together that it might not have thought up without this visual stimulus.

—Nigel Holmes,
Designer's Guide to Creating
Charts & Diagrams

Charts

Designer's Guide to Creating Charts & Diagrams by Nigel Holmes (1984, Watson-Guptill, 1515 Broadway, New York, NY 10036)

Created by the art director responsible for the charts and diagrams in *Time* magazine, this book provides carefully organized and accessible background on the various types of charts, suggestions on how to analyze information, and numerous examples and common errors. Particularly useful is the chapter on specific assignments, which takes the reader through the analysis of data and creation of charts for nine different problems. (Some problems have multiple audiences and hence multiple solutions.) Although the book predates desktop publishing's time-saving production tools, its conceptual and analytical approach is not the least bit dated.

Using Charts and Graphs: 1000 Ideas for Visual Persuasion by Jan V. White (1984, R.R. Bowker, 245 West 17th St., New York, NY 10011)

We didn't count, but this book probably does have a thousand ideas. And because the emphasis is more on geometrical than conceptual approaches, many of them can be executed with today's electronic drawing tools. (The book itself does not provide that how-to.)

The Visual Display of Quantitative Information and Envisioning Information by Edward Tufte (1983 and 1990, respectively, Graphics Press, PO Box 430, Cheshire, CT 06410)

Tufte's books demand careful attention but they reward the reader with a fundamental understanding of how words, numbers, and pictures can best be combined to communicate statistical information. The author doesn't believe in making a chart look like a video game; he holds that if the numbers are boring, you've got the wrong numbers. The keys to good information design, he says, are simplicity of design and complexity of data. His historical examples are alternately delightful and obscure; collectively they constitute an impressive catalog of what has been called cognitive art.

Clip Art

Canned Art: Clip Art for the Macintosh (1990, Peachpit Press, 1085 Keith Ave., Berkeley, CA 94708)

Although the title suggests that this is a Macintosh resource, over half of the 15,000 clip art images in this sample book are available in PC formats. A cover page for each of over 35 vendors indicates available formats. Reproduction of images is at about 25 percent of original size. If you use clip art in your publications, this $29.95 digest is an economical purchasing guide to the many clip art packages available.

Dover Pictorial Archive Book Catalog (Dover Publications, 31 East 2nd St., Mineola, NY 11501)

Electronic clip art is fairly expensive; traditional clip art is not. For years, Dover Books has been one of the largest suppliers of public domain (copyright-free) art. Their catalog lists over 300 books, with very few costing more than $10; many of them are less than $5. All you need to do is crop and scale the art and manually paste it onto the camera-ready pages. Permission and additional fee required for publication rights.

Comstock Desktop Photography (Comstock, The Comstock Building, 30 Irving Place, New York, NY 10003)

Comstock Desktop Photography contains 449 professional stock photographs in black-and-white TIFF files (256 shades of gray) for CD-ROM. Compatible with PC and Mac systems. Rights for in-house publications and composites granted with purchase; permission and additional fee required for publication rights.

The Computer Culture and the Future

In addition to being extraordinary tools, computers hold a mirror to some aspects of the culture we live in. As such, they've inspired a number of interesting books by some good and provocative writers.

Computer Lib/Dream Machines by Ted Nelson (revised edition, 1987; Tempus Books, One Microsoft Way, Redmond, WA 98052-6399)

Considered the first cult book of the computer culture, it was first published in 1974, a few months before the announcement of the Altair. The visionary material from the first edition—with its prediction of user-friendly systems, computer-aided instruction, image synthesis, and more—and the new material added to the 1987 edition are served up in small bites in a quirky, nonlinear form that makes a kaleidoscope of the computer and its place in our lives.

The Media Lab: Inventing the Future at MIT by Steward Brand (1987, Viking, 40 West 23rd St., New York, NY 10010)

Apple Fellow Alan Kay has said that "The best way to predict the future is to invent it." And the Media Lab at MIT may well be where the future of publishing, broadcasting, film, and recording is being invented. *Whole Earth Catalog* founder Steward Brand spent several months there, and in addition to providing an in-depth tour of the Media Lab, he offers his view of what it means in the larger media lab that we all live in.

The Soul of a New Machine by Tracy Kidder (paperback edition, 1981; Avon Books, 959 Eighth Ave., New York, NY 10019)

The story of the creation of the Eagle computer is told as a technological and human drama. Wonderfully written (the book won a Pulitzer Prize), it's a very enjoyable way to increase your understanding of computers.

Desktop-Published Classics

A great deal has been written about desktop publishing. The two books listed here simply showed what the technology could do and in the process either inspired or convinced a great many people that this particular emperor had clothes after all.

Whale Song: A Pictorial History of Whaling and Hawaii by MacKinnon Simpson and Robert B. Goodman (1986, Beyond Words Publishing, 112 Meleana Place, Honolulu, HI 96817)

This very beautiful history of nineteenth-century whaling does not in itself have anything to do with desktop publishing, except in demonstrating that the technology could be used for the craft of pictorial storytelling. Not only was this the first coffee-table book created using desktop publishing techniques, but it was produced from 300-dots-per-inch LaserWriter output on a special paper from S.D. Warren (with color separations done traditionally).

When [Media Lab director] Nicholas Negroponte and I originally discussed what this book might be about, he suggested, "It's about quality of life in an electronic age." A few months later he added, "It's a primer for a new life-style." Later still he mentioned, "I was still in my pajamas at ten-thirty this morning after I had been doing Lab work, through e-mail on my computer, for several hours. Maybe what we're talking about is 'The right to stay in your pajamas.'"

—Stewart Brand,
The Media Lab

Zen & The Art of the Macintosh: Discoveries on the Path to Computer Enlightenment by Michael Green (1986, Running Press, 125 South 22nd St., Philadelphia, PA 19103)

You don't need to use a Mac to appreciate this passionately personal exploration of early desktop computer art. A crazy quilt of fantastic bit-mapped graphics and 1980s zen musings, this book is a testimonial to as well as a reflection on the incredible seductiveness of computers.

Graphic Design: Formal and Historical Perspective

Graphic Style from Victorian to Post-Modern by Steven Heller and Seymour Chwast (1988, Harry N. Abrams, 100 Fifth Ave., New York, NY 10011)

A lavishly illustrated review of commercial art (from books to posters to shopping bags), this volume may not relate to your average business publication, but it is glorious to look at and shows how graphic design has interacted with popular tastes ranging from the Victorian to the punk.

The Grid by Allen Hurlburt (1978, Van Nostrand Reinhold, 115 Fifth Ave., New York, NY 10003)

Allen Hurlburt, who was art director of *Look* magazine for many years, provides a brief and useful introduction to the history of grids along with a collection of grids created by top designers for newspapers, books, and magazines.

How to Understand and Use Design and Layout by Alan Swann (1987, North Light Books, 1507 Dana Ave., Cincinnati, OH 45207)

This book is organized as a three-section design course. The first section has the reader work with simple shapes and lines as a way of exploring proportion before bringing type, color, illustration, and photography onto the evolving page. The second section shows the elements of design applied to a wide variety of products (books, magazines, packaging, and posters). And the final section looks at the evolution of the design for specific products, including a print ad, a newsletter, a direct-mail insert, a full-color brochure, and a poster.

Publication Design: A Guide to Page Layout, Typography, Format and Style by Allen Hurlburt (1976, Van Nostrand Reinhold, 115 Fifth Ave., New York, NY 10003)

An illustrated review of significant developments in magazine design from the 1930s to the 1970s, this book covers a lot of ground briefly and well. Geared to the professional designer, the samples reproduced serve as a gallery of photography and art from a graphic design perspective.

Paul Rand: A Designer's Art (1985, Yale University Press, 302 Temple St., Princeton, NJ 06520)

Paul Rand is one of the giants of contemporary graphic design. This book collects several of his essays on design and displays a wide range of his work, including familiar trademarks (IBM, ABC, and Westinghouse), advertisements, and book and magazine covers.

Thirty Centuries of Graphic Design: An Illustrated Survey by James Craig and Bruce Barton (1987, Watson-Guptill, 1515 Broadway, New York, NY 10036)

Brief commentary and lots of reproductions are accompanied by a chronology of people and events for each era. Available in paperback, this is a useful addition to the library for the desktop designer who wants a sense of the history and traditions of graphic design.

In my view a great many well-conceived pieces of design are successful simply because they make full visual and creative use of a limited number of design elements. First, see how well the work develops using one element. Then sparingly introduce the other ingredients, making sure that they do not overwhelm the design. Never use anything for its own sake; always consider and justify its inclusion as a contributor to the overall effect.

—Alan Swann,
How to Understand and
Use Design and Layout

The designer is confronted, primarily, with three classes of material: a) the given—product, copy, slogan, logotype, format, media, production process; b) the formal—space, contrast, proportion, harmony, rhythm, repetition, line, mass, shape, color, weight, volume, value, texture; c) the psychological—visual perception and optical illusion problems, the spectator's instincts, intuitions, and emotions as well as the designer's own needs.

—Paul Rand,
A Designer's Art

Working with Style: Traditional and Modern Approaches to Layout and Typography by Suzanne West (1990, Watson-Guptill Publications, 1515 Broadway, NY, NY 10036)

This is really three books in one. The first two provide overviews of different approaches to designing the printed page—the traditional style, as old as the Rosetta stone and formalized on a foundation of Renaissance aesthetics; and the modern style, which grew out of Gestalt psychology, Bauhaus philosophy, and the Swiss school of graphic design early in this century. Each book is designed in the style it describes, so that you experience the style as you read about it. The third is a workbook with exercises for exploring and applying the information presented earlier.

Graphic Design: Tips and How-To Information

Editing by Design: A Guide to Effective Word-and-Picture Communication for Editors and Designers by Jan V. White (1982, R.R. Bowker, 245 West 17th St., New York, NY 10011)

Jan White has written many books about graphic design. The great benefit of this one is that it focuses on the interaction of words and pictures in a way that tries to bridge the gap between the way editors and graphic designers approach publications. In the desktop publishing environment, where traditional roles are being redefined, this perspective is especially useful.

Graphic Idea Notebook: Inventive Techniques for Designing Printed Pages by Jan V. White (1980, Watson-Guptill, 1515 Broadway, New York, NY 10036)

This book is bursting with ideas for how to treat various design components on the printed page. The material is broken out into usefully informal categories such as getting attention, mug shots, boxes, breaking up text, direction, motion and change, and so on. The book is delightfully written as well as playfully formatted, with easy-to-find ideas. It is virtually all photos, drawings, and geometric shapes, with very direct annotations on using the visual ideas displayed.

Looking Good in Print: A Guide to Basic Design for Desktop Publishing by Roger C. Parker (1990, Ventana Press, PO Box 2468, Chapel Hill, NC 27515)

A good introduction to the general principles of graphic design written for the hands-on desktop publisher who is a novice designer. Particularly useful are the makeover section, showing "before" and "after" versions of different kinds of publications, and the sections showing how the same elements—headlines, text, and illustrations—can be designed into very different-looking pages.

Notes on Graphic Design and Visual Communication by Gregg Berryman (revised edition, 1984; William Kaufmann, Inc., 95 First St., Los Altos, CA 94022)

Slim, inexpensive, and chock-full of useful information, this book is a well-organized collection of notes from the author's 15 years of teaching graphic design. In an age when many books have more white space than substance, this one's a gem.

The Verbum Book of Electronic Page Design by Michael Gosney and Linnea Dayton (1990, M&T Books, 501 Galveston Drive, Redwood City, CA 94063)

The heart of this book is a series of case histories in which different designers describe the development and production of a specific project. All the major page layout programs are represented, but even more useful than the technical how-to is the insight into the design process. You follow one designer fiddling with a piece of paper to develop a folding brochure, another reflecting on the

---

A clear area of white space can be as dramatic as a picture (especially if the picture is mediocre, as many often are). It gives the eye a place to rest. It can be a foil to the text: an "empty" contrast to the "full" areas that thereby makes the full areas appear even fuller. It can help to organize the material on the page. It can tie successive pages together by repetition of identifiable areas. White space, if used well, is the cheapest addition to the publication's roster of weapons.

—Jan White,
Editing by Design

It is not possible to dig a hole in a different place by digging the same hole deeper and bigger.... If a hole is in the wrong place, then no amount of digging is going to put it in the right place. Vertical thinking is digging the same hole deeper; lateral thinking is trying again somewhere else.

—Edward de Bono,
cited in The Design Concept

relative merits of spontaneity and efficiency in computer design, and another demonstrating how his graphic design work is constructed in an architectural way. A gallery section displays work of additional designers accompanied by brief production notes. Other books in the Verbum series focus on PostScript illustration and digital painting.

Inspiration

Design Annuals

Flipping through any of the annual collections of leading work in editorial and advertising graphic design is a good way to stimulate ideas. These books also help you keep a finger on the pulse of the latest trends in typography, layout, illustration, and photography. They include *AIGA Graphic Design*, *Communication Arts Annual*, *Art Directors Annual*, and *Graphis Annual*.

The Design Concept : A Guide to Effective Graphic Communication by Allen Hurlburt (1981, Watson-Guptill, 1515 Broadway, New York, NY 10036)

Beginning with an overview of theories on the creative process, this book provides a useful look at the development of an idea. It is illustrated throughout with examples of leading work in advertising, editorial, and information design. The case histories are presented as recollections from a very impressive cast of designers (Paul Rand, Saul Bass, Brad Thompson, George Lois, Milton Glaser, Herb Lubalin, Lou Dorfsman, and Henry Wolf).

Forget All the Rules About Graphic Design (Including the Ones in This Book) by Bob Gill (1981, Watson-Guptill, 1515 Broadway, New York, NY 10036)

Bob Gill is a graphic designer, illustrator, and film-maker who describes his approach to design as taking ordinary boring problems and redefining them so that they are interesting or unique. This book is a collection of such problems and Gill's solutions to them. The title should give you a pretty good sense of his attitude, except that there are no rules in the book to break, just inventive ideas to inspire you.

Ideas on Design by the Pentagram Group (1986, Faber & Faber, Inc., 50 Cross St., Winchester MA 01890)

Through briefly annotated examples of the work of the Pentagram Group, this collection provides a glimpse into how designers come up with some of their ideas. Among the many examples: The colors and typography of a street sign inspire the sign for a boutique called Street Shoes; the relationship of a university health sciences department and the hospital with which it is affiliated is abstracted into a geometric logo, and a collection of found objects triggers the creation of an alphabet.

Newsletters

Editing Your Newsletter: How to Produce an Effective Publication Using Traditional Tools and Computers by Mark Beach (third edition, 1988; Coast to Coast Books, 1507 Dana Ave., Cincinnati, OH 45207)

This well-balanced guide covers the basic aspects of planning, developing, designing, and producing a newsletter. Chapters on design, typography, and graphics are well illustrated with diverse samples of real and fictional publications, and the chapters on production, printing, and distribution provide useful introductions to these areas. There is very little information about electronic page assembly, which is not a shortcoming in such a useful book, except that the subtitle promises more than it delivers. The Resources section includes lists of newsletter directories, workshops, and awards.

Intuition...encourages the mind to jump away from the unexpected, and helps to produce ideas that are surprises as well as solutions....

If good designers have anything in common, it is that they all seem to be equipped with a subconscious sponge, capable of absorbing a wide and unrelated range of stimuli to be tucked away at the back of the mind for future use. A builder's yard or a factory are as likely to provide a fruitful scrap of inspiration as a book on Islamic calligraphy or a visit to the Louvre. But how did that scrap become part of a design solution? Logic? Intuition? Lateral rationalisation? Maybe thinking by jumping is as close a description as we can get.

—Ideas on Design

When we studied our mailing list, we found 158 households that no longer belong. We pay about half a dollar to print, label, and mail one newsletter. The bad addresses represented $79 per issue—$948 per year. That's almost $1,000 per year we were tossing into the wastebasket.

—anecdote from
Editing Your Newsletter

Paper

Laser Paper Sample Kit (1988, Portico Press, PO Box 190, New Paltz, NY 12561)

This kit provides five sheets each of 14 different white papers for the user to test in his or her laser printer. An accompanying 12-page report is an accessible introduction to paper in general (brightness, opacity, smoothness and so on) and to its use in laser printers. A chart provides specifications for 49 papers suitable for use in laser printers as well as information about available weights, sizes, and matching stock for envelopes, business cards, and so on. Future kits will be devoted to specialty papers (labels, envelopes, and overhead transparencies) and colored papers.

Production and Printing

Getting It Printed: How to Work with Printers and Graphic Arts Services to Assure Quality, Stay on Schedule, and Control Costs by March Beach, Steve Shepro, and Ken Russon (1986, Coast to Coast Books, 2934 Northeast 16th Ave., Portland, OR 97212)

This book covers much of the same ground that the standard production references, such as *Pocket Pal,* do. But as the subtitle suggests, it also offers advice on how to specify and prepare your work, what you can and cannot expect from printing technologies, and how to work with your printer to get the best possible result. It's practical, technical but accessible, and peppered with anecdotes from publishers and printers.

The Graphic Designer's Handbook by Alastair Campbell (revised edition, 1987; Running Press, 125 South 22nd St., Philadelphia, PA 19103)

Originally published in England, this handbook is a reference to printing options and terms, including paper and binding, page imposition, proof marks, copy-fitting tables, halftone screens, and so on. The color pages, which are numerous, include tint charts. Brief introductory chapters focus on the design process.

Graphics Master 4 by Dean Phillip Lem (fourth edition, 1988; Dean Lem Associates, Inc., PO Box 25920, Los Angeles, CA 90025)

This printing reference is as up to date on desktop publishing as any we've seen. The hardcover, spiral-bound format with heavy card stock makes it a pleasure to use, and it includes two essential tools of the trade: a line gauge (calibrated for the 6-picas-per-inch conversion that has been adopted in electronic page layout programs) and a proportion scale for sizing art. Color tint charts are printed on both coated and uncoated stock, with die-cut tint masks (one black and one white) so that you can isolate any tint from the surrounding colors. The typeface display is extensive for a general reference guide, and the character-count guide includes information for Linotype (and hence Adobe), Bitstream, and Varityper systems. It is not inexpensive ($69.50), but it is a valuable reference aid for the serious desktop designer.

Pasteups & Mechanicals: A Step-by-Step Guide to Preparing Art for Reproduction by Jerry Demoney and Susan E. Meyer (1982, Watson-Guptill, 1515 Broadway, New York, NY 10036)

Close-up photographic sequences take you through the techniques of the traditional art department. And although many of these are replaced by your computer (inking rules and rounded corners, for example), many of them are not (scaling, cropping, and silhouetting photographs—even pasting in type corrections).

Before installing paper into your printer tray, lightly "fan" the paper with your fingers to separate each sheet and to discard any of the cut edges (also known as flashing). The goal is to begin with fresh, flat sheets, free of lint or other small debris that could impair printer performance or lead to premature wear on delicate printer parts.
                              —Laser Paper Sample Kit

Use of the term desktop publishing applied to the graphic arts...can be misleading, for the publishing process encompasses much more than is presently available from desktop publishing systems. In addition to typographic composition, page makeup and laser-printed pages, the process of publishing requires the use of multi-color, high-fidelity halftone reproduction..., large volume, high-speed press runs of multi-page signature forms, ability to print on a variety of different paper stocks, different binding and finishing operations, distribution and many other factors.
                              —Dean Phillip Lem
                              Graphics Master 4

When the printing plate is made, the printing image is rendered grease receptive and water repellent, while the non-printing areas are rendered water receptive and ink repellent. On the press the plate is mounted on the plate cylinder which, as it rotates, comes into contact successively with rollers wet by a water or dampening solution, and rollers wet by ink. The dampening solution wets the non-printing areas of the plate and prevents the ink from wetting these areas. The ink wets the image areas which are transfered to the intermediate blanket cylinder. The paper picks up the image as it passes between the blanket cylinder and the impression cylinder.

—Pocket Pal

Pocket Pal: A Graphic Arts Production Handbook (50th Anniversary edition,1989; International Paper Co., 6400 Poplar Ave., Memphis, TN 38197)

An inexpensive and concise guide to the history, process, and language of printing, this has been the standard reference for 50 years. If you have no other reference guide to the world of printing, don't pass up this $6.25 bargain.

Software

Corel DRAW! (COREL Systems Corporation, 1600 Carling Ave., Ottawa, Ontario, Canada, K1Z 8R7)

Corel's premier graphic illustration program CorelDRAW! is rapidly becoming a standard among PC-based desktop publishers. Since its introduction in January 1989, the software has been awarded top marks by many of the major trade publications for its power, speed, and ease of use.

FoxPro (Fox Software, Inc., 118 W. South Boundary, Perrysburg, OH 43551)

FoxPro does everything you would expect database software to do. More importantly, however, it does those things more quickly than most other products. It uses the dBASE programming language, which makes it easy to combine its database strengths with Ventura's formatting muscle.

GoScript (LaserGo, Inc., 9369 Carroll Park Dr., San Diego, CA 92121)

If you don't have Adobe's PostScript, this software is the next best thing. With it, you can take a Ventura chapter printed to file, and output it using a dot-matrix printer. Very handy for on-site prototyping using a laptop printer.

Hotshot Graphics (Symsoft, 444 first St., Los Altos, CA 94022)

Hotshot Graphics is a picture processor for PC Graphics. It allows you to manipulate graphics in much the same way a word processor allows you to manipulate text. We used it to capture, edit, and convert many of the screen images in the Project section of this book.

Softkick Plus (Aristocad, Inc., 1650 Centre Pointe Dr., Milpitas, CA 95035)

If you have an EGA or VGA screen instead of a full-page display, this software is a must. Although it doesn't quite take the place of a full-page display, Softkicker speeds up your Ventura work considerably. Another Aristocad product, VP To The MAX, turns Ventura Publisher into a full-featured word processor.

Style, Grammar, and Usage

The Chicago Manual of Style (thirteenth edition, 1982; The University of Chicago Press, 5801 Ellis Ave., Chicago, IL 60637)

In addition to setting forth rules for proper punctuation, use of numbers, tables, mathematics, references, notes, and bibliographies, this widely used reference provides an overview of the entire publishing process, from securing rights and permissions through design and typography to printing and binding. The 1982 edition begins to reflect the impact of technology on the editing process, although it stops short of desktop publishing.

The Elements of Style by William Strunk, Jr. and E.B.White (third edition, 1979; Macmillan Publishing Co. Inc., 866 Third Ave., New York, NY 10022)

Of all the many books on style, this is the most universally embraced classic. It is a simple, straightforward model of the lessons it imparts.

If the student doubts that style is something of a mystery, let him try rewriting a familiar sentence and see what happens. Any much-quoted sentence will do. Suppose we take "These are the times that try men's souls." Here we have eight short, easy words, forming a simple declarative sentence. The sentence contains no flashy ingredient such as "Damn the torpedoes!" and the words, as you see, are ordinary. Yet in that arrangement they have shown great durability; the sentence is almost into its third century.

—The Elements of Style

The Transitive Vampire: A Handbook of Grammar for the Innocent, the Eager, and the Doomed by Karen Elizabeth Gordon (1984, Times Books, 201 East 50th St., New York NY 10022)

This entertaining and delightfully unorthodox guide uses odd and whimsical words, characters, and illustrations to beguile you into understanding the parts of a sentence and how to put them together properly.

Type

Desktop Publishing Type & Graphics by Deke McClelland and Craig Danuloff (1987, Harcourt Brace Jovanovich, 124 Mt. Auburn St., Cambridge, MA 02238)

This volume serves as an annotated type spec book for the faces available for desktop publishing through 1987, and as a visual reference to the appearance of lines, screens, fountains, and patterns at various resolutions in the desktop publishing environment. It includes directories for Symbol, Dingbats, Cairo, Mobile, some foreign-language and notation fonts. Chapters on point size, spacing, leading, and line length provide visual aids to understanding the interaction of these aspects of type.

Font & Function (Adobe Systems, 1585 Charleston Road, PO Box 7900, Mountain View, CA 94039)

In addition to displaying the fonts that they sell, Adobe's oversize type catalog is full of information and ideas about using type. And you can get it free by calling 1-800-29-ADOBE.

Herb Lubalin: Art Director, Graphic Designer and Typographer by Gertrude Snyder and Alan Peckolick (1985, American Showcase, 724 5th Ave., New York, NY 10019)

Graphic designer Herb Lubalin brought a new meaning to typographic design. This is a loving tribute and testimonial to his talent by colleagues. It is a book devoted entirely to Lubalin's designs, from logos to typefaces to magazines. If you are the least bit intrigued by letterforms, the lifework of this designer will delight and inspire you.

Inversions by Scot Kim (1981, Byte Books, 70 Main St., Peterborough, NH 03458)

Computer programmer and artist Scot Kim has taken ordinary words and rendered them with a magician's sense of visual trickery. Some words read the same right side up and upside down, some words are hidden inside their opposites, some repeat into infinity. Although the book is more likely to be classified as wordplay than typography, it is a delightful way to learn about letterforms, symmetry, and visual perception.

A Manual of Comparative Typography: The Panose System by Benjamin Bauermeister (1988, Van Nostrand Reinhold, 115 Fifth Avenue, New York, NY 10003)

The premise of the PANOSE system is that type, like trees and birds, can be identified by noting special features. The result is a type specimen book in which distinctive features of the letters of each face included are circled. Whether or not you use the system itself, the visual display can be extremely useful for educating your eye to the nuances of type. Although the book is not specific to desktop publishing, it's interesting to note that the author is the technical support manager at Aldus Corporation.

MacTography Type Sampler (1990, Publishing Solutions, Inc., 326-D North Stonestreet Ave., Rockville, MD, 20850)

A DTP type specimen book, this looseleaf volume displays more than 2800 PostScript fonts from more than 30 manufacturers, for Macintosh and IBM-compatible computers. For each typeface, a complete character set is shown in 24-point type followed by a paragraph set 10/12 justified and/or a line of 24- or 36-point display type and a line showing the range from 4 to 36 points. The initial cost is $75, with an update available for $80.

Typographic Communications Today by Edward M. Gottschall (1989, The MIT Press, 55 Hayward St., Cambridge, MA 02142)

An in-depth look at the evolution of typographic design in this century, this book includes samples of work by all the great names in the relatively brief history of graphic design—from El Lissitzky and Jan Tschichold to Paul Rand, Herb Lubalin, and Lou Dorfsmann—along with opinions they've expressed in speeches, articles, and interviews over the years. Chapters on typographic milestones classify over 200 typefaces in 9 basic categories, with a complete alphabet of upper- and lower-case letters for each face and some with notes on their designs. This lavish, oversize book—it measures 10-3/4 by 14-1/2—will set you back the cost of a good desk accessory, but you get more than 900 illustrations, 500 of them in color.

Typography & Typesetting: Type Design and Manipulation Using Today's Technology by Ronald Labuz (1988, Van Nostrand Reinhold, 115 Fifth Ave., New York, NY 10003)

A very readable overview of the history, technology, and aesthetics of typography, this book is well illustrated, well designed, and thoughtfully put together. A wide range of sample documents includes pages from newspapers, books, magazines, and advertising.

Ventura Publisher

Desktop Power Series (New Riders Publishing, PO Box 4846, Thousand Oaks, CA 91360)

This is a series of books that contain examples of Ventura Publisher style sheets. Each sample style sheet incorporates all the paragraph tag specifications necessary to format it, as well as illustrations of how the example will look when it is printed. Included in the series are such titles as, "Style Sheets for Business Documents," "Style Sheets for Newsletters," and "Style Sheets for Technical Documents."

Ventura: The Complete Reference by Marilyn Holt and Ricardo Birmele (1989, Osborne/McGraw-Hill, 2600 Tenth St., Berkeley, CA 94710)

This book is a useful deskside reference volume for general users of Ventura Publisher. Its three sections cover all aspects of Ventura, from the basics to working with publications composed of several chapters, as well as the Professional Extensions. An Alphabetical Reference explains each command and dialog box option.

Mastering Ventura, by Matthew Holtz (second edition, 1989, SYBEX Inc., 2021 Challenger Drive, Alameda, CA 94501)

This is an easy-to-use tutorial that helps to decipher Ventura's sometimes arcane features. Because it provides information missing from Ventura's software manuals, this book is a must-have for the serious Ventura user.

When a computer unit is making end-of-line and hyphenation and justification decisions, it counts the number of spacebands (...the spaces between words). The width of each spaceband is determined by dividing the amount of available space by the total number of spacebands in a particular line. The amount of actual space taken up by a spaceband will therefore vary from line to line.... Thus, if five spacebands are regularly used for a paragraph indent, the indent will vary from paragraph to paragraph because the spacebands will be larger in some lines, smaller in others.... A general rule to keep in mind is that whenever you type two successive spacebands, you are making an error.

—Ronald Labuz
Typography & Typesetting

Magazines and Newsletters

There are a great many magazines covering both the computer field and the field of graphic design—far too many to describe even briefly in these pages. *PC Magazine, PC World,* and *BYTE* are among the many that keep technology-hungry users up to date on the latest products. *Art Direction, Communication Arts,* and *Print* display the best editorial and advertising work in this country, and *Graphis* is a source for international coverage. The following publications are of special interest to people working in desktop publishing.

Publish! (PCW Communications, 501 Second St., San Francisco, CA 94107)

With its clear focus on desktop publishing tools and process, *Publish!* is a useful source not only for information about the technology but also for insight into how organizations are using it and coping with the good, the bad, and the uncertain. It speaks with equal success to designers making the transition from traditional to desktop production and to businesses of all kinds which, as a result of this technology, find themselves increasingly involved in publishing concerns. Monthly, $39.90 per year.

Step-by-Step Electronic Design (Dynamic Graphics, 6000 N. Forest Park Drive, Peoria, IL 61614)

This newsletter lets you sit by the side of professionals to see how they combine the art and mechanics of electronic design and illustration. It covers a wide variety of projects and software, is clearly written and illustrated, with six to eight color pages in each issue. It also includes excellent columns on typography and high-resolution output. Monthly, $48 per year.

Verbum: Journal of Personal Computer Aesthetics (Verbum, PO Box 15439, San Diego, CA 92115)

This well-produced gallery of computer art explores desktop technology's leading edge, not only in the art it displays but in the production of the magazine as well. In addition to print, it covers the video-multimedia-hyper-media spectrum, acknowledging that we're fast dissolving the distinctions that gave us these labels in the first place. The journal includes reviews of art-related hardware and software and a much-needed "Against the Grain" column, which cuts through some of the hype surrounding the electronic marketplace. For sample pages, see the Magazine section of Chapter 6. Quarterly, $24 per year.

Some [Linotronic] service bureaus... insist that you send your system file and a collection of the font files you've used, or at least a detailed list of all the font files you've used.... You may also have to supply TIFF...files for the graphics included in your pages. That's because the page layout file doesn't include the graphic elements themselves; instead it includes a command to get and print each graphic component at the appropriate point in the printing process. If the TIFF...file isn't on the disk you supply to the service bureau, it won't be available when it's called and...you may end up with a rough bitmap or a blank box in place of your detailed illustration or scanned image.

—Steve Hannaford,
Step-by-Step Electronic Design

GLOSSARY

Abandon A sort of "multiple undo" command on Ventura's File menu that lets you return to the last saved version of your document.

alignment The placement and shape of type relative to the margins. See also *centered, flush left, flush right, justified, ragged right,* and *wraparound text.*

alley The space between two columns of text.

ascender The portion of a lowercase letter, such as b or f, that rises above the x-height.

ASCII An acronym for "American Standard Code for Information Interchange," the form in which text-only files are stored. These files include all characters, tabs, and carriage returns but not character and paragraph formatting such as italic, boldface, hanging indents, and so on.

Assignment List The list of paragraph tag names, file names, or text attributes that appears in the Side-Bar at the left of the computer screen.

Auto-Numbering A dialog box available on the Chapter menu that allows you to automatically number a sequence of similarly tagged paragraphs.

bad break A line break that is visually jarring, such as a page that begins with the suffix "ing" or a column that ends with a single word. See also *orphan* and *widow.*

base page The underlying frame, automatically created by Ventura, that is found on each Ventura page. It can be manipulated in the same manner as a user-created frame.

baseline An imaginary line on which the letters in a line of type sit. The baseline aligns with the bottom of the x-height of the characters, and descenders of letters such as g and p drop below the baseline.

Big First Char A first letter set in enlarged and sometimes decorative type for graphic emphasis. This facility is available by selecting the Special Effects dialog box from the Paragraph menu.

bit-mapped The representation of a character or graphic as a series of square dots or pixels that sometimes print with jagged edges. See also *paint-type graphics.*

bleed art Any photo, illustration, or tint that runs off the edge of the page.

blurb Text that summarizes an article, usually set smaller than the headline and larger than the running text. Sometimes used interchangeably with "breakout."

body text The main text, also called body copy or running text, usually set in 9- to 12-point type in continuous paragraphs.

border A printing frame around text, graphics, or an entire page. Borders range from simple hairline rules to decorative and thematic graphic elements.

breakout A sentence excerpted from the body copy and set in large type, used to break up running text and draw the reader's attention to the page. Also called a pull quote or blurb.

bullets Dots or other single characters used to designate items in a list.

> **TIP**
>
> Unless you specify a specific Inter-Line space, Ventura will insert a value that is 120% of the current paragraph tag. You can calculate the value by multiplying the type size by 1.2, or keep a chart handy:
>
> | Type size | Default Inter-Line | |
> |-----------|------------|--------|
> | 6 point | 1 point | 6/7 |
> | 7 point | 1.5 points | 7/8.5 |
> | 8 point | 1.5 points | 8/9.5 |
> | 9 point | 2 points | 9/11 |
> | 10 point | 2 points | 10/12 |
> | 11 point | 2 points | 11/13 |
> | 12 point | 2.5 points | 12/14.5|
> | 13 point | 2.5 points | 13/15.5|
> | 14 point | 3 points | 14/17 |

TIP

You can automatically center text vertically in a frame by opening the Paragraph menu, choosing the Alignment dialog box, and selecting Middle Vertical Alignment.

TIP

To turn a chapter you've already created into a template, open that chapter and save it under a new name using the Save As option from the File menu. Then remove from it all the text and graphic files that you won't need to reuse each time. Finally, resave the template chapter using the Save option from the File menu.

byline The name of the author of an article.

callout A label that identifies part of an illustration.

camera-ready Photographs, art, and complete pages in a form that the printer can photograph for making printing plates.

cap height The height of a capital letter in a given font and size.

caption The text describing a photograph or illustration.

center axis The imaginary center line through a page, a text block, or a piece of art.

centered Aligned along a center axis.

chapter The basic unit of a publication created in Ventura. It is made up of all the imported text and graphic files, combined with text and art created within Ventura, whose placement and format are defined within an ASCII text file with a .CHP filename extension.

character An individual letter or symbol.

clip art Public domain art, either in books or on disks, that you can use free of charge and without credit in a publication.

clipboard An electronic holding place for the most recent text or graphic cut from a Ventura frame or chapter. Ventura maintains three clipboards; one each for entire frames, text, or graphic objects. Whatever is on the Clipboard can be pasted into the current document. Note, however, that when you shut down, whatever is on the clipboard is lost.

column guides Nonprinting frame boundaries that help you visualize the margins of text that you type or import. You can display column guides through the Show/Hide Column Guides command on the Options menu.

column rules Thin vertical rules separating two columns of type.

Column Snap A command on Ventura's Options menu that causes text and graphics frames being moved or placed to snap to the nearest column guide.

condensed type Type in which the individual character is narrower than normal, without any change in the height.

continued line A line of text indicating the page on which an article continues or the carryover line on the subsequent page that identifies the story being continued. Also called a jumpline.

copy-fitting Editing text to fit a specified space.

copyright Ownership of a work by the writer, artist, photographer, or publisher.

counter The white space inside rounded letters such as a, e, and p.

crop To trim a graphic to fit a space without reducing the size of the graphic.

crop marks Intersecting lines indicating where a page is to be trimmed. Ventura's automatic crop marks will print only if the paper on which you are printing is larger than the page size you have selected.

cropping tool A small hand-shaped cursor that appears when you crop images within a graphic frame.

crossbar The shape of Ventura's Frame mode cursor.

deck A line following the headline that gives more information about a newsletter, magazine, or newspaper story. Also called a tagline.

cursor keys The set of four keys that can move the cursor in the directions indicated by the arrows on the keys: up, down, right, or left.

default A preset value or option that is used unless you specify otherwise.

descender The portion of a lowercase letter, such as g or y, that drops below the baseline of the type.

deselect To turn off a command by clicking on it when it is currently selected. Also to cancel the selection of text and graphics in the publication window by clicking elsewhere on the page.

dialog box A box displayed on the screen that enables you to select or specify options and values.

digitize To convert an image into a series of dots stored by the computer so that the image can be manipulated and placed in publications.

dingbat A decorative or symbolic device used to separate items on the page or to denote items on a list.

discretionary hyphen A hyphen inserted manually by typing Ctrl-Hyphen. A discretionary hyphen shows on-screen as a small box only when you activate Show Tabs & Return, and it prints only if it is needed to break a word at the end of a line.

display type Large type, often boldface, used for headlines, breakouts, and other attention-getting text.

double-sided A page that is printed on both sides of the paper when you select Sides: Double in the Page Layout dialog box (available from the Chapter menu). See also *single-sided* and *facing pages*.

download To send printer fonts from your computer to your printer. You can let Ventura automatically download a font each time your use it, or (to save time) you can manually download a font. Fonts that you download manually remain in the printer's memory until you turn off the printer.

downloadable fonts Individual fonts that you can buy and install in your desktop-publishing system.

dpi Dots per inch.

drag To hold down the mouse button while you move the pointer to a new location on the screen.

drag-place To drag the mouse diagonally, defining the width of a graphic or text frame before you place it.

draw-type graphics See *object-oriented graphics*.

drop cap An enlarged initial letter that drops below the first line of body text. See also *stick-up cap*.

dummy A term that means different things in different organizations. It can be a rough preliminary sketch of a publication or story, an early proof with type and rough art in place, or a mock-up of an entire publication.

ellipsis Three dots (...) used to indicate an incomplete thought or that text has been deleted from a quote. To achieve a properly spaced ellipsis, press and hold Alt-Shift as you type 193 using the keyboard number pad. You can embed an ellipsis by inserting <193> into your document's text file.

em dash A dash the size of an em space, inserted by typing Ctrl-].

em space A typographic unit equal to the point size of the type being used. For 10-point type, an em space would be 10 points. To insert an em space in Ventura, press Ctrl-Shift-M .

Encapsulated PostScript (.EPS) A file format that enables you to print line art with smooth (rather than jagged) edges and to see and resize the graphic on-screen as it will print. The .EPS files are created by Ventura when you print to a file using a PostScript width table. (Ventura appends its default file extension of .C00 to such files.) These images can be printed only on PostScript-compatible printers. The .EPS files produced by graphic drawing programs (such as Corel Draw or Illustrator) can be directly imported into a Ventura chapter.

en dash A dash the size of an en space, inserted by typing Ctrl-[.

en space A space half as wide as an em space, inserted by pressing Ctrl-Shift-N. In this Glossary, the space between each term and its definition is an en space.

face The name of a typeface, such as Times Roman or Helvetica.

facing pages Two pages that face each other in a printed publication. In Ventura, you can select Sides: Double in the Page Layout dialog box on the Chapter menu. You can select the Facing Pages view from the View menu to see facing pages together on the screen.

figure space A space as wide as one number in the current font size.

filename extension Three characters to the right of the period that complete a DOS filename.

fill A pattern or texture inside a rectangle or other closed shape. Ventura has no built-in fill patterns (other than percent gray fills), but you can import graphics with fills from other programs.

Fill Attribute A dialog box on the Graphic menu that allows you to define a percent gray fill for a graphic object drawn using Ventura's built-in graphics tools.

flush Aligned or even with, as in flush left or flush right text.

flush left Aligned along the left edge or margin.

flush right Aligned along the right edge or margin.

fold marks Dotted or dashed lines on camera-ready art that indicate where to fold the printed piece.

folio The page number. It may or may not correspond to Ventura's internal page numbering scheme.

font In desktop publishing, sometimes used interchangeably with "face" to refer to the entire family of letters of a particular shape or design, such as Helvetica. In traditional typesetting, font refers only to one size and style of a given typeface, such as 10-point Helvetica roman or 12-point Helvetica bold.

font metric A list of character widths and heights for a particular font that is stored in a file.

footer See *running foot.*

format The overall appearance of a publication, including page size, paper, binding, length, and page-design elements such as margins, number of columns, treatment of headlines, and so on.

formatting Type and paragraph specifications that are applied in a word-processing or page layout program.

for position only A photocopy or photostat of a piece of art pasted in place on the camera-ready page to indicate the position of the actual art that is to be stripped in by the printer. Usually written as FPO.

TIP

Ventura employs different filename extensions for the files with which it works. For example, Ventura uses .CHP for chapter files, .CAP for text capture files, .PUB for Ventura Publications, .INF for its configuration information file, .IMG for image files that have been translated into Ventura's internal GEM format, and .STY for style sheet files.

TIP

When you want to force Ventura to redraw its screen—for example, when it has become cluttered with text-editing changes—press Esc.

TIP

Sometimes, when you click on a frame that overlays another frame, its handles don't appear. That's because Ventura may be confused as to which frame you mean to manipulate. If you press Ctrl as you click on the frame, Ventura cycles among all possible frames at that location. You can perform successive clicks until the frame you need to manipulate is active, with its handles showing.

frame A rectangle used to hold a graphic object or a text file. Each underlying page in a Ventura chapter is a frame.

Frame Setting mode One of four Ventura modes. In this mode, you create and modify the dimensions and properties of frames into which you import text or graphic images.

galley Traditionally, proofs of type before it is arranged on the page; used for proofreading and layout. (The term derives from the long, shallow metal trays used to hold metal type after it had been set.) In desktop publishing, you may still want to print galleys to the specified column width in your page layout program for proofreading.

gatefold A paper fold in which one or two sides of an oversize page fold in toward the middle of the sheet.

Gothic-style typefaces Sans serif typefaces.

Graphic Drawing mode One of four Ventura modes. In this mode, you create images using Ventura's built-in graphic drawing tools.

greeking Simulating text as gray bars in order to speed screen display (an option available through Ventura's Set Preferences command). Also used to refer to dummy Latin text to show the look of a document without the actual words.

grid A series of vertical and horizontal rules used in the design process to determine placement of text and graphics on the page.

gutter The space between two facing pages. Sometimes used to refer to the space between two columns of text.

hairline rule A very thin typographic rule. In desktop publishing, the width of a hairline rule varies depending on the resolution of the printer. To create a hairline rule in Ventura, give the rule a height of 0.25 fractional points.

halftone The representation of a continuous-tone photograph or illustration as a series of dots that look like gray tones when printed. Also called a screened halftone because traditionally the original image is photographed through a finely ruled screen, the density of which varies depending on the printer's capabilities. In desktop publishing, photographs can be screened during scanning.

handles Used in Ventura to refer to the eight small solid rectangles that surround a selected graphic.

hanging indent A paragraph style in which the left margin of the first line extends beyond the left margin of subsequent lines. To create a hanging indent in Ventura, define the First Line as an Outdent in the Paragraph menu Alignment dialog box.

header See *running head*.

headline The title of an article or story.

I-beam The shape Ventura's pointer assumes when you select the Text Editing mode.

image A graphics file in which is stored a graphic that is made up of a bit-mapped image. Pictures formatted as TIFF and PC-Paintbrush .PCX images are examples of bit-mapped files. See also *line art*.

image area The area inside the page margins. Some page elements, such as page-number markers, are placed outside the image area.

imagesetter An output device, such as the Linotronic, that produces high-resolution pages from desktop-generated files.

TIP

When you want to change the specifications for a single paragraph to body text, you don't have to change to Paragraph Tagging mode. Simply click the text tool anywhere in the paragraph, and press F10. That is Ventura's default function key assignment for the Body Text paragraph tag. You can change that assignment, if you wish. You can also assign an already defined paragraph tag name to any function key, making it available for tagging in Text Editing mode.

TIP

To kill a widow when a one-line caption or headline runs over, try changing the alignment to justified. Be sure to check the printout to determine if the justified spacing is acceptable.

TIP

Many service centers that provide Linotronic output base their page rate on a maximum printing time, such as 8 minutes per page. Anything beyond that time is charged as overtime. For very complex pages, some service centers recommend creating a PostScript file of your document. The procedure for making a PostScript file is to Print to a Filename, using a PostScript .WID file, and assigning .EPS to the resulting file (rather than to Ventura's default .C00).

insertion point A blinking vertical bar indicating where the next text block will be typed or pasted. The position of the insertion point is set by clicking the I-beam on the page while in Text Editing mode.

Inter-Line spacing The space between the baseline of one line and the baseline of the line below it.

italic type Type with letters that slant toward the right, often used for display text and captions. See also *oblique type*.

jaggies The stairstepping effect of bit-mapped art and type created by diagonal lines in a technology that is based on square pixels.

jumpline See *continued line*.

justified Type that is flush, or even, on both the right and left margins.

kerning The process of adjusting the space between characters, generally done only in headlines and other display type. To remove space between letters (while in Text Editing mode), highlight the letters and press Shift-Left Arrow. To add space, highlight the letters and press Shift-Right Arrow.

kicker A phrase preceding a headline that provides information about the story.

landscape A horizontal page orientation that is wider than it is tall.

layout The arrangement of text and graphics on a page.

leader A rule, often dotted, that moves the eye from a callout or label to the part of the illustration it describes.

leading The distance from the baseline of one line of text to the next, measured in points. See also *Inter-Line Spacing*.

letterspacing The amount of space between letters. You can control letterspacing by using the Paragraph Typography dialog box on the Paragraph menu.

Linotronic A PostScript-compatible output device that can print files created on a desktop system at resolutions up to 2540 dots per inch.

line art A graphics file where the image is made up of discrete, mathematically defined objects. See also *image*.

Line Attribute A dialog box from the Graphic menu that allows you to modify the line style of graphics created in Ventura. See also *Fill Attribute*.

line break In Ventura, line break specifications are used to position paragraphs vertically relative to each other.

Line Snap A command on Ventura's Options menu that causes text and graphics frames being moved or placed to snap to the nearest baseline of the current body text specification.

lpi Lines per inch.

logotype A company, product, or publication name designed as a distinctly recognizable unit.

margin The distance from the edge of the paper to the image area occupied by text and graphics.

masthead Traditionally, the listing of staff, ownership, and subscription information for a periodical. Masthead is sometimes used to refer to the typographic treatment of the publication name on the cover, although this is more accurately called a nameplate.

measure The length of a line of type, traditionally expressed in picas.

mechanical Traditionally, a piece of artboard with type galleys, line art, and "for-position-only" photostats in place and with tissue overlays marked for color. In electronic publishing, a mechanical is the final camera-ready page, either from a laser printer or an imagesetter, with position-only stats keyed to flat art that is to be stripped in by the printer. Also called a keyline, pasteup, or camera-ready page.

menu A list of commands that appears when you point to any of the items listed just above the Ventura screen work area (Edit, View, Chapter, Graphic, and so on).

menu bar The area at the top of the screen containing menu names.

modular layout A format in which different elements on a page or spread are designed as self-contained units.

monospacing Letterspacing that is the same for all characters regardless of their shape or width. Traditional typewriter characters are monospaced. See also *proportional spacing*.

nameplate The typographic design of a publication's name as it appears on the cover of the publication.

negative leading A type specification in which there is less space from baseline to baseline than the size of the type itself (for example, 40-point type with 38-point leading). Negative leading is often used with larger type sizes set in all caps in order to tighten up the text unit.

nonbreaking space Space inserted between two words so that they cannot be separated by a line break.

object-oriented graphics Graphics created as a series of mathematically defined curves and lines. They can be resized without causing distortion or moiré patterns. Also called draw-type graphics. See also *line art*.

oblique type A slanted style of a roman typeface. The letters, for the most part, maintain their original forms except for the slant, whereas italic letters have a different shape from their roman counterparts. See also *italic type*.

orphan The opening line of a paragraph isolated at the bottom of a column or page, separated from the rest of the paragraph.

outside margin The space between the outside trim and the text.

overline A brief tag, over a headline, that categorizes a story. Also called a kicker or an eyebrow.

page layout The size, orientation, number of pages, and margins for a document; specified in Ventura's Page Size & Layout dialog box.

page view The amount of the page you can see on the screen, which varies with the size of your monitor and the view selected from Ventura's View menu. The choices are Reduced, Normal (1x), or Enlarged (2x) view. You can also employ a Facing Pages view if you have specified double-sided pages in the Page Layout dialog box from the Chapter menu.

paint-type graphics Graphics represented by square dots or pixels, which can be individually manipulated on-screen. These graphics may be distorted or lose resolution when resized. See also *bit-mapped*.

Paragraph Tagging mode One of four Ventura modes. In this mode, you define and apply typographical attributes to individual paragraphs.

pasteup Traditionally, the process of assembling mechanicals by pasting galleys and line art in place. In desktop publishing, traditional pasteup has largely been replaced by electronic page assembly in Ventura and other page

Resizing paint-type graphics and scanned images sometimes produces moiré patterns and other distortions. To avoid this problem, enter a frame width and height in the Sizing & Scaling dialog box that is an exact multiple of the images' original size.

layout programs. But if your publication is oversize, or if you have an existing logo or position prints for art to be stripped in by the printer, you may still need to do some pasteup for camera-ready pages.

perspective The representation of three-dimensional objects on a flat plane as they appear to the eye.

pica A traditional typographic measurement, composed of 12 points. A pica is actually equal to a little less than 1/6 inch, but in desktop publishing you will generally see it expressed as 1/6 inch.

PICT format A Macintosh file format for saving object-oriented graphics.

picture window A rectangle that indicates the position and size of art to be stripped in by the printer.

pixel Short for "picture element." It is the smallest dot or unit on a computer screen. The clarity of screen resolution depends on the number of pixels per inch on the monitor.

placeholder A frame that will hold text or graphics that you leave in place in an electronic template so that you can later place, paste, or type new items over the placeholder and retain the same spacing relative to other elements on the page.

point The basic measurement of type. There are 12 points to a pica, and 1 point equals about 1/72 inch.

pointer The icon that moves on the screen as you move the mouse. The shape of the pointer depends on which mode is active.

point size The distance from the highest ascender to the lowest descender. See also *point*.

portrait A vertical orientation for pages or photographs. See also *landscape*.

PostScript A page description language developed by Adobe Systems and used by many laser printers and high-resolution typesetters. It is as close to a standard as there is in desktop publishing at this writing.

printer font A mathematical description of every character in a font, which enables a printer to print characters in any size at the best resolution possible on that printer.

Most VGA screens won't display custom letter spacing accurately enough for a smaller value to be noticed. Therefore, it's usually better to set Ventura's on-screen kerning threshold value to more than 18 points. This will also speed up your screen's refresh rate.

printer port The place where a printer connects to a computer. It can be either a parallel printer port (where data communcation occurs one byte at at time) or a serial printer port (where data is communicated in a serial stream of bits). Most laser printers use serial ports to communicate with computers.

proofread To check typeset material for spelling, punctuation, alignment of elements, and other details and to be sure that corrections have been made properly. Standard proofreading marks can be found in many printing reference guides, style manuals, and dictionaries.

proportional spacing Letterspacing that is proportional to the shape of a letter. Computer typefaces are proportional, with the m and the w, for example, taking up more space than the i and the l. See also *monospacing*.

proportion wheel A tool used to calculate the percentage of enlargement or reduction of a piece of art to fit the space specified on a page.

publication A collection of Ventura chapters that can be printed as a whole. For example, a book, with each of its chapters formatted as a Ventura chapter, can be collected, organized, and printed as a Ventura publication.

pull quote See *breakout*.

TIP

To import new text into a story you've already placed into a frame, set the insertion point by clicking the text tool where you want to add the new text. Choose Load Text/ Picture from the File menu, and click on the Destination: Text Cursor option. Then click OK and indicate which file is to be imported. Ventura inserts the new text file at the insertion point and forces all subsequent text farther down in the existing text frame(s).

TIP

If you become impatient with moving the cursor to access commands that you need to use over and over again, here are some handy shortcuts.

For this command...	Use...
Hide/Show Side-bar	Ctrl-W
Hide/Show Tabs	Ctrl-T
Reduced View	Ctrl-R
Normal View	Ctrl-N
Enlarged View	Ctrl-E
Activate Frame mode	Ctrl-U
Activate Paragraph mode	Ctrl-I
Activate Text mode	Ctrl-O
Activate Graphic mode	Ctrl-P
Go to page	Ctrl-G
Save	Ctrl-S

ragged right Text alignment that is even or flush on the left margin and uneven on the right.

RAM An acronymn for "Random Access Memory." This is where the computer stores information temporarily while you're working with it. If you lose power or shut down before saving to disk, whatever is in RAM at the time is lost.

recto The right-hand page.

repeating frame A dialog box available from the Frame menu. It allows you to duplicate a frame (with its contents) on every, or each right or left, page in a Ventura chapter. Repeating frames are useful when formatting complex headers or footers or when placing an identical graphic image on every page.

registration The alignment of two of more elements, such as a color tone within a box, so that they appear seamless.

resolution The clarity or fineness of detail visible on-screen or in the final printout, expressed as dots per inch. In printed material, the resolution is dependent on the printer's capacity, which in the current desktop technology ranges from 300 dots per inch in most laser printers to 2540 dpi in Linotronic 300 imagesetters.

reverse White letters or rules against a black or color background.

ROM An acronymn for "Read Only Memory." ROM is where the computer stores permanent system information. Because data is permanently burned into ROM chips, their data can be recalled and used any time the computer is powered up.

Roman-style typefaces Typefaces with serifs.

roman type Vertical-style type, as opposed to italic or oblique. In Ventura's type style options, roman type is called Normal; in some word-processing programs, it is called Plain.

rounded-corner tool The tool used in Ventura's Graphic mode to draw squares and rectangles with rounded corners.

rules Lines in typography, measured in points.

runaround text See *wraparound text.*

running foot A line at the bottom of the page with information similar to that in a running head.

running head A line at the top of the page that helps orient the reader within a document, which may include such information as title, author, chapter, issue date, and page number.

running text See *body text.*

sans serif A typeface without finishing strokes at the ends of the characters. (From the French *sans,* meaning "without.")

scale To calculate the degree of enlargement or reduction of a graphic so that it fits the space allotted for it. A proportion wheel is often used to scale art.

scanner A hardware device that reads information from a photograph or other piece of art into a collection of dots that can be stored as a bit-mapped file on a hard disk, manipulated in various software programs, and placed electronically in a page layout program.

screen A tint, a percentage of either black or a second color, behind text or art. Also called a tone.

screen dump A bit-mapped image of the screen, which can be printed directly to a printer by pressing Shift-Print Screen if you have loaded GRAPHICS.COM before you loaded Ventura Publisher.

screen font The character set that is displayed on-screen as pixels and that calls up the respective printer font when you print a publication.

script Typefaces that simulate handwriting.

scroll bars The gray bars on the right and bottom sides of the computer screen used to move horizontally or vertically around the page. Ventura's Assignment List also has a vertical scroll bar.

select To indicate where the next action will take place by clicking the pointer on text or graphics or by dragging the cursor across the text.

selection box A box in a dialog box that contains an option.

self-mailer A printed piece designed to be mailed without an envelope. The area for the mailing label and postal indicia, if there are any, must be designed in accordance with postage regulations.

serif A line or curve projecting from the end of a letter form. Typefaces with these additional strokes are called serif faces.

set solid Type set without any leading between lines, specified, for example, as 14/14.

show through Printing on one side of the paper that can be seen on the other; commonly found in lower-quality paper stock.

sidebar A smaller, self-contained story inside a larger one, usually boxed with its own headline to set it apart from the main text.

signature A large printed sheet that, when folded and cut, becomes multiple pages in a publication.

silhouette A photograph from which a background image has been removed, outlining a subject or group of subjects.

single-sided Refers to publications printed on only one side of the paper. When you select Sides: Single from the Page Layout dialog box, Ventura assumes that your publication is single-sided and displays only one page at a time. In this case, you won't be able to select the Facing Pages option from the View menu. See also *double-sided*.

small caps Capital letters that are smaller than the standard uppercase characters for that typeface and size. In Ventura, small caps are 2 points smaller than the current font's cap height.

spread Two facing pages in a publication.

stacking order The order in which graphics objects overlap on-screen. The order can be manipulated through the Bring to Front and Send to Back commands on the Graphic menu.

stick-up cap An enlarged initial letter extending above the body text; used as a graphic element to draw attention to the beginning of a story or chapter. Called Big First Characters in Ventura, stick-up caps can be automatically generated using the Special Effects dialog box from the Paragraph menu.

stripping The assembling of all photographic negatives or positives necessary to create a printing plate of the entire page. Halftones and color separations are often stripped into the film created from an electronically assembled page.

style Traditionally, style refers to the broad characteristics of a typeface (such as serif or sans serif).

TIP

To speed up printing when you want to proofread text and don't need to see graphics, click on the Hide All Pictures on the Options menu. When you later print the chapter, you'll be given the option of whether to print the graphics as well. Not printing them can result in a significant increase in printing speed.

TIP

You can modify the size of small caps for any paragraph tag by using the Attribute Overrides dialog box from the Paragraph menu. You create small caps by first highlighting the letters to be small capped, clicking on Upper Case in the Assignment List (if the letters are not yet capitals), and then clicking on Small in the Assignment List.

TIP

You can change from one style sheet to another at any time. Choose Load Diff Style from the File menu, and scroll through the list of .STY filenames to find the one with the paragraph tags you want to use. If you do so, however, remember that the same paragraph tag names on any two style sheets does not guarantee identical type specifications.

TIP

It is wise to document your style sheets using the Print Stylesheet option in the Update Tag List dialog box available from the Paragraph menu. Once you've generated the style sheet documentation file, format it with Ventura's built-in STYLOG.STY style sheet, and print it. If you save the hard copy with an example of the chapter, you can save yourself a lot of time when you later have to duplicate a typographical design.

style sheet A Ventura-generated file that holds typographical and formatting information for all of a named group of paragraph tags. Each Ventura chapter must be associated with a single Style Sheet; Ventura chapters collected into a Ventura publication can each be assoicated with different style sheets.

surprint To print one image over another, such as type over a graphic.

tabloid A large-format publication, usually half the size of a standard newspaper.

target printer The printer on which the final output will be printed.

template An electronic prototype of a Ventura chapter that provides the layout grid and style sheet for similar publications.

Text Editing mode One of four Ventura modes. In this mode, you edit text files imported into a Ventura chapter and directly modify the attributes of selected portions of text. Any changes you make while in Text Editing mode are automatically stored in the imported file when you save the chapter.

thin space A fixed space, the width of a period, inserted by pressing Ctrl-Shift-T. See also *em space* and *en space*.

threaded text Text imported or typed as a single file, connected in Ventura's memory from one frame to the next and from one page to the next. When you cut, add, or move copy from any frame in a threaded text file, Ventura automatically adjusts subsequent text across as many pages or frames as needed to maintain the link between all the text in the file.

tick marks Marks on rulers showing the increments of measure. The larger the page view in Ventura, the finer the increments on the ruler.

TIFF files Short for "Tagged Image File Format," a format for electronically storing and transmitting bit-mapped, gray-scale, and color images.

tint A percentage of black or a color.

tone See *tint*.

tracking In Ventura, the amount by which every letter in a word or sentence within a paragraph tag is placed closer together or further apart.

trim In commercial printing, the size of the page after it is cut during the binding process.

verso The left-hand page.

vignette A graphic in which the background fades gradually until it blends with the unprinted paper.

weight The density of letters, traditionally described as light, regular, bold, extra bold, and so on.

white space The areas of the page without text or graphics; used as a deliberate element in good graphic design.

widow A short last line of a paragraph, especially troublesome when it is isolated at the top or bottom of a page or column or when it appears in a caption.

width The horizontal measure of letters, described as condensed, normal, or expanded.

TIP

To move to the next page or
spread, press Page Down. To
move to the previous page or
spread, press Page Up. To go to
a particular page in the chapter,
press Ctrl-G and enter the number of the page to which you want
to go.

width table A file (with the extension .WID) that holds information about the height and width of each character in a given font. Width tables are especially useful when moving Ventura chapters between computers that use different output devices—thus ensuring that a chapter formatted and proofed on one printer will be identically formatted and print correctly on another printer.

wraparound text Text that wraps around a graphic. Also called runaround text.

WYSIWYG An acronym for "What You See Is What You Get." Pronounced wizzy-wig, it refers to the representation on a computer screen of text and graphic elements as they will look on the printed page.

x-height The height of the main body of a lowercase letter, excluding ascenders or descenders.

zero point The point at which the 0 on the horizontal ruler intersects with the 0 on the vertical ruler. You can change the current zero point at any time by clicking and dragging the 0,0 rulers' intersection to any place on your screen.

INDEX

CREDITS

The sample documents reproduced throughout this book are reprinted by permission.

Chapter 1

No Crack poster, copyright © Do It Now Foundation 1987-88; AIGA Media and Technology insert, copyright © AIGA Boston 1986; *War and Peace in The Nuclear Age*, copyright © WGBH Educational Foundation 1988; *Leadership*, copyright © Weisz Yang Dunkelberger Inc. 1987

Chapter 3

Radon manual, copyright © 1988; GTech brochure, copyright © GTech Corporation 1988; Image Set Services, copyright © ImageSet Design 1988; Giraffe Project acknowledgment, copyright © Scot Louis Gaznier 1988; *The Numbers News*, copyright © American Demographics 1988; *Hardwood Herald*, copyright © Hardwood Manufacturers Association 1988; Kidney Foundation annual report, by permission of The National Kidney Foundation of Maryland; *The Wildman Herald*, copyright © 1988; Solebury School newsletter, copyright © Scot Louis Gaznier 1988; Academic Press listings, copyright © Academic Press, Inc. 1988; Statement of Purpose, copyright © Do It Now Foundation 1987; *Newservice*, copyright © Do It Now Foundation 1987; *Dateline!*, copyright © GTech Corporation 1988; *TeleVisual Market Strategies*, copyright © Telecommunications Productivity Center 1986; Medic Alert annual report, copyright © Tom Lewis, Inc. 1988; Roosevelt University annual report, copyright © Roosevelt University 1986; *TeleVisual Market Strategies*, copyright © Telecommunications Productivity Center 1986; *Verbum*, copyright © Donovan Gosney Inc. 87/88; *A Guide to Better Signs*, copyright © Communications Design Group 1986; *Worldnet*, by permission of the United States Information Agency; GTE folder, copyright © Weisz Yang Dunkelberger Inc. 1987-88; *Communique*, copyright © Kate Dore, Dore Davis Design 1987; *FLASH*, copyright © Nautilus Books, Inc. 1988; Superlearning catalog, copyright © Barbara Lee/Folio Consulting 1988; *Signal*, copyright © Point Foundation 1988; *Longevity*, copyright © Omni Publications International Ltd. 1988

Chapter 4

The Voter's Guidebook, copyright © New York City Charter Revision Commission 1988

Chapter 5

Midwives Benefit flyer, copyright © John Odam 1988; Student Recital flyer, copyright © Diane Landskroener 1988; VideoFashion Monthly, copyright © VideoFashion, Inc. 1989; Brown Bag Lunch flyer, copyright © WGBH Educational Foundation 1986; Design Systems Personnel, copyright © Michael J. Sullivan 1989; April–Eric poster, copyright © AIGA/Boston 1988; WPFW Radio Poster, copyright © Richard J. Steele 1987; World Trade Institute program, copyright © Communications Design Group 1988; Holiday Inn Conference folder, copyright © Carol D. Finkelstein 1989; Drugs & Alcohol folder, copyright © Do It Now Foundation 1987-88; Yerba Buena Ave. real estate flyer, copyright © Zetatype Desktop Publishers 1988; Colligan's Stocton Inn folder, copyright © Carla Bond Coutts 1987; Royce Investment Group folder, copyright © Letter Perfect Typesetter, Ltd. 1989; Infractions folder, copyright © Infractions 1987; Family Programs, copyright © The Art Institute of Chicago 1987; Historic Hudson Valley folder, copyright © Historic Hudson Valley 1988; *inFidelity*, copyright © Keith Yates Audio 1987-1988; Clackamas College brochure, copyright © Clackamas Community College 1988; Pitney Bowes brochure, copyright © Weisz Yang Dunkelberger Inc. 1987-88; Success Encyclopedia, copyright © Showcase Publishing Company 1990; Washington D.C. Visitors Association annual report, copyright © Richard J. Steele 1987; *Why Design?*, copyright © Watzman + Keyes Information Design 1987; European Terracotta Sculpture folder, copyright © The Art Institute Of Chicago 1987; Arthur D. Little brochure, copyright © Michael J.

Sullivan 1989; ML Technology Ventures 1987 Annual Report; ML Media Partners 1987 Annual Report; Subscription Programs brochure, copyright © The Art Institute Of Chicago 1988; *Islam and the West*, copyright © Foundation for Traditional Studies 1988; Sacramento Regional Foundation Yearbook, copyright © Sacramento Regional Foundation 1987; Alaska Official State Vacation Planner

Chapter 6

Water Rights, copyright © Howard Smallowitz 1989; *Application Success Stories*, copyright © Zetatype Desktop Publishers 1988; *Housing Insights*, copyright © Howard Smallowitz 1989; *Inside Qualified Plans*, copyright © Shearson Lehman Hutton Inc. 1989; *NOOZ*, copyright © WGBH Educational Foundation 1986; *Consumer Markets Abroad*, copyright © American Demographics 1988; *Perspectives*, copyright © Transamerica Life Companies 1988; *National Gallery of Art* newsletter, copyright © Richard J. Steele 1987; *ThePage*, copyright © Page-Works 1987-88; *Newservice*, copyright © Do It Now Foundation 1987; *Friends of Omega*, copyright © Omega Institute 1987; *Indications*, copyright © Index Group, Inc. 1988; *O'Connor Quarterly*, copyright © O'Connor Hospital 1988; *The Freeze Beacon*, copyright © John Odam 1987; *Strategy*, copyright © Shearson Lehman Hutton Inc. 1989; *Dear Nipper*, copyright © BMG Music 1990; *AmeriNews*, copyright © Kate Dore, Dore Davis Design 1987; *Re:*, copyright © ImageSet Design 1988; *Litigation News*, copyright © American Bar Association 1988; *Washington College Magazine*, copyright © Washington College 1987-88; *Backtalk*, copyright © Texas Back Institute 1987; *American Demographics*, copyright © American Demographics 1988; *Business North Carolina*, copyright © The News and Observer Publishing Co. 1987-88; *Science Digest*, copyright © Frank Kendig and *Science Digest* 1988; *Heartcorps*, copyright © Heart Corps, Inc. 1988; *Mother Earth News*, copyright © The Mother Earth News Partners 1989; *Trips* copyright © The Banana Republic 1989

Chapter 7

Table Specification Guide, copyright © Geiger International; the book end catalog, copyright © Lisa Menders 1987; Beverly Hills Auto catalog, copyright © Beverly Hills Motoring Accessories 1988; Concept Technical Manual, copyright © Oscar Anderson 1988; Davidson Software catalog, copyright © Julie Gibbs 1988; School of Visual Arts catalog, copyright © School of Visual Arts Press, Ltd. 1988; Clackamas College catalog, copyright © Clackamas Community College 1988; *Portland State Quarterly*, copyright © 1988; *Mathcad*, copyright © Michael J. Sullivan 1989; Fitzgerald, Abbott & Beardsley presentation folder, copyright © Fitzgerald, Abbott & Beardsley 1987; Indelec information sheet, copyright © Michael J. Sullivan 1989; Infrared Optics data sheet, copyright © Two-Six Inc. 1988; Questor Inlets data sheet, copyright © Extrel 1988; product information sheets, copyright © Smith & Hawken 1990; MasterCard International 1988 Annual Report, copyright © MasterCard International 1988; College Auxiliary Services, copyright © College Auxiliary Services, SUNY New Paltz 1987; Northeastern Illinois Regional Transit Authority Report, copyright © First Chicago Corporation 1990; Medic Alert Annual Report, copyright © Tom Lewis, Inc. 1988; Cutco Industries Annual Report, copyright © Letter Perfect Typesetter, Ltd. 1989; Traffic/Archive form, copyright © WGBH Educational Foundation 1986; Camera Billing Form, copyright © WGBH Educational Foundation 1986; Employee Information form, copyright © Geiger International; Bank of California Bonus Enrollment form, copyright © The Bank of California 1989; Proposal Evaluation form, copyright © Earthwatch 1987; Admission form, copyright © Clackamas Community College 1988; InFractions order form, copyright © Infractions 1987

Project 6

Group photo, single portrait, and flower photo, copyright © Comstock 1986; photo of woman, copyright © Dion Ogust 1991

The manuscript for this book was prepared and submitted to Microsoft Press in electronic form. Text files were processed and formatted using Microsoft Word.

Cover design by Don Wright
Cover photograph by Walter Wick and Studio 3, Inc.
Interior text design by Don Wright and Ronnie Shushan
Principal production art and coordination by Peggy Herman
Principal proofreading by Kathleen Atkins
Color separations by Wescan Color Corporation, Redmond, WA

Text composition by Ricardo Birmele and William J. Teel, Jr., in Palatino with display in Futura Bold Condensed Italic, using Ventura Publisher® with an IBM-compatible computer and the Linotronic 300 laser imagesetter.